# LLOYD GEORGE
## AND
# FOREIGN POLICY

*Volume One*

Lloyd George and Foreign Policy

Caricature by Leslie Ward ("Spy") from *Vanity Fair*
(National Library of Wales)

# LLOYD GEORGE

# and Foreign Policy

VOLUME ONE
The Education of a Statesman: 1890–1916

MICHAEL G. FRY

McGILL-QUEEN'S UNIVERSITY PRESS
Montreal and London   1977

© McGill-Queen's University Press 1977
ISBN 0 7735 0274 2
Legal deposit second quarter 1977
Bibliothèque nationale du Québec


Design by Anthony Crouch MGDC
Printed in Canada by
The Hunter Rose Company


*This book has been published with the help of
a grant from the Social Science Research Council
of Canada using funds provided by the Canada Council*

*for Maria*

# CONTENTS

# CONTENTS

# PREFACE

This study is not a biography of David Lloyd George. I leave that monumental task to the more courageous. Rather I have attempted, in this volume, to investigate Lloyd George's role in the conduct of British foreign policy from the last decade of the nineteenth century to December 1916. My concern is with diplomacy, imperialism, and strategy. A second volume will examine the premiership and the near quarter-century of prophecy, prescription, and frustration.

The pattern is familiar enough. The young Lloyd George, ambitious and open-minded, becomes part of the decision-making process of the Liberal government from 1908. He combines the roles of critic and policy-maker during the war and becomes prime minister in December 1916. As head of a coalition government he exercises first an episodic and then a decisive influence on the conduct of foreign policy until October 1922. Finally, he becomes a rebellious elder statesman and an erratic commentator on events until his death in March 1945. In retracing the pattern, all his biographers, with one exception,[1] have treated foreign policy as a secondary consideration, apart from the years of his premiership. They bound from the Boer War to Agadir and from the 1914 crisis to the Peace Conference. They tarry until Chanak, sweep forward to Lloyd George's encounter with Hitler in 1936, and end with his public statements on the origins and conduct of the Second World War. I hope to redress the balance somewhat, relate Lloyd George to dissent and decision-making, and add to the understanding of both his fascinating career and British foreign policy in the twentieth century.

Lloyd George, like Joseph Chamberlain and Winston Churchill, became a supremely controversial figure, subject to both passionate and even scurrilous attack, and romantic adulation. He could

1. W. Watkin Davies, *Lloyd George: 1863–1914.*

attract and repel in dangerous proportions. The Lincoln of Wales, the resurrected Pitt, the new Castlereagh was also the Welsh upstart, the poseur playing Moses, the Sultan beyond rehabilitation, the spellbinder unmasked. Liberals denounced him as an assassin and an apostate. The Labour Party regarded him as a threatening competitor and a potential wrecker, while Tories viewed him as an intolerably disruptive force. Squiffs, Simonites, and Samuelites, Socialists and Conservatives found common cause in their fears. Distrust of Lloyd George became fashionable. No story about him was too bizarre to believe; he would plot policy on the top of a bus, plan a social revolution on the Riviera, misplace treaties and agreements, and put off Hitler in order to attend the Eisteddfod.

One further parallel with Churchill's career is inescapable. Colleagues tended to regard both as unreliable, unstable and unsafe, lacking in principle, unsound of judgement, and prone to error. Lloyd George, in rebuttal, argued that the problems which beset England after 1922 remained unsolved largely because hate-filled and jealous men of inferior ability abused his legacy, excluded him from power, and shifted the responsibility for their own failure onto his shoulders. Insignificant mediocrities and party hacks shunned intuitive genius and as a result the British Empire faced mortal danger in 1939. Predictably the Churchills rallied to the thesis and the cause.[2] Randolph Churchill, congratulating Lloyd George on a recent speech in March 1936, the best, he said, he had ever heard in Parliament, thanked Lloyd George for supporting his father and claimed, "all save you two are pygmies." Two years later, on receipt of the first volume of Lloyd George's Peace Conference memoirs, Winston Churchill described the work as "a marvel" and noted, "all now thrown away—not even by traitors—only muffs and boobies." Historians seem all too ready to concur.

We are now, however, in the second phase of the historiography of Lloyd George, muting extremes and indulging in neither crude obloquy nor hagiography. Polemic has not disappeared, but

2. R. Churchill to Lloyd George, 11 March 1936, LGP, G/4/5/77; W. Churchill to Lloyd George, 17 Oct. and 10 Dec. 1938, ibid., G/4/5/33 and 34. Brendan Bracken agreed that Lloyd George had saved Britain in 1918, and that Baldwin and Chamberlain had thrown away his victory. (Bracken to Lloyd George, 13 June 1940, ibid., G/6/4/2.) Even Lord Robert Cecil conceded this point. (Cecil to Lady Asquith, 1 Feb. 1944, Cecil Papers, Add. 51073.)

praise is less lavish and more deserved, and criticism is detached and understanding.

Lloyd George has captured my imagination and seduced my interest. I have pursued him in the private papers and the official archives, and the documents have led me where I had hoped to go. When one measures the qualities of the man against the dimensions of the problems he faced, one becomes appreciative of his achievements, and even indulgent toward his failures. Just as Churchill's reputation slowly returns to earthly proportions so Lloyd George will gain his rightful place. He may never become entirely respectable but his reputation will rest safely beyond mere abuse. Indeed, in many respects he stands above his contemporaries as the most significant figure in British politics in the first half of the twentieth century.

# ACKNOWLEDGEMENTS

The sustained and generous support of the Canada Council and Carleton University enabled me to complete this study. I am also grateful for assistance from the publication funds of the Norman Paterson School of International Affairs, Carleton University, and for a grant in aid of publication from the Social Science Research Council of Canada, using funds provided by the Canada Council.

Professor W. N. Medlicott, former Stevenson Professor of International History at the London School of Economics and now senior editor of *Documents on British Foreign Policy 1919–1939*, has continued to assist and encourage my work. I have profited greatly from conversations with and the writings of Kenneth Morgan of the Queen's College, Oxford. James Bayer of the University of Western Ontario, Professor J. O. Baylen, Georgia State University, Professor N. M. Fieldhouse of McGill University, Lawrence Pratt of the University of Alberta, and especially Christopher Wrigley of Loughborough University aided my research. Christopher Wrigley's research assistance was, in fact, invaluable. I should add that John Grigg graciously provided me with selected translations from the memoir of Lloyd George by D. R. Daniel.

I essentially completed this manuscript at the end of 1973, after a final excursion into the archives in the summer of that year. At that time two important books were published which relate to my work. Kenneth Morgan's *Lloyd George: Family Letters, 1885–1936* (Cardiff: University of Wales Press) contains much of the family correspondence recently deposited in the National Library of Wales, Aberystwyth. As usual, Kenneth Morgan's scholarship was impeccable, and I have cited his volume where possible. In the cases where I found letters or parts of letters not published by him I cited the appropriate file of the Lloyd George Papers in the National Library of Wales. John Grigg's *The Young Lloyd George*, relying heavily on the papers placed in the National Library of Wales, dealt only with the years up to the end of the Boer War.

## ACKNOWLEDGEMENTS

Inevitably, for the earlier period, we have covered some of the same ground, but our objectives, emphases, and interpretations differ in varying degrees.

I have worked in a number of private and public archives, and several libraries, as the bibliography shows. I wish to thank the staffs of these libraries and archives, and especially those who serve at the Beaverbrook Memorial Library, the Bodleian Library, the British Museum, the National Library of Scotland, the National Library of Wales, and the Public Record Office. I have sought permission to use and to quote from the papers deposited in the archives and libraries identified in the bibliography. I thank the trustees, executors, and holders of copyright who granted me permission to do so, and apologize for any oversights in this regard. Transcripts of Crown-copyright records in the Public Record Office appear by permission of the Controller of H. M. Stationery Office. I am grateful to the National Library of Wales for allowing me to use illustrations from their collection.

Finally, I must express my deep appreciation for the lasting friendship and unfailing hospitality of D. Gareth Jones of Penarth.

MICHAEL G. FRY
OTTAWA

# ABBREVIATIONS

| | |
|---|---|
| *BDOW* | *British Documents on the Origins of the War, 1898–1914* |
| Cab | Cabinet Minutes and Papers |
| CID | Committee of Imperial Defence |
| *DDF* | *Documents diplomatiques français, 1871–1914* |
| FO | Foreign Office |
| LGP | Lloyd George Papers, Beaverbrook Memorial Library, London |
| *Parl. Deb.*, H. of C. | Parliamentary Debates, House of Commons |

*I*

# The Problem:
# The Man and
# the Sources

Lloyd George, in his vocation, which was to secure and exercise political power at the centre of an apparently indestructible Empire, demonstrated greatness rather than grandeur. He was the exemplar of brilliance not nobility, a superb arriviste who remained insubstantial in certain fundamental ways. He was not, however, a vulgarian, seeking to wield power for its own sake; nor was he a naïve man for whom to exercise power was to attempt to understand its implications. Lloyd George had a sense of service and purpose; there were great ends to be pursued, great causes to be followed in the course of a political career.

He attempted to wrap himself in an aura of mystery which biographers would not be able to unravel.[1] He never gave or revealed himself fully to any political associate, and he challenged historians to penetrate the layers of his personality and belief system. They would all fall short, in his view; the enigma would

---

1. Lloyd George to Basil Murray, 4 Feb. 1932, LGP, G/248; Basil Murray, "L.G.", preface.

remain.[2] Moreover, Lloyd George himself, those in Wales who remained devoted to him, perhaps in self-delusion, and exasperated English observers constructed images of this remarkable parvenu, which by definition contained elements of distortion. Myth compounded the mystique. Lloyd George did not rise from abject poverty and defy intolerable oppression, he was not a Nonconformist zealot, and he was never an uncomplicated enragé. He did not love small nations to the point of unrealism, he had not prevented war in 1911, he could not have secured Bulgarian intervention on the allied side in 1915, and he did not reward Chaim Weizmann's applied scientific prowess with the Balfour Declaration of 1917.

At the core of the problem and of a study such as this stand Lloyd George's memoirs of the war and the peacemaking. In the summer of 1922 Lloyd George, encouraged by Frances Stevenson and Sir Maurice Hankey, secretary to the cabinet, began preliminary work for the war memoirs.[3] He rejected Lord Beaverbrook's offer of £80,000, to avoid being in his clutches according to Miss Stevenson, and accepted a bid of £100,000 from Thornton, Butterworth and Hearst for a two-volume work. In the last week of August at Criccieth he made further decisions. Hankey recommended Maj.-Gen. E. D. Swinton, the military historian, as principal research assistant. Swinton accepted and Lloyd George planned to devote part of September to the project. Influenced perhaps by his wife, he was able to tell Thomas Jones "that he had made up his mind not to make any money out of the book but to pay expenses and give the whole of the rest to some war charity.... He said that he did not wish people to be able to say that he had made money out of the war, and that 'old Carnegie', had kept him out of the workhouse."[4]

Swinton began work in September and Hankey expressed amazement at Lloyd George's ability to plunge into such an under-

2. A. G. Gardiner described him as full of fascination and disquiet, the unknown factor of the future and the potential romance of the contemporary political scene. He was "the most piquant and the most baffling figure in politics." (A. G. Gardiner, *Prophets, Priests and Kings*, 129–37.)

3. T. Jones diary, 8 and 31 July and 12 Nov. 1922; T. Jones minute, 1922; T. Jones to wife, 20–23 Aug. 1922; T. Jones to Hankey, 8 Sept., and Hankey to T. Jones, 22 Sept. 1922, T. Jones Papers, A/1, X/7, and P/1; Lord Lee of Fareham, "A Good Innings," Lee of Fareham Papers, II, 926–27.

4. Andrew Carnegie made a substantial financial gift to him at the end of the war.

taking. He seemed determined to complete the project, but the next few weeks demanded other things of the prime minister. In November, in the aftermath of defeat, he and Swinton turned again to the task. By January 1924, however, progress was increasingly impeded by ill-health, the pressure of politics, and journeys abroad. In addition, Lloyd George had become a very highly paid journalist.[5] He contemplated changing his memoirs into a history of his personal role in the war, written by Swinton, to which Lloyd George would contribute several chapters.[6] Dissuaded from this course, he permitted the project to languish, although preparatory work went on.[7]

The delay testified to his vigorous activity in other fields, in spite of which he was able to produce *The Truth about Reparations and War Debts* (1932) and other minor pieces.[8] Meanwhile, the literary efforts of Churchill, Beaverbrook, and a host of political and military biographers, along with the publication of Field-Marshal Sir Henry Wilson's diaries in October 1927, presented an irresistible challenge to self-vindication. As Lloyd George told Hankey, *they* knew how hard *they* had worked to pull the country through, whatever claims were made by or on behalf of others, and clearly "I must publish my story." [9]

Lloyd George did not, however, return to the task in any sustained way until August 1932. Recuperation from illness and absence from office, if not detachment from political activity, gave him a period of relative leisure until the fall of 1934. Prompted by his entourage and by General Jan Smuts,[10] Lloyd George

5. T. Jones, *Lloyd George*, 268. Lloyd George signed with the United Press Association of America in November 1922, and later wrote for the Hearst group and others for handsome fees. Sales of his memoirs were predictably high; volumes one and two of the *War Memoirs* reached over 108,000 and over 76,000 respectively by March 1936.

6. Swinton to Lloyd George, Jan. 1924, Swinton to Ironside, 14 Dec. 1922, Hankey to Swinton, 25 Jan. 1924, LGP, G/216; Swinton's draft chapters, ibid., G/217 and 218.

7. Lloyd George visited the battlefields of the First World War in August and September 1929 to refresh his memory and prepare for the writing of his memoirs. (A. J. Sylvester, *The Real Lloyd George*, 174–76.)

8. For example, his prefatory note to P. Guedalla, ed., *Slings and Arrows*.

9. Lloyd George to Hankey, 11 Oct. 1927, LGP, G/8/18/4. Lloyd George and Hankey deplored the revelations in Wilson's diaries. Lloyd George urged Hankey to publish his own account. (Hankey to Lloyd George, 2 Dec., and Lloyd George to Hankey, 11 Dec. 1930, ibid., G/8/18/15 and 16.)

10. M. Thomson, *David Lloyd George*, 25–26, and T. Jones, 267–73. Smuts

responded to a cluster of stimuli. He was the last of the great figures of the war to attempt an explanation. His memoirs would serve, therefore, as a monumental rebuff to his detractors. He would, in comparison with them, avoid suppressing or distorting evidence, seek out the truth, and mete out justice to the living and the dead. Lloyd George knew what would sell and the financial return was now a consideration. He would relive the war, the greatest event of his life, as he wrote, and add a literary dimension to his reputation. Finally, he would, through his memoirs, warn of recent errors and current dangers, and offer solutions to guide the world to safety.[11] Personal vindication, discrediting of enemies, diagnosis of and remedy for society's ills, Lloyd George offered them all, particularly as the 1919 treaty system came under challenge. His memoirs were not meant to be the last fling of a virtually extinct statesman.

Lloyd George, at Churt or travelling abroad, demonstrated remarkable vigour and control for a man in his early seventies. He completed the six-volume *War Memoirs* by January 1937, and by December 1938 had published two volumes on the peacemaking. This feat was also a testimony to his research assistants and secretaries, with A. J. Sylvester most prominent and valuable, aided by Miss Stevenson, Malcolm Thomson, and others.[12]

In certain ways Hankey, who acknowledged his debt to Lloyd George, "materially and spiritually,"[13] and described himself on

---

was clearly the "old comrade of the Great War" who urged Lloyd George to write lest judgement go against him by default. (Lloyd George to Hankey, 10 April 1933, LGP, G/212.)

11. Lloyd George to N. Collins (*News Chronicle*), 24 Nov. 1932, LGP, G/211. Lloyd George planned to add a chapter relevant to the current disarmament negotiations. He wanted to show the time-lag between placing orders for armaments and their production, and to prove that, if existing armaments were reduced and surpluses destroyed, no power could re-equip its army in less than a year. See also the preface to his *The Truth About the Peace Treaties*, I, 5–6.

12. Sylvester to R. Morris, 27 March 1934, LGP, G/21/1/30; Sylvester to N. B. Ronald (FO), 25 Sept. 1933, Sylvester to Lloyd George, 12 Oct. 1933, and Hankey to Sylvester, 22 May 1933, ibid., G/213, G/20/2/85, and G/239; notes of conversation between Lloyd George, A. F. Kerensky, Bruce Lockhart, and Sylvester, 7 Sept. 1933, ibid., G/240. M. Thomson began research for a projected book by Lloyd George on disarmament. (Thomson to Lloyd George, 25 July 1932, ibid., G/29/2/1.) Much of the evidence on this process of research and writing is in ibid., G/211–215 (correspondence on memoirs), G/219–230 (drafts of memoirs), and G/231–252 (material for memoirs).

13. Hankey to Lloyd George, 30 March 1933, ibid., G/212.

one occasion as the intellectual valet of his hero and former chief,[14] played the vital role. Above all else perhaps Hankey, advising, suggesting, encouraging, and warning, provided an intellectual anchor to the past, helping Lloyd George to explore and recapture shared experiences. He also provided a basis for judgement and restraint. An unrepentant and unyielding Lloyd George, determined not to surrender control of his official papers and willing to face legal action, was not an easy pupil.[15] The world must realize that "I am on my defence—that for fifteen years I have borne with a stream of criticism polluted with much poison and antagonism. My shelves here groan under...mutilated, bowdlerised distorted quotations. I must in all justice, not to myself but to the public and posterity, tell the whole truth."[16]

On the other hand only the prime minister could give permission to publish official documents. Clear precedents were lacking, and Lloyd George was exempt from the obligations of neither his privy councillor's oath nor the Official Secrets Act. Hankey, persona grata with both Prime Minister Ramsay MacDonald and Stanley Baldwin, handled the matter. When the first extracts from the *War Memoirs* were due to appear in the *Daily Telegraph* in April 1933 Hankey persuaded Lloyd George to consult the leaders of the government. Baldwin knew that Hankey had aided Lloyd George, and would, in all probability, act on his advice.[17] The position was regularized; Lloyd George, to avoid publishing material detrimental to the public interest, would rely on Hankey's judgement and impartiality, and Hankey would "clear" the volumes on behalf of the government.[18]

Hankey bestowed the government's imprimatur and applied a seal of approval. He participated actively in the preparation and

14. Hankey to Lloyd George, 23 July 1929, Lloyd George Papers (National Library of Wales, Aberystwyth), 20462C; notes of dinner party, 29 Oct. 1936, LGP, G/208. Austen Chamberlain, Churchill, and Hankey were prominent.

15. Lloyd George to Addison, 3 Oct. 1934, LGP, G/1/4/4.

16. Lloyd George to Hankey, 18 April 1934, ibid., G/212.

17. Hankey to Lloyd George, 8 April 1933, ibid. Only Churchill had followed this procedure. Grey and the others had not consulted Hankey and the cabinet office. As MacDonald was busy with his impending visit to the United States, Hankey suggested consulting Baldwin.

18. Lloyd George to Hankey, 10 April 1933, ibid. When thanking Simon for permitting Sylvester to copy telegrams on Russian affairs, Lloyd George promised to use them with discretion and with the public interest in mind. He agreed to submit his manuscript to Hankey, Simon, Baldwin, or the prime minister. (Lloyd George to Simon, 7 Oct. 1933, ibid., G/214.)

writing processes,[19] guiding the use of documents, and establishing working relations with government departments, and their historical branches.[20] Not only did this procedure permit Hankey to facilitate and control Lloyd George's use of documents, it also enabled him, and through him the government, to avoid injury to the living and harm to the current international situation. Lloyd George, for instance, was persuaded to suppress a chapter entitled "Czar's Future Residence," containing references to the wartime antimonarchical movement in Russia and personal attacks on the tsar, in deference to the king who deplored the use of cabinet minutes and Foreign Office dispatches for such purposes.[21] Although the Peace Conference memoirs were generally acceptable, the Colonial Office opposed publication of a chapter on Palestine, regarding it as unhelpful in the current situation. Moreover, Lloyd George was asked to avoid giving offence to Italy and Turkey, to omit any reference to reparations which might aid German propaganda, to minimize Keynes's role in 1919, and to amend his reparations statistics. However, as Hankey conceded in July 1938, even though publication of the memoirs might disturb the international scene marginally, nothing Lloyd George wrote could make the Czech crisis any worse than it already was.[22]

At the same time Hankey attempted, not always successfully, to erase error. He provided a not infallible check on the author's fading memory. He guided, usually from sympathetic motives, the selection of specific chapters and sections,[23] and he was a mine of

19. Ibid., G/212.

20. Hankey to Lloyd George, 9 and 27 April 1934, ibid. Hankey would consult the Foreign and Dominions Offices over the chapters on American entry into the war, the Imperial War Cabinet, and peace moves. Vansittart refused Lloyd George permission to publish certain material relating to the Imperial War Cabinet. Lloyd George was also prevented from using the telegrams from Madrid relating to the peace moves in 1917.

21. Hankey to Lloyd George, 9 April 1934, ibid.

22. Hankey to Lloyd, 11 July 1938, ibid., G/8/18/38 and 39.

23. Hankey to Lloyd George, 30 March 1933, ibid., G/212. Hankey suggested that a chapter on the 1916 peace negotiations would serve the public interest at that time. In 1938 Hankey urged Lloyd George to extend his treatment of Dominion participation at the Peace Conference, to emphasize the role of the Dominions and to support "your main point" that the decisions at Paris were not taken hastily under the stress of unbalanced emotions and temporary crises. They were the result of lengthy deliberations involving the allies and the Empire Delegation. Specifically, Hankey advocated a chapter on the naval, military, and air clauses of the peace treaty. Lloyd George had insisted on voluntary service as the basis for the future Germany army, following the advice of the CIGS and

information even to the extent of preparing notes on personalities, issues, and policies.[24] Moreover, Hankey primed Lloyd George on changing official interpretations of wartime policies,[25] and warned him of sources of opposition likely to arise both before and after publication.[26]

In not the least difficult of his tasks, and one which he shared with Lloyd George's assistants and family, Hankey never ceased to attempt to neutralize the venom and bitterness which so frequently marred the author's judgements of his former colleagues. He insisted, in April 1934, that Lloyd George could make a unique contribution to history, fully documented and of sustained value, only if he retained a sense of dignity. Hankey conceded that Lloyd George had laboured under an excessive degree of provocation, but he urged him to refrain from sinking to the level of answering taunt with gibe and indictment with denunciation. Hauling national heroes from their pedestals Hankey likened to a churchman marshalling evidence against the saints. The process was painful, bitter, and against the public good; he therefore repeatedly urged Lloyd George to soften his criticism of politicians such as Walter Runciman, Churchill, Neville Chamberlain, Ramsay MacDonald, and Philip Snowden, and of military leaders such as Field-Marshals Haig and Robertson.[27] Even with the aid of the king, Hankey was clearly more successful on some occasions, as for example with reference to Churchill, than on others.[28]

---

the Empire Delegation, and had intended the German disarmament clauses to be the prologue to general disarmament. (Hankey to Lloyd George, 11 July 1938, ibid., G/8/18/39.)

24. Hankey prepared a note on Robert Cecil and the blockade question, and led Lloyd George through the intricacies of the strategic debates of 1915. (Hankey to Lloyd George, 9 May and 22 March 1933, ibid., G/212.)

25. Hankey to Lloyd George, 16 April 1934, ibid. Hankey advised that the General Staff had become decidedly hostile towards offensives of the Passchendaele brand; Lloyd George's denunciation should seal the matter.

26. Hankey to Lloyd George, 11 July 1938, ibid., G/8/18/39. He warned that the Treasury would demand omission of precise references to Keynes. Others would attack his treatment of Turkey. Friends of President Wilson and Robert Cecil would protest against the chapters on the League, demanding emphasis on Anglo-American cooperation rather than rivalry. Hankey could see the current value of such a change of emphasis.

27. Hankey to Lloyd George, 16 and 19 April 1934 and 16 July 1936, ibid., G/212; Lloyd George to Lord Sandon, 14 Dec. 1934, ibid., G/215.

28. Hankey, on behalf of the king, urged Lloyd George to omit some critical passages on Ramsay MacDonald, and Clive Wigram asked for more generous treatment of both MacDonald and Snowden. Lloyd George, however, insisted

Hankey performed one other service: he recommended that Lloyd George employ Basil Liddell Hart. Just as Hankey had scrutinized the political and diplomatic material, so Liddell Hart, strong on military affairs, and familiar with and critical of writers of the "Western Front school," could advise on strategic questions.[29] Lloyd George, who already enjoyed a relationship of mutual high regard with Liddell Hart, accepted Hankey's suggestion readily and established a working arrangement with Liddell Hart which lasted beyond the outbreak of the Second World War. Liddell Hart provided invaluable assistance; he read the whole manuscript, gave very detailed comments, based upon his vast knowledge of military history, and helped gather information through interviews with survivors of high rank.[30] In many respects, therefore, the memoirs were bred by Lloyd George, Swinton, and Sylvester, out of Hankey and Liddell Hart; a not unimpressive pedigree even if the offspring never did it justice.

Some of Lloyd George's former colleagues and others also gave assistance. Lord Reading and Sir Eric Geddes offered general advice, while Lord Lee of Fareham, on strategy and food production, Sir Joseph Maclay, on shipping, Smuts, on the League of Nations, Sir John Stavridi, on the Graeco-Turkish affair and on the Balkans generally, Chaim Weizmann, on the Middle East, and Soviet Ambassador Ivan Maisky and the historian Sir Bernard Pares, on Russia, made contributions of varying content and value.[31]

In terms of motive, tone, and ultimate execution, however, Lloyd George retained control of his memoirs. They are in many

---

that since he had been frank about old colleagues he could not suppress references to MacDonald about activities which the Labour leader had undertaken deliberately and in good conscience. (Hankey to Lloyd George, 19 April 1934, Wigram to Lloyd George, 23 April 1934, and Lloyd George to Wigram, 25 May 1934, ibid., G/214.)

29. Hankey to Lloyd George, 11 April 1933, ibid., G/212. Liddell Hart, receiving thirty guineas per article, would assist for a fee of one hundred guineas for three or four days' work.

30. Lloyd George–Liddell Hart correspondence, ibid., and Liddell Hart Papers; B. Liddell Hart, *The Memoirs of Captain Liddell Hart*, 2 vols. (London, 1965), I, 347, 353, 357–70. Liddell Hart and Lloyd George regarded each other with a measure of respect and shared similar views on the war. (Liddell Hart to Lloyd George, 14 Jan. 1935, LGP, G/212.)

31. F. Stevenson to Sir J. Stavridi, 22 Jan. 1936; correspondence in LGP, G/214 and 215; F. Stevenson to Lee, 1 May 1933 and 3 Aug. 1934, and Lee to F. Stevenson, 3 Aug. 1934, Lee of Fareham Papers, Lloyd George file.

ways a remarkable achievement, whatever their historical and literary shortcomings. They have been rendered obsolescent in part by the opening of the official files and the availability of the Lloyd George papers, but they remain decidedly valuable. This is particularly so because they reveal much of their author, and indeed they are an extension of his character and personality.

The historian who takes up the challenge and joins in the pursuit of Lloyd George encounters two significant obstacles: his elusiveness in the archives and a mountain of biographical material which is quantitatively impressive and qualitatively depressing. With the theme of foreign policy the historian meets a third problem: Lloyd George's first love politically was Wales and domestic issues dominated much of his thought and energies. He knew Wales and could identify himself directly with social and economic problems; he learned about foreign policy at a different rate and through somewhat different processes.

The historian experiences a sense of the ludicrous, born of frustration, when, after rejoicing in the demise of the fifty-year rule and witnessing the opening of government archives and private collections, he finds himself complaining about the inadequacy of research material. Perhaps it was naïve to expect otherwise in relation to Lloyd George. His papers at the Beaverbrook Library are an extensive, impressive, but uneven collection. They are detailed from December 1916 to 1922, adequate in some ways even to 1941, but disappointing for the earlier years, particularly before 1908. Weighty for instance on Ireland, they are less useful for foreign policy.[32] The papers deposited in the National Library of Wales do not compensate adequately.[33] Perhaps the files and diary held by William George will help, but doubtless the challenge involved in studying foreign policy will remain.

At the root of the matter lies Lloyd George's use of letters, notes, memoranda, and marginalia; one must indeed squeeze the archives until the pips squeak.[34] Apart from his correspondence

32. Researchers interested in the years of office should not ignore the G series, on the assumption that its contents are relevant only to the post-1922 period.

33. K. O. Morgan, ed., *Lloyd George: Family Letters, 1885–1936* (hereafter cited as Morgan, *Family Letters*), and note 39.

34. Lloyd George also cast doubt on the value of some of his correspondence. He told his brother that he had written home about his parliamentary achievements very largely to please Uncle Lloyd, who worried lest he were inactive. Thus his letters would picture him as full of confidence, when in fact he was

with Dame Margaret, Uncle Lloyd, and other members of his family, Lloyd George's epistolary efforts are rarely impressive and are frequently disappointing.[35] More letters came in than went out, Lloyd George's use of secretarial assistance was at best erratic, and a coordinated filing system appeared only tardily to bring some measure of order. Lloyd George's extensive family correspondence, his press articles, and his other writings suggest that although he was no master of, certainly he had no aversion to, the written word. He preferred, however, other means through which to transact his political business. As a busy minister he wrote only rarely to those with whom he was in almost daily or at least regular contact. When his life became more complicated even his letters to his family became less frequent and Lloyd George utilized, mastered, and eventually excelled in the sometimes dangerous art of personal contacts and soundings.[36] The working breakfast became a political forum, meals were political vehicles, golf permitted gossip, and private conversation and the intimate conference, so often leaving less of a trail, became his forte. He relied on his ability to convince deputations, cabinets, committees, and conferences by both seductive and dictatorial displays of authority, or by sheer charm and humour. This is why the diaries of the perceptive editor of the *Manchester Guardian*, C. P. Scott, are so valuable. No one understood Lloyd George better than Hankey in this regard, and when he wrote of the visit to Hitler his mental picture was of Lloyd George at every meal squeezing information out of his host.[37] Inevitably then, and tragically, much passed between Lloyd George and his colleagues that was never written down and almost certainly other material was lost or destroyed.

The papers of his contemporaries likewise yield a scanty harvest of letters and notes from Lloyd George and a rather thin return on foreign policy. The letters exchanged with C. P. Scott, for example, are far less revealing than Scott's diaries. Moreover, some

---

usually relieved "at having got through without a spill." (Lloyd George to W. George, 19 May 1917, LGP, I/2/2/74.)

35. Lloyd George's letters to Herbert Lewis do not negate this conclusion.

36. T. Jones, 267. Lloyd George complained in December 1917 that he was receiving no letters from home. His wife replied that she wrote every day, "if they are ever handed to you." (Dame Margaret to Lloyd George, 3 Jan. 1918, LGP, I/1/2/32.)

37. Hankey to Lloyd George, 10 Oct. 1936, LGP, G/212.

archives remain closed to general research while "official" studies are in process; others, more infuriatingly, are opened selectively, at the whim of their owners or trustees, often perhaps for sound enough reasons but sometimes for seemingly trivial considerations. Of the available collections of private papers, none are more important in relation to foreign policy than those of the secretariat: Philip Kerr, Edward Grigg, Thomas Jones, and Hankey. All four collections, however, relate more fully to volume two of this study.

The private archives, moreover, are no substitute for the official files although many of them contain large quantities of government documents, and the Lloyd George papers hold more than most. Inevitably duplication occurs but on rare occasions a memorandum or paper appears in a private source that has escaped the official eye. Furthermore, the personal marginalia provide an important bonus for those who are able to consult government papers in private collections. Any attempt by officialdom to obstruct such access is detrimental to research, but again, there may appear to be sound reasons for such obstruction.

However, the records of the cabinet, supported by the files of the Foreign Office, the Committee of Imperial Defence, and other relevant departments, provide the indispensable basis for research into policy formulation and execution. They contain Lloyd George's memoranda and the responses thereto. They permit the historian to follow him through cabinet, departmental, and conference debate. Yet, whether one marvels at or laments the record, the official files do not compensate completely for the absence of a diary, and the presence of so few magisterial declarations of force and clarity, stating fundamental principles of policy. Historians must, nevertheless, probe the composition of his ideas and the layers of his personality, and seek out those factors most relevant to political action.[38]

From the rich, if narrow, cultural, religious, and political milieu of North Wales and Nonconformism, Lloyd George made the transition relatively easily to London and wider fields. He was

38. For example, K. O. Morgan, *David Lloyd George: Welsh Radical as World Statesman*, and his "Lloyd George's Premiership, A Study in Prime Ministerial Government"; C. Hazlehurst, *Politicians at War, July 1914 to May 1915* (London, 1971).

conscious that there was little in his background that counted for much in English society: a Welsh solicitor from an obscure sect and without a university education who apparently was not born to succeed. He and his family lacked the crucial combination of leisure, financial resources, inclination, and acceptability that ensures social prominence. Lloyd George remained devoted to visual and even sensual experiences: to travel, scenic beauty, the theatre, opera, thundering sermons, and choral music. These were the things that stirred his emotions, and he enjoyed life in London, and in London–Welsh society.

Over the years his feeling for Wales became distant, but while he sought escape from Welsh constraints, he continued to draw strength from his roots. Wales, while marking him as a provincial, gave him a popular following to the point of adulation, the imagery of his oratory, and a secure political base from which to grow. Indeed, Lloyd George was returned in the 1931 election without ever having set foot in his constituency during the campaign. Moreover, he could rely for the greater part of his career on the support of a loving and indulgent family.[39] Welsh and Nonconformist causes, which he served, identified him initially with Gladstonian liberalism, and a nationalism that was both cultural and political. But neither Wales and Nonconformism nor Gladstone's political construct could contain him. Joseph Chamberlain provided an alternate model of political radicalism and how to get on.

To that end Lloyd George brought immense abilities and attributes: boundless energy, resilience and determination, courage and imagination, creativity and vision, a sharp and open mind, a strong nerve, a silver tongue, an unfettered intellect, extremely good health, a capacity for hard work, a thick skin, and an intuitive grasp of political realities. These talents, an obsession with politics, and a driving ambition subdued but never erased a degree of insecurity; hence his egocentricity, his vanity, and his search for comfort and praise. Lloyd George was conscious of his gifts and powers to the point of experiencing a sense of innate superiority over his contemporaries. Indeed, he came to believe

39. Richard Lloyd to Lloyd George ("Dearest Boy"), Dec. 1907–Feb. 1917, LGP, I/1/1/1–48; Lloyd George to W. George, 6 March 1917, *ibid.*, I/2/2/63; correspondence with his wife and other members of his family, Lloyd George Papers (National Library of Wales), 20422C-20439C, 20461C-20477C; Morgan, *Family Letters.*

in a personal destiny,[40] which complemented his deism and his acceptance of the idea of a supreme will guiding the historical process. Lloyd George was neither inhibited by Nonconformist convictions nor weighed down with spiritual ballast, and his favourite line from Victor Hugo, "Let us march with our faces towards the dawn," was not a message of humility. Nevertheless, his career reflected an unresolved contest between competing forces: between the cognizance of his powers on the one hand, and a sense of uncertainty on the other. The Chinese concept of the unity of opposites helps one to understand Lloyd George.

Entrenched oligarchies, the aristocracy, and established institutions impressed Lloyd George only selectively; usually he regarded them as vulnerable. On the platform and in the courtroom he assailed the authority of landowners and the bench, of business and brewers, of the universities, the House of Lords and the Church of England, and of all visible forms of vested interest and privilege. He challenged them and was willing to risk the wounds and damn the consequences.

Parliament, and then office, confirmed that there was room at the top and especially at the summit of the Liberal party. The divisions in Liberal ranks provided opportunities for Lloyd George. Indeed, for him political parties were ephemeral rather than deiform institutions, and were acceptable only to the extent that they met current challenges. The House of Commons itself might retain both its powers and prestige, but Lloyd George used as effectively the podium, the pulpit, and the press.[41] Talent, moreover, was not hereditary and mandarins should not be allowed to stifle initiative and experimentation. Consequently, while Lloyd George used the bureaucracy, he laced the drink with his own intuition and with information from less orthodox sources. Confrontations with officialdom were, therefore, probable.

Lloyd George cast himself then as an activist, a critic, and an iconoclast, aroused by a perceived set of antagonists, by forms of opposition and condescension. Temperamentally he was suited to

40. Uncle Lloyd fed this belief. Lord Riddell commented on it, and evidence exists of Lloyd George's interest in the occult. (Riddell diary, 21 May 1913, Lord Riddell, *More Pages From My Diary 1908–1914* (London, 1934), 152; LGP, G/42/1/10.)

41. Lloyd George to Northcliffe, 21 March 1913, LGP, C/6/8. He thanked Northcliffe for his generous treatment during the Marconi affair and concluded, "I know the power you wield."

the role and his hard, even cruel, mouth betrayed the fact, just as his sparkling blue eyes advertised a sense of humour. Lloyd George had a high propensity for violence. He fought old campaigns over again when current struggles were lost, and he battled enemies even as they faded away. He justified any means of attack and in this invites comparison with Cleon.[42]

Lloyd George acted in this way to a large degree in the Boer War, but that experience also sharpened his awareness of the fact that compromise and conciliation were at least as potent weapons as militancy and confrontation. He became both emotional and calculating, persistent and patient, a politician of instinct and judgement. This dualism governed his political behaviour. Both the compulsion to challenge and the will to conciliate became integral parts of his political style. By this rule he fostered the image of the proud, Celtic Nonconformist, resisting assimilation and the anglicizing process, but making whatever adjustments were necessary in order to function effectively in British political life.

In this way Lloyd George demonstrated his continuing independence while achieving a *modus vivendi* with convention and the consensus. He never permitted himself to be either overawed or tamed. He rejected the inappropriate and the inconvenient and took up what he regarded as realistic and relevant. He genuflected to certain rules and conventions so that he could defy others and he both lived up to and lived down his past. Perhaps this dual posture reduced his credibility and even his effectiveness politically. Nevertheless this was the authentic Lloyd George.

Had Lloyd George remained a Welsh nationalist, or an immaculate, radical dissenter at Westminster, the analysis would be simpler. In fact, the essence of his political career was evolvement, largely through a process of response and reaction to political realities, issues, and crises. The political youth, however precocious, did not retain the man, yet the man did not entirely escape the youth. The maturing process was complex and it is as absurd to see Lloyd George simply discarding radical assumptions for, say, the realism of the Foreign Office, as it is to detect a fully developed set of ideas in the man of twenty-five. Youthful hints of

42. Speeches at Newcastle, 9 Oct. 1909, Guedalla, *Slings and Arrows*, 121, and Plymouth, 8 Jan. 1910, Lloyd George, *Better Times*, 266–77.

awareness of broader horizons do not constitute a mature political credo. Personality traits and strands of character may be set early and remain constant; ideas change, expanding and contracting.

Lloyd George's assumptions, ideas, and patterns of thought were exposed to new experiences and influences as he moved from Llanystumdwy to London by way of Criccieth and Portmadoc. He reconsidered, reassessed, and reformulated his views; he selected, confirmed, and rejected ideas, gave greater weight to some than others, controlled and gave free rein as he built up an integrated system.

Lloyd George sought out new challenges, he experimented, investigated alternatives, mastered his brief, and spun a political web *en courant* of inherent and adopted strands. This evolvement, this taking on of the layers of political maturity, of office and power, was not an indiscriminate process. Yet there was frequently an element of the unexpected, of the romantic and even of the irrational in his conduct. Indeed, to make Lloyd George a thoroughly rational figure is to ignore an important dimension of the man. He functioned at times almost as if devoted to a rule of paradox and became a brilliant political schizophrenic who evidently expected to carry the license of opposition into Downing Street and an imaginative freedom of thought into the halls of diplomacy.[43] He expected, in effect, the best of all worlds, where he could enjoy both freedom and power, and this expectation was a constant feature of his behaviour.

The political battle, for instance, was irresistible; it was his emancipation and became his life's work. Lloyd George realized that he could achieve national prominence only within the Liberal party.[44] No alternative existed, and yet his links with that party were always special and at times even tenuous. Centripetal and centrifugal forces pulled him into and yet thrust him away from the Liberal fold; and after the Boer War and the securing of office he could not rest easily in any wing of the party, whatever his popular image. Despairing observers discovered that, beyond the mere fact that he was Welsh, Lloyd George was not even a

43. Guedalla, *Slings and Arrows*, Lloyd George's prefatory note.
44 Lloyd George to Herbert Lewis, 31 Dec. 1931, LGP, G/1/1/20. Lewis advised him to break with party politics and to assume the role of "world statesman." (Lewis to Lloyd George, 15 Dec. 1931, ibid., G/12/1/19.) Others had offered the same advice in 1923, but Lloyd George admitted that "I find it hard to avoid a scrap."

predictable radical. He continued to work within the Liberal party while retaining possession of his own political future, to the extent of exploring arrangements across party lines.

Contemporary responses, therefore, become understandable. Sydney Buxton, the postmaster-general, remarked in April 1907: "Yes, none of us know what Lloyd George is up to."[45] He seemed capable of sheer opportunism, a dangerously irresponsible and alien figure without conviction, integrity, loyalty, or principle.[46]

In terms of policy the tap-root was largely but not exclusively radical; the mature root system was widespread. In the realm of domestic politics, beyond purely Welsh matters, Lloyd George eventually synthesized radicalism and Nonconformism with the New Liberalism. He fused concern over education, disestablishment, temperance and political privilege, as befitted a Free Churchman, with free trade and progressive taxation policies, and a determination to secure social reform through state intervention. In this process, Lloyd George established a relationship with the Liberal Imperialists, but benefited from the brief upsurge in the political importance of Nonconformist radicalism, for perhaps as many as 200 of the members of Parliament elected in 1906 were Free Churchmen. In addition, he drew on the theories of social imperialism, and identified in part with those who searched for national efficiency and competence.[47] Conviction united with political realism and personal ambition to demand this synthesis. Lloyd George became convinced that the nation deserved a more comprehensive and vigorous alternative to socialism and he was the first prime minister to fight a general election to defeat the Labour Party.

A similar process marked his response to the problems of foreign policy. Indeed, to prosper politically, Lloyd George was

45. A. Chamberlain, Politics from Inside . . . 1906–1914 (London, 1936), 65–66.
46. J. S. Sandars to Garvin, 12 May 1910, Garvin Papers, box 57. Sandars, Balfour's private secretary, dubbed Lloyd George "the perfervid Celt"; W. M. Conacher, "The Lloyd Georgics," 43–54.
47. M. Richter, The Politics of Conscience (London, 1964); S. H. Beer, British Politics in the Collectivist Age (New York, 1965); G. R. Searle, The Quest for National Efficiency (Berkeley, 1971); B. Semmel, Imperialism and Social Reform: English Social and Imperial Thought 1895–1914 (Cambridge, Mass., 1960); A. Marwick, The Deluge (New York, 1965). The social imperialist and national efficiency movements advocated economic planning, social engineering, state intervention, and the efficient allocation of resources to produce social progress, economic growth, disciplined modernization, redirected patriotism, preparedness, and national and imperial security.

forced to develop a familiarity with foreign and defence questions. To do so he selected from and synthesized competitive, disparate, and even alien assumptions and ideas. Initially he was most but not solely in sympathy with dissenting and pacific dogma held by those who sought to establish reformed rules of international conduct. Once in Parliament, if not earlier, and then in office, he attempted to reconcile this dogma with the Hobbesian thesis of conflict and with the rules of Darwinian international behaviour; in effect with the current wisdom of the Foreign Office and the defence departments. He became more concerned with the world as it was and rather less with what it might become, although he was never devoid of either reforming zeal or prescience.

This particular attempt at a synthesis meant for instance that while Lloyd George retained his faith in armaments limitation, as chancellor of the exchequer he sanctioned unprecedented levels of expenditure for national and imperial defence. Moreover, he did not permit his audiences during the First World War to forget that fact. He understood the equation relating capabilities to policy goals, as well as that relating aims to popular appeal. Where the theses of pacificism and national interest were not reconcilable, Lloyd George invariably championed the latter cause. It followed that he and Sir Edward Grey, the foreign secretary of Liberal Imperialist convictions, were able to establish an impressive degree of rapport on policy matters between 1908 and 1914. Radical colleagues such as Lord Loreburn and John Burns retained few illusions about the maturing Lloyd George.

The outcome, itself a complex and never fully stable integration of ideas, is easier to identify than the process, Lloyd George's political education. How rapidly and fully did the fusion of views take place, and how often did he regress in a fit of nostalgia? Assumptions, seemingly discarded, could re-emerge, and discrepancies between his public pronouncements and private conversations were not unknown. Part of the problem lies in the intellectual constructs of observers who see unyielding dichotomous relationships between, for instance, radicalism and imperialism, and idealist and realist assumptions about foreign policy. Such constructs are as unsound as those which rely on simple progressions between fixed points. The Boer War, the debates over naval preparedness and a continental strategy, the Agadir crisis, the decision for war in 1914, and the challenge of war itself were the decisive events, but Lloyd George was more the hawk in

1911 than in 1914. The complex of ideas, the product of synthesis, determined that Lloyd George would, in the 1914 crisis, seem first to divide and then help unite the cabinet, the Liberal party, and the nation.

These syntheses on domestic and foreign policy meant that Lloyd George became a progressive reformer and an architect of national and imperial security.[48] He saw himself as a centrist, as an alternative to extremism. In December 1916 he created an administration from broadly based political and apolitical talent with the self-made man prominent. The government was meant to transcend narrow partisan considerations and provide the potential for national reconciliation.[49] In the postwar era he attempted to perpetuate and even institutionalize what he saw as more representative of the popular will than were the party faithful. Fusion proved to be a disillusioning and ultimately humiliating experience that did much to destroy his credibility. As he left office and on into the eventide of his life, however, he insisted that he had remained true to certain principles and ideals. Those who disagreed had simply failed to understand him.[50]

He had become convinced that the silent man was neither strong nor effective. He believed the orators were the actors in the twentieth century, for they could generate psychological power, and that his own gifts were essentially those of a man of eloquence and action. The charisma of a commanding presence and an expressive voice, combined with a will to act, were the characteristics which Lloyd George admired and felt he possessed. In other words he valued in others what he saw in himself.

Lloyd George was a superbly equipped and formidable politician, but he overplayed his hand and outstayed his welcome.[51] The longer he governed the less he inspired trust and confidence. Once out of office he could excite the politically young and fill the House of Commons when he spoke. Most politicians could not deny some association with him, many admitted past intimacies

48. Roosevelt to Lodge, 18 March 1917, *Selections from the Correspondence of Theodore Roosevelt and Henry Cabot Lodge, 1894–1918*, 2 vols. (New York, 1925), II, 503–504.

49. A. C. Murray, *Master and Brother: Murrays of Elibank* (London, 1945), 82; Lady Dorothy Neville, *My Own Times* (London, 1912), 104.

50. C. P. Snow, *New Statesman and Nation*, 226–27; V. Bonham-Carter, *Winston Churchill as I Knew Him* (London, 1965), 161–65.

51. Viscount Samuel, *Memoirs* (London, 1945), 87–89; Lord Salter, *Memoirs of a Public Servant* (London, 1961), 61, 69.

and current flirtations, but no party in power embraced him. The weight of inscrutability, unpredictable behaviour, and distrust proved too heavy. There was too much to forgive and forget, and Lloyd George could match anyone in bitterness.[52] His political career was, in consequence, a progression of massive achievement and self-destruction. He became a great but tragic figure, and ultimately an isolated giant.

52. Lloyd George to F. Guest, 18 Feb. 1935, LGP, G/215. Lloyd George described Passchendaele as the most terrible moment of the war and the most miserable of his life. Next to it, in terms of personal misery, he placed the events of 1928 when those "malignant insects," his fellow Liberals, were "buzzing and biting around my head." After Herbert Samuel denounced his views on a negotiated peace in 1939, Lloyd George wrote to Lord Mottistone: "I am glad you snubbed Samuel. I do not dislike Jews. I have had many friends amongst them. I know their hatred of hog flesh; that ought to induce them to disown Samuel as their spokesman, for I know him well, and I tell you he is, always has been, and ever will be, until he gets to the bosom of Abraham, a swine of the swiniest. Then Abraham will hate him as he would putrid pork." (Lloyd George to Mottistone, 9 Oct. 1939, ibid., G/15/4/4.)

# 2

# Ideas and
Realities

The last thirty years of the nineteenth century witnessed a cultural
and political renaissance in Wales which helped mould the young
Lloyd George.[1] He was caught up in radical, Nonconformist, and
nationalist movements which bit deep into those who by hard
work and sheer ability had raised themselves into the professions,
local prominence, and even notoriety. As a young attorney,
orator, municipal politician, and journalist, Lloyd George forged a
future for himself.[2] Undeterred by critical and even hostile
commentary, he moved rapidly into more elevated political
circles. Logically his fortunes lay with the Welsh group within
that collection of interests which passed for the Gladstonian
Liberal Party. Once in the House of Commons, in April 1890,
Lloyd George devoted himself predictably and militantly to Welsh
and Nonconformist causes.[3] He explained away the concentric
circles of criticism which his conduct provoked: he was a Celt, an

---

1. K. O. Morgan, *Wales in British Politics, 1868–1922* (Cardiff, 1963).
2. Lloyd George to D. R. Daniel, Dec. 1887 and 5 July 1888, LGP, G/40/1.
3. *Caernarvon and Denbigh Herald*, 28 March and 4 April 1890, and *Liverpool Mercury*, March and April 1890, ibid., H/107; W. George, *My Brother and I*, 132-33.

alien, inscrutable to the dull-witted English. At the same time he recognized the danger of sustained extremism. To extract power from within the Liberal Party and yet retain a certain independence from it he must make reconciliations with the hierarchy, and act responsibly. He understood that the prolonged absence from power corrupts.

How well was Lloyd George equipped to deal with questions of defence, foreign, and imperial policy; how did his opinions develop in the years before he took office in December 1905? Lloyd George was not a particularly contemplative or introspective person concerned with fashioning great mental edifices. He did not pass through any deep intellectual or penetrating philosophical experience and pause to examine its implications in the shadow of a great mentor. Clearly there was no hint of the intellectual in action, and his command of English and Welsh, rather than of European languages, did not induce profound reasoning about the European state system let alone the nature of international relations. Indeed, by reducing the problems to a relatively simple set of propositions, he demonstrated his refusal to concede a mystique to international affairs.

Lloyd George was widely rather than well read, in history, law, biography, and politics, but the cumulative impact seemed more descriptive than analytical, more emotional than cerebral.[4] Newspapers, periodicals, and pamphlets were no doubt as significant for him as any other corpus of literature. Indeed, the question is less what Lloyd George read and more his motive for reading: to pass examinations, to qualify, to extract facts, historical parallels, and quotations in order to underpin his political activities and oratory.

Three sets of influences affected his ideas about foreign policy: the lingering stimuli of Wales and Nonconformism; humanitarianism and radical dissent as funnelled through Gladstone; and a youthful sense of broader considerations, sharpened by the struggle over current policy issues which pitted Liberal against Unionist and Liberal against Liberal.

From Wales and Nonconformism, Lloyd George derived a view of international affairs which he invariably expressed in

4. The French Revolution, the functioning of empires, and the American Civil War interested him; Lincoln, Robespierre, and Cromwell attracted him, and he read Carlyle, Macaulay, Gibbon, Hallam, Burke, Henry George, Hugo, Dumas, Ruskin, and Scott. He could read French and Latin.

religious or moral terms. An eternal force of light and goodness, God's law to some audiences, provided for human freedom and happiness, order in nature, and peace. The antithesis, a force of darkness and evil, bred injustice, waste, and war. This code governed all nations and for this reason Lloyd George denounced the jingo and his "Rule Britannia." God ruled the waves and his law did not permit even England to exploit the earth and its peoples.[5] Wales could not remain loyal if immorality ruled in London. On the other hand a state which upheld the moral, Christian, or natural law commanded the devotion of all its subjects. It followed that statesmen were free to conduct foreign policy in conformity with higher principles than those of realpolitik. They had a choice to exercise which ultimately came down to that of war or peace. War, Lloyd George argued, was an immoral, inhumane, and irrational act to which only a depraved government would resort. Welsh audiences in particular could be forgiven, therefore, for assuming that he was a pacifist.

At the political level, Lloyd George opposed war as wastefully expensive and a threat to social and economic reform. He saw it as benefiting bankrupt conservatism, invariably fatal to liberalism and, consequently, as a source of decay. War, in fact, was a conspiracy of the few against the many, of the oligarchy against the people. Finally, Lloyd George charged, governments launched wars to divert attention from domestic injustice and to retain power by arousing an unhealthy and spurious patriotism. The Tories, he suggested in October 1905, had avoided major conflicts since the Boer War, but had waged costly colonial wars against native peoples.[6] They were, in fact, a decadent, secretive, and inept élite. The remedy lay in a democratizing process, in the mobilizing of a peace-loving public opinion, and securing parliamentary scrutiny of foreign policy. Successive Conservative governments, Lloyd George suggested, curtailed debate on defence estimates and foreign affairs in a patent attempt to evade control. If Parliament was not effective then Lloyd George would turn to the nation at large, to the popular will. This was a

---

5. W. George, 27–80; Lloyd George speech at York, 30 Jan. 1905, P. Guedalla, *Slings and Arrows*, 209; W. Watkin Davies, *Lloyd George*, 15–39; Sir A. T. Davies, *The Lloyd George I Knew*, 22–39. The attraction of preachers such as Hugh Price Hughes enhanced this theme.

6. Speech at Kirkcaldy, 27 Oct. 1905, LGP, A/13/2/8.

Gladstonian appeal in effect, to resist demands for continuity in policy in the name of national unity.

Lloyd George, however, was not a pacifist and had offered himself for military training, for motives that remain obscure, in a local volunteer militia in June 1882.[7] He accepted the concept of a permissible war, fought for great principles and ennobling causes, such as the expulsion of the Turk from Europe, and struggled with the resulting dilemmas. How could a corrupt oligarchy wage a morally defensible war; was not war itself a political and social regenerator; what of legitimate national interests and self-defence; and how else could nations deal with deviate international behaviour? In fact he often resembled the atheist who shakes his fist at heaven when disaster strikes.

Lloyd George took the existence of a separate Welsh race to be self-evident. The Welsh were a distinct entity, a nation enjoying their own language, traditions, culture, and pastimes. They loved nature, oratory, divine law, and chapel; the English, in contrast, were a nation of footballers, stock exchange brokers, and drinkers.[8] The Celts, like the Jews, had not wielded independent political power, but had survived the rise and fall of empires. Surely this demonstrated their higher virtue and demanded that they continue to resist alien values and institutions. Moreover, Lloyd George claimed, Welsh patriotic feelings were part of all that was best in nineteenth-century Europe, where patriotism provided the creative driving force of the nationalist movements. Races, once prostrate in the face of tyranny, had achieved emancipation and self-respect. Patriotism not party politics gave freedom to the oppressed and liberty to the imprisoned. It "raised the destitute...and bent monarchies to its will."[9] The force of patriotism was morally indestructible, and in fact the hope of the future.

"God still selects nationalities to be missionaries of his ideas," Lloyd George argued, as he claimed the right of national self-determination, if not of a nation state, for Wales. Nations were

---

7. Within a year of entering parliament he challenged the War Office decision not to support the volunteer corps at Festiniog, Merionethshire, which he described as a "splendid recruiting ground." (25 June 1891, *Parl. Deb.*, H. of C., cccLIV, 1523.)

8. Speeches at Cardiff, 5 Feb. 1896, LGP, A/8/2/7, and Aberystwyth, Dec. 1896, H. du Parcq, *Life of David Lloyd George*, I, 144–48.

9. Speech, 12 Oct. 1894, LGP, A/7/3/31; du Parcq, I, 59, 148.

created by a higher force than the decrees of statesmen. They could not be made or destroyed by legislation; they were not mere legal entities. Bulgars would not become Turks because Lord Salisbury, the Tory leader, wished them to be so; Wales would not disappear because of the petulant sneers of ten thousand Balfours.[10] He who loved Wales, loved justice and freedom. God knew how dear to him was his Wales, and by inference all small nations. They were the streams, Lloyd George romanticized, which did not lose their identity in the great rivers, and without which those rivers would dry up.[11] Undoubtedly Lloyd George viewed international politics to some extent in terms of race.

Gladstone's declaration of faith in the public law of Europe and his apparent devotion to the idea of a European concert attracted Lloyd George as a solution to international anarchy. The great powers, harmonious in spirit and motive and under the moral leadership of England, would agree to outlaw all selfish, unilateral acts and uphold the freedom and rights of all nations. Conference diplomacy and pacific procedures would supplant the mechanics of the balance of power. In one of his earliest forays, in November 1880 at the age of 17, Lloyd George, attacking a Unionist opponent, Ellis Nanney, in the *North Wales Express*, defended the Concert of Europe as most likely to preserve peace, inspire England with a love of freedom and ensure her security. Gladstone's policy should therefore receive the blessing of all patriotic Welshmen and Liberals.[12] These considerations also demonstrated how his Welsh nationalism merged into an identification with a broader British nationalism. Wales, with her distinct identity, could function best within the United Kingdom. In this way Lloyd George came to share a sense of superiority; an Englishman must lead Europe, and if so, why not a Scot or a Welshman?

Whether Britain should follow an isolationist policy remained a moot point. It was a question of both disliking foreign entanglements, justified in the name of the balance of power, and being attracted to intervention in support of great causes. Under Canning, Lloyd George argued as early as November 1880, the Tories

---

10. Speeches at Criccieth, 30 Jan. and 3 Feb. 1892, LGP, A/7/1/4 and 6; W. George, 128–29; L. S. Amery, *My Political Life*, 3 vols. (London, 1953), I, 89.

11. Speech at Cardiff, 27 Oct. 1916, LGP, H/107.

12. Brutus article, 19 Nov. 1880, *North Wales Express*, du Parcq, I, 37–39.

had fought oppression and aided Europe's emerging nations to secure liberty.[13] Under Lord Salisbury, the same party was "barren of statesmen." In a more significant attack, in January 1898, Lloyd George ridiculed Lord Salisbury as a secretive, craven, and faltering prime minister and foreign secretary who inspired neither fear in Europe nor confidence at home.[14] He ignored England's glorious mission to protect oppressed nationalities, without regard for her own interests or material gain. Under Salisbury, Lloyd George charged, England the missionary crusader had become the pedlar and the huckster. She must oust him and thereby save her honour.

The Armenian crisis and the related question of Crete's desire for independence from Turkish rule or union with Greece had provoked Lloyd George's assault on Salisbury in 1898. The Turk, the oppressor of liberty, ravaged Christian peoples in an orgy of misrule. He also posed a perpetual threat to the peace and, Lloyd George declared, must be expelled from Europe. Salisbury, like Disraeli before him, had betrayed Britain's honour by permitting the Turks to slaughter the defenceless Armenians. This neglect, Lloyd George insisted in October 1898, was the darkest blot on British foreign policy. Salisbury had offered protection for the price of Cyprus, kindness for a fee, Christianity with a dividend, and had then failed to keep his word. Tory immorality again, but then "we were great Christians under that eminent Jewish statesman, Disraeli."[15]

Lloyd George found only one source of comfort in Salisbury's Near Eastern policy: the suggestion that Britain had probably backed the wrong horse in the Crimean War.[16] For the rest, the sultan had jeered at Britain's representations, rejected any reform program, and used Foreign Office notes as cigarette papers, saying, "I will not be robbed of my pastime. I have murdered Christians for centuries past and I will not forego similar pleasures in the centuries to come."

Gladstone, in contrast, Lloyd George noted, had championed Bulgar, Armenian, and Montenegrin. He had mobilized and even

13. Brutus article, 5 Nov. 1880, *North Wales Express*, ibid., I, 35–36.

14. Speeches at Bangor and Colwyn Bay, 13 and 14 Jan. 1898, LGP, A/8/4/1 and 3.

15. Speech at Haworth, 24 Oct. 1898, ibid., A/8/4/27.

16. Speech, 29 April 1901, *Parl. Deb.*, H. of C., XCIII, 115–21.

at times defied a reluctant Concert, and had acted in the name of Christian justice. Surely he was the fountain of truth.[17]

As late as 1940, Lloyd George returned to the theme. He worshipped Gladstone, he said, and Disraeli's temporary eclipse of him would not prevent a glorious resurrection of Gladstone's reputation. After another long and devastating period of war, Lloyd George predicted, nations would return to Gladstone's ideals and accept his doctrine on national rights and the dangers of armaments.[18]

Lloyd George advocated multilateral not unilateral disarmament and again expected England to provide Europe with moral leadership.[19] He was therefore opposed to governments which, misled by experts and demands for limitless expenditure, actually fed the arms race. England, he charged in November 1899, contributing to a tragic escalation of cost and fear, was "really taking the initiative, we are forcing the pace and when bad times come the taxation will be so enormous as to be absolutely oppressive." Lloyd George argued for the exercise of the common sense of the layman. As an alternative to current policies, he demanded in June 1904 that Britain honour the resolutions of the first Hague Conference of 1899, opt for arbitration procedures and support the humanizing of warfare. This policy, he argued, would render the Empire secure.[20]

Domestically, Lloyd George insisted, bloated armaments, like war, undermined the pursuit of reform. He attacked inflated defence estimates as immoral.[21] Military establishments he criticized as instruments of repression and a source of employment and power for a vigorous but decadent aristocracy. In the process he challenged the integrity of Joseph Chamberlain, the colonial

---

17. Brutus article, 19 Feb. 1881, *North Wales Express*, du Parcq, I, 53–56. Lloyd George never joined the Balkan Committee, which concerned itself with the subject peoples of the Ottoman Empire. (T. P. Conwell-Evans, *Politics from a Back Bench, 1904–18* [London, 1932], x–5; H. N. Fieldhouse, "Noel Buxton and A. J. P. Taylor's 'The Trouble Makers'," in M. Gilbert, ed., *A Century of Conflict 1850–1950* [London, 1966], 175–98.)

18. Lloyd George to Lord Crewe, 16 April 1940, LGP, G/5/5/1, and Crewe Papers, C/31.

19. Speech, 27 July 1899, *Parl. Deb.*, H. of C., LXXV, 547–49.

20. Speeches at Carmarthen, 27 Nov. 1899, and Alexandria Palace, 4 June 1904, LGP, A/9/1/25 and A/12/1/65.

21. Speeches, 27 Feb. and 23 March 1896, and 27 July 1899, *Parl. Deb.*, H. of C., XXXVII, 1298–1300, XXXVIII, 1699–1700, and LXXV, 547–49.

secretary, long before the Boer War.[22] The War Office, he charged in 1895 and 1896, gave preferential treatment to the Kynoch Company of Birmingham. Subsequently, on two occasions in 1898, Lloyd George declared publicly that Wales had bred heroes and statesmen when Birmingham was still a swamp. Now Birmingham lived off the profits of war, as the recent disturbances on India's northwestern frontiers revealed. He denounced this "electro-plated Rome, its peddling imperialism and its tin Caesar." Chamberlain, Lloyd George insisted, the former highwayman turned darling of the Primrose League, was England's "tawdriest statesman."[23] He had neglected the morally and economically sound policy goals of arms limitation, retrenchment, reform, and peace.

Lloyd George believed nevertheless that national and imperial security depended upon naval supremacy. He tended therefore to attack the inefficiency of the defence establishment rather than to deplore expenditure upon it. Only the third sea lord, the efficient Sir John Fisher, escaped criticism and even earned praise.[24] Lloyd George rejected the need for Britain to imitate the European powers and create a large army. He insisted, however, on the need for a strong navy to defend the Empire, protect commerce, assure national security, and prevent panic in times of crisis.[25] Indeed, the white Dominions must share the burden.[26]

On occasion, as in March 1896, Lloyd George opposed not the development of a new naval base but the government's failure to locate that base at Pembroke Dock.[27] The Conservative government, ignoring both its election promises and the fact that Pem-

22. Speeches at Bangor, 4 July 1895, LGP, A/8/1/25, and 16 July 1896, *Parl. Deb.*, H. of C., XLII, 1642.

23. Speeches at Swansea, 4 Feb. and 14 Dec. 1898, LGP, A/8/4/8 and 32.

24. Speeches at Bangor, 15 Dec. 1896, Blaenavon, 4 June 1903, Glasgow, 24 Jan., Bilston, 12 May, and Kingston, 19 Oct. 1905, ibid., A/8/2/2, A/11/1/43, A/13/1/3 and 14, and A/13/2/7, and 14 Aug. 1901, *Parl. Deb.*, H. of C., XCIX, 805–806. He compared Tory incompetence with the superior record of the French. France, spending only £40 million on defence in 1901, had built an effective military machine. Although her navy was weak, she received value for her expenditures.

25. London *Echo*, 20 Feb. 1903, du Parcq, II, 391.

26. Speech, 27 July 1899, *Parl. Deb.*, H. of C., LXXV, 547–49.

27. Speeches, 28 May 1895, ibid., XXXIV, 524–26, and 26 and 30 March 1896, XXXIX, 211–16, 429–30; Lloyd George to Richard Lloyd, 27 March 1896, du Parcq, I, 172–73. He had also demanded harbours for Wales in the summer of 1892.

broke Dock was the finest harbour in the land, could not understand that the Admiralty was obsessed with the southern coast and had grievously neglected western and eastern ports. Fortified naval bases on these coasts were vital in time of war, Lloyd George maintained, and the development of Pembroke Dock would repair the neglect in the west. Thus in the course of one argument he sought to provide for investment and employment in Wales, national security, and political support for himself.

This seeming ambivalence was present in Lloyd George's attitude toward free trade. On the one hand he insisted that causal links existed between the perpetuation of free trade and the maintenance of peace. Britain continued to avoid war with the Great Powers because of the influence of free trade. The South African war had demonstrated this to be so. Why had the Great Powers, he asked, not intervened in a war which they detested and which had demonstrated Britain's vulnerability? The answer was that Europe's commercial lobbies would not permit an attack on a nation devoted to free trade. Yet at the same time he associated free trade with the quest for naval supremacy and imperial security. Free trade spawned shipbuilding and seamanship, both of which fostered maritime greatness.[28]

The issue of free trade also became for Lloyd George a source of empathy with British nationalism. He denounced protection not only as misguided imperialism and a Tory ramp but also as unpatriotic defeatism. Joseph Chamberlain came to embody all these heresies when in 1903 imperial preference replaced South Africa as the central issue.[29] Lloyd George's explanation was not profound but in a series of distressingly repetitious speeches he made some telling points. He described imperial preference as political quackery, born in Germany and adopted by a colonial secretary who posed as the new Bismarck. This misguided politician promised a Zollverein, imperial consolidation, and social reform, but was in fact a false prophet, a mere political spasm, an epileptic. Chamberlain, previously a man of courage and ability, would lead the Empire astray. Britain must, Lloyd George warned, avoid the errors of the United States and Germany, and remain devoted to an empire of commerce and free trade. Protection was

28. Speeches at Paisley, 2 Dec. 1903, and Perth, 24 Nov. 1904, Guedalla, *Slings and Arrows*, 62–63, 36.

29. Speeches at Aberearn, 5 June, Pembroke Dock, 2 Oct. 1903, and Bradford, 2 March 1904, LGP, A/11/1/45, A/11/2/19, A/12/1/22.

the very policy which hindered their search for commercial supremacy. Arthur Balfour he ridiculed as having no policy beyond that of raising revenues through tariffs to avoid progressive taxation and to finance the production of weapons of war.[30]

Lloyd George developed a quite elementary philosophy of empire by inductive reasoning from selected historical examples, but did not forge a theory of imperialism in the manner of the disciples of Lord Cromer, Britain's former consul-general in Egypt, and Sir Alfred Milner, Britain's high commissioner in South Africa during and after the Boer War. Nor had he any first-hand knowledge of the Empire apart from his visit to Canada in 1899. In fact, initially his views were essentially partisan; the Empire, beyond the white Dominions, was a brutal, unjust, and aggressive creation of the Tories. From Afghanistan to Zululand Conservative policies, fathered by Disraeli and adopted by Salisbury and Chamberlain, were wantonly barbarous and indefensible.[31] Native peoples did not even benefit from humane, enlightened, civilizing, paternalistic rule, which Nonconformists and evangelical radicals demanded as fervently as any Social Darwinian, with his racial arrogance, pride in authoritarian government, and sense of duty. In March 1901, for instance, Lloyd George denied that humanitarian considerations justified military action against the Ashanti.[32] He would accept a colonial war at a tenfold cost to bring about the abolition of slavery, and to end the practice of human sacrifice in West Africa. In fact the government, he declared, had imposed forced labour and unfair taxation on the Ashanti and had then acted to suppress a purported insurrection.

In the same vein, in 1903, Lloyd George condemned Chamberlain's administration in East Africa, and the oppressive taxation imposed on South Africa.[33] These policies, he insisted, forced natives into the mines to provide cheap labour, and encouraged

30. Speech at Alexandria Palace, 4 June 1904, ibid., A/12/1/65; Lloyd George to H. Lewis, 28 Nov. 1904, H. Lewis Papers, file 19.

31. Brutus article, 19 Nov. 1880, North Wales Express, du Parcq, I, 37–39.

32. Speech, 19 March 1901, Parl. Deb., H. of C., xci, 438–43. He reported to his brother that he gave Chamberlain a "thoroughly good trimming" and that "Jo" became very angry. (Lloyd George to W. George, 19 March 1901, W. George, 183.)

33. Speeches, 2 and 19 March 1903, Parl. Deb., H. of C., cxviii, 1199–2000, and cxix, 1267–71.

polygamy. They were on a par with Spanish practices in South America and merely soiled Britain's image in a quest for profits.

Lloyd George had attacked Gladstone's decision to occupy Egypt by force in September 1882 for similar reasons. He saw it as a fraudulent financial ramp and as deviate behaviour. No danger existed to the Suez Canal to justify it. The Khedive was as guilty as Arabi Pasha, the nationalist leader, and foreign control was a grave injustice perpetrated on the Egyptian people. Locked in poverty by the oppressive taxation of a corrupt government, they yearned for liberation. Arabi Pasha, rising from humble origins, provided an opportunity for emancipation.[34]

Initially then, Lloyd George regarded most imperial ventures as a denial of human liberty and national rights. He did not believe, however, that empires could not serve higher causes, and that the British Empire specifically was doomed not to do so. England, supported by a cluster of autonomous, liberal, white Dominions, could be the fulcrum of a humane, prosperous, and secure Empire which would be a legitimate focus of national pride in, for example, Ottawa, as well as in London. Indeed, loyal Welshmen, again identifying with a broader British patriotism, could rest proudly in that Empire, and some could make a contribution to its greatness. In so doing they would serve Wales, the United Kingdom, and the British Empire. The Boer War both demonstrated and accelerated the development of such views, and in the long run Lloyd George would match the likes of Milner and Lord Curzon, former Viceroy of India, in their devotion to the Empire and its security. In another way this is understandable; radicals can be more nationalist and imperialist because they are not as internationalist in outlook as are the members of a traditional élite who, by reason of education and travel, tend to be more cosmopolitan.

Lloyd George went to Westminster in April 1890 with a receptive mind. His first parliamentary comment on foreign affairs came in May 1892, on the Suez Canal Company. He was exposed to debate over foreign policy and the dogma of imperial security at a particularly critical time, when Gladstone, Lord Rosebery, former foreign secretary and Gladstone's future successor as Liberal prime minister, and Salisbury challenged one other. These were years when a sense of vulnerability bred uncertainty and experimentation in policy, which the orgy of celebration at the Diamond

34. Speech, 13 Nov. 1882, LGP, A/6/1/2 and du Parcq, I, 41–42.

Jubilee of 1897 could not conceal. France and Russia, in combination, from January 1894, were menacing imperial competitors in Africa, India, and Asia. Imperial Germany and her allies might also challenge as the Ottoman and Manchu dynasties wavered or proved troublesome. The security of Egypt seemed threatened and some in London regarded the fleet as inadequate to meet all global contingencies. In such circumstances perhaps only a dedicated Marxist or pacifist would argue that alliances, defence planning, and naval preparedness were utterly inadmissible, and concepts such as the balance of power irrelevant. Who else would insist that the Foreign Office was devoid of reason and that Britain could afford to discount the Russian problem?

The practitioners of Liberal foreign policy, the models whom Lloyd George observed, were scarcely a uniform or even united group. They diverged on several issues, with Rosebery in frequent confrontation with Gladstone, John Morley, the chief secretary for Ireland, and Sir William Harcourt, the chancellor of the exchequer, who were opposed to a forward policy in the Nile valley and favoured détente with France. Rosebery, supported by Edward Grey, the future foreign secretary and a Liberal Imperialist, preferred to expand British control over Egypt and the Sudan. Indeed, Rosebery was and remained decidedly hostile to France and the Franco-Russian entente; for him Britain's imperial enemies lay in Paris and St. Petersburg.

Lloyd George found merit in both views. He retained his reverence for Gladstone,[35] but preferred the seemingly modern and exciting Rosebery to the more pedestrian Harcourt, and became contemptuous of Morley.[36] Indeed, when Harcourt retired in 1898 as Liberal leader in the Commons, Lloyd George suggested that he had been less in touch with the younger spirits than Rosebery, whose imperial sympathies were greater. He described Rosebery as the finest foreign secretary since Lord Palmerston.[37] While not matching Gladstone on the Near East he had outdone Salisbury. But Rosebery did not invariably satisfy

35. On Gladstone's death, Lloyd George described him as a saint and as the greatest leader of men since Napoleon. (*Caernarvon Herald*, 20 May 1898, LGP, A/8/4/19.) Lloyd George told Herbert Lewis in 1907 that he felt Gladstone would be remembered most for putting the "Alabama" affair to arbitration. (Lewis diary, 28 April 1907.)
36. D. A. Hamer, *John Morley* (London, 1968), 333–34.
37. *Daily Telegraph*, 15 Dec. 1898, du Parcq, I, 191.

Lloyd George, who found his actions often unpredictable. In August 1892 Lloyd George asked Tom Ellis, the Liberal deputy-whip, "What is the truth about Rosebery? Does he mean mischief? The outlook is rather gloomy as far as foreign affairs is concerned."[38]

In January 1899, on the heels of the Fashoda crisis, Lloyd George declared himself in favour of consolidationist imperial policies, whereby Britain could defend the Empire as economically as possible.[39] He would oppose expansionist and annexationist moves. Given the extent of the Empire on the eve of the Boer War, however, to favour consolidation scarcely made one an anti-imperialist. Indeed, the South African conflict would soon demonstrate that Lloyd George did not intend that his career or the prospects of the Liberal party should founder on self-destructive extremism and suicidal confrontations over the future of the Empire. Liberals, in his opinion, must challenge the monopoly of patriotism and imperialism which the Tories claimed.

Lloyd George had denounced Salisbury not only for his weakness in face of the Turk but also as a menace to imperial security. On both counts the prime minister was a source of national humiliation.[40] After bullying Venezuela, refusing arbitration, and making preposterous claims in order to seize gold-bearing areas, Salisbury had meekly yielded to United States pressure. He had jeered at the kaiser's incapacities at a time when German commerce was ousting British trade from China and world markets. Even a small republic in South Africa could defy London. Despite her naval and military resources, Britain under Salisbury could neither resist any great power nor fulfil her obligations. Her treaty rights in Madagascar, her commercial privileges in Siam, and her trade throughout Africa were seemingly forfeit to French claims.

38. Lloyd George to Ellis, 16 Aug. 1892, T. Ellis Papers, f. 686.
39. Speech at Manchester, 18 Jan. 1899, LGP, A/9/1/1.
40. On Salisbury's death, however, Lloyd George ranked him with Gladstone, Bismarck, and Disraeli as a great leader. He praised the tranquil dignity of his dispatches, his wise retreat to avoid war with the United States, his restraint over Fashoda, and his lack of responsibility for the Boer War. Balfour's government, labouring under the loss of Chamberlain, Hicks-Beach, and Salisbury, was "a miserable rump." (Speeches at Caernarvon, 25 Aug. 1903, and Chester, 28 July 1905, ibid., A/11/2/8 and A/13/2/3.) Perhaps Lloyd George spoke in this way to impress the Liberal Imperialists and for immediate political advantage.

*33*

Indeed, Salisbury might give Wales or Yorkshire to France if she pressed the issue.[41]

Yet while Lloyd George denounced Salisbury's appeasement of the United States he also applauded America as the most significant example of a progressive political and social experiment, and was an advocate of close Anglo-American relations and cooperation among the English-speaking peoples. The confrontation with France at Fashoda provides a further example of his ability to fuse radical and patriotic tendencies. On the one hand he lamented Salisbury's hesitations in the face of Britain's hostile, imperial rival. The French, gambling on Salisbury's willingness to yield, had squeezed the indiarubber dummy at Fashoda. The situation was dangerous but, Lloyd George argued, Britain must meet the challenge even at the risk of war. He agreed with Rosebery that she could not relinquish the Nile valley. However, he preferred to avoid war and so, he insisted, did Théophile Delcassé, the French foreign minister. France would give up her claims to Fashoda and would settle in reasonable fashion for access to the Nile. Britain, for her part, should respond in like manner, and disavow the bullying and hectoring Tory chancellor of the exchequer, Sir Michael Hicks-Beach. Should war result with France, the navy would ensure victory, but Britain's success would be illusory and even dangerous. She would have defeated the only democratic power in Europe, at a time when France also faced domestic enemies who threatened her political institutions. France, England, and democracy would suffer, and "the throned Philistines of Europe would laugh and applaud." Like the *Manchester Guardian* and Morley, Lloyd George deplored a breach with Britain's ideological counterpart in Europe.[42]

Predictably, Lloyd George, in contrast to Rosebery, welcomed the Entente Cordiale in April 1904, both as a solution to Anglo-French differences and Britain's imperial predicaments, and as an

41. Speeches at Penarth, 28 Nov. 1896, Kettering, 12 Nov. 1897, Bangor and Colwyn Bay, 13 and 14 Jan. 1898, Haworth, 24 Oct. 1898, Swansea, 14 Dec. 1898, and Southport, 27 May 1899, ibid., A/8/2/21, A/8/3/26, A/8/4/1, 3, 27, and 32, and A/9/1/13. Lloyd George later conceded, on 25 July 1900, that although Britain had grounds for war with France over Madagascar, Salisbury had concluded rightly that British trade there did not justify war. (*Parl. Deb.*, H. of C., LXXXVI, 1206.)

42. Speeches, 24 Oct. 1898, 18 Jan. 1899, and 27 Jan. 1900, LGP, A/8/4/27, A/9/1/1, and A/9/2/6; H. Spender, *The Fire of Life* (London, n.d.), 53. Their conversation on the Thames embankment has received undue weight.

essentially Liberal policy.[43] Lord Lansdowne, the foreign secretary, in defiance of Chamberlain who earlier had courted Germany, had begun an era of cooperation between two free and democratic peoples.[44] He had created an atmosphere of public courtesy in Anglo-French relations, taken a vital step toward the pacification of Europe, and had helped secure the Straits of Gibraltar in the event of war. In turn, Lloyd George warned, Liberals must stand guard over the Entente lest the reckless Tories attempt to challenge France again in the Nile valley or elsewhere in Africa. While Lloyd George derived satisfaction from Chamberlain's failure to secure an alliance with Germany, he regretted the decline in London's relations with Berlin. He deplored both Tory hostility toward Germany and the swaggering, bellicose tone of German diplomacy, and subsequently sought an Anglo-German understanding.[45]

The evidence on Lloyd George's attitude toward Russia in these years, and indeed to 1914, suggests that he was much more concerned with Russia as an imperial competitor than as the persecutor of liberalism. His unrelenting hostility toward the Turk did not affect this attitude. Lloyd George periodically attacked Russia's encroachments in China and Manchuria, her lack of respect for the Open Door policy, and the commercial and imperial threat she presented generally. He deprecated any sign of weakness in the face of Russian diplomatic pressure or provocation, and he welcomed the alliance with Japan in January 1902, while deploring the attendant possibility of war.[46] During the Dogger Bank incident of October 1904 Lloyd George described the action of the Russian fleet as "most insolent and unjustifiable," and her explanation as "unsatisfactory and unacceptable." He applauded, however, the resort to arbitration as a truly Liberal step by Lansdowne.[47]

43. Speeches, 8 March and 19 April 1905, *Parl. Deb.*, H. of C., cxlii, 755–59, cxlv, 631–36, and at Kirkcaldy, 27 Oct. 1905, LGP, A/13/2/8. Lloyd George was with Rosebery when the Entente Cordiale was announced. Rosebery denounced the step as folly, and forecast war with Germany. (Lloyd George, *War Memoirs*, i, 1.)

44. He voted in favour of the Channel Tunnel proposal in June 1890.

45. Speech at Kingston, 19 Oct. 1905, LGP, A/13/2/7.

46. Speeches at Bangor, 1 Feb. 1899, and Southport, 27 May 1899, ibid., A/9/1/2 and 13, and 21 and 22 March and 26 July 1901, *Parl. Deb.*, H. of C., xci, 703–706, 899–901, and xcviii, 272.

47. Speech, 19 April 1905, *Parl. Deb.*, H. of C., cxlv, 631–36; article in *North Wales Observer*, 28 Oct. 1904, LGP, A/12/2/38.

An examination of Lloyd George's voting patterns in the House of Commons until December 1905 adds little. For all but three years the Tories ruled and then Lloyd George voted, with only rare exceptions, against the estimates and expenditures of the Foreign, Colonial and War Offices, and of the Admiralty. The Liberal leaders could rely on him at least to that extent. When Gladstone and then Rosebery governed, from August 1892 to June 1895, Lloyd George was scarcely a prominent renegade in significant divisions. On 11 September 1893 he joined with the thirty-nine MPs who voted to reduce the salary of the secretary of state for war; a week later, on 18 September, he and eighteen others challenged the salary of the first lord of the admiralty. These gestures against the Liberal government were, however, isolated instances, and Lloyd George did not vote on the Army and Navy estimates in 1894 and 1895.

Furthermore, on those occasions when Lloyd George judged Liberal imperial policy, as in the case of Henry Labouchere's motion of 20 March 1893 on Sir G. Portal's mission to Uganda, he supported that policy and, in this instance, voted against the motion. The decision of April 1894, in the month following Gladstone's resignation, to declare a protectorate over Uganda, was confirmed in June. Lloyd George did not join the small group voting against this step and thus demonstrated his support for Rosebery's policy.[48] He voted against the Liberal hierarchy and with the radical Labouchere only in July 1897, in the two divisions over the Jameson Raid report.[49] Of course, when Salisbury returned to power in 1895, Lloyd George criticized the Foreign Office for its handling of the Uganda railway project. On this issue he made much of his humanitarian concern for the interests of the Masai people.[50]

Conformity, therefore, marked his voting patterns, rather more than dissent. Lloyd George had neither matched Labouchere in the estimates debates nor the Irish MPs in their extremism. On 5 June

48. Lloyd George did not vote in any of the divisions on Uganda between 1892 and 1894 except on 20 March 1893.

49. The two divisions were on the Birrell amendment and the Stanhope motion on 19 and 27 July 1897. Curiously, Lloyd George made no public references to Cecil Rhodes, and, like all the radicals, failed to press the inquiry into Chamberlain's conduct in the Jameson Raid until February 1900.

50. He had voted against further financial support for the Dongola Expedition on 5 Feb. 1897, and opposed the Uganda Railway Bill on 7 May 1900.

1902 he voted with the majority of the House in an expression of gratitude to the army for its victory in South Africa,[51] a not unrevealing commentary on his reactions to the Boer War.

51. He voted against the government's proposal on 31 July 1901 to award a grant to Lord Roberts and repeated this gesture over Lord Kitchener's grant on 5 July 1902, only to reverse his position on the latter question.

# 3

# "A Brave and Clever Little Man"

The Boer War was the single most important event in Lloyd George's early career and certainly the most controversial. To some he showed himself capable of sheer duplicity and naked ambition, acting with scant regard for truth, loyalty, and honour. Others regarded the Boer War as Lloyd George's noblest hour, when he fought courageously from impeccable motives and risked all for the sake of principle. Neither view is acceptable.

Lloyd George had followed events in South Africa,[1] but the crisis which matured in the late summer of 1899 found him in Western Canada.[2] By mid-September he prepared to hurry back to England for war seemed inevitable. "The prospect oppresses me with a deep sense of horror. If I have the courage I shall protest with all the vehemence at my command against the outrage which is perpetrated in the name of human freedom."[3] He joined

1. Lloyd George to his wife, 14 Feb. 1896, Morgan, *Family Letters*, 99; speech, 28 Nov. 1896, LGP, A/8/2/21.
2. Lloyd George to W. George, 13 June 1899, W. George, *My Brother and I*, 176. He was a guest of the minister of the interior, combining an investigation into emigration with a holiday.
3. Lloyd George to W. George, 18 Sept. 1899, ibid., 177.

contempt to condemnation: "Today I read in the Canadian papers that those London chipmunks (a quivering, nervous little animal) have been screeching for war. I wonder how many...would face a Boer rifle." The government could not, in his opinion, draw back, and were damned. "If they go on the war will be so costly in blood and treasure as to sicken the land. If they withdraw they will be laughed out of power." Such sentiments were sincere but private, and Lloyd George warned his wife against revealing publicly his hope "that the English will get a black eye." However, in early October he made it known to his constituents that he would oppose "this blackguardish action."[4]

When Lloyd George, fit and buoyant, arrived back in England shortly after the outbreak of war on 11 October, a trace of ambivalence remained in his attitude. The Boer advance demanded considered reflection. To his brother Lloyd George confided that he agreed with the *Chronicle* rather than "Labby."[5] "Boers have invaded our territories and until they are driven back, Government entitled to money to equip forces to defend our possessions. In my opinion, the way these poor hunted burghers have been driven in self-defence to forestall us, aggravates our crime. There is something diabolical in its malignity."

In other words the Boers had committed an act of aggression, and military operations were justified to restore the situation territorially.[6] But the English were guilty of far greater crimes. They were responsible for provoking an unnecessary and what he forecast would be a long and costly war.

His only speech of the emergency session, delivered on 27 October, made no mention, therefore, of Boer responsibility or error.[7] The government, intent on both subjugating the Boers and

---

4. Lloyd George to his wife, 24, 25, and 27 Sept. and 2 Oct. 1899, Morgan, *Family Letters*, 122–23; Lloyd George, message, 18 Sept., for release at a meeting at Caernarvon, 6 Oct. 1899, LGP, A/9/1/20.

5. Lloyd George to W. George, 16 Oct. 1899, W. George, 177. "Labby" was the radical MP, Henry Labouchere. See A. L. T. Thorold, *The Life of Henry Labouchere* (London, 1913), and R. J. Hind, *Henry Labouchere and the Empire, 1880–1905* (London, 1973).

6. Lloyd George to his wife, 23 and 24 Oct. 1899, Morgan, *Family Letters*, 123–24.

7. Lloyd George to his wife, 27 Oct. 1899, Morgan, *Family Letters*, 124, and speech, 27 Oct. 1899, *Parl. Deb.*, H. of C., LXXVII, 782–83. Perhaps Lloyd George had not meant to speak so soon, although he had supported Stanhope's amendment, censuring the government's conduct of the prewar negotiations. (J. H. Edwards, *The Life of David Lloyd George*, I, 201.)

concealing that policy, had declared war on a bogus franchise issue. Similar injustices existed at home, "but when the Uitlanders of the Transvaal, including Jews and others, claimed electoral reforms, the country did not hesitate to go to war on their account. This was not merely wrong but a palpable act of hypocrisy."

In Lloyd George's view the government had set out not only to mislead but also to excite public opinion, and influence the by-election.[8] They had misrepresented the concessions granted by Paul Kruger, president of the Transvaal Republic. Someone had been guilty of either negligence or deliberate forgery. The colonial secretary was above such practices, Lloyd George concluded, with exaggerated care, and therefore the blame must lie with officials in South Africa.

This speech, whatever its merits and however heartfelt, was an error, both politically and tactically. Such intemperance helped rally the government's supporters and divide the Liberals. It also made it more difficult for Lloyd George to join in the demand to punish Kruger. Lloyd George did not speak again in Parliament until February 1900. On the public platform, however, in an emotional and dangerous atmosphere and in the aftermath of "Black Week" he met patriotic jingoism with radical fervour.[9] "Lloyd George nights" became exciting occasions, providing memorable confrontations.[10]

He made five significant speeches, three in Wales, one in London, and one at the Palmerston Club at Balliol College, Oxford.[11] His approach was more constructive and the content became somewhat philosophical. The nation must, Lloyd George insisted, reject militarism and the resort to hostilities, for war undermined liberalism, arrested progress, diverted resources from social reform, and brutalized those who waged it. This lament for a

8. At the by-election held at Bow and Bromley on 28 October the Conservative won a resounding victory over the Liberal candidate. Lloyd George spoke against the war at Bow on 20 October. (*Manchester Guardian*, 21 Oct. 1899.)

9. K. O. Morgan, *Wales in British Politics*, 178–80; E. Stokes, "Milnerism," *The Historical Journal*, 5, no. 1 (1962), 47–60.

10. Lloyd George to W. George, 20 Jan. and 7 March 1900, W. George, 178. The jingoes and Chamberlain were disappointed, as if the anticipated political returns from the war had not materialized. Some Liberals felt that a quiet but powerful undercurrent of pacific opinion existed and would surface.

11. Speeches at Carmarthen, 27 Nov. 1899, Flint, 29 Dec. 1899, Criccieth, 1 Jan., London, 9 Jan., and Oxford, 27 Jan. 1900, LGP, A/9/1/25, A/9/2/1, 2, and 6, and *Manchester Guardian*, 10 Jan. 1900. See also speeches at Bangor, 10 July, Llangeitho, 18 Oct. 1901, LGP, A/10/1/19 and 27.

nation was an elegy for the British as well as the Boers. Lloyd George's expressed concern was for the moral health of Britain, the future of liberalism, and the welfare of the Empire. He would campaign, therefore, as had John Bright, Richard Cobden, and Gladstone. He was no pacifist, but the war in South Africa could not claim the elevated position of a just conflict. It had been necessary neither to secure British supremacy in South Africa nor to revenge Majuba. "There may be something to be said for a war so long as it is entered upon for an unselfish purpose. The influence of a war must always be brutalising at best, but still, if you enter upon it for an unselfish purpose there is something which almost consecrates the sacrifices, bloodshed and suffering endured. But when you enter upon a war purely and simply for the purposes of plunder, I know of nothing which is more degrading to the country or more hideous in its effects on the mind and character of the people engaged in it."[12] He intended to focus on the essential question: the injustice of the war not its conduct.[13] In this way he could actually applaud the contribution of the Welsh Fusiliers to the campaign, and champion "our gallant men."[14]

The government, "floated into power on beer" and led on by Joseph Chamberlain, had deliberately built up its forces and found a pretext for war, forcing Kruger to strike out against impossible terms. Inspired by gold and diamond merchants, Germans, profit-seeking plutocrats, conspiratorial Jews, and cowardly Uitlanders, the government, in a fit of militarist imperialism, had ignored the arbitration procedures so recently accepted at the Hague Conference and were bent on annexations. Moreover, Lloyd George suggested, Britain was isolated in this criminal and immoral endeavour. Europe's intellectuals, and the governments of France, Germany, and the United States, were infuriated. The powers had not intervened only because they suspected, rightly, that the war would exhaust Britain.[15] Only the Turks had offered

12. Lloyd George to W. George, n.d., W. George, 182; speeches, 18 Oct. 1901, LGP, A/10/1/27, and 25 July 1900, *Parl. Deb.*, H. of C., lxxxvi, 1210–11.
13. Lloyd George to W. George, 1 Feb. 1900, H. du Parcq, *Lloyd George*, ii, 223.
14. *Manchester Guardian*, 2 March 1900; statements, 13, 15, 16, and 19 March 1900, *Parl. Deb.*, H. of C., lxxx, 727, 905–906, 1155–56, 1267–68.
15. On 10 July Lloyd George pointed to the fact that the government were forced to ask the Japanese to handle the Boxer revolt. (*Parl. Deb.*, H. of C., lxxxv, 1107.)

support.[16] This was logical because the Boer leaders, and even Kruger, were pacific, moderate, progressive, and liberal.[17] Britain's historic role as the champion of the weak and the shield of the oppressed was in jeopardy. To Welsh audiences, Lloyd George emphasized that Britain had attacked God-fearing, bible-reading farmers who sought freedom as had the old Welsh Covenanters.[18]

He made one positive suggestion: while they could not make humiliating approaches to Kruger, the government could attempt to secure a settlement through the mediation of the United States.[19] The agreement must protect the Kaffirs and award the fullest possible measure of self-government to South Africa, within the Empire.[20] Lloyd George acknowledged in April 1900, against the background of significant British military successes, that the peace, prosperity, and demilitarization of South Africa depended on the establishment of British rule. He insisted, however, that war *à outrance* and annexation of the Boer Republics were unacceptable and, indeed, unnecessary methods to achieve supremacy in South Africa and a strengthened Empire.[21] Canada and Australia, Lloyd George claimed, assisted Britain in time of war no matter who the enemy, while Ireland opposed involvement in any conflict. Britain, he urged, must neither emulate Spain's record in Cuba nor Russia's in Poland; let the tsar retain the unique distinction of annexing a white, independent nation.

The Liberal party was sorely divided. Lloyd George, claiming to be in sympathy with Lord Rosebery on several issues, chose to regard Rosebery's response to the war almost as deviate behaviour, brought on by Chamberlain's nefarious influence. This explained

16. He praised W. E. H. Lecky as "our greatest historian" who, though a Conservative and an imperialist, opposed the war.

17. Speech, 6 Feb., *Parl. Deb.*, H. of C., lxxviii, 758–67, and *Manchester Guardian*, 7 Feb. 1900.

18. Lloyd George to W. George, 26 May 1900, W. George, 181–82. Expressing admiration and sympathy for the "brave Boers," Lloyd George insisted that victory was far distant. Disease was spreading among the British forces, and within months the public would realize the horrors of the whole affair.

19. *Morning Herald*, 29 Jan. 1900, du Parcq, ii, 223.

20. Speech, 2 March 1900, *Manchester Guardian*, 3 and 14 March 1900.

21. Lloyd George to W. George, 3 April 1900, W. George, 179; speeches at Bangor, 11 April, and Caernarvon, 24 April 1900, LGP, A/9/2/13 and 15. He used the press to prepare the ground for these meetings, emphasizing the issue of freedom of speech, and accusing his opponents of organizing a mob to attack him. (*Manchester Guardian*, 11, 12, 14, and 25 April 1900; *Western Mail*, 6 and 10 April 1900, LGP, A/9/2/11 and 12.)

why Rosebery and the Liberal Imperialists, such as Edward Grey, Richard Haldane, and Herbert Asquith, stood by the government. Lloyd George joined the Stop-the-War Committee after attending a peace rally at the Exeter Hall in London on 11 January 1900. In an emotional atmosphere of religious fervour those present resolved to use all legal means to oppose the war.[22] Lloyd George took the committee's proposals to a Liberal meeting on 14 February, chaired by the party's leader in the House of Commons, the moderate Sir Henry Campbell-Bannerman, but he met with little success. Campbell-Bannerman opposed the war and deplored both Chamberlain's activities and the attitude of the Liberal Imperialists, but like the majority of the party, he could not embrace Lloyd George. The grassroots National Liberal Federation was torn in the same way as the hierarchy. At its meeting, from 26 to 29 March, Lloyd George stood with the president, Dr. R. S. Watson, Charles Trevelyan, and Frederick Maddison against a Dr. Lunn and a Professor Massie.[23] He pleaded, however, for understanding and reconciliation so that the Tories would not benefit unduly and Liberals might reunite once the war was over.

From this point Lloyd George faced the problems which resulted from his attempt to reconcile four aims. He was committed to oppose the war and never wavered; he was bound to work for a particular type of peace settlement; he must not further divide and injure the Liberal party; and he must show that he was both humanitarian and patriot. Lloyd George could afford neither to compromise unduly his convictions nor to ignore political realities. It was not easy to predict the effect of a particular issue on his standing in majority Liberal, radical, or Welsh circles. Unless he could influence Campbell-Bannerman and his followers, he might succeed merely in isolating and destroying himself politically. How wise was it to continue to confront the Liberal Imperialists? To court one faction might make him *persona non grata* with another and with the electorate. These were testing dilemmas and the degree of cool calculation in Lloyd George's responses must not be exaggerated.

22. *Manchester Guardian*, 13, 18, and 22 Jan. and 15 Feb. 1900.
23. Speech at Nottingham, 27 March 1900, LGP, A/9/2/9, du Parcq, II, 238, and *Manchester Guardian*, 28 March 1900; R. Spence Watson, *The National Liberal Federation from its commencement to the General Election of 1906* (London, 1907), 239-75.

These difficulties became more acute as the war escalated and turned decisively in Britain's favour in the spring of 1900, and as the prospect of an election emerged. He could neither recant nor compromise easily, even in the face of hostile constituents and the threat of defeat, should Chamberlain force a dissolution to capitalize on the war fever.[24] Indeed, Lloyd George insisted on holding public meetings lest his case fail by default and silence bring defeat. "Ruffianism" must not triumph.[25]

Moreover, he could not ignore the conduct of the war and the evident incompetence of the authorities.[26] Information filtering back from South Africa provided Lloyd George with a superb if tragic vehicle. Exploitation of it might call into question his patriotism though not his humanitarianism. To the extent that it embarrassed Chamberlain, it might, however, rally Liberal opinion.

Medical staffs were overworked, supplies were inadequate, hospitals were primitive and crowded, and, Lloyd George noted, British soldiers preferred capture by the Boers to torture in their own ambulances. The War Office had sent a force of 50,000 to attempt a task requiring 220,000 men. The army was ill-served and the government could hardly pass the blame to the soldiers in the field. Lloyd George turned the War Office's incredibly feeble defence, that suffering was present in all wars, into an attack on Chamberlain, feeling free to increase the official casualty figures tenfold. If suffering was inevitable, why had Chamberlain been so reckless in the prewar negotiations? The answer was obvious: the colonial secretary was already on the hustings and was willing to sacrifice lives in order to win the general election.[27]

In addition, Lloyd George charged, Chamberlain's war had resulted in untold suffering because of barbarous acts against

24. Lloyd George to W. George, March and 22 March 1900, W. George, 179; du Parcq, II, 226.

25. Lloyd George to H. Lewis, 13 April 1900, H. Lewis Papers, file 230.

26. Lloyd George to W. George, 27 June 1900, W. George, 182; speeches, 25 and 29 June, and 30 July 1900, Parl. Deb., H. of C., LXXXIV, 909, LXXXV, 163–69, and LXXXVII, 58. Also questions put on 10, 16, and 20 July 1900, ibid., LXXXV, 1107, and LXXXVI, 105–107, 646.

27. Speeches, 29 June and 25 July 1900, Parl. Deb., H. of C., LXXXV, 163 69, and LXXXVI, 1199–1212. Lloyd George, two other Welsh MPs, John Morley, and Labouchere supported Sir W. Lawson's motion to reduce Chamberlain's salary. Edward Grey and R. B. Haldane opposed it and Campbell-Bannerman did not vote. The motion was soundly defeated.

Boer women, children, and property. It had become a campaign of extermination, and would result in a lengthy military occupation. On this issue Lloyd George was questioning the actions of the army in the field.

He risked further confrontations with the colonial secretary before dissolution on 25 September 1900. After condemning Chamberlain's references to and use of captured correspondence between unnamed members of Parliament and certain Boers, which placed all members opposed to the war under suspicion of treason, Lloyd George reactivated the issue of War Office contracts. He had already referred to it in a speech at Bangor in April. Using precisely the tactics he had just condemned, he asked whether certain firms, through a certain gentleman in Birmingham who had influence with a member of the government, benefited from unfair practices when submitting tenders to the War Office. Such firms, Lloyd George suggested, obviously were doing well out of the war.[28]

Yet, naturally, Lloyd George was determined to show that he was not an unpatriotic radical whose motives bordered on treason. He claimed that he was neither the "pro-Boer" nor the "Little Englander" of the Tory press. He could no more vote money to than confidence in the government but maintained that he was guilty merely of fearless criticism.

Inevitably the election was hard fought. As Lloyd George told Herbert Lewis, "Men who have speculated heavily in South Africans threaten my life. I mean politically.... I am going for Chamberlain and everybody in the hope that I may distract attention from my own iniquities."[29] His courageous, fiery, and emotional election speeches attacked the cost of the war, Chamberlain, and the excessive profits of Birmingham armaments manufacturers.[30] He countered the indictment that the Boers fought on only in the hope of a Liberal victory with more evidence on the war's conduct and the government's failure to negotiate a just settlement. He linked the war cleverly with domestic problems and the lack of reform. John Morley was impressed. "Lloyd George

28. Speech, 8 Aug. 1900, ibid., LXXXVII, 1008–14.

29. Lloyd George to H. Lewis, 20 Sept. 1900, H. Lewis Papers, file 230.

30. Colonel Platt received on 29 September Chamberlain's written denial of Lloyd George's indictment of profiteering from the war. (*Caernarvon Herald*, 12 Oct. 1900, LGP, A/9/2/41.)

is in some ways the most satisfactory—a brave and clever little man who ought to have a good future."[31]

In the course of the election campaign, however, Lloyd George made a further conciliatory, patriotic gesture, his third since the war began.[32] He conceded that the merits of any war still being fought were difficult to judge. Perhaps he was honestly mistaken; Kruger, another Tory in fact, was possibly as guilty as Chamberlain. In any case, the Transvaal Republic and the Orange Free State had ceased to exist. Restoration of the *status quo ante* was impossible and Lord Roberts, the commander-in-chief, must settle South Africa's political future. Canada should be the model. She had a "French" prime minister and a Scot for her national hero. Freedom had bred loyalty in Quebec and must be the basis of the new government of South Africa.

Lloyd George was re-elected with an increased majority, on 6 October 1900, but Liberal opposition to the war continued to be hampered by several factors. The divided party with its radical heritage was ill-equipped to fight on the issues raised, and Liberals were loath to injure the war effort and risk charges of treason. Patriotism and the need for national unity were effective forces until the conflict threatened to drag on interminably. Lloyd George ceased to clear the Boers and charge the government with sole responsibility for the outbreak of the war. Liberals were hesitant. Socialist and trade union support, with Keir Hardie and John Burns prominent, was not sufficiently weighty and in fact could be a liability. Moreover, the independently-minded Hugh Price-Hughes, editor of the *Methodist Times*, undermined radical unity.[33] Campbell-Bannerman, welcoming the new *Liberal Monthly* in October 1900, diagnosed the predicament:[34] the Liberal Publications Department was unable to exploit the war and foreign policy questions generally, even during the election. Yet, as he pointed

31. Morley to Harcourt, 13 Oct. 1900, A. G. Gardiner, *The Life of Sir William Harcourt*, 2 vols. (New York, n.d.), II, 523–24; Lloyd George to his wife, 3 Aug. 1900, Morgan, *Family Letters*, 125.

32. Speeches in his constituency, 15, 17, 19, 21, and 25 Sept., at Newton, 9 Oct., Bangor, 7 Nov., and Liverpool, 30 Nov. 1900, LGP, A/9/2/27, 26, 25, 29, 32, 45, 46, and 48; du Parcq, II, 238–45; *Manchester Guardian*, 2, 6, and 8 Oct. 1900.

33. D. P. Hughes, *The Life of Hugh Price-Hughes* (London, 1905), 542-62; Jack Jones, *The Man David*, 102, 109; Sir A. T. Davies, *The Lloyd George I Knew*, 22.

34. Campbell-Bannerman to Bryce, 20 Oct. 1900, Campbell-Bannerman Papers, Add. 52517

out, Liberals must attack "Chamberlainism" and its iniquitous "vulgarity, recklessness, caddishness and snobbery," which debased public life and was a more deadly evil than jingoism itself.

W. T. Stead in the *Review of Reviews*, the new publication *War Against War*,[35] Leonard Courtney, Charles Hobhouse, Philip Stanhope, Sir William Harcourt, Sir Wilfrid Lawson and Frederick Harrison led a press and pamphlet campaign.[36] They worked in organizations such as the South Africa Conciliation Committee, the Transvaal Committee, the Stop-the-War Committee, and with the Liberal Publications Department. They were aided by the *Manchester Guardian*, guided by C. E. Montague and L. T. Hobhouse, the *Morning Leader*, the *Star*, and subsequently by the *Daily News*, under R. C. Lehmann and then A. G. Gardiner.[37] This campaign provided Lloyd George with both intellectual and emotional sustenance as well as a legitimate opportunity to enter the newspaper business.[38] However, he contributed little enough to the press and the evidence in his correspondence is thin.[39]

Lloyd George did not need to alter his tactics at all, however, to follow Campbell-Bannerman's advice. In the new session of Parliament he deliberately pursued his vendetta with Chamberlain. On 10 December 1900, he returned to the question of possible conflicts of interest between the private activities and public duties of ministers.[40] Chamberlain had established the

35. J. S. Galbraith, "The Pamphlet Campaign in the Boer War," *Journal of Modern History*, 24, no. 2 (1952), 111–26; J. O. Baylen, "W. T. Stead and the Boer War: The Irony of Idealism," *Canadian Historical Review*, 40, no. 4 (1959), 304–14; "W. T. Stead's, 'History of the Mystery' and the Jameson Raid," *Journal of British Studies*, 4, no. 1 (1964), 104–32.

36. L. Courtney Papers, vols. 7 and 8; F. Harrison Papers; G. P. Gooch, *Life of Lord Courtney* (London, 1920).

37. J. L. Hammond, *C. P. Scott of the Manchester Guardian* (London, 1934), 78–80; H. Spender, *The Fire of Life*, 109–24; H. A. Taylor, *Robert Donald* (London, n.d.), 20; J. A. Spender, *The Life of Sir Henry Campbell-Bannerman*, 2 vols. (London, 1923), I, 319. The E. T. Cook Papers contain no correspondence with Lloyd George.

38. Lloyd George to his wife, 20, 23, and 31 Aug. 1900, Morgan, *Family Letters*, 126–27; G. Cadbury to Lloyd George, 18 Dec. 1900, Lloyd George Papers (National Library of Wales), 20462C; *Manchester Guardian*, 26 Feb. and 1 Dec. 1900; speeches, 25 Sept. 1900 and 7 Nov. 1901, LGP, A/9/2/32, A/10/1/32.

39. Surely Stead's writings were a source of inspiration and information, but the Stead papers contain no letters to or from Lloyd George, and I have found only one letter, Stead to Lloyd George, 13 Dec. 1900, Lloyd George Papers (National Library of Wales), 20462C.

40. Speech, 10 Dec. 1900, *Parl Deb.*, H. of C. LXXXVIII, 397-421. He was

guidelines for the Colonial Office in 1885. A minister must avoid both direct or indirect association with and investment in a private company which did business with the government. The colonial secretary, Lloyd George charged, had broken his own commandments. Firms with which he was involved made profits from Admiralty and War Office contracts, and from providing accommodation for Boer prisoners in Ceylon.

Thus, Lloyd George inferred, as the Empire expanded firms contracted. Impropriety prevailed which set dangerous precedents and required an explanation. After this statement, Lloyd George's praise of British standards of official conduct in comparison with those of the United States, and his denial of having made any charges against either Joseph or Austen Chamberlain, were ignored. He had challenged a public hero, defaced a monument, and in a way calculated to have the maximum political effect. This assault on Chamberlain might provide Liberals with a unifying cause.[41]

His comments on the war and the peace settlement were intended to reinforce this effect.[42] The government, he charged, seemed willing to permit both the humiliation of Lord Kitchener, Roberts's successor as commander-in-chief, and the escalating savagery. It seemed content to bring famine and create a refugee problem in South Africa, as it drove the Boers to a desperate extremism and gambled with a native uprising. Should the European powers intervene, Lloyd George warned, Britain would be hard pressed to protect her national and imperial interests.

He poured ridicule on Chamberlain's attitude toward peace negotiations. The colonial secretary, the Mephistopheles of South Africa, talked of fair treatment for the Boers and yet denounced as treachery any such demand from his opponents. Perhaps, Lloyd George suggested, he had not eliminated the possibility of changing his allegiances again and returning to the pro-Boer party. In

---

aided before and during the debate by H. Spender and the revelations of *The Star*. (Spender, *Fire of Life*, 61–63; du Parcq, II, 249–50; J. L. Garvin, *The Life of Joseph Chamberlain* (London, 1934), III, 613–16.) See also his speech in London, 12 December, *Manchester Guardian*, 14 Dec. 1900.

41. He did not, however, pursue this charge resolutely. (Lloyd George to his wife, 14 March 1902, Morgan, *Family Letters*, 129–30.)

42. He gave credence even to press reports that Kitchener would shoot all his prisoners. (Speech, 17 Jan., *Manchester Guardian*, 18 Jan. 1901.); speeches, 15 Dec. 1900 and 11, 14, and 27 June 1901, *Parl. Deb.*, H. of C., LXXXVIII, 875, 894–99, XCV, 51–52, 409–10, and XCVI, 67–68.

the meantime, despite the advice of the sagacious Kitchener and a seemingly more moderate Sir Alfred Milner, Chamberlain haggled over debts and constitutional issues, and had aborted the Middleburg negotiations. This was typical of a man who preferred to finance this and other wars through loans rather than taxation on mining profits and higher incomes, and who was bent on evading parliamentary scrutiny of his policies.[43]

In fact, Lloyd George insisted, the government offered only a Cromwellian peace. They intended to replace independence with servitude, deprive the Boers of their land, and offer farms to imperial yeomen and British war veterans. Chamberlain planned to establish a crown colony, with Milner as governor. Political control would remain in London for an unspecified period with only an indefinite promise of self-government. Lloyd George warned that the Boers would not surrender on such terms. They had no faith in a government which had treated them as Gladstone had dealt with Egypt; Chamberlain had been prominent in both administrations.

Despite his reference to Egypt, Lloyd George called for an honourable, "Gladstonian peace." The settlement should fuse British supremacy with freedom and justice for South Africa. There should be an amnesty and no military occupation, but the Boers should pay an indemnity. They and all white inhabitants should enjoy immediate autonomy and self-government, if not full independence. In this way Britain would control foreign and defence policies and yet avoid the costs of postwar reconstruction.[44]

Whatever the impact of the positions he had adopted, Lloyd

43. Statements, 11, 12, 15, 18, and 29 March, 29 April, 6 June, 4, 8, and 25 July, and 1 Aug. 1901, *Parl. Deb.*, H. of C., xc, 1212–13, 1326–27, xci, 185–86, 302–08, xcii, 214, xciii, 115–21, xciv, 1274–75, xcvi, 890–908, 1142, xcviii, 166–68, 844, 899–904, 911; speeches, 17, 20, and 23 April and 15 May 1901, LGP, A/10/1/7, 10, 8, and 12.

44. Speeches, 28 Dec. 1900, LGP, A/10/1/1, 18 Feb., 19 and 25 March, and 2 Aug. 1901, *Parl. Deb.*, H. of C., lxxxix, 397–407, 421–22, xci, 472–75, 1189–92, and xcviii, 1135–50; *Liverpool Daily Post*, 19 Jan., and *Caernarvon Herald*, 22 Feb. 1901, LGP, A/10/1/3 and 5. Before the debate of 18 Feb. he agreed not to move the amendment drawn up by Courtney and approved by Campbell-Bannerman, but opposed by Morley, Sir W. Harcourt, and Labouchere. The amendment called on the government to offer the Boers equal rights for all white inhabitants, protection and justice for all natives, and complete local autonomy but under British control. (Campbell-Bannerman to Ripon, 16 Feb. 1901, Spender, *Campbell-Bannerman*, i, 321–22.)

George worked for a Liberal reconciliation at the National Liberal Federation meetings at Rugby in February and at Bradford in May 1901.[45] The various problems and the attempted compromises, however, amounted to giving with one hand and taking back with the other. This was particularly so when the issue became that of the concentration camps, since Lloyd George was now a prominent member of the League of Liberals against Aggression and Militarism.[46]

The question of the camps inevitably involved further criticism of the army's conduct which in turn revived accusations of lack of patriotism, defeatism, and treason.[47] Undeterred, and in advance of Campbell-Bannerman, Lloyd George, with Stead and Emily Hobhouse,[48] spelled out the terrible details: inhumane detention of Boer women and children, distressingly high mortality rates, starvation and disease, and inadequate supplies of food, clothing, medical services, and accommodation, made worse by the refusal to permit inspection by Joshua Rowntree and other independent observers. Such policies, Lloyd George declared, were degenerate and foolish. They represented a triumph of reaction and "a recrudescence of barbarism." They stripped the Empire of all morality, resulted in a passionate hatred of British rule in Africa, and were perpetuated because, "either the people have degenerated or they are represented by the most cowardly Ministers that ever existed."

Lloyd George had appealed to the Liberal party to reunite and,

45. Speeches at the N.L.F. meetings, 27 Feb. and 15 May 1901, *Manchester Guardian*, 28 Feb. and 16 May 1901; Spender, *Campbell-Bannerman*, i, 325; Haldane to Milner, 3 March 1901, V. Halperin, *Lord Milner and the Empire* (London, n.d.), 116–17. Lloyd George counselled withdrawal of an amendment to the Birrell resolution aimed at Milner, but more on procedural and tactical than on policy grounds. He wanted the N.L.F. to pursue party unity and to help bring a liberal peace to South Africa immediately on the cessation of hostilities, not at Chamberlain's pleasure. He did not want the recall of Milner to become a central and divisive issue.

46. *Manchester Guardian*, 22 and 25 April 1901; A. M. Scott to Lloyd George, 11 Dec. 1901, LGP, A/1/11/1.

47. Speeches, 24 May, 17, 21, and 27 June, 4 July, and 2 and 15 Aug. 1901, *Parl. Deb.*, H. of C., xciv, 1179–81, 1195–98, xcv, 451–53, 573–83, 1055, xcvi, 152–54, 890–908, xcviii, 1135–50, and xcix, 1031–36, 1048; Lloyd George to W. George, 3 July 1901, du Parcq, ii, 257–58; speech, 10 July 1901, LGP, A/10/1/19.

48. Lloyd George encouraged her to publish information on the concentration camps. (Spender, *Fire of Life*, 115; A. T. Bassett, *The Life of the Rt. Hon. John Edward Ellis* [London, 1914], 171–96.)

indeed, Campbell-Bannerman and other moderate Liberals had moved in his direction. Yet, at the same time, unity was jeopardized as the Liberal Imperialists responded by fêting Milner on his return to London in May. Lloyd George had cut deep in his attack on the war and on those Liberals who "consorted with infamy" and with Milner. As Harcourt noted, he "is a red flag to a good many of the Liberal Imperialists."[49] In radical circles, however, Lloyd George's standing was enhanced.[50]

In the summer of 1901 two courses of action were open to the Liberals. They could permit the profound disagreements over the war to continue, hoping that these differences would not fatally impair unity. The Liberal party would remain divided for the duration of the war. No compromise would emerge, based, for instance, on the acceptance of a policy of ultimate British supremacy in South Africa and on an agreement permitting Liberals to continue freely to attack the government's war policies. Lloyd George preferred to seek an accommodation by elevating those issues which would permit the party to close ranks behind Campbell-Bannerman. He had not, however, ruled out the possibility of an alternative leader or a compromise arrangement. On 9 July 1901, at the Reform Club, Liberals agreed in fact to differ on South Africa. They did not work out a compromise policy, although they voted confidence in Campbell-Bannerman's leadership. The Liberal Imperialists retained both their freedom and standing within the party, and the pro-Boers were able to continue their campaign against the government but not under the banner of official Liberal policy.[51]

Lloyd George was not satisfied with this decision and, ironically, like the Liberal Imperialists but with different motives and expectations,[52] looked in Rosebery's direction. Obviously Lloyd George could join with Rosebery more readily than any Liberal Imperialist in an indictment of Milner. While Lloyd George

49. Harcourt to his son, 18 June 1901, Gardiner, *Sir William Harcourt*, ii, 530; D. A. Hamer, *John Morley*, 338–39.

50. Scott to Hobhouse, June 1901, Hammond, *Scott*, 77. He denounced Grey as "hopeless by conviction," Asquith as corrupted by his surroundings, and Haldane as in league with Milner.

51. Lloyd George was present at the Reform Club meeting but did not speak. (*The Times*, 10 July.) See also H. W. McCready, "Sir Alfred Milner, the Liberal Party and the Boer War," *Canadian Journal of History*, 2, no. 1 (1967), 13–44, and A. M. Gollin, *Proconsul in Politics* (New York, 1964), 38, 55–59.

52. Grey to J. A. Spender, 21 Dec. 1901, Spender Papers, Add. 46389.

recognized the need for cooperation under Campbell-Bannerman, he stated publicly that Rosebery was indispensable to the party and the nation. Rosebery proved in fact thoroughly unpredictable and uncooperative, but Lloyd George naïvely persisted with the idea, at least until February 1902.[53] His speeches from early October 1901, a preface to the meeting of the General Committee of the National Liberal Federation, held at Derby in December, explored the interrelated propositions of Liberal unity, Campbell-Bannerman's leadership, and Rosebery's contribution.[54]

At Derby Lloyd George supported those resolutions which he regarded as moderate.[55] These were declarations calling for improved conditions in the concentration camps, peace negotiations, and the dispatch of a commissioner to South Africa to secure a settlement. Lloyd George insisted that the commissioner should be like Lord Durham, impartial and unprejudiced, bearing no responsibility for and being in no way compromised by involvement in the war. He must investigate conditions rather than state terms, and the government would do well to avoid publishing beforehand its peace proposals. Milner was obviously unsuitable. Meanwhile the Liberal party, Lloyd George argued, must express its regret at the suspension of constitutional government and the establishment of martial law in Cape Colony.

Lloyd George found much to applaud in Rosebery's celebrated and at first sight conciliatory speech at Chesterfield, which seemed to augur well for party unity. Two days later, on 18 December 1901, he was scheduled to address the Birmingham Liberal Association.[56] That notorious occasion, which almost cost him

---

53. John Dillon reported on 5 May 1903 that "Rosebery quite recently had made advances to Lloyd George, the most able of the Radicals, and Lloyd George had responded." (W. S. Blunt, *My Diaries: being a personal narrative of events, 1888–1914*, 2 vols. [London, 1919], II, 53.) Rosebery remained a siren. (R. R. James, *Rosebery* [London, 1963], 476; Marquess of Crewe, *Lord Rosebery*, 2 vols. [London, 1931], II, 651; Scott diary, 11 June 1916, Scott Papers, Add. 50902; A. J. P. Taylor, ed., *Lloyd George: A Diary by Frances Stevenson*, 26.)

54. Speeches, 7, 18, 23, and 31 Oct. and 7, 15, and 23 Nov. 1901, LGP, A/10/1/25 and 27, du Parcq, II, 253–55, LGP, A/10/1/29 and 32, du Parcq, II, 264, and LGP, A/10/1/39.

55. Statement, 4 Dec. 1901, ibid., A/10/1/40, du Parcq, II, 273–75; Watson, *National Liberal Federation*, 261. He pressed, unsuccessfully, for a more formal and fuller recognition of Campbell-Bannerman's leadership.

56. Speech, dictated and handed out to reporters, 18 Dec. 1901, LGP, A/10/1/42, G/31/1/58. His speech at the peace meeting in Bristol on 6 Jan. 1902 contained similar themes. (Ibid., A/19/2/1.) Rosebery had urged the Liberal

his life, is of importance here for what Lloyd George would have said had the mob permitted him to speak. He praised Rosebery, although not unreservedly, for the Chesterfield speech was not free from ambiguity, calling as it did for peace negotiations and condemning Milner, but refusing to criticize the conduct of the war. Lloyd George pleaded for Liberal unity, based upon the demand for an amnesty for the Boers and a peace which offered representative government. The Derby resolutions were, he said, a platform for all Liberals to adopt. Rosebery had pointed the way and the Liberal Imperialists would follow his lead in a surge of grateful repentance.

Lloyd George was either naïve or desperate to think that Liberals could be so easily reconciled.[57] Frederick Cawley's compromise amendment, moved in the House of Commons on 21 January 1902, starkly revealed the difficulties of Lloyd George's position.[58] In the debate he insisted that he had opposed the war out of love for the motherland. All sensible people preferred conciliatory peace terms and yet they could disagree on the merits of the war itself.[59] He could not accept, however, an amendment explicitly supporting the effective prosecution of the war as well as denouncing the government's failure to secure a rapid peace. Campbell-Bannerman's capacity for error seemed greater, therefore, than Rosebery's in this matter, for by supporting the resolution he "has been stripped of all his principles and left on the veldt to find his way back the best way he could."

The Liberal party, Lloyd George pleaded, must not pawn its heirlooms to achieve fraudulent unity and a spurious popularity. The government was not immortal and Liberals would have their day if they refused to exchange their "undeserved unpopularity" for a "well merited contempt." Little wonder that in February Lloyd George told Herbert Lewis that he regarded himself as the most unpopular man in England.[60] A majority of Liberals

---

party to "wipe its slate clean" and become a viable, modern alternative to a vulnerable government. See also J. Amery, *Life of Joseph Chamberlain* (London, 1951), IV, 20–22. Basil Zaharoff has been accused of helping to incite the mob. (D. McCormick, *Peddler of Death* [New York, 1965], 78–80.)

57. Speech, 15 Feb. 1902, LGP, A/10/2/9; du Parcq, II, 309–20.

58. Speech, 21 Jan. 1902, *Parl. Deb.*, H. of C., CI, 537–43. He abstained on the vote.

59. W. George, 187; Lloyd George to his wife, 25 March and 18 April 1902, Morgan, *Family Letters*, 132, 134.

60. Lewis diary, 16 Feb. 1902; Lloyd George to his wife, 5 and 6 March 1902, Morgan, *Family Letters*, 127–28.

confirmed their support for Campbell-Bannerman, and Rosebery and the imperialist wing formed the Liberal League in an act of disengagement.

The war itself was in its final phase and Lloyd George made his last effective parliamentary statement on the situation on 24 April 1902.[61] He questioned War Office statistics, which showed that three times as many Boer soldiers as were known to exist had been killed, and asked how a phantom army could continue to haunt Kitchener. Beneath such ridicule lay Lloyd George's continued admiration for the Boer guerrillas' exploits.[62]

The truth was that, unlike the government, Lloyd George declared, he understood the intense pride and patriotism of small nations. A man's love for his country varied in inverse ratio to its size. The experts were understandably baffled and indeed all estimates were futile when men fought in defence of a heartfelt cause. Britain's assault on the Boers had the flavour of the Panama scandal; the shareholders had expected instant profits at a small cost, the directors were re-elected on that speculative and misleading prospectus, but the profiteers sat in the government. After that appropriate final thrust Lloyd George, sensitive to the charge that he had neglected domestic and Welsh issues, turned to Arthur Balfour's Education Bill. Peace came to South Africa on 31 May 1902.

Certain conclusions seem permissible. Lloyd George worked hard, read the Blue Books, and hit out with great vigour. He courted and pursued controversy, but frequently he was on the defensive against equally bitter attacks from outside and within the Liberal party. Clearly his conduct was not above reproach. His judgements were far from profound on many issues and were not sufficiently free from political intent. True enough, the government and its military and civilian experts had miscalculated. Its position was not free from subterfuge and hypocrisy, and spurious motives were hardly absent. Conditions in the concentration camps were deplorable and had continued to be so for far too long. United States opinion was hostile and ministers might have been more impressed than they were by the threat of intervention from a Continental League, inspired by the Dual Entente. On the

61. Statements, 17, 25, and 28 Feb., 4, 7, and 20 March, and 24 April 1902, *Parl. Deb.*, H. of C., ciii, 87–92, 169–70, 1015–16, 1029, civ, 346–47, 455–60, 802–09, cv, 638–58, and cvi, 1244–47; speeches, 15 Feb. and 3 April 1902, and 28 Jan. 1903, LGP, A/10/2/9 and 15, A/11/1/5.
62. Lloyd George to his wife, 12 March 1902, Morgan, *Family Letters*, 129.

other hand, neither President McKinley nor President Roosevelt had contemplated involvement, and the cabinet was justifiably concerned lest Russia make advances in East Asia, while Britain was embroiled in South Africa.

Lloyd George misunderstood the situation, or merely sought political advantage, when he focused his assault on Chamberlain rather than on Milner. The colonial secretary had become involved in war more by ineptness and miscalculation than design. Milner, however, had been determined to ensure British supremacy in South Africa, by peaceful means if possible, or, with few regrets, by war if necessary. Furthermore, Milner's desire to annex, unite, and anglicize South Africa so that it could become an independent state within the Empire did not meet Lloyd George's desiderata for peace.

Lloyd George's view of the war was in one sense limited and short-term for he saw it as an issue between white races, between the moral Boers and the less laudable English. The native question and the possible consequences of placing black peoples under Boer rule, the progressive qualities of which were scarcely proven, completely escaped him, despite his humanitarian concern over the treatment of the native peoples. In addition, his allegations of a plutocratic conspiracy, with the government emerging as a mere tool of Jews, unscrupulous mine-owners, financiers, and jingoes, were neither convincing nor elevated. Nor did Chamberlain's personal profit motive exist, as distinct from his political opportunism. The attack on his honour was not justified and Lloyd George would deserve severe censure but for the extenuating circumstances.

Nevertheless his responses were defensible to some degree. Chamberlain and his colleagues undoubtedly called the election to make political capital out of the war. Moreover, Lloyd George was forced to combat even more serious charges: a lack of patriotism and even traitorous conduct. Little wonder he fought to the limit in self-defence. Throughout the whole affair, however, Lloyd George apparently laboured under the handicap of a single unsound premise: that public opinion would revolt against the war and react against the blatant electioneering of the government. The public proved him wrong and the lack of unity within the Liberal party compounded his predicament.

Yet he performed an essential national service with singular courage. He exposed error and folly, and provided an alternative policy to prolonged war and annexation. Lloyd George insisted that creative statesmanship could forge a working relationship between the white races in South Africa. He also helped combat the moral stultification which stems from the pursuit of national unanimity, however dubious or sordid the cause. He contributed to dissent and insisted that dissent was a sign of national health. At the same time he issued a warning lest the nation become militaristic and reactionary. A government could, for a righteous cause, in the pursuit of freedom, and after exhausting all other remedies, he had argued, resort to war. The American Civil War, for instance, had brought social and moral benefits, although its costs and consequences provided a terrible warning. In struggles where the moral enthusiasm of the nation was aroused, as in the conflict with the despotic Bonaparte, Lloyd George would support Britain in defiance of the world, but the Boer War was no such conflict. In fact, as Lloyd George told an audience in Edinburgh, the war had uncovered a national conceit, a debased form of patriotism, and revealed a malignant sense of racial superiority.[63] Joseph Chamberlain, the popular imperialist and demagogue, had aroused the worst in the nation. In sum the Boer War was unworthy of Britain. It reduced her to the level of Spain, Russia, and Turkey, and he could not remain indifferent.

Finally, however, Lloyd George's evolving position threatened his credibility, especially because of the degree of political opportunism involved. He was sincere in his opposition to the war, romantically attracted to the Boers, and genuinely distressed by the inhumanity of the campaigning. Yet Welshmen fought in the British army and their service was a source of pride to him. Understandably concerned to counteract the image of himself created by the Tory press, which equated his conduct with treason, Lloyd George had sought a compromise. The Boers' case was just, but ultimately he denied that he was any more a pro-Boer than John Bright was a Russophile in opposing the Crimean war or Chamberlain "a nigger" in opposing the Afghan and Zulu wars.[64] Even on the question of responsibility for the outbreak of war Lloyd George accepted an amended interpretation which rested on arguments justifying defensive action against the

63. Speech, 31 Oct. 1901, LGP, A/10/1/29. By this he meant a claim to racial superiority over other white races, not over the peoples of Afro-Asia.
64. Speech, 7 Oct. 1901, ibid., A/10/1/25.

Boer invasion. Then he tended to argue that the war was unnecessary rather than immoral. Ultimately, he acknowledged that Britain could not lose prestige by courting Kruger, although he advocated a negotiated rather than a dictated peace settlement. His terms were less harsh than Milner's and Lloyd George expected the Boers to accept them. They were based, however, on the assumption that British rule and supremacy in South Africa would be restored. Lloyd George's peace settlement would not threaten Britain's imperial interests.

These modifications affected Lloyd George's attitude toward imperialism. The Boer War confirmed for him that morally disparate types of imperialism existed.[65] The old Tory imperialism still flourished, exploiting, costly, and ultimately self-destructive. In contrast was a form of imperialism based on consent and the recognition that possession of an empire imposed duties and obligations. Britain must make her Empire an instrument of freedom, toleration, progress, and peace. It would be secure, function economically, maintain free trade, and not impose intolerable burdens on any member. This Empire, Lloyd George argued, would survive when all other empires had passed away, for unity came from freedom, power from justice, and loyalty from equality. This concept of Empire permitted him to declare, "I also am an imperialist. I believe in Empire; its enemies are my enemies." It followed that the need for imperial security could become a constant theme of his oratory.

Lloyd George's responses to postwar issues in South Africa, therefore, reflect more than a vendetta with Chamberlain.[66] Johannesburg was a sewer, he charged, land settlement schemes had failed, Transvaal finances were in chaos, and South Africa's economy floundered. Consequently the Boers were not becoming loyal citizens of the Empire. Moreover, when Milner's cheap labour policy, the Chinese Labour Ordinance of February 1904, was passed, Lloyd George interpreted it as a violation of all civilized codes, which introduced slavery into the Empire to serve the mine-owners' interests.[67] Lloyd George made Chamberlain

65. Speeches, 27 Jan. 1900 and 21 Nov. 1901, ibid., A/9/2/6 and A/10/1/36.

66. Speeches, 30 April, 23 and 30 June 1903, and 8 March 1905, *Parl. Deb.*, H. of C., cxxi, 1008–12, cxxvi, 191–95, 947–49, and cxlii, 755–59, and 4 June 1903, LGP, A/11/1/43. He branded the expedition against the Mullah of Mudug as humiliating folly. The Sudan was disturbed by, and Italy and Abyssinia were disgusted with British policy.

67. Speeches, 24 March, 19 May, and 21 July 1904, *Parl. Deb.*, H. of C., cxxxii, 658–62, cxxv, 396–99, and cxxxviii, 877–83.

morally responsible, notwithstanding the fact that Alfred Lyttelton had replaced him as colonial secretary in October 1903.

By attempting to redefine imperialism, Lloyd George clearly hoped to contribute to Liberal unity. He called on all Liberals to support policies which could demonstrate that the propensity for good in imperial rule outweighed the propensity for evil. He indicted the Tory record, from the loss of the American colonies to the Boer War, as disastrous. The Conservatives had squandered the heritage. It followed that the future must be entrusted to more rational, progressive, and prescient men.[68]

The Liberal party, however, was in a state of disrepair. Mere cabals had replaced cohesive organization and the party seemed either leaderless or overled. Campbell-Bannerman, despite his growing stature and attempts at consolidation, speculated as late as January 1903 on whether the party would founder.[69] If the "Leaguers" joined Chamberlain all was at an end.

The Boer War, however, had a dual effect. It pointed the way to reconciliation even while it threatened to produce disintegration. In the years before 1906 two sets of forces were at work, alternately wounding and healing the Liberal party, but eventually the patient was restored to some kind of health. Liberals came to accept Campbell-Bannerman as a leader with political skill, patience, and courage enough to defy the pretenders. He beat off the final conspiracy in 1905 and became prime minister. Rosebery, petulant and bewildering, had proved to be no alternative.

The Conservatives undermined their own solidarity. They committed or were the victims of a series of blunders, and showed a deadly ability to weaken their position. Under the languishing leadership of Balfour and in the wake of Chamberlain, the Conservatives drove wedges into their own unity. They then presented the Liberals with the unifying issue of free trade.

Liberal reconciliation was built on three other foundations. First, important sections of the party began to discover sufficient common ground in policy revaluation to make cooperation more than mere contrivance. Secondly, all feasible alternatives foundered for those who investigated other political pastures. Finally, in December 1905, cooperation proved to be the only path to

---

68. Speeches, 19 March 1903, ibid., cxix, 1267–71, 4 April 1903, 30 Jan., 4 March, and 6 May 1905, LGP, A/11/1/27 and A/13/1/4, 9 and 13.

69. Campbell-Bannerman to Bryce, 26 Jan. 1903, Campbell-Bannerman Papers, Add. 52517.

office. These factors were as obvious to Asquith as to Campbell-Bannerman or Lloyd George.

The Liberal Imperialists had challenged Gladstonian policies and had jeopardized party unity. Even at the height of the Boer War, however, they had not acted with unrelieved extremism. They had rarely boycotted attempts to achieve an accommodation and had mixed a measure of tolerance with more unyielding attitudes. Moreover, some Liberal Imperialists were less extreme than others, Asquith being milder than Haldane or Grey. While they championed Milner during the war, they generally despised Chamberlain. Consequently, Lloyd George's attack on the colonial secretary won a measure of Liberal Imperialist support.

The Liberal League, as Herbert Gladstone warned Campbell-Bannerman in April 1903, undoubtedly contained those who would rest more easily with the Unionists, some who were attracted by political alternatives beyond both parties, and others who wished to remain within but alter decisively the complexion of the Liberal party.[70] The movement to foster national efficiency, social imperialism, and collectivism attracted Haldane particularly, and Grey and Asquith to a lesser degree. They explored it briefly in the milieu of the Coefficients Club from November 1902.[71] This flirtation, however, did not survive the debate on protection. Free trade Liberal Imperialists could not support Chamberlain's panacea, and his speech of 15 May 1903 helped undermine more than Conservative electoral prospects.[72] Asquith carried the campaign against Chamberlain and did so brilliantly, as Liberals supported a policy of progressive taxation rather than tariffs to raise revenue for reform. Opposition to Balfour's Education Act of 1902 had provided a further basis for Liberal unity. The party fought the 1905 election on the familiar slogans of free trade, peace, retrenchment and reform, but the Liberal Imperialists were ready to control the defence and foreign policies of the new government.

70. Gladstone to Campbell-Bannerman, April 1903, ibid.
71. The Coefficients Club, organized by the Webbs and Leo Amery, was an attempt to maintain common ground for social imperialists from all parties and from outside political parties.
72. Beatrice Webb said that while Sidney preferred the Empire as "the unit of consideration" for policy matters, he could not accept protection. (B. Webb to Bertrand Russell, June 1903, Bertrand Russell Papers.) See also B. Webb diary, 9 July 1901 and 1 March 1904, B. Webb, *Our Partnership*, ed. B. Drake and M. J. Cole (London, 1948), 217, 283.

Herbert Gladstone, despite the gloom of disunity, had astutely assessed the pretenders. Grey had no popular following; the office of lord chancellor would buy Asquith, who was forced to earn money at the bar and could not afford to lead an opposition movement. Asquith was bitten by social aspirations and was driven on by the "little snob" Margot, but he sought office not martyrdom.

One incident revealed the trend. In February 1904 all the important Liberal Imperialists save Haldane joined in the vote against the Chinese labour proposals; in effect against Milner personally as much as in opposition to the government. Milner thought he had "squared" Asquith but, as Leo Amery reported, Asquith had ratted, and Margot was already choosing wallpaper for Number 10.[73] He had dropped Milner just as he would rid himself of Churchill and Haldane. Ambitious and never reluctant to manoeuvre, Asquith at least ran consistently. Milner ultimately served under Lloyd George.

Herbert Gladstone had described Lloyd George as "a typical cadger" who wanted office, suffered from a swollen head, and probably saw himself as the leader of the party.[74] He cited as evidence Lloyd George's "arrangement" with R. W. Perks, leader of the Liberal Imperial Council, during the Khaki election. This charge was surely unfounded but Gladstone's comment was a significant one. Lloyd George's preference for confrontation was tempered by an appreciation of the value of conciliation. Political realism made him recoil from extremism. In any case he did not regard all Liberal Imperialists with unrelieved suspicion or contempt; he seemed to admire, for instance, Asquith's intellectual qualities.[75]

Furthermore, his attitudes towards domestic, imperial, and foreign policies were evolving and maturing. The Boer War had made him a national figure, and demonstrated his ability to move men. Lloyd George sensed the opportunities that lay ahead for a

---

73. Amery to Milner, 26 Feb. 1904, Gollin, *Proconsul in Politics*, 65.

74. In September 1903 Campbell-Bannerman refused to chair a meeting addressed by Lloyd George, for family reasons. (Campbell-Bannerman to J. B. Smith, 19 Sept. 1903, J. A. Spender Papers, Add. 46388.)

75. K. Robbins, *Sir Edward Grey* (London, 1971), 112; Lloyd George to his wife, 16 May 1902, 6 July 1905, Morgan, *Family Letters*, 135, 142; W. George, 271–72, 276–77; Taylor, *Lloyd George: A Diary*, 3, 31, 78; F. Lloyd George, *The Years that are Past*, 19; D. Sommer, *Haldane of Cloan* (London, 1960), 236, 344, 346, 352–53.

politician of courage, skill, and ambition; he expected a place in the cabinet. Finally, the Boer War had demonstrated the danger of leading dissent in matters of imperial and foreign policy. Lloyd George knew that he could not again risk dissociation from the Empire, and all that it meant in the Edwardian age.

# 4

# Maturing in an Interlude

Campbell-Bannerman's government, which took office in December 1905, represented an uneasy alliance rather than a mature consensus. Campaign promises and election manifestoes provided certain guidelines, but few could predict how the cabinet would function and what priorities it would pursue. In retrospect, the well-worn labels of "Radical" and "Liberal Imperialist" attached to individual ministers seem perhaps more convenient for historians than valid, for far more complex relationships existed. Social origins were disparate, intimacies were the exception, intellectual content varied, and so did political acumen and appetite. Radicals were not a homogeneous group and they indulged in inconsistent and politically divergent behaviour. The debate over foreign policy up to the outbreak of war in August 1914 was not a simple confrontation between patriotic imperialists and radical dissenters, with the latter group exasperating the Foreign Office. The behaviour of Lloyd George, Morley at the India Office, and Haldane at the War Office, demonstrated that fact, and Charles Hardinge, permanent under-secretary at the Foreign Office until 1910, described Campbell-Bannerman as the best ever prime minister with regard to the conduct of foreign affairs. An analysis of Edward Grey's policies in the years before 1914 reveals three phases rather than one. Only in the second phase, between 1909 and 1912, when the implications for Britain of the ententes with France and Russia, the Moroccan crises, and the naval race became evident, were there serious cabinet confrontations, resulting in the "Grey must go" campaign of the winter of 1911–1912. For the rest, the Foreign Office enjoyed relative immunity from attack.

Lloyd George preferred the Home Office and considered the Local Government Board and the Post Office so as to avoid losing contact with Welsh affairs, but finally he accepted the Board of Trade.[1] His biographers treat his tenure of that office almost exclusively in terms of domestic and commercial policies. Virtually as a postscript some note his brief participation in the Colonial Conference of 1907 and his contributions on the Chinese labour question. This period until April 1908, however, is not devoid of significance. Some impetus was given to the development of his synthesis of radicalism and patriotic imperialism. Office strengthened his commitment to the Liberal party and the Board of Trade did not divorce him from foreign and imperial affairs. His involvement in the formulation of foreign policy was very limited, however, and his participation in the discussions on the Baghdad Railway was virtually an isolated case.

The evidence on Lloyd George's views is less than satisfactory. His role in cabinet debate is obscured by the inadequacy of Campbell-Bannerman's reports to the king.[2] Lord Esher, a member of the Committee of Imperial Defence, lamented how infrequently and briefly the prime minister wrote to the monarch, and with justification. The files of the Foreign Office are often more revealing about relatively minor officials than are cabinet records about ministerial opinion.[3] The Algeciras conference, South Africa's constitutional development, the Hague Conference of 1907, Britain's relations with the European powers, with Turkey and the United States, and particularly the defence estimates appear in

1. Unsigned note to Campbell-Bannerman, 5 Dec. 1905, Campbell-Bannerman Papers, Add. 52518. Lloyd George had been ill and had gone to North Italy with his brother. He did not return to London until 3 December. See also A. Carnegie to Morley, 17 Dec. 1905, Morley Papers, Eur. D.573/66; Cambon to Rouvier, 25 Oct. 1905, *DDF*, 2, viii, 79.

2. Cab 41/30 and 31; Campbell-Bannerman Papers, Add. 52512 and 52513.

3. The Lloyd George Papers contain little above routine importance on foreign policy for 1906 and 1907.

Campbell-Bannerman's reports, but he omitted the details of discussion. Lloyd George for instance was mentioned specifically only once, with regard to the settlement of the railway strike in November 1907.

In addition, the Board of Trade was not normally on the distribution list for Committee of Imperial Defence papers.[4] Lloyd George was not at this time a member of the CID, and he did not attend a meeting of that body until its ninety-ninth session on 14 May 1908. Consequently, the records of the CID are unrevealing, and in some cases curiously so. The Board of Trade participated in the investigation of the Channel Tunnel scheme in 1906, and in the preparations for the Hague Conference in 1907, but there is no evidence of Lloyd George's personal involvement. The issue of the freedom of the seas took on greater significance in May 1907 when Prince von Bülow, the German chancellor, declined to discuss naval arms limitation at the Hague Conference.[5] The Admiralty in turn insisted on the maintenance of the right of blockade and the means to control merchant shipping in wartime. Lloyd George, however, was not prominent in the debate between the Sea Lords and certain radical ministers. Perhaps he did not doubt the prime minister's sincere intent to secure progress toward arms limitation and a system of arbitration. Perhaps also he sympathized with the Admiralty's position on the freedom of the seas.

As president of the board of trade, Lloyd George seldom received Foreign Office letters, dispatches, and memoranda, and his heavy departmental duties generally pointed elsewhere than to the Foreign Office's preserve.[6] Lloyd George's opportunity,

4. CID paper, 4 May 1908, Cab 38/14/3.

5. Inter-Departmental Committee to consider the subjects for discussion at the Second Peace Conference, 11 April 1907, Cab 37/87/42, and 28 May 1908, Cab 37/93/68; Foreign Office memoranda, 12 April, 31 May, and 3 June 1907, Cab 37/88/43, and Cab 37/89/63 and 65; CID papers, 15 May, Cab 38/11/20, and 19 June 1906, Cab 38/12/31; memorandum, 25 Aug. 1906, Cab 38/12/49. See also A. J. A. Morris, "The English Radicals Campaign for Disarmament and the Hague Conference of 1907," *Journal of Modern History*, 43, no. 3 (1971), 367–93; H. S. Weinroth, "The British Radicals and the Balance of Power, 1902–1914," *The Historical Journal*, 13, no. 4 (1970), 653–82, and "Left-Wing Opposition to Naval Armaments in Britain before 1914," *Journal of Contemporary History*, 6, no. 4 (1971), 95–120.

6. Board of Trade files, B.T. 12/42–53, 1900–1908, yield as little as the circulated memoranda. (See, for example, Dec. 1905, on commercial negotiations with Rumania, Cab 37/81/187.)

to develop familiarity with foreign policy matters was, therefore, limited, but this situation should not be regarded as indicating an intrinsic lack of interest and concern on his part. With the single exception of his defence of free trade, however, Lloyd George made no major speech on foreign policy during these years. Even then he did little more than reiterate his belief in the existence of causal bonds between free trade, commercial expansion, and national prosperity on the one hand, and disarmament, brother-hood, and peace on the other. Free trade was a dogma of oratory, the path to the promised land.[7]

The conventions governing the conduct of Campbell-Banner-man's cabinet also had their impact. Ministers were expected to settle interdepartmental problems without reference to the cabinet. The prime minister, in consultation with the relevant minister, largely determined what matters came before cabinet, although the foreign secretary and others enjoyed discretionary powers in this regard. The prime minister also decided to a great extent on the distribution of memoranda to the cabinet. These conventions helped neutralize controversy and avoid divisive debate. Moreover, these were not years of crisis. The cabinet made few momentous decisions on foreign policy. It never overruled Grey on any major question, and the defence estimates neither dramatized political differences nor threatened social reform.

The cabinet's devotion to domestic questions is very evident. They debated foreign and defence policy at length on a mere sixteen recorded occasions in more than two years, and even then the service estimates dominated those deliberations. Moreover, Grey's method of conducting policy anaesthetized potential opposition. He was placed and placed himself, until 1909, largely beyond searching and detailed scrutiny. The cabinet was subject to Foreign Office practices and zealous professionalism. Secrecy undermined the potential for dissent, but never completely, for some of Grey's colleagues knew more at the time than they sub-sequently revealed.

Lloyd George's understanding of the intricacies of foreign policy was not, therefore, greatly enhanced. He was insulated from controversy and committed to policy decisions largely by inex-

7. Lloyd George, *Better Times*; speeches, 5 Jan. 1906, 23 Jan. and 1 Nov. 1907, and 28 Feb. 1908, LGP, B/4/1/10, B/5/1/3 and 30, and B/5/2/8; speeches, 12 March 1906 and 15 July 1907, *Parl. Deb.*, H. of C., CLIII, 1023–36, and CLXXVIII, 437–47; A. Chamberlain, *Politics from Inside*, 53, 87.

perience. He had neither reasons nor an issue on which to confront the Foreign Office. He was on the whole a compliant colleague, a state of affairs which Welshmen loyal to the Crown and devoted to Lloyd George applauded. Lord Loreburn, the lord chancellor, and James Bryce, at the Irish Office, were the persistent if ineffectual critics of Grey, and it was Haldane, Grey's friend and confidant, who irritated the French and the Foreign Office in 1906. Lloyd George identified himself with a relatively uncontroversial, economical, apparently pacific, and untested Liberal foreign policy, the ultimate implications of which remained largely unexplored. Clearly, and understandably, he shared the desire to place cabinet loyalty at a premium. Avoidance of controversy would prevent a schism, and Liberal solidarity after years of troubled opposition seemed eminently preferable.[8]

Lloyd George had become a national figure with a political image which identified him with radical dissent. He was expected to help ensure that the Liberal government pursued arms limitation, arbitration and conciliation procedures, and concert diplomacy, and perpetuated a non-entangling, morally defensible, and pacific Entente with democratic France which did not preclude a rapprochement with Germany. Grey must mediate between Europe's alliance groups, pacify the Continent, and ensure that Britain fostered détente and did not become involved in war. Lloyd George's role, positive or negative, in any serious departure from these policies would affect his public image, his relationship to Grey and the Foreign Office, and his standing within the cabinet. While Campbell-Bannerman was prime minister, Lloyd George was not particularly troubled. On the other hand he had already demonstrated his concern for national prestige and imperial security, and a capacity for compromise.

In fact, Lloyd George and Grey ultimately came together to a greater degree than either subsequently conceded, and their rapport was surely more important than either Lloyd George's rhetoric or his opposition to inflated defence estimates. Arthur Ponsonby, a Liberal critic of Grey, even understated the case when in January 1913 he commented on Grey, "He would be a

8. E. T. Cook described Lloyd George as more vulgar but less bitter than Chamberlain. His wild man image on the platform actually increased the impact of his reasonableness when people met him. They noted with surprise "he is quite a moderate man after all." (J. W. Robertson Scott, *The Life and Death of a Newspaper* [London, 1952], 292, 354.)

good friend for Lloyd George and Lloyd George would be a good friend for him."[9] Certain contemporaries understood in part the process through which Lloyd George passed, among them Lord Esher and more especially J. L. Garvin, editor of *The Observer*. The latter was perceptive enough in his diagnosis when he told Lord Northcliffe, the newspaper proprietor, in November 1907, "Were we not right about Lloyd George. The man is maturing very rapidly. Having tasted the pleasures of a solid and statesmanlike success, tinsel triumphs will henceforth be less attractive to him. He will follow this up, bid high and go far."[10]

This makes all the more interesting the interpretation of the whole period from 1906 to 1914 that Lloyd George entrenched in his memoirs, in which there is little attempt to distinguish between various phases.[11] First of all, he contrasted pacific, Francophile radicals with belligerent Tories and Liberal Imperialists. The former group he described as consistent in attitude, devoted to principle, and in search of détente. The latter, he suggested, had turned on France and then on Germany, preferring policies of confrontation.

Lloyd George insisted that Grey had seized virtually a free hand, while radicals had remained innocent, uninformed, and devoted to domestic affairs. A secretive Grey and an inner clique had controlled foreign and defence policies, and the foreign secretary was more frank with Dominion representatives than with his colleagues. Neither the cabinet nor the Dominions, Lloyd George charged, were informed about "our military commitments." He himself, he claimed, had become aware of them only during the Agadir crisis and the cabinet was not enlightened until 1912. Furthermore, he suggested, Grey had deceived the cabinet on the question of whether he had committed Britain to assist France and Russia in a European war. Grey had denied that any bond existed but had given the contrary impression to the Dual Entente.

Lloyd George argued that he had accepted Grey's assurances in good faith and that the military appreciation by Henry Wilson, director of military operations, in August 1911, had confirmed Grey's interpretation. All was apparently contingent on a German

9. Z. S. Steiner, *The Foreign Office and Foreign Policy 1898–1914* (Cambridge, 1969), 84–85; L. Masterman, "Recollections of David Lloyd George," 160–69.

10. Garvin to Northcliffe, 7 Nov. 1907, Garvin Papers, box 59.

11. Lloyd George, *War Memoirs*, I, 1–4, 27–31, 35–36, 40, 43, 55–60.

attack on Belgium. He personally had never questioned the fact that Britain must discharge her treaty obligations to Belgium in such an eventuality.

Two conclusions followed from Lloyd George's analysis. First, that the theory of collective responsibility did not apply; Lloyd George and those who had been excluded and uninformed for so long were free of responsibility for the outbreak of war in 1914. Second, that the violation of Belgian neutrality provided an irresistible moral and legal argument for involvement in war. No analysis could have been more convenient for its author.

If Lloyd George had a theory of history it was that personalities were the vital forces determining the unfolding of events. His revelations about Grey were meant not only to establish a thesis about foreign policy but also to demonstrate that the foreign secretary was the antithesis of himself. In the course of the exposé, Grey would be revealed as both weak and yet in control. Moreover, Lloyd George insisted, Grey was typical of the generation of political leaders who served Europe so inadequately before and during 1914. He lacked courage, vision, resolution, imagination, great intellectual quality, breadth of mind, and firmness. He was not fit for high office and in 1914 the populace and the military grasped the initiative from "the hands of quivering and hesitant statesmanship." A powerful and secretive Grey had, under Lloyd George's pen, become simultaneously a feeble and inadequate Grey. He was thus doubly condemnable by virtue of almost contradictory qualities.

But for his family and secretariat, Lloyd George would have gone even further.[12] His brother warned against the vitriolic attacks on Grey contained in an early draft of the *War Memoirs*. He urged Lloyd George to avoid an apologia and to present an objective and authoritative account of permanent value, reflecting well on himself but not creating sympathy for Grey. Lloyd George made changes and concessions, but he insisted that Grey's reputation was not based on achievement. He was a calamitous foreign secretary before 1914 and "by 1916 he was in a blue funk, thoroughly paralysed by the jeopardy into which he had plunged us." Moreover, he had been a bitter opponent after the war, and

12. W. George to Megan Lloyd George, 14 May, W. George, *My Brother and I*, 238–39; Lloyd George to W. George, 28 May, and W. George to Lloyd George, 30 May 1933, LGP, G/211.

Lloyd George felt relieved of any debt of camaraderie. Hankey, a neutral observer, "thoroughly approves" the amended draft, Lloyd George noted.[13] While he had been indulgent toward Asquith's failures and defects, "the charlatans and skunks I deal faithfully with. Grey certainly belongs in my opinion to the first category."[14] Such comments are more revealing of Lloyd George in 1933 than of Grey. Like G. M. Trevelyan's defence and Grey's own memoirs they require more than marginal emendation. Lloyd George's *War Memoirs* in fact do justice neither to Grey nor to himself.

Lloyd George participated to some extent in the decision-making process from 1908. E. L. Woodward noted as much in 1933, suggesting that Lloyd George seemed to have forgotten how important he had been.[15] He had become so consumed by the war itself that he had lost sight of his position both before and during July 1914. Woodward pointed to several instances: Lloyd George's involvement in the special cabinet committee on Foreign Affairs in January 1911, the Mansion House speech, the preparations for Haldane's mission in 1912, and his role in the cabinet decisions after Haldane's return from Berlin. Woodward concluded that he could not accept Lloyd George's view of Grey. The publication of the German documents had damaged Grey's image, but as in the case of Lord Castlereagh, the truth would emerge in the end.

Arthur Murray, Grey's parliamentary private secretary before 1914, agreed:

13. Beaverbrook read the amended draft and endorsed it as truthful and a proper deflation of Grey. (Beaverbrook to F. Stevenson, 31 May 1933, LGP, G/211.)

14. An unsigned "Appreciation of Lord Grey of Fallodon," in LGP, G/8/10/3, describes Grey as an impassive, dignified and insular aristocrat who concealed what emotions he possessed beneath a frigid exterior. He was contemptuous of foreigners and of all ideas he did not share or understand. His singular achievement was to remain in office and yet avoid public criticism. Grey kept the last and greatest commandment to the full, "Thou shalt not be found out." He made no sacrifice for others and yet inspired sacrifice in his own service; he preferred fauna to his fellow men, and his supreme claim to prominence was that he helped plunge Europe into war. A blunter man might have smashed the web enmeshing the nations; a more unscrupulous man might have limited the conflict or have won over enough allies to end the war rapidly. Grey, however, turned the war from a calamity into a cataclysm.

15. Woodward to Mrs. H. A. L. Fisher, 11 Dec. 1933, ibid., G/214.

*I propose to take the opportunity of dealing with some of the mis-statements (to use no stronger term) about Grey and his policy contained in Lloyd George's War Memoirs.*

*Lloyd George gives the impression that he was—up to the war period—kept almost completely in the dark by Grey as to the essential features of foreign affairs and policy. As to that I have a note in my Diary to the effect that at the end of 1910 my brother Alick (who was then Chief Whip) came to me and said that Lloyd George had said to him that although he (L.G.) was specially interested in Foreign Affairs in that he was called upon to provide the money for huge Naval Estimates, he was kept in the dark in regard to the essential features of our Foreign Policy. He knew practically nothing, he said, of what was going on and he demanded that all important papers should be sent to him.*

*I wrote Tyrrell a few days ago asking him for his recollection of the incident and I have a letter back from him confirming it as set out above.*[16]

As to the scheme for a cabinet committee to review foreign policy, Murray noted:

*I am to some extent confirmed in my view that it was set up, by a note in my Diary of a conversation at the end of 1911 between Alick and Lord Loreburn in which the latter referred to the absurdity of "five amateurs", Asquith, Grey, Lloyd George, Winston and Haldane meeting together in July 1911 and deciding, without consulting their colleagues in the Cabinet, to land 150,000 men in France in the event of war. Did the above perhaps constitute the Committee?*
*In any event my recollection is quite clear that after the incident at the end of 1910 no further complaint came from Lloyd George as to being kept in the dark about Foreign Policy; so presumably he was satisfied with the arrangements that had been made—except of course in respect to the Ambassador's letters.*

Lord Crewe, secretary of state for India between 1910 and 1915, replied "that though I should like to record my complete dissent from these attacks, yet they appear to be expressions of opinion, however unjust, not mis-statements of fact."[17] He recalled a

16. Murray to Crewe, 12 Oct. 1933, Crewe Papers, C/14 .
17. Crewe to Murray, 18 Oct. 1933, ibid.

similar situation when Sir William Harcourt had asked to see Foreign Office papers in 1894 and, lamenting the fact that he had not kept a diary, observed:

> *but so far as my remembrance goes there was no regular Cabinet Committee in the sense of one being set up at a Cabinet meeting, but that this body of five, representing the Departments specifically interested, was called together from time to time by Asquith, and that this method satisfied the Chancellor of the Exchequer. I was a member of the C.I.D. from 1908 and I knew about the "conversations" which excited Loreburn so much from intimate talks with Asquith and Grey. Probably one may now admit rather too much was done by interchange of views between the inner circle of Ministers, but this is a necessary defect of a too large Cabinet, and Lloyd George would not have complained of it had he always been one of those consulted.*

Murray responded that Crewe's letter helped "show how unjustifiable are the attacks, coming as they do from one whose character and attitude during the pre-war weeks gives him less right than anyone else to put pen to paper on the subject of Grey." Crewe, Walter Runciman, president of the board of agriculture in 1914, J. A. Pease, president of the board of education in 1914, and those "who know L.G. and his ways," should defend Grey. Murray himself intended to ask Lloyd George publicly why, if Grey had been so remiss in not making Britain's attitude over Belgium clear to Berlin, he himself had never proposed such a step to the cabinet.[18]

Neither Woodward nor Murray, however, offered evidence for the period when Lloyd George was president of the board of trade. Grey and his officials inherited the Moroccan crisis of 1905 and began to formulate a Continental policy which pivoted on and reinterpreted the Entente with France. This policy was based on the assumption that Germany was the most probable threat to British security, the balance of power, and peace.[19] Grey there-

18. Murray to Crewe, 20 Oct., and Crewe to Murray, 24 Oct. 1933, ibid.
19. Grey to Spender, 19 Oct. 1905, J. A. Spender papers, Add. 46389; Grey to Campbell-Bannerman, 4 Sept. 1907, Campbell-Bannerman Papers, Add. 52514. In general one should consult Steiner, *The Foreign Office*, 83–213, G. Monger, *The End of Isolation* (London, 1963), 236–331, M. L. Dockrill, "The Formulation of a Continental Foreign Policy in Great Britain, 1908–1912,"

fore permitted and subsequently encouraged staff talks with France and Belgium. Lloyd George and the majority of the government remained uninitiated and the cabinet discussed the Algeciras conference only once, in March 1906.[20] Similarly, the Foreign Office settled the Akaba affair with Turkey without reference to the cabinet,[21] which also did not formally discuss the memorandum of 1 January 1907 by Eyre Crowe, head of the Western Department of the Foreign Office.[22]

Lloyd George was also not prominent in the concurrent attempts to improve the public atmosphere in relations between London and Berlin, but he became involved with the Anglo-German Friendship Committee, formed in November 1905.[23] One of his officials, W. H. Dawson, in the Labour Department of the Board of Trade, assumed that Lloyd George's sympathies lay with those who favoured détente with Germany and the neutralizing of any naval rivalry. Dawson saw Lloyd George, the German ambassador Count Metternich, and himself as devoted to the same goals: social reform, Anglo-German rapprochement, and the pacification of Europe.[24] Lloyd George's speech to the World Peace Congress in London in the summer of 1908 seemed to confirm these assumptions.

When Grey pursued the other foundation of his European policy, the Entente with Russia, he reported but twice to the cabinet, in March 1907.[25] His request for secrecy was to a large extent met. Morley actually welcomed the Russian entente on behalf of the India Office and gave no lead to the radical or socialist critics,[26] who launched their protest in a letter to *The*

---

(Ph.D. thesis, University of London, 1969), Z. S. Steiner, "Grey, Hardinge and the Foreign Office, 1906–1910," *The Historical Journal*, 10, no. 4, (1967), 415–39, and S. R. Williamson, *The Politics of Grand Strategy: Britain and France Prepare for War, 1904–14* (Cambridge, Mass., 1969), 1–88.

20. Prime minister to the king, 7 March 1906, Cab 41/30/46.

21. Cab 41/30; Ripon to Campbell-Bannerman, 27 April 1906, Campbell-Bannerman Papers, Add. 41225; Monger, *End of Isolation*, 297.

22. Cab 41/31; Viscount Morley, *Memorandum on Resignation* (London, 1928), xvi–xvii; Cab 37/86/1. This last source contains merely a xeroxed copy and provides no circulation list.

23. Cab 41/30; A. T. Bassett, *The Life of John Edward Ellis*, 245; E. D. Morel to Russell, March 1915, Bertrand Russell Papers.

24. Dawson to Lloyd George, 2 Jan. 1907, W. H. Dawson Papers, f.187. See also H. Lewis diary, 28 April 1907.

25. Cabinet meetings, 6 March and 20 March 1907, Cab 41/31/7 and 10.

26. Grey's applause for Morley's role in the negotiations with Russia was

*Times* of 11 June 1907, signed by Ramsay MacDonald, J. A. Hobson, and others.[27] The letter attacked the policy of establishing closer relations with an autocratic regime which perpetuated an iniquitous social and political system, and exploited anti-Semitism. Moreover, the dissenters charged, the agreement betrayed Persia and violated the nationality principle in order to sustain the balance of power. Such a policy would isolate Germany and divide Europe into military blocs.

Grey, however, was unmoved. Parliament was in recess during the last months of 1907 and he did not present the Entente until the throne speech, on 29 January 1908. Lloyd George did not identify himself with the opposition to Grey. Furthermore, when Grey finally informed the cabinet on 6 May 1908 that Edward VII would meet the tsar at Reval, Lloyd George made no protest.[28] In the ensuing parliamentary uproar in June he also avoided any hint of criticism. By this time of course he was chancellor of the exchequer in Asquith's government, but there is no evidence that he considered the Russian entente particularly distasteful. On 4 June 1908, in the supply debate on the Foreign Office estimates, which focused on the arrangement with Russia, Lloyd George stood by Grey against his radical and Labour opponents. Perhaps he followed Morley's lead. In any case, Lloyd George had always shown greater concern for Russia the imperial enemy than Russia the foe of liberalism.

Lloyd George also contributed to the development of Liberal policy toward the Empire. Campbell-Bannerman's administration fostered self-government and the establishment of Dominion status for white communities. It hoped to stimulate imperial unity through the acceptance of common interests and joint involvement in their pursuit by the members of the Empire. Lloyd George claimed to have done more than merely support the

---

profuse. (Grey to prime minister, 31 Aug. 1907, Campbell-Bannerman Papers, Add. 52514.) See also S. E. Koss, *John Morley at the India Office, 1905–10* (New Haven, Conn., 1969), J. A. Murray, "British policy and opinion on the Anglo-Russian Entente 1907–14," (Ph.D. thesis, Duke University, 1957), A. W. Palmer, "The Anglo-Russian Entente 1907," *History Today*, 7, no. 11 (1957), 748–54, Monger, *End of Isolation*, 284–87; Carnegie to Morley, Sept. 1906, Morley Papers, Eur. D.573/56.

27. *The Times*, 11 June 1907; M. Beloff, *Lucien Wolf and the Anglo-Russian Entente 1907–1914* (London, 1951).

28. Cabinet meeting, 6 May 1908, Cab 41/31/50.

government's policy toward South Africa in 1906.[29] The Board of Trade, moreover, established trade commissioners in all self-governing colonies as a practical and symbolic act.

Lloyd George participated in the preparations for and the conduct of the Colonial Conference which met in April and May 1907. He made a contribution, sometimes rather ill-tempered, to the discussions on commercial and trade matters, but added nothing to the debate on foreign and defence policy.[30] However, the question of creating an imperial communications and transportation facility, the "All-Red Route," interested him. In guarded exchanges with Sir Wilfrid Laurier, the Canadian prime minister, Lloyd George promised that his department, while impressed with the problems involved, would continue to explore the scheme.[31] His concern did not waver, as Churchill reported to Crewe in May 1908. "Sir Thomas Shaughnessy of the CPR is in England and Lloyd George wants to examine him before the 'All Red Route Committee'. I am therefore summoning the Committee for 4:30 on Tuesday at the Board of Trade....Hitherto Lloyd George has been the 'motor muscle'. His new office places him in some difficulty and the Colonial point of view certainly requires strong special representation." Crewe replied, conscious of the financial difficulties involved, "As you say, Lloyd George's position becomes curious; he now has to be devil's advocate, a new role for him."[32]

Lloyd George's departmental duties also involved him in the problem of the Baghdad railway. Grey disliked the prospect of a German presence in the Persian Gulf, beyond her commercial interests, and viewed the Baghdad railway as a menace to the British position in Persia and Mesopotamia. By November 1906

29. E. T. Cook, "Liberal Colonial Policy," *Contemporary Review*, 51 (April 1907), 457–68, and "Eight Years of Liberal Imperialism," *Contemporary Review*, 105 (Jan. 1914), 1–11. Lloyd George continued to insist that Campbell-Bannerman, abetted by John Burns and himself, was the principal architect of South African constitutional change. The Campbell-Bannerman papers contain only one letter relating to Lloyd George and the constitutional future of the Boer republics. (F. J. S. Hopwood to Lloyd George, 5 May 1906, Campbell-Bannerman Papers, Add. 52518.)

30. Minutes of the Colonial Conference of 1907, Cab 18/11A.

31. Lloyd George to Laurier, 18 July 1907, Laurier Papers, M.G. 26, G.1(a), vol. 468. Laurier was interested in the development of a sea and rail link between Britain, Canada, and Australia.

32. Churchill to Crewe, 15 May, and Crewe to Churchill, 16 May 1908, Crewe Papers, C/7.

he had prevailed on France and Russia to join in representations to Germany to force participation in the railway and its probable extension to the Persian Gulf. At that point, Grey, Asquith, the chancellor of the exchequer, Morley, and Lloyd George met as a cabinet committee to outline a policy.

The Baghdad Railway Committee made its recommendations in May 1907.[33] It concluded, in line with Grey's views, that British interests, strategic, political, and commercial, demanded that her participation be assured permanently and on equitable terms. Britain must secure complete rights for the construction and control of the railway from a point north of Baghdad to the Persian Gulf, and equality of treatment must be instituted for all participants along the whole railway. The committee expected British capital to finance the section under British control, and British contractors to build the harbour works at Baghdad, Bussorah, and Koweit. Finally, while Germany's initiative must be recognized and her role confirmed, Britain expected full representation on the railway's regulatory boards, and the creation of an international administration once the railway reached the Gulf. This policy led to considerable difficulties with France and Russia, and raised the unwelcome prospect of Franco-German cooperation. Grey retreated, but of significance here is the fact that Lloyd George had participated in the formulation of a policy in defence of imperial interests.

A year later, while Lloyd George was still at the Board of Trade, a sub-committee of the CID took up the question.[34] Lloyd George's participation was interrupted, however, when he became chancellor of the exchequer and he did not sign the committee's final report of 26 January 1909. His contributions consisted largely of

33. Memorandum to Cambon and Benckendorff, 4 June 1907, BDOW, vi, 355–56. However, the Foreign Office circulated a Report of the Baghdad Railway Committee, dated 26 March 1907. (Cab 37/87/36.) This report was by an inter-departmental committee which may have assisted the cabinet committee. It was signed by R. P. Maxwell, R. Ritchie, W. H. Clark, W. Tyrrell, and A. Parker. The Board of Trade position is not identified but no dissenting opinions were recorded.
34. The CID sub-committee was a successor to the cabinet committee and began its investigation in March 1908. (Report of a sub-committee of the CID to consider questions relating to the Persian Gulf and the Baghdad Railway, 26 Jan. 1909, Cab 38/15/2.) (See also Oliver Esher and M. V. Brett, eds., Journals and Letters of Reginald Viscount Esher, 4 vols. (London, 1934–38), ii, 296, 367 (hereafter cited as Esher Journals).

questions to expert witnesses.[35] However, at the first meeting, on 2 March 1908, Lloyd George noted that the problem of establishing a protectorate over Bahrein and other questions were in fact part of the much larger issue of British control over the whole of the Persian Gulf. The principle of policy involved, he suggested, was whether Britain needed to establish some sort of control over the Gulf in order to maintain her commercial and political supremacy in that area.

In the light of trade statistics, Lloyd George concluded that, commercially, Bahrein was very important. He agreed with the Foreign Office that Britain must establish a general jurisdiction as a preface to declaring a protectorate and securing complete control. The issue was one of method; Lloyd George suggested "squaring" the sheikh by offering a guaranteed cash subsidy in return for Britain taking over the Customs. Lloyd George obviously was not turning away from the prospect of increased imperial responsibilities.

There remained the question of defence policy but this did not become a *cause célèbre* until the debate over the naval estimates for 1908–09. The cabinet discussions in the preceding two years resulted in compromises offering security and economy without serious provocation to Germany.[36] The disarmament conference of 1907 at The Hague, moreover, temporarily provided grounds for radical optimism.[37] Admiral Sir John Fisher, now first sea

35. Report, proceedings, and appendices, and Foreign Office memorandum, British Interests in the Persian Gulf, App. 2, Cab 16/10. Churchill replaced Lloyd George on the sub-committee, joining Esher, Morley, and Grey. Lloyd George did not attend the meeting of the CID which discussed the final report. (CID meeting, 25 Feb. 1909, Cab 38/15/4.)

36. Between February and July 1906 the cabinet approved 1906–07 naval estimates providing for three Dreadnoughts and a saving of £2.5 million. The cabinet also eliminated a proposed increase in the War Office estimates of £1,630,000, and Haldane demonstrated how to reduce the army by 20,000 men. On 13 February 1907 the cabinet reduced the naval estimates by a further £1 million and provided for only two Dreadnoughts for 1907–08. (Cabinet meetings, 21 Feb., 21 March, 10 and 13 July 1906, 13 Feb. 1907, Cab 41/30/43, 50, 68, and 69, and Cab 41/31/3.) Fisher did not challenge these decisions (Esher to M. V. B., 21 Dec. 1906, *Esher Journals*, II, 209–10.)

37. Final decisions on the 1907–08 construction program awaited the results of the Hague Conference. Should it fail the cabinet would authorize a third capital ship. Should it succeed they would consider eliminating one of the two projected Dreadnoughts. In fact the 1907–08 estimates showed finally a reduction of only £450,000 and were set at £31,419,500. (Cabinet meetings, 25 April and 5 June 1907, Cab 41/31/16 and 21.)

lord, had identified himself with a policy of economy and efficiency. He had risen from obscure origins, challenged convention, and seemed to respect neither political reputations nor traditions. His exploitation of the press was unmatched by any sea lord and he was almost more of a model for Lloyd George than an opponent. Haldane, for his part, operated on a tight financial rein at the War Office.

Lloyd George questioned two decisions: the Dreadnought program itself and the move toward a concentrated Home Fleet. He deplored the former because it forced the pace of competition, was "a piece of wanton and profligate ostentation," and could threaten social reform.[38] He was ready to oppose both developments if they became injurious to Anglo-German relations. However, he objected specifically neither to the decision of October 1906, confirming the concentration of the battle fleet in home waters, nor to the decision to complete the Rosyth naval base. He accepted the fact that a Liberal government must look to the requirements of national defence, and never departed from this position before 1914.

The final months of 1907 brought complications which endangered cabinet unity, questioned certain policy assumptions, and disturbed the harmony between the Admiralty and the government. The Hague Conference had failed and the Admiralty was about to demand a third Dreadnought. The German Naval Law, announced in November 1907 and enacted in February 1908, seemed to threaten the future naval balance and jeopardise the state of Anglo-German relations. It helped activate a CID study of the probability of an invasion. The Unionists demanded a sharp riposte, two Dreadnoughts for one, while the Liberal and radical press reminded the government of its domestic program and priorities. All this at the same time as Campbell-Bannerman's anticipated retirement and the resulting cabinet reorganization.

Lloyd George could hardly escape the dilemma. He expected promotion and he lamented the failure of the Hague Conference. In public, he could desert neither the cause of retrenchment and reform nor that of national and imperial security. His respect for Fisher as a man of efficiency was apparently undiminished. Yet he had enjoyed a cordial conversation with the kaiser during his

38. A. J. Marder, *From the Dreadnought to Scapa Flow* (London, 1961), i, 56; Lloyd George, *War Memoirs*, i, 6.

visit to England in the fall of 1907. Germany was a model of social reform, and Wilhelm had encouraged him to tour Germany.[39] Moreover, as Lloyd George subsequently reported to his friend D. R. Daniel, he did not believe that the kaiser supported the policy of Admiral von Tirpitz as a preparation for war. The German navy was essentially a diplomatic weapon because "he does not want to go to conferences to settle the rights of his country in the Orient and other places without something he can point over his shoulder to when his enemies are slow to listen—power. He has felt his weakness in the past. That is why he is in such a hurry to get his navy. Not because he wants war but he wants a bludgeon in his hand."[40]

The Admiralty's proposals of December 1907, for an enlarged construction program and an increase of £2 million over the previous year's figures,[41] confronted the cabinet's desire to avoid any rise in the naval estimates.[42] Weighing political and public expectations against virtually unavoidable technical and inflationar factors, the cabinet reached an initial compromise in late January 1908, authorizing an increase of £1.25 million.[43]

Fisher was not satisfied; perhaps the expanded construction program was threatened. He manipulated the press in his favour, therefore, through Garvin and Lord Northcliffe.[44] Such machinations invoked the question of cabinet secrecy and with Lewis Harcourt, first commissioner of works, in the lead, the government challenged Fisher in early February.[45] Harcourt pointed out that a

39. Memoranda on naval matters, LGP, B/2/7B/1, 2, 3, 4, and 5 and on the invasion study, B/2/4/1 and 2; Fisher to Lloyd George, n.d., ibid., B/1/3/1, in which Fisher asked him to return the Admiralty memorandum on invasion; Fisher to Lloyd George, 17 Dec. 1907, ibid., B/1/3/2, in which Fisher insisted that he had always opposed Rosyth, and had reduced it from a £10 million to a £3 million establishment. See also Cambon to Pichon, 13 Nov. 1907 and 18 Nov. 1908, DDF, 2, II, 198, 558.

40. D. R. Daniel, "Memoirs of David Lloyd George," III, Daniel Papers, 2914.

41. The Admiralty called for six unarmoured cruisers, sixteen destroyers, and £500,000 for submarines, in addition to two capital ships.

42. Esher diary, 8 Dec. 1907, Esher Journals, II, 268.

43. Cabinet meeting, 29 Jan. 1908, Cab 41/31/39, and Campbell-Bannerman Papers, Add. 52513.

44. A. M. Gollin, The Observer and J. L. Garvin, 1908–1914: A Study in Great Editorship (London, 1960), 35–53, and J. L. Garvin Papers, box 56 and metal boxes 1 and 7.

45. Esher diary, 7 Feb. 1908, Esher Journals, II, 280–84; Fisher to Garvin, 7 Feb. 1908, Garvin Papers, metal box 7, and Gollin, The Observer, 43–45. Harcourt reapplied the pressure on 6 February.

combined vote of radicals, Labour, and the Unionists in parliament could defeat the government. The cabinet was determined to reduce the naval estimates by £1,340,000 and had appointed a committee comprised of Lloyd George, Reginald McKenna, president of the board of education, and Harcourt to seek ways of implementing this policy. Fisher rebuffed Harcourt, insisting that the estimates, already reduced by £¾ million were "at their irreducible minimum."[46]

Campbell-Bannerman made no mention of a cabinet committee in his reports to the king,[47] but Lloyd George and Churchill dined with Fisher on 4 February. They were both more civil and more disposed to compromise than Harcourt, although Lloyd George repeated the latter's threat that Admiral Sir Charles Beresford was prepared to replace Fisher and accept a reduction of £2 million.[48] Fisher remained firm and Lloyd George attempted a new approach the next morning; if Fisher accepted the required reduction this year "he might have any sum he pleased next year." In his account to Garvin, Fisher stated that "however Lloyd George came à la Nicodemus and squared that."[49]

Lloyd George then accompanied Fisher to a special meeting of the Board of Admiralty at which Fisher advised against threats of resignation to force the government's hand. The board maintained, nevertheless, that in view of the reduction of £¾ million in their original proposals, they must now hold firm. Fisher subsequently convinced the prime minister of the merits of the Admiralty's position and Campbell-Bannerman so instructed

46. Some confusion over figures and personalities clearly existed then and since. When Fisher argued that the estimates were already reduced by £750,000 he meant that the increase was reduced from £2 to £1.25 million (the increase already virtually conceded by Campbell-Bannerman on 29 January). McKenna's support for the Admiralty was undoubtedly for the £1.25 million increase rather than the earlier demand for an additional £2 million. Marder wrote that five members of the cabinet contemplated resignation: Harcourt, McKenna, Lloyd George, Crewe, and Burns. (Marder, *Dreadnought to Scapa Flow*, I, 138.) In fact no cabal existed; Esher excluded Crewe, McKenna was malleable, and Lloyd George went to great lengths to square Fisher. (*Esher Journals*, II, 283.)

47. D. Sommer, *Haldane of Cloan*, 209–10. He states that a cabinet subcommittee of Lloyd George, Harcourt, and McKenna, established to review the navy estimates, proposed a reduction of £1,300,300, only for Fisher to defeat them.

48. Gollin, *The Observer*, 44.

49. Fisher to Garvin, 14 Feb. 1908, Garvin Papers, metal box 7, and Gollin, *The Observer*, 53.

Asquith. To soften the blow, Haldane would prune £300,000 from the army estimates.[50]

Campbell-Bannerman convened the cabinet on 10 February 1908 to review naval estimates which still showed an increase over the 1907–08 figures of £1,300,000. The cabinet in fact trimmed a further £400,000 from them, leaving, however, the vote for new construction intact.[51] They confirmed this actual increase of £900,000 on 17 February and two days later Haldane's army estimates were duly reduced by £300,000.[52]

Lloyd George accepted the compromise as the best attainable and one guaranteed to preserve cabinet unity. He took no part in the parliamentary and press controversy, leaving others to lead the assault of the Radical Disarmament Committee, and Asquith to defend the government. The increase in the naval estimates was under £1 million and seemed unavoidable; the new construction program was hardly provocative and Fisher seemed satisfied. Efficiency, reasonable economy, and security were all served, and Haldane had swallowed his pill. Lloyd George could rest as content as the loss, in the previous November, of his beloved daughter Mair would permit.

Before him lay new challenges. Lloyd George's promotion, in view of his record and the need to retain a balanced cabinet, was assured. His precise office, however, could not be decided without some contention. Morley's claims could not be ignored, and Lord Esher worried lest Asquith, the new prime minister, give Lloyd George excessive freedom to curtail defence spending. Lloyd George, moreover, scarcely helped his own case by being less than discreet.[53] Walter Runciman, financial secretary to the Treasury, actually threatened resignation if Lloyd George were elevated. As

50. The whole episode hardly suggests that the prime minister was senile and indolent. He was, however, on the verge of a serious illness and resignation. Moreover, Haldane and the Admiralty had clearly fought an inter-service battle, each trying to avoid reductions in their estimates at the expense of the other. (Fisher to Garvin, 7 Feb. 1908, Gollin, The Observer, 43–44.)

51. Cabinet meeting, 10 Feb. 1908, Cab 41/31/41. Lord Tweedmouth, first lord of the admiralty, fought this decision to no avail. (Tweedmouth to Campbell-Bannerman, 11 Feb. 1908, Gollin, The Observer, 52.)

52. Cabinet meetings, 17 and 19 Feb. 1908, Cab 41/31/43 and 44.

53. Esher to Fisher, 25 March 1908, Esher Journals, II, 298. Esher wanted Asquith to come to prior terms with Lloyd George to fix the size of the naval estimates for the next two years. Lloyd George, after checking with Morley, threatened resignation unless he was made chancellor of the exchequer. He showed scant respect for Asquith in private and leaked news of government

Lord Emmott, chairman of the Ways and Means Committee, explained, "Runciman's reason is that he does not consider Lloyd George's personal probity above suspicion, while he knows that Lloyd George would sacrifice anyone and allow any amount of suspicion to fall on anyone to save himself if a scandal occurred." [54]

Lloyd George became chancellor of the exchequer, assuring Asquith of his loyalty, that charges of a breach of trust over appointments were baseless, and that he would keep the Treasury free from any hint of protection. [55] More revealing were Lloyd George's protestations that "Men whose promotion is not sustained by birth or other favouring conditions are always liable to be assailed with unkind suspicions of this sort. I would ask it therefore as a favour that you should not entertain them without satisfying yourself that they have some basis of truth."

The Foreign Office seemed greatly concerned at the promotion of Asquith, Lloyd George, and Churchill, who became president of the board of trade. [56] Despite the fact that Lloyd George had been neither a controversial nor a difficult minister, Crowe and Hardinge were disturbed by his role in the recent debate over the naval estimates. He seemed, like Churchill, to be a meddling amateur, bent on reducing defence spending and likely to search for that ultimate in futility, a naval agreement with Germany. L. T. Maxse, editor of the *National Review* and a Germanophobe, warned Andrew Bonar Law of the same dangers; they must not tolerate "treachery at the Exchequer." [57]

Sir William Tyrrell, Grey's private secretary, while sharing these apprehensions, revealed a hint of the understanding of Lloyd George demonstrated by Garvin in November 1907. [58]

---

appointments to the press. (Esher diary, 10 April 1908, *Esher Journals*, ii, 303.) See also H. Montgomery Hyde, *Carson* (London, 1953), 241.

54. Emmott diary, April 1908, Emmott Papers, i, 1907–11, f.67–68.

55. Lloyd George to Asquith, 11 April 1908, Asquith Papers, file 11; R. Jenkins, *Asquith* (London, 1964), 201–202.

56. Hardinge-Villiers correspondence, Nov. 1907, Sir C. Hardinge and Sir F. Villiers Papers, FO/800/24; Dockrill, "Continental Foreign Policy," 20–22.

57. Maxse to Bonar Law, 5 June 1908, Bonar Law Papers, 18/4/66.

58. Tyrrell to Bertie, 3 April 1908, FO/800/165. The Foreign Office understood that Cruppi, minister of commerce, had invited Lloyd George to Paris where he would be entertained by the French president, Cruppi, and the British Chamber of Commerce. Bertie replied that the visit had been engineered by Walter Behrens, "a Musical Jew," Paris representative of the Linotype Company, president of the Chamber of Commerce, and a friend of Cruppi. Behrens was anxious to promote trade in cheap French wines and to secure a decoration

Grey had instructed Tyrrell to inform Sir Francis Bertie, the ambassador to France, of Lloyd George's expected arrival in Paris on 10 April 1908. Tyrrell explained "that Lloyd George belongs to that section of the Cabinet which is described as Germanophil whose love for the Fatherland, however, has decreased in proportion to the length of time he has been in office. A pleasant stay in Paris may contribute to complete his conversion and anything you could say or do in that direction would be of great use. Moreover, he is in all likelihood soon going to a higher post than he occupies at present in the Government."

In other words Lloyd George was following a predictable pattern: the responsibilities of office were moderating his extremism. Tyrrell's analysis obviously was too simple. Nevertheless Lloyd George's political education had moved ahead even in these relatively uneventful years at the Board of Trade.

---

or a knighthood for himself. (Bertie to Tyrrell, 4 April 1908, FO/800/165.) Lloyd George's private secretary, W. H. Clarke, a nephew of Sir George Buchanan, would accompany him.

# 5

# At Home and Abroad: 1908

Lloyd George, residing at No. 11 Downing Street from April 1908, had entered a decisive period in his political education. The years of domestic and international calm were ending and he could avoid neither involvement nor controversy.

J. L. Garvin anticipated great things of Lloyd George. He attempted, like Tyrrell, to fit the chancellor of the exchequer into that pattern of predictable behaviour which results when a conventional radical matures in office. Lloyd George, however, did not simply discard a form of radicalism and adopt the views of the Foreign Office and the Admiralty. When Asquith's government debated the problems of naval preparedness and Anglo-German relations Garvin inevitably became somewhat disenchanted.

Lord Courtney of Penwith, an ally of the Boer War, feared exactly what Garvin anticipated, and not without evidence. Consequently, he came to disapprove thoroughly of Lloyd George, and the Mansion House speech of 1911 brought the final disillusionment. Lloyd George appeared corrupted by office, and seduced by officialdom. He seemed willing to threaten both Germany and the peace of Europe.[1]

1. Garvin to Lee, 16 Oct. 1910, Lee Papers, Garvin file; G. P. Gooch, *Life of Lord Courtney* (London, 1920), 566.

Both Garvin and Courtney had misjudged their subject to some extent. In the spring of 1908 Lloyd George still expected, as he had in 1906, as great a degree of continuity in British foreign policy as the international situation would permit. He welcomed evidence of continued harmony with the United States and Japan, and hoped that the Ententes with France and Russia would remain intact. After all, they permitted an economical defence of imperial interests and he regarded them as innocent of commitment and aggressive intent. Lloyd George continued to value the Ententes as an expression of improved relations rather than as a decisive weight in the European balance of power. He knew nothing officially about the staff talks with France and Belgium.

From this basis Lloyd George still expected Grey to seek a détente with Germany and provide moral leadership to Europe. The Admiralty in turn must offer economy and efficiency, for Lloyd George's devotion to arms limitation was as strong as ever. Indeed, his lengthiest letters dealt with that subject. What constituted a satisfactory margin of naval superiority would depend rather less on expert forecasts and more on financial and political factors.

Lloyd George maintained, however, that a Liberal government must provide for national and imperial security. He argued, therefore, that a naval agreement with Germany must leave Britain supreme and, as the Foreign Office demanded, must precede any political arrangement. The terms of the political agreement were a matter for negotiation, but Lloyd George was unlikely to press for a settlement that was unacceptable to Grey. Clearly he subscribed to certain compelling assumptions as to how a Liberal government must fulfil its responsibilities to the nation and the Empire.

Much depended on the foreign secretary, and here even C. P. Scott of the *Manchester Guardian*, shared Lloyd George's confidence:

> *I was very grateful to you for communicating with Sir Edward Grey and I return his kind letter. I saw him at the Foreign Office next day, and he gave me all possible help and information. On the armaments question in so far as he spoke of it he seemed to me fair and moderate and I was particularly glad to hear his views. His general policy of "cards on the table" seems to me admirable and if an understanding could be come to with Germany on that basis it would*

*cut the ground from the feet of the panic mongers and solve half our difficulties.*[2]

Both Grey and Lloyd George were understandably concerned for cabinet and party unity. Indeed, Lloyd George became almost as prominent in settling as in creating quarrels over defence estimates. Ultimately he deviated from the Cobdenite economic doctrine that enlarged defence spending endangered social reform and free trade. He became prepared, however reluctantly, to finance reform *and* rearmament through progressive taxation policies and loans.

Although the Treasury plunged Lloyd George more deeply into domestic affairs, it also provided wider opportunities for him to influence foreign and defence policies. Administrative practices changed but little under Asquith; departmental autonomy, minimum possible interference from the cabinet, and extensive use of ad hoc committees remained normal procedure.[3] However, expanded sources of information were open to Lloyd George and more material above the routine crossed his desk or breakfast table. His relationship to the Foreign Office and the defence departments changed, and in the cabinet he carried more weight. His speeches took on greater authority; even his excursions abroad assumed national significance. Automatically he became a member of the CID, taking his place for the first time on 14 May 1908.[4] Lloyd George attended only two of its fifteen meetings before May 1911 and submitted no memoranda.[5] Yet his participation in sub-committees brought direct contact with the debate over

2. Scott to Morley, 25 March 1909, Morley Papers, Eur. D.573/60.

3. Treasury files, 1908–15, T. 2, 3, 5 (correspondence with the Admiralty), 6, 7, 9, 12 (correspondence with the Foreign Office), 13, 27, 108, T. 114/1, T. 142/1/2, and T. 147/1; C. Hazlehurst, "Asquith as Prime Minister, 1908–1916," *English Historical Review*, 85 (1970), 502–31.

4. CID, 14 May 1908, Cab 38/14/5 and Cab 2/2; J. P. Mackintosh, "The Role of the Committee of Imperial Defence before 1914," *English Historical Review*, 77 (1962), 490–503; Lord Hankey, *The Supreme Command, 1914–1918*, 2 vols. (London, 1961), I, 60–76; S. W. Roskill, *Hankey, Man of Secrets 1877–1918* (London, 1970), I, 94–105.

5. CID, 14 May 1908 to 30 May 1911, Cab 38/14/5 to Cab 38/18/42, Cab 2/2, and conferences and committees on defence, Dec. 1905–12, Cab 18/24. Lloyd George took very little part in the preparations for and the proceedings of the Conference on the defence of the Empire, 28 July to 19 Aug. 1909 (Cab 18/12A and 12B), nor in the deliberations of May 1911.

national and imperial defence, and the invasion problem.[6] Such exposure brought a greater understanding of the official view of the realities of the European situation and the German problem. A crisis might even induce Lloyd George, for all his reservations, to accept a policy of confrontation with Germany in support of France. If so, he would cross a crucial political and intellectual threshold.

In November 1907 Campbell-Bannerman had appointed a sub-committee of the CID to investigate the threat of invasion. It held sixteen meetings between November 1907 and July 1908. Lloyd George became a member in April and joined in the deliberations on 29 May.[7] There he listened to what Lord Esher described as a "masterly performance" by Arthur Balfour, the Conservative leader, which left the gathering "dumbfounded," and without a question to pose.[8] On 22 October Lloyd George attended the CID meeting which accepted the unanimous report of the sub-committee.[9]

The report affirmed that so long as Britain retained naval supremacy against any reasonably probable combination of powers, invasion was unlikely. Permanent loss of the command of the seas, however, would mean that, whatever the state of home defences, subjection to the enemy was inevitable. The sub-committee recommended that the army be able to repel surprise attacks, and also be able to compel an invader to attack with a force of sufficient magnitude to prevent it evading the navy. The size of such a force was put at 70,000. Consequently, the report concluded, should 100,000 men be needed for the defence of India in an emergency, the army for home defence must be adequate to force the enemy to launch and enable Britain to repel an invasion force of 70,000.

Lloyd George had helped formulate and had endorsed conclusions which were founded on the existence of a potential

6. Sub-committee on the military requirements of the Empire as affected by India, 1 May 1907, Cab 38/13/20; Sub-committee on the military requirements of the Empire as affected by Egypt and the Sudan, 11 March 1909, Cab 38/15/5: Sir G. N. Nicholson memorandum, 6 Nov. 1911, BDOW, vii, 639, 626–29.

7. Sub-committee on invasion, Nov. 1907 to 28 July 1908, Cab 16/3A; miscellaneous papers, and memoranda, 3, 6 June 1908, Cab 1/7.

8. Balfour statement, 29 May 1908, Cab 38/14/7; Esher Journals, ii, 316–20.

9. CID, 22 Oct. 1908, Cab 38/14/10; Report of a sub-committee to reconsider the question of overseas attack, 22 Oct. 1908, Cab 38/14/11; Esher Journals, ii, 352.

German threat, and had accepted the remedy of naval supremacy. No doubt he had reservations about the diagnosis if not the cure. Moreover, although the staff talks with France and Belgium remained secret, the General Staff had referred directly in early June to possible future military operations in Europe to aid an ally and uphold the continental balance of power.[10]

Calculations about the defence of India, however, still dominated the related debate on the preparation of an expeditionary force. Winston Churchill, demonstrating his ability to produce prodigious amounts of paper on subjects scarcely related to his own department, challenged the War Office's 1908–09 estimates.[11] Initially, he demanded reductions in what he described as a dangerous, provocative, and expensive striking force of 166,000 men. Then he condemned the expeditionary force as irrelevant to full-scale war against either Russia over India, or against Germany to restore the European balance of power. It was a feckless compromise, a mere expedient which would satisfy neither the radicals nor the conscriptionists.

Haldane's reply of 26 June 1908 was not free from ambiguity and equivocation,[12] but his first sentence could scarcely have been more explicit. " Mr. Churchill's paper seems only to contemplate a campaign upon a large scale in India, and leaves out of account the possibility of our being called upon to operate on the Continent of Europe or in other parts of the world such as the nearer East." However, Haldane then identified the Expeditionary Army of 100,000 exclusively with the defence of India, thereby discounting the possibility of involvement in more than one major theatre, and disguising the fact that Europe already stood higher in the War Office's list of priorities than India. Deliberately or not, he added to the obfuscation as he listed the requirements for home defence, overseas garrisons and bases, and training establishments.

A copy of Haldane's paper exists preserving Lloyd George's questioning marginalia. Haldane presented two hypotheses: on the evidence of her naval program Germany planned an attack on

10. S. R. Williamson, *The Politics of Grand Strategy*, 98–99. He cites a General Staff memorandum of 2 June. No copy remains in the Lloyd George papers.

11. Churchill memoranda, 17 and 27 June and 3 July 1908, Cab 37/93/83 and Cab 37/94/89 and 93, and LGP, C/18/3/3, 4 and 6.

12. Haldane memorandum, 26 June 1908, LGP, C/18/3/5. The Public Record Office conceded the value of "illuminating marginalia" and yet closed those files of the Lloyd George papers containing official papers. (Public Record Office, *Handbook No. 4, List of Cabinet Papers 1880–1914* [London, 1964], ix.)

or an invasion of England; second, Britain's "treaty obligations" or a menace to the balance of power by "a strong and aggressive power" might compel her to intervene in Europe "to assist and reinforce her Continental allies." Clearly, both these scenarios threatened Lloyd George's hopes for an Anglo-German détente and an economical defence policy, and he questioned them, at least privately if not officially. Obviously too, the second hypothesis was potentially more disturbing than the first, except to the extent that it remained shrouded in the ambiguity surrounding the primary function of the expeditionary force. Lord Esher, a defence critic whom Lloyd George did not discount, helped perpetuate this situation in his anxiety to defend the army. He was fully aware of the War Office's plans, and regretted them, but he did not enlighten Lloyd George.[13]

In a statement to his constituents on 21 July 1908 Lloyd George unreservedly praised Haldane and the Territorial Army, urging all Welshmen to support the scheme.[14] He described the Territorial Army as a purely defensive organization based on the voluntary principle and vital to national security. Indeed, all those who loved freedom and their native land should aid in its success. The army, Lloyd George pointed out, faced dual tasks in the event of war; the Regular Army and its Special Reserve must defend Britain's overseas possessions while the Territorial Army would aid in providing security against invasion.

In October 1908 Asquith appointed a sub-committee of the CID to examine the European implications of defence in the wider context of imperial security. Asquith, Lord Crewe, the colonial secretary, Reginald McKenna, first lord of the admiralty, Esher, and Haldane dominated the proceedings with Charles Hardinge, Grey's permanent under-secretary, and the military and naval experts prominent. Their report was adopted by the CID on 24 July 1909.

Lloyd George was not a member of the sub-committee nor did he attend this CID meeting.[15] No copy of the report survives in his

13. Esher to Lloyd George, 22 May 1908, *Esher Journals*, II, 313–14; Esher memorandum, for the chancellor of the exchequer, 30 May 1908, Cab 37/93/69; Esher diary, 7 and 22 May and 12 Nov. 1908, *Esher Journals*, II, 310–12, 359. Esher gave the impression that imperial defence still dominated military planning.
14. Statement, 21 July, *The Times*, 22 July 1908.
15. Report of the sub-committee on the military needs of the Empire, 24 July

papers, but CID memoranda were now circulated to him as a normal procedure. He may not have heard of Hardinge's guarded and disarming references to the military conversations with France, but he can hardly have been unaware of the policy recommendations. The cabinet would rule on Britain's involvement in the event of war. However, the fundamentals of an incipient continental strategy were proposed. The sub-committee, rebuffing Admiral Fisher, encouraged the General Staff to plan for involvement in a European war to aid France, Belgium, and even Holland in the event of German aggression. Specifically they should seek to provide a reserve contingent to reinforce the left of the French army, while the Admiralty concentrated on plans for economic warfare.[16]

The significance of these proposals may have passed Lloyd George by, but it seems unlikely. He was no doubt better informed than he subsequently claimed and was disturbed by the nature of the information becoming available to him. He did not complain, however, when Asquith and Grey failed to submit the sub-committee report to the cabinet as a whole. Further developments waited on the Agadir crisis.

Lloyd George also participated in the Sub-committee on Aerial Navigation, which was established in October 1908, under Esher, and reported on 28 January 1909.[17] At the second meeting, on 8 December, they took evidence from C. S. Rolls and Major B. F. S. Baden-Powell. Lloyd George questioned Rolls on the impact of bombing from dirigible balloons and the Wright brothers' machines on towns, forts, and naval bases. He probed Baden-Powell on the use of balloons and aeroplanes for search and scouting. Furthermore, Lloyd George expressed interest not only in the comparative merits of planes and balloons as a source of air power, but investigated the relationship of air power to the problem of invasion. Specifically he asked whether aerial surveillance of ships, and troop and materiel concentrations in German

---

1909, Cab 38/15/15; CID, 24 July 1909, Cab 38/15/14; Williamson, *Politics of Grand Strategy*, 108–12.

16. The sub-committee had not ruled out landings in Belgium to cover Antwerp.

17. Sub-committee of the CID on aerial navigation, 23 Oct. 1908 to 28 Jan. 1909, Cab 16/7 and Cab 38/15/3. Haldane, McKenna, and service advisers were the other members. Lloyd George did not attend the first meeting on 1 December.

ports, could detect whether Germany was planning an invasion of Britain.

Lloyd George signed the final report which was accepted by the CID on 28 January 1909.[18] It concluded that they could not assess adequately the dangers to Britain resulting from the development of air power until Britain herself possessed airships. However, the committee decided that rigid airships, rather than aeroplanes, would be of great value to the navy for scouting and possibly destructive purposes. They might also prove useful to the army. The other recommendations dealt with the financing and control of research and development.[19] The sub-committee had not been particularly demanding, but Lloyd George's involvement was not irrelevant to his dramatic proposals of August 1910.

Lloyd George's principal task of course was at the Treasury. In a fundamentally important memorandum of 18 May 1908 he listed the critical variables of finance and politics which the government must weigh as it pursued the twin goals of social reform *and* national security.[20] Lloyd George assumed that the cabinet agreed on the need to avoid additional taxation except in unforeseen and very exceptional circumstances. He forecast, however, that at current taxation levels revenues would increase by only £1.5 million. Expenditures would rise by £9.5 million, the navy alone consuming an additional £2 million. Old age pensions, Lloyd George suggested, had priority and he hoped that his estimate of naval expenditures would prove to be inflated. He predicted nevertheless a deficit for the 1909–10 fiscal year of £7,759,000 unless he could reduce the National Debt charge by £3 million, or cut the costs of the army and the civil service.[21]

His critics accused Lloyd George of using statistics as adjectives, and to be sure accuracy was not always his forte, but the trend was clear. Defence expenditures had risen rapidly since 1893–94, but the size and efficiency of the armed forces had not grown in proportion to these increases. The Liberal government,

18. CID, 25 Feb. 1909, Cab 38/15/4.
19. Both the navy and the army should experiment with airships and balloons, but private enterprise should experiment with aeroplanes.
20. Memorandum, 18 May 1908, Cab 37/93/62, and LGP, C/14/1/2.
21. Lloyd George to W. George, 12 May 1908, W. George, *My Brother and I*, 220. He predicted increases of £1,400,000 for education, £1,300,000 for civil expenditures, and £4,800,000 for old-age pensions.

he insisted, had a less than satisfactory record. Total government expenditures in 1908–09 were some £3.5 million above the levels of 1905–06, and defence expenditures were reduced in the same period by less than £2 million.[22] They would therefore face attacks both from the Unionists and from within their own party.

A week later he took the message to Parliament. He endorsed the maintenance of naval superiority over Germany by a margin of three or four to one, financed to date from current expenditure rather than loans.[23] The government, he said, was nevertheless pledged to reduce defence costs and to finance an enlarged program of social reform. He wanted to eliminate wasteful and unnecessary outlays on armaments, for which Britain, where navies were concerned, was more responsible than any other power. Only then would they remove the mutual fear and distrust so evident in Britain and Germany, and so clearly fed by the press. If Parliament bowed before the service departments he would be forced either to reduce government expenditures and delay reform, or raise taxes. Lloyd George, however, had not in fact ruled out a resort to the capital market.

Three days later he assured Lord Courtney and the deputation representing the forthcoming Seventeenth International Peace Congress that he sympathized fully with their aims. He would look favourably on their request for a grant to support the Congress and for a modest annual sum to help maintain their permanent bureau in Berne.[24] He agreed with Courtney that expenditures incurred in aid of the peace movement were justifiable because they would lead both to greater economies in defence costs and to international harmony. Both Asquith and Grey knew, according

---

22. Lloyd George's statistics showed the following:

$$\left. \begin{array}{l} \textit{Defence Expenditures}\text{—Army, 1905–06—£28,479,000} \\ \text{Navy, 1905–06—£33,152,000} \end{array} \right\} = £61,631,000$$

$$\left. \begin{array}{l} \text{—Army, 1906–07—£28,501,000} \\ \text{Navy, 1906–07—£31,472,000} \end{array} \right\} = £59,973,000$$

$$\left. \begin{array}{l} \text{—Army, 1908–09—£27,459,000} \\ \text{Navy, 1908–09—£32,319,000} \end{array} \right\} = £59,778,000$$

Haldane took exception to the statistics on army expenditures which, while accurate, misled the cabinet by disguising various other factors which had unavoidably contributed to their growth. He saw little prospect of reducing the 1909–10 estimates to £27 million. (Haldane memorandum, 25 May 1908, Cab 37/93/67.)

23. Speech, 25 May 1908, *Parl. Deb.*, H. of C., clxxxix, 863–75.

24. *Daily News*, 28 May 1908, LGP, C/33/1/6.

to Lloyd George, that the government must encourage projects to promote détente and seek to remove the fierce passions which led to war. All that remained, Lloyd George assured Courtney, was to decide how the government would dispense its grants. He promised to press the case of the peace movement as the most deserving of all.

Although Esher described Lloyd George as "determined to get two millions off the army," [25] the chancellor was happy to see Churchill lead the assault on the War Office's estimates. [26] Political considerations largely governed his conduct. He was willing to compromise with Haldane, [27] but ready to share Churchill's victory. [28] In any case, Anglo-German relations and the naval question were more vital.

At Grey's invitation and with no suggestion of unwarranted interference he met with Count Metternich, the German ambassador, on 14 and 28 July 1908. [29] Metternich's preliminary observations were not devoid of significance or interest. He described Lloyd George to Chancellor Bülow as a prominent minister who thought imperially and was respected by the Unionists. In opposition, Lloyd George had occasionally attacked Germany but he was now of a conciliatory frame of mind, regretting the current popular Germanophobia.

Lloyd George acknowledged that Britain's diplomatic support of France had upset Germany, but he assured Metternich that France did not harbour warlike intentions. Both Lloyd George and Grey insisted that the future of Anglo-German relations pivoted on the naval question. They agreed that "every Englishman would spend his last penny to preserve their superiority at sea."

25. Esher diary, 23 July 1908, *Esher Journals*, II, 329. Asquith reported that Lloyd George opposed expenditures on ranges for the territorial army. (Cabinet, 22 July 1908, Cab 41/31/64.)

26. Haldane memoranda, 19 and 25 May 1908, Cab 37/93/63 and 67; D. Sommer, *Haldane of Cloan*, 212–17; Esher to Knollys, 26 June, and diary, 26 June and 8 July 1908, *Esher Journals*, II, 324–27.

27. Esher diary, 13 and 22 June, and McKenna to Esher, 12 June 1908, *Esher Journals*, 320–24; Esher to Lloyd George, 22 May, ibid., 313–14, and Esher-Lloyd George conversation, 29 May 1908, ibid., 319; Esher memorandum, for Lloyd George's guidance, 30 May 1908, Cab 37/93/69; Lloyd George to W. George, 7 Sept. 1909, W. George, 230.

28. Esher diary, 26 June 1908, *Esher Journals*, II, 326.

29. Lloyd George, *War Memoirs*, I, 7–17; Metternich to Bülow, 16 July and 1 Aug. 1908, *Grosse Politik*, XXIV, 8217, 99–102, and 8219, 110–15. Radicals understood that Lloyd George was opposed to the freedom of the seas. (S. Koss, *Sir John Brunner, Radical Plutocrat, 1842–1919* [Cambridge, 1970], 232.)

Lloyd George made light of England's military capabilities and denied any intention to threaten or attack Germany with the fleet. He suggested, however, that the formidable German army, when supported by a powerful fleet, presented a real danger to England. Metternich argued that a political agreement must precede a naval treaty, but Lloyd George disagreed categorically; precisely the reverse must prevail. He admitted, however, that the Dreadnought policy was an error and assured Metternich that Britain would abstain from further qualitative competition.

Moreover, Lloyd George felt that the recent correspondence between the kaiser and Lord Tweedmouth, former first lord of the admiralty, should have been published, to demonstrate the emperor's friendship, and to provide an opportunity to initiate confidential discussions on naval expenditures. Significantly, and without regard for the radical point of view, Lloyd George suggested that secret, confidential, and unofficial conversations were more likely to secure a naval agreement than gatherings such as the Hague Conference or official, formal exchanges.

Grey seemed to agree fully with Lloyd George on all points except on the publication of the kaiser–Tweedmouth correspondence. It would have been surprising, of course, had they permitted the ambassador to witness a difference of opinion, although such spectacles are not unknown. Esher was eminently satisfied. Lloyd George apparently had assured Metternich that he was prepared to borrow £100 million to maintain Britain's relative naval strength. "It is rather splendid of Lloyd George," Esher noted.[30]

Within days Lloyd George was called on to defend the government's old age pension proposals against Austen Chamberlain, the Tory financial critic, who advocated delay in their implementation because of the serious situation in Europe.[31] The international situation was always threatening to a degree, Lloyd George asserted. New enemies replaced old, Germany replaced France, and the process would continue until nations turned from the arms race to the rational settlement of disputes. In fact, Britain's relations with France and Russia were now appreciably more cordial in Africa and the Far East, and the government would not permit the press to bring about a crisis with Germany. Therefore

---

30. Esher diary, 23 July 1908, *Esher Journals*, ii, 329–30.
31. Speech, 25 July 1908, *Parl. Deb.*, H. of C., cxcii, 680–93.

they would implement social reform, secure in the knowledge that Britain commanded the seas and was safe from invasion. He intended initially to raise taxes to pay for old age pensions. Should the nation's security seem threatened, he would turn to the capital market.

Grey was not present at Lloyd George's second meeting with Metternich on 28 July. The ambassador blamed British policy, French expectations, and the "poisonous press" for the dangerous decline in Anglo-German relations. Lloyd George, refusing to compromise on the question of naval supremacy, suggested that further competition would be both futile and dangerous. It would leave Britain's margin of superiority intact and activate other tendencies in British opinion which he personally deplored. The naval race would restore the militarists and the Conservatives to power, pledged to implement tariff reform so as to raise revenues for defence expenditures and conscription.

To help counter these regressive trends, Lloyd George urged, Germany must accept an agreement to reduce the tempo of naval construction and to establish a ratio of three to two in capital ships. She would cooperate thereby with "the peace-loving Liberal Government" which would hold power for the next three or four years. Lloyd George also assured Metternich that the Liberal government interpreted security needs in terms of a two-power standard, which required a fleet not twice the size of that of Germany but as large as the combined power of the German and the next largest navy. He suggested, in conclusion, that Berlin's willingness to build even one less Dreadnought a year would eliminate British hostility toward Germany.[32]

From this meeting Lloyd George went almost immediately to address a rowdy session of the Peace Congress.[33] He called for reform, the peaceful settlement of international disputes, and an end to the arms race, so that improved Anglo-German relations and peace would prevail. Armaments created fear and tension. It followed, Lloyd George insisted, that the supremacy achieved through an arms race was merely temporary and ultimately futile. It would result eventually in an actual threat to national security.

32. Lloyd George, *War Memoirs*, i, 14–16.
33. Speech at the Queen's Hall, 28 July, LGP, C/33/1/7, Metternich to Bülow, 29 July, *Grosse Politik*, xxiv, 8218, 104–107, and French chargé to Clemenceau, 29 July 1908, *DDF*, 2, ii, 417.

Lloyd George suggested that they consider the situation as viewed from Berlin. Britain, despite her current supremacy, had pioneered the Dreadnought without just cause and had launched the naval race. Moreover, to be secure against invasion, she claimed the protection of the two-power standard. Germany made no similar claim in military terms. Who could deny that Germany was justified in fearing alliances that threatened her with aggression, and in taking seriously the hatred expressed in the *Daily Mail* and *The Times*. Lloyd George demanded therefore an Anglo-German settlement, a détente between two powerful and progressive states, in line with the understandings reached with Russia, France, and the United States.

*The Times* charged him with irresponsible and amateur behaviour.[34] The danger from Germany was "serious enough to render the attack which Lloyd George made upon the Two Power Standard for the Navy last night at the Peace Congress singularly reckless and inopportune." Lloyd George denied that he had made any attack on the two-power standard and asked for a retraction.[35] The government, he argued, was committed to the two-power standard. He had interpreted its policy to the Peace Congress as he had to Metternich. Perhaps the din of the suffragettes had obscured his words. He would not, however, withdraw any of his observations on Anglo-German relations, the European situation generally, or the attitude of the British press. *The Times* was not impressed and described Lloyd George's "approval of the expressed policy of his own Government" as "somewhat begrudging."[36] This confrontation clearly affected the controversy which developed over Lloyd George's perambulations in Europe.

Lloyd George left for Germany on 1 August, accompanied by the journalist Harold Spender and Charles Henry, the Liberal MP.[37] Much of the criticism of his subsequent conduct is unjustified.[38]

34. *The Times*, 29 July 1908.
35. Lloyd George to *The Times*, 29 July, *The Times*, 30 July 1908.
36. *The Times*, 1 and 3 Aug. 1908.
37. They motored across France and toured southern and western Germany. On 20 August they arrived at Frankfurt-on-Main, visited Berlin on 21 August and then, via Hamburg, Bremen, and Bremerhaven, embarked for Southampton on 25 August.
38. Lloyd George insisted that he intended merely to gather information on welfare programs. He denied having any mandate from the government to explore political matters, and suggested that any discussions he had held on Anglo-German relations "arose accidentally out of the visit" and were **very**

Grey demonstrated no anxiety at the outset that Lloyd George would in any way embarrass the government or undermine the value of the king's visit to the kaiser at Cronberg. A memorandum on the substance of the July conversations with Metternich was in fact used to help prepare the king.[39]

The royal meeting at Cronberg, on 11 and 12 August, exploring the possibility of opening negotiations for a naval agreement, proved abortive. Grey decided, therefore, to suspend the talks. Hardinge reported at length on 16 August on the lack of progress, and Grey informed the cabinet.[40]

By that time Lloyd George, indiscreetly perhaps but in good faith, had publicly committed himself.[41] On 12 August, while at Carlsbad, he gave an interview to the *Neue Freie Presse* of Vienna. He deplored the current levels of tension in Europe and the malevolent role of the press in both England and Germany, and called for a naval agreement and an Anglo-German accord as essential to world peace. "I believe," he was reported as saying, "that we must work for the conclusion of an entente between England and Germany in order that we may be able to devote ourselves wholly to the task of peace, progress and social reform." In issuing this statement, and apart from the dubious tactical wisdom of the interview, Lloyd George had every reason to assume that he enjoyed Grey's confidence. He was, as far as he knew, not acting at variance with government policy; King Edward and he were about the same business.

The Cronberg discussions, however, had altered Grey's policy. The Foreign Office, understandably, was anxious to rein in the itinerant Lloyd George and to curb his tongue. Hardinge and Eyre Crowe were particularly exercised lest the chancellor speak too freely when he visited Berlin. The French government naturally was concerned.[42]

---

cordial. (Press release, 26 Aug., *The Times*, 21 and 27 Aug. 1908; Lloyd George, *War Memoirs*, I, 17.) *Berliner Tageblatt*, 18 Aug., and Harold Spender argued that his real motive was to pursue *The Plan* and help secure a naval agreement. (H. Spender, *Fire of Life*, 161.)

39. Grey memoranda, 31 July and 6 Aug. 1908, *BDOW*, VI, App. 111, 779 and 111, 173–74.

40. Hardinge to Grey, 15 Aug., ibid., 116, 183–84, Hardinge memorandum, 16 Aug. 1908, ibid., 117, 184–90; Cab 37/94/108 and 109.

41. Spender, *Fire of Life*, 165; du Parcq, *Lloyd George*, III, 516; *The Times*, 15 Aug. 1908.

42. French chargé (Berlin) to Pichon, 17 Aug., French chargé (London) to

Churchill's inopportune speech at Swansea on 15 August served to exacerbate these apprehensions.[43] The Times professed to see a joint conspiracy to undermine Grey's authority and, after chastizing Churchill for his effusions, attacked Lloyd George openly. Its Berlin correspondent, citing the Frankfurter Zeitung, suggested that he intended to visit Berlin via St. Blasien in the Black Forest, the favourite summer resort of Admiral Tirpitz. Forsaking his departmental duties, "The Chancellor of the Exchequer, in the course of his wanderings upon the Continent, has chosen to unbosom himself to a casual newspaper correspondent at Carlsbad for the purposes of publication." Such indiscretions were not only disconcerting but superfluous, The Times suggested. Far more authoritative and official sources than could be mustered in "informal press interviews at an Austrian watering place" had invited the powers in the past to consult with Britain on arms limitation, but to no avail. Repetition was not required and "In any case we think these crude pronouncements upon international politics are as much to be deplored as Mr. Churchill's vituperative rhetoric. The foreign policy of Great Britain is too gravely vital a matter to be taken out of the high plane of states-manlike guidance by inexperienced politicians in a hurry."

The Times continued to lament these dangerous and damaging "demi-semi-official utterances in England and demi-semi-private missions on the Continent," which implied a lack of unity and purpose in government policy. It noted furthermore that Grey and Asquith had returned to London on 20 August to deal with the matter.[44] The prime minister agreed that day at Grey's request to warn Lloyd George against public discussion of the naval question which might cause offence in Berlin and increase German opposition to a naval agreement. Asquith immediately telegraphed Lloyd George to advise him that the kaiser had insisted that Germany could not modify her naval program, and that he seemed to resent

---

Pichon, 18 and 22 Aug. 1908, DDF, 2, ii, 423, 424, and 426; M. L. Dockrill, "The Formulation of a Continental Foreign Policy in Great Britain, 1908–1912," 26. Hardinge raised the matter with Grey, and Crowe asked that Lloyd George be urged to say nothing at all in Berlin. The Times Paris correspondent, referring to Lloyd George as "this unwise pacifist," noted how the French were disturbed by his ill-advised actions. (The Times, 21 Aug. 1908.)

43. The Times, 15, 17, and 18 Aug. 1908, and R. S. Churchill, Winston S. Churchill (Boston, 1967), ii, 270, 511–14.

44. Asquith to Lloyd George, 20 Aug. 1908, FO/800/101, and The Times, 20 Aug. 1908.

any British suggestions about construction policies. German opinion would likely harden if public exchanges took place and Lloyd George should avoid any such conversations. Asquith promised that the cabinet would discuss a reply to the kaiser when it had received more information.

Whether Lloyd George had already heard of the outcome of the Cronberg meeting is impossible to say, but Asquith's telegram was the first official notification to him that tactical considerations dictated a different approach. In reply, Lloyd George assured the prime minister that he did not intend to consult anyone in Germany on international affairs and would devote himself exclusively to investigating pension schemes.[45] He had, Lloyd George noted, uncovered a good deal about the situation and would report immediately on his return but reaffirmed that "I shall certainly make no public statement on the subject." In defence of his press interview Lloyd George claimed that " My interview in the Vienna Neue Freie Presse was purely a repetition of statements made by you and Sir Edward Grey." With full justification he insisted that he was behaving with circumspection and loyalty.

In Frankfurt, on 20 August, Lloyd George had denied that his visit had any political significance and refused to be interviewed. Moreover, on arrival in Berlin on 21 August he disclaimed any intention of trespassing on Foreign Office territory. He had no wish to become an "international complication." The Times welcomed what it described as an admission by Lloyd George that he was unsuitable and even incompetent to handle such negotiations, and hoped that "political dilettanti" on both sides of the North Sea would take note.[46]

That Lloyd George had intended to seek out Bülow and that the German chancellor wanted to avoid him if at all possible is beyond question.[47] Clearly, until checked by Asquith and discouraged by

45. Lloyd George to Asquith, 21 Aug. 1908, FO/800/101, and Asquith Papers, file 11.

46. The Times, 21 and 22 Aug. 1908.

47. Bülow to German Foreign Office, 21 Aug., Stemreich to Bülow, 21 Aug., Bülow to German Foreign Office, 22 Aug., and Stemreich to Bülow, 22 Aug. 1908, Grosse Politik, xxiv, 8233, 138, 8234, 138, 8235, 139; The Times, 17 Aug. 1908. Lloyd George, as late as 21 August, seemed intent on seeing Bülow at Hamburg or Nordeney. Bülow's own newspaper had already deplored the idea of premature and self-defeating conversations. Via Stein, the Berlin correspondent of the radical Frankfurter Zeitung, he helped dissuade Lloyd George from further approaches. See also Sir F. Oppenheimer, Stranger Within (London, 1960), 183.

the German Foreign Office, he had hoped to initiate informal conversations, but timing was the crucial factor. Up to the point when he received Asquith's telegram in Berlin, Lloyd George could justify his intentions as consistent with government policy as he understood it when he left England.

Grey confirmed as much when he explained to the French chargé d'affaires on the following day that the Anglo-German conversations had made no progress, Britain had warned Germany that she would match her naval construction, and he expected Lloyd George to conform to government policy.[48] He informed the French chargé of the meetings with Metternich in July and suggested that the chancellor's principal concern during his visit to Germany was to study welfare schemes. "If, however, he were to be approached with regard to the naval question he would no doubt in private conversation express our views, for this question had now become the one subject of interest to the exclusion of all other political questions between England and Germany." These are not the words of a foreign secretary in despair with a maverick colleague.

However, Grey's equilibrium was disturbed that very day. On 21 August the *Daily Telegraph* carried an article entitled, "Mr. Lloyd George's Mission, Journey to Berlin, An Exchange of Views," which gave an account of Harold Spender's interview with the *Berliner Tageblatt*. Spender had insisted that Lloyd George had abandoned his visit to St. Blasien because of lack of accommodation and not because of Admiral Tirpitz's presence there. The chancellor had been unaware that Tirpitz was even at St. Blasien. However, Spender assured the press, although Lloyd George had travelled throughout Germany to study welfare programs, anyone who knew him realized that he had never lost sight of his mission of peace. Of course, Lloyd George was not prime minister and had no mandate from the cabinet. He could not initiate negotiations, but he was willing to discuss matters should the German government present him with an opportunity. In fact, Lloyd George believed that an Anglo-German conference on arms limitation could reach an agreement. Finally, Spender promised, the Liberal victory at the next election would be a further guarantee that Britain would pursue a pacific policy.

48. Grey to Bertie, 26 Aug. 1908, BDOW, vi, 120, 194–95. Clemenceau was amazed at Lloyd George's "crass ignorance" of foreign affairs. (Sir P. Magnus, *King Edward the Seventh* [London, 1964], 412–13.)

Grey, enclosing an account of the interview, assured Asquith that, assuming a public statement was desirable at that time, Spender's views were unobjectionable and harmless.[49] He pointed out, however, that it was very risky for a minister travelling abroad to comment on international affairs when he was out of touch with the Foreign Office.[50] Warming to the question, Grey assured Asquith that he would remain silent while no harm resulted. However, should injurious effects develop, he would insist on the disavowal and humiliation of Lloyd George, or offer his own resignation with all its inconvenient consequences. His principal concern, Grey indicated, was that in the wake of excessive public debate over arms expenditures, Britain might be suspected of seeking a deal with Germany to forestall a naval race. For instance, someone might hint that Britain would use the Baghdad Railway, Morocco, or some other political question to purchase a naval limitation agreement with Germany. Obviously Grey was concerned about French sensitivity, and feared that Lloyd George, despite Asquith's restraints and the news that policy had changed, would be unable to resist an opportunity to negotiate in Berlin.

Asquith, alarmed by Grey's threats, agreed substantially with his analysis. He suggested that Lloyd George should have refused all interviews with the press, although one could not say to what degree he had authorized Spender's outburst.[51] However, the prime minister noted, to go around with a second-rate pressman as secretary was ill-advised; to be interviewed through him was absurd. Lloyd George's indiscretions were harmless enough, but he had written to him and, without delivering a reprimand, had made their distaste quite plain. Lloyd George would be brought to heel. Finally, Asquith noted, Lloyd George seemed to feel that during his travels he had discovered new truths about the international situation. The errant neophyte would enlighten them on his return. Grey acquiesced and Lloyd George gave no cause for further dispute.[52] The foreign secretary, however, rather petu-

---

49. Grey to Asquith, 22 Aug. 1908, FO/800/100; Grey to Spender, 23 Aug. 1908, J. A. Spender Papers, Add. 46389.

50. Esher to M.V.B., 22 and 23 Aug. 1908, *Esher Journals*, II, 332–33.

51. Asquith to Grey, 24 Aug. 1908, FO/800/100.

52. Lloyd George in fact made a speech in Hamburg on 23 August to business leaders on the need for an Anglo-German armaments agreement. The king, Lord Knollys, and Bertie were very upset by the whole affair. Esher and Mrs. Keppel apparently interceded with the king on Lloyd George's behalf, con-

lantly deplored Churchill's plan to spend his honeymoon in Berlin; an unhappy choice, in Grey's opinion.[53]

Deprived of the excitement of interviews with the kaiser and Chancellor Bülow, Lloyd George had settled for dinner with Theobald von Bethmann Hollweg, then secretary of the interior, and a working breakfast with Bülow's secretary.[54] The former charged the Entente powers with attempting to encircle Germany. Lloyd George attempted to show Bethmann Hollweg that Britain's intentions were pacific, but that she must retain her naval supremacy over Germany. Neither Bethmann Hollweg nor Bülow's secretary, however, offered any hope of a naval agreement.

Lloyd George, impressed by the former's comments on Britain's decadence and loss of will, "left Berlin gravely disturbed." In his view the German élite, while retaining a certain friendship for Britain, were now gravely suspicious of her policies. The German people were fanatically patriotic and restless, and German economic and military power was remarkably developed. On the other hand her business, industrial, and commercial leaders seemed opposed to the folly of war. Grey's task therefore was to appeal to those elements in Berlin who were rational, moderate, and pacific; in fact to Germany's influential doves. A rapprochement was even more necessary and was still attainable. One might question his optimism. However, should Germany menace Britain's national interests and security Lloyd George would respond to the challenge. In that regard the cabinet must face the consequences of the negative results of the Cronberg negotiations.

---

vincing him that the chancellor was an imperialist at heart. (Sir S. Lee, *King Edward VII: A Biography* (London, 1925–27), ii, 654–55; Magnus, *King Edward*, 412–13; W. S. Blunt, *My Diaries*, ii, 300, 305; Dockrill, "Continental Foreign Policy," 29–30.)

53. Grey to Asquith, 12 Sept. 1908, FO/800/100.

54. Lloyd George, *War Memoirs*, i, 17–19; Spender, *Fire of Life*, 163–65; French chargé (Berlin) to Pichon, 23 Aug. 1908, *DDF*, 2, ii, 428.

# 6

# Between Panic and Parsimony

The failure at Cronberg, the deteriorating European situation, and the fear that Germany could effectively challenge Britain's naval supremacy forced Grey, Asquith, and the king to look more favourably on the Admiralty's demands.[1] McKenna, the new first lord, had accepted a recommendation for four or possibly six Dreadnoughts in May 1908.[2] Fisher now suggested that Britain should lay down six, seven, or even eight Dreadnoughts in 1909 to meet the two-power standard plus ten per cent, which Asquith accepted as official policy in November.[3]

These demands were bound to provoke the Treasury. Lloyd George's dislike for McKenna was already well developed and in September 1908 they clashed over a rather revealing incident. Badgered by Churchill, who faced a difficult unemployment

1. Grey to Spender, 23 Aug. 1908, Spender Papers, Add. 46389.
2. Fisher to Esher, 5 May 1908, *Esher Journals*, II, 309; McKenna memorandum, 20 July 1908, LGP, C/24/3/1.
3. A. J. Marder, *From the Dreadnought to Scapa Flow*, I, 145–59; and H. S. Weinroth, "Left-Wing Opposition to Naval Armaments in Britain before 1914," 108–10.

situation in the North and a cotton strike, Lloyd George approached McKenna. "I have been much exercised upon unemployment in the engineering and shipbuilding trades, which Churchill tells me is acute and increasing, especially on the Clyde and Tyne. We have discussed possibilities of allowing a few ships from next year's programme to be laid down at once so as to maintain a more even level of construction up to the end of March without increased unrest. I am still quite uncommitted in opinion, but I feel that the question deserves serious and immediate attention." [4] He proposed that they meet in London.

McKenna offered to meet Lloyd George at Asquith's home in Scotland, but rejected his proposal outright.[5] The Admiralty could not lay down any more capital ships before March 1909, beyond the scheduled program. The sea lords preferred to evaluate the performance of the Dreadnoughts and certain German capital ships before recommencing construction. In any case, McKenna pointed out, the shipyards were behind in their current orders because of strikes. Lloyd George's scheme would require supplementary estimates, and yet the Treasury had refused him funds for an experimental airship. However, even if it were supported by the Treasury, McKenna regarded the idea as unsound.

Lloyd George was infuriated.[6] Surely McKenna could not think, unless he had misunderstood the proposal, that Churchill and he were suggesting that the Admiralty should lay down two or more battleships without consulting the prime minister. Even if they were capable of such disloyalty, McKenna had no right to infer that treachery was coupled with stupidity. He resented McKenna's lecture on procedure; Churchill's imaginative scheme merited investigation. McKenna's view, however, prevailed.

On 8 December 1908 McKenna recommended a construction program of six Dreadnoughts, involving an increased expenditure of almost £3 million.[7] The cabinet, on 18 December, accepted

4. Lloyd George to McKenna, 11 Sept. 1908, Asquith Papers, file 20, and McKenna Papers, 3/20/1; Churchill memorandum, July 1908, Cab 37/94/107.
5. McKenna to Lloyd George, 12 Sept. 1908, LGP, C/5/12/1, and Asquith Papers, file 20.
6. Lloyd George to McKenna, 16 Sept. 1908, LGP, C/5/12/2. The misunderstanding in part stemmed from Lloyd George's failure to point out to McKenna that Churchill envisaged advancing the construction of auxiliary vessels only, not capital ships.
7. McKenna memorandum, 8 Dec. 1908, Cab 37/96/164.

navy estimates which showed an increase of £2,900,000,[8] but they inserted a reservation to the effect that they would review the decision on two of the six Dreadnoughts in January. All agreed that they must ensure a substantial margin of superiority in 1911 and 1912, but the pace of the German program would govern Britain's actual rate of construction. On the other hand, this decision gave Fisher the opportunity to campaign for eight Dreadnoughts.[9]

Lloyd George had entered the discussions relieved that the recent Franco-German dispute was settled and expecting to approve moderate defence estimates.[10] He took the reservation to be a defeat for McKenna, and lavished praise on Churchill for helping smash McKenna's "fatuous estimates." Lloyd George told his brother, that he, Churchill, Morley, and Grey had checked the Admiralty's demands and removed at least temporarily the threat to his own financial plans.[11] Seemingly content, Lloyd George left for Cannes.

Early in the new year, however, he faced fresh and disturbing evidence.

> The Admiralty mean to get their 6 Dreadnoughts . . . [they] have had very serious news from their Naval attaché in Germany . . . McKenna is now convinced we may have to lay down 8 Dreadnoughts next year!!! I feared all along this would happen. Fisher is a very clever person and when he found his programme was in danger he wired to Davidson for something more panicky—and of course he got it.
>
> Can we not secure reliable information on this through the Foreign Office—or even through the German Embassy as to what the Germans are really doing.
>
> Frankly I believe the Admirals are procuring false information to frighten us. McKenna feels his personal position and prestige is at

8. Asquith report, 19 Dec. 1908, Cab 41/31/74; Sir A. Fitzroy, Memoirs, 2 vols. (London, 1927), II, 370.

9. Fisher worried lest the current programs result only in a slim lead of eighteen to thirteen by 1912. This did not meet the two-power standard. Germany might, by accelerating her program, complete seventeen or even twenty-one Dreadnoughts by April 1912.

10. Lloyd George to W. George, 10 Nov. 1908, W. George, My Brother and I, 247.

11. Lloyd George to Churchill, 21 Dec., R. S. Churchill, Winston S. Churchill, II, 515, and Lloyd George to W. George, 19 Dec. 1908, W. George, 222.

*stake. He has postponed his visit to the South of France in order to organise the intelligence for the next fight.*

*Could you not get Grey to write to the Embassy or see Metternich? I do not believe the Germans are at all anxious to hurry up their building programme, quite the reverse. Their financial difficulties are already great. Why should they increase them?*[12]

The cabinet returned to the estimates in early February 1909 and debated whether and under what circumstances four or six Dreadnoughts were required.[13] They instructed McKenna to furnish an estimate of projected British and German naval expenditures up to 1912.[14]

At this stage it became apparent to Lloyd George that Grey now supported the Admiralty and that the Foreign Office regarded him as leading a "little navy party."[15] This confrontation has provided the basis for all interpretations of the 1909 naval debate, but it must not obscure other considerations. Lloyd George was perfectly justified in claiming in his memoirs, concerning this occasion at least, that "I never resisted any addition to the strength of the Navy which would provide a reasonable margin of security against the increases in the German Navy."[16]

On 2 February he wrote to Asquith.[17] He did so with great

12. Lloyd George to Churchill, 3 Jan. 1909, Churchill, *Winston S. Churchill*, II, 516–17.

13. Churchill memorandum, 2 Feb., Cab 37/97/19, and LGP, C/24/3/2, and Cabinet meeting, 2 Feb. 1909, Cab 41/32/2.

14. McKenna memoranda, 5 Feb. 1909, Cab 37/97/24 and 25, and LGP, C/24/3/3.

15. Churchill memorandum, 8 Feb. 1909, Cab 37/97/27, and LGP, C/24/3/4; Harcourt memorandum, 24 Feb. 1909, Cab 37/98/37; Marder, *Dreadnought to Scapa Flow*, I, 146. According to Hardinge, Grey was prepared to resign over this issue as early as December 1908, and possibly Lloyd George had misinterpreted Grey's original position. (Foreign Office memoranda, 18 and 22 March 1909, Cab 37/98/46 and 47, and M. L. Dockrill, "The Formulation of a Continental Foreign Policy in Great Britain, 1908–1912," 110–14; Fitzroy, *Memoirs*, II, 372; L. Masterman, *C. F. G. Masterman, A Biography* [London, 1939], 115, 123–24.)

16. Lloyd George, *War Memoirs*, I, 5. He explained that he had opposed the Admiralty's program as excessive and provocative, and that he had favoured building commerce-protecting not capital ships. Germany's principal concern was military not naval preparedness, he wrote, and British public opinion had expected a naval agreement.

17. Lloyd George to Asquith, 2 Feb. 1909, LGP, C/6/11/2, and Asquith Papers, file 21.

difficulty; the draft letter was replete with changes, and the deletions are as revealing as the final version. The navy estimates, he wrote, threatened to reopen all the old controversies that had torn the party apart for years. To save it from a sterile and squalid disruption, Asquith must not commit himself prematurely to the ill-considered demands of the Admiralty. He must give due consideration to the views of Morley, Churchill, and the other dissenters in the cabinet. The government, Lloyd George insisted, was bound by its election pledges to reduce the gigantic expenditure on armaments. Many Liberals took these pledges seriously; a £3 million increase would chill their zeal, an increase of £5 or £6 million would "stagger" them. The people, he warned, were losing confidence in the government because of its legislative failures and its unfulfilled promises. Navy estimates of £38 million would transform disaffection into sedition and end the usefulness of the current parliament. The government would fall if it did not reverse Tory policies. Lloyd George accepted the goal of national security as the paramount one, but he assumed that no incompatibility existed between that primary goal and their pledges on retrenchment.

He rejected McKenna's analysis of the reasons why Germany had accelerated her naval program. The German government was attempting to regulate employment by postponing or anticipating various programs. In this case the shipbuilding industry was depressed and, to offset unemployment, the government had decided to lay down certain ships a few months earlier than planned.[18] Here was economic wisdom, Lloyd George suggested, advanced thinking similar to the course he and Churchill had recommended to McKenna in September. No Machiavellian scheme existed in Berlin. The Admiralty was full of "panic-mongers," and he saw no evidence that Germany intended to anticipate her 1910 program for allegedly sinister motives. Economic indicators and indices would govern her decisions. In any case Berlin could not conceal an accelerated program, and should a real threat emerge Britain could respond accordingly.

Lloyd George rejected McKenna's proposal as sheer folly for "on one hypothesis it is extravagant and on the other it is inadequate." If Germany adhered to her original scheme, four

18. He had witnessed the stagnation of the German shipbuilding industry in August 1908. (*The Times*, 11 and 27 Aug. 1908.)

Dreadnoughts were enough; if Germany began her 1910 program in 1909 the Admiralty's plan for two additional Dreadnoughts laid down in March 1910 was an inefficient and ineffective response. Clearly, Lloyd George charged, McKenna had no intention of being tied to his own estimates should the situation deteriorate. He asked for £100,000 to lay down two Dreadnoughts in March 1910, but if Germany were to accelerate her 1910 program, he would require an additional sum of between £200,000 and £300,000. Should Germany actually attempt to complete twenty-one Dreadnoughts by 1912, the Admiralty's plans would be simply absurd. In sum, McKenna's policies were hand-to-mouth, un-businesslike, and unsuited to an emergency. They were, in fact, a weak compromise, attempted for fear of the German navy on one hand and of radical opinion on the other.

Lloyd George proposed an alternative scheme which, without appearing to menace Germany, would preserve Britain's naval supremacy, reassure public opinion, and demonstrate that the government had a long-term plan to guard against invasion and ensure national security. Moreover, his proposal would, he assured Asquith, give the cabinet some flexibility in adapting the rate of construction to current needs, within a larger scheme already sanctioned by Parliament, and in providing for supplementary votes should unforeseen circumstances arise. The government would be able to stabilize the shipbuilding industry, preserve cabinet control over the naval experts, permit long-term Treasury planning, avoid fluctuating rates of construction, and secure a rational, efficient, and economical policy. Lloyd George claimed to offer the optimum answer to the situation: a powerful fleet, built without placing a crushing burden on the taxpayer—an annual naval vote of £32 million would suffice—and ultimately conducive to an Anglo-German détente. In conclusion, Lloyd George assured Asquith that he sought only "to serve you as my chief and to save Liberalism from the barren mangling up I fear is unavoidable if we indulge in the extravagant and ill-digested policy of the Admiralty. It will disappoint every businessman in the country, it will disgust most Liberals and it will bring disaster to the government."

Lloyd George meant this letter to be a conciliatory move rather than an uncompromising statement of the "economist" case. He wanted to heal the divisions and reconcile divergent interests. McKenna, however, would have to retreat.

Asquith's reply seemed encouraging.[19] He indicated that there was agreement among Lord Crewe, Grey, and other members of the government that naval supremacy must be ensured through an adaptable program, founded on information not rumour and permitting amendment without friction, misunderstanding, and delay. He urged Lloyd George to develop his plan in greater detail.

Lloyd George, in reply, promised a paper on naval defence. He also proposed that the prime minister make a statement to Parliament, warning that the government might need special powers to prepare for an accelerated naval program commencing in April 1910.[20] The Admiralty must be able to begin collecting materials to enable them to construct four additional ships should they be required. This was the first hint of the "four now and four later" solution.

In anticipation of Asquith's support (in retrospect an exaggerated and even naïve expectation), Lloyd George produced his memorandum. He proposed that the German Navy Law be matched with a British Defence Act of equal duration.[21] Parliament would sanction a five-year program to construct twenty Dreadnoughts. Legislative consent would govern any acceleration of this program, but it would enable the Admiralty to watch developments in Germany and respond appropriately.

As he warmed to the idea Lloyd George seemed to suggest that the Admiralty might in effect build now and pay later, should an emergency arise. They could accelerate construction and pay when the financial resources became available within the five-year period. Parliament would control the total proportions but not the annual dimensions of the program. The sea lords could plan in advance and begin each year's construction of four ships on the first day of every financial year. The result, Lloyd George forecast, would be an adequate margin over Germany in the first three years and a clear preponderance in the final two years. Finally, he suggested, to guard against sudden bursts of German construction, the government must ensure that sufficient plant existed to produce guns and turrets for at least twelve Dreadnoughts per year.[22] Hardly the proposals of a chancellor of the exchequer

19. Asquith to Lloyd George, 8 Feb. 1909, LGP, C/6/11/4.
20. Lloyd George to Asquith, 8 Feb. 1909, ibid, C/6/11/5.
21. Lloyd George to W. George, 9 Feb., W. George, 223, and Lloyd George memoranda, Feb. 1909, LGP, C/24/3/6 and C/24/3/7.
22. Lloyd George calculated that by 31 March 1911 Britain would have

insensitive to national security, although Esher's response was surely exaggerated. "Lloyd George, in his heart, does not care a bit for economy and is quite ready to face Parliament with any amount of deficit, and to 'go' for a big Navy. He is plucky and an Imperialist at heart, if he is anything. Besides he despises the stalwarts on his own side....Lloyd George realises that in 1912 we shall be in danger of having hardly a one power naval standard. Winston cannot see it."[23] As he told Lord Knollys, the king's private secretary, "George will some day drift over to the Tories....George is a round man in a square hole. He believes in the Navy but is just now hampered by the fact that he is a representative radical. So he is dragging on the tail of Winston."

Lloyd George felt that his scheme met all requirements, but the issue of four or six Dreadnoughts remained unresolved. Nor had Fisher given up hope of eight. At the cabinet, on 15 February 1909, Churchill, Lewis Harcourt, John Burns, president of the local government board, and Morley faced Grey, Walter Runciman, president of the board of education, Crewe, and Sydney Buxton who supported McKenna's request for six Dreadnoughts.[24] Lloyd George offered his compromise scheme which, however, merely created new divisions. The prime minister, Crewe, and Grey agreed in principle with Lloyd George, but Runciman and Harcourt were opposed, on the grounds that it would undermine parliamentary control. The cabinet decided therefore to establish a committee, comprised of Asquith, Grey, Morley, and Lloyd George, to reach a settlement with the Admiralty.

In defiance of this evidence Asquith blamed the extremism of Lloyd George and Churchill for the lack of progress. With more justification he deplored their hints of resignation and manipulation of the press.[25] So did J. A. Spender of the *Westminster*

---

twelve Dreadnoughts ready for service, to Germany's nine. Britain would enjoy an overwhelming lead in pre-Dreadnoughts. The German program would give her twenty-five Dreadnoughts by 1915; if Britain built eighteen or twenty Dreadnoughts in the next five years she would have thirty by 1915, or thirty-four including ships of the "Nelson" class.

23. Esher diary, 12 Feb., and Esher to Knollys, 12 Feb. 1909, *Esher Journals*, II, 370; Marder, *Dreadnought to Scapa Flow*, I, 160.

24. Cabinet meeting, 15 Feb. 1909, Cab 41/32/4. The basic issue of four as against six Dreadnoughts was refined to a possible solution of four now and two later, although Fisher, McKenna, and Grey now aimed for eight.

25. Asquith to his wife, 20 Feb. 1909, J. A. Spender and C. Asquith, *Life of Herbert Henry Asquith, Lord Oxford and Asquith*, 2 vols. (London, 1932), I, 254.

*Gazette,* but even he noted that Lloyd George did not regard a program providing for six Dreadnoughts as necessarily either reckless or aggressive.[26]

At the cabinet committee Lloyd George further investigated the danger presented by Germany's capacity to expand her production of gun mountings and turrets. The government should, he advised, instruct those firms able to manufacture this equipment that it would place orders with them for the projected twenty Dreadnoughts in the next five years, only if they expanded their productive capacity to sixty turrets per year. Lloyd George expected these firms to respond under the threat of competition from government arsenals, even though the emergency productive facilities might at time lie idle.[27] Indeed, he seemed prepared to grant the government powers to coerce industry so that Britain could build up to twelve Dreadnoughts in a crisis.

One result of the prolonged and detailed discussions of 23 February was that Lloyd George and Fisher apparently disagreed only on whether the Admiralty should plan year by year, as Fisher preferred, or on the basis of the five-year scheme.[28] When McKenna insisted that the navy must have a margin in Dreadnoughts over Germany in 1914 of twenty-eight to twenty-three, and in 1915 of thirty to twenty-five, Lloyd George made no complaint whatsoever. He had felt all along that the Admiralty's interpretation of German motives was faulty, its projections unsound, and its remedies crude. When McKenna defended his forecasts of German construction Lloyd George responded with the charge of "extraordinary neglect on the part of the Admiralty that all this should not have been found out before." McKenna replied that Lloyd George had dismissed his warnings as "contractors' gossip."[29] However, the Admiralty's desired margin of superiority over Germany which Lloyd George had just accepted required a construction ratio of three British to two German

26. Spender to Lloyd George, 18 Feb. 1909, Spender Papers, Add. 46388; W. Harris, *J. A. Spender* (London, 1946), 82, 95–96. Spender interpreted Lloyd George's position as permitting only four Dreadnoughts, on the assumption that the cabinet would decide later whether to order two additional ships if the German threat materialized.

27. Lloyd George memorandum, Feb. 1909, LGP, C/24/3/7.

28. Conference minutes, 23 Feb. 1909, Asquith Papers, file 21. Asquith, Lloyd George, Grey, McKenna, Fisher, and Jellicoe were present.

29. Jellicoe memorandum, 24 Feb. 1909, A. T. Patterson, ed., *The Jellicoe Papers,* I. *1893–1916* (London, 1966), 17.

Dreadnoughts. As the German program envisaged four capital ships that year, Lloyd George would be forced to accept the Admiralty's case for six Dreadnoughts unless a compromise formula emerged. Indeed, he might accept six to avoid eight.

On the following day Asquith brought the cabinet closer to a decision; the basis was the immediate authorization of four Dreadnoughts, with the possibility of four additional ships from the 1910 program being laid down not later than 1 April 1910, should circumstances warrant them. Asquith viewed the decision as a victory for naval preparedness[30] but it cannot be regarded as an outright defeat for Lloyd George, except in the sense that his five-year plan had failed to carry the cabinet. Throughout the debate he had not lost sight of the primary goal, national security, and never did so in the prewar years.

Predictably, Fisher was not satisfied, and he forced McKenna to seek Asquith's assurance that eight ships would be laid down and would constitute part of the 1909 program.[31] Lloyd George objected, demanding that the prime minister resist McKenna's attempt to reinterpret the agreement.[32] They were not committed to lay down eight Dreadnoughts that year, while merely postponing payment on the second four until the 1910–11 financial year; the case for the second four Dreadnoughts would be reviewed later. He and his supporters had worked to reach a compromise, but if McKenna attempted this manoeuvre a schism was unavoidable. Grey had suggested, Lloyd George noted, that McKenna had the substance, leaving Lloyd George merely the shadow, but now the Admiralty would take even that away from him. He must insist on the original interpretation of the 24 February decision.

The cabinet, on 5 March 1909, clarified the matter.[33] The Admiralty would lay down four Dreadnoughts in July and October 1909. The government could place orders for materials, gun mountings, and other essential equipment for an additional four ships which, if they were authorized, would be laid down on 1 April 1910. The navy estimates for 1909–10 showed an increase of £2.75 million. By April 1912, if eight ships were built, Britain would have twenty Dreadnoughts in commission and an ample

30. Asquith to his wife, 25 Feb. 1909, Spender and Asquith, *Asquith*, i, 254.
31. McKenna to Asquith, 25 Feb. 1909, LGP, C/6/11/6.
32. Lloyd George to Haldane, 25 Feb. 1909, ibid., C/4/17/1.
33. Cabinet meeting, 5 March 1909, Cab 41/32/5.

margin over Germany. Lord Emmott's view was "that the government might just as well have gone the whole hog. It does not seem likely that either Winston or Lloyd George would have resigned. Even if they had, what would they have done? Fisher says, it is reported, 'of course we are going to build the second 4. Why we have named them: 1. Winston, 2. Churchill, 3. Lloyd, and 4. George'."[34]

Significantly, Tory rather than radical criticism of this decision was pronounced and effective, helping to sustain the campaign for eight Dreadnoughts in an atmosphere made more extreme by Lloyd George's April 1909 budget. This campaign, aided by the disturbing but convenient evidence of the Austrian and Italian Dreadnought programs, which activated further Foreign Office support for the Admiralty, proved irresistible. On 21 July 1909, the cabinet confirmed that the Admiralty could place preliminary orders for equipment, materials, and gun mountings for the four extra capital ships. They would be laid down in April 1910, would be in commission by the spring of 1912, and would not prejudice the 1910–11 program.[35] Lloyd George made no attempt to obstruct this decision; he accepted the Admiralty's case as proven. Political considerations were, of course, not absent.

In his budget statement of 29 April 1909 Lloyd George had warned of the inescapable costs of the Dreadnought program, and had accepted the possibility of eight rather than four new ships.[36] Indeed, he had stated specifically that he did not present sobering financial facts as arguments against the program. He had declared that, whatever the cost, the government would not shirk its duty. They must ensure against invasion, and guarantee the security of the nation's commerce and freedom. As in the past they must also be prepared to safeguard Europe's liberties. The government could not fail, for if it did, "Such a stupendous act of folly would, in the present temper of nations, not be Liberalism but lunacy. We do not intend to put in jeopardy the naval supremacy which is so essential not only to our national existence, but, in our judgement,

34. Emmott diary, 28 March 1909, Emmott Papers, 1907–1911, f.151; A. M. Gollin, *J. L. Garvin and The Observer*, 72–76; Marder, *Dreadnought to Scapa Flow*, I, 162–63.

35. Cabinet meeting 21 July, Cab 41/32/26, McKenna memorandum, 14 July, Cab 37/100/97, and Churchill memorandum, 20 July 1909, Cab 37/100/99; Gollin, *The Observer*, 77, 89; Marder, *Dreadnought to Scapa Flow*, I, 170–71.

36. Speech, 29 April 1909, *Parl. Deb.*, H. of C., IV, 475, 478–81.

to the vital interests of Western civilisation." Rational analysis, however, must replace fear. "It would also be an act of criminal insanity to throw away £8 millions of money, which is so much needed for other purposes, on building gigantic flotillas to encounter mythical Armadas." Need must govern expenditure; they must not build "navies against nightmares" nor waste millions to appease an "unreasoning panic." Finally, he had suggested, "It is the business of a Government to follow with calmness, as well as with courage, the middle path between panic and parsimony, which is the only safe road to national security." Should the government decide to lay down eight Dreadnoughts by 1 April 1910 he would propose suitable financial arrangements; should four capital ships suffice he would divert the money to social programs or to the relief of the local ratepayers.

If Arthur Ponsonby's response was representative, Lloyd George had balanced superbly well.[37] Worried by the direction of government policy and the indifference of Liberal MPs, he saw Lloyd George as a saviour:

> Your Budget will, if it has not already, completely alter this atmosphere. I talked to a large number of members on Thursday night, both Labour and Liberal. There was real enthusiasm and the intensity of it I could measure in each case by the genuineness of their radical views. I don't hear Cabinet secrets nowadays. . . . But the net result to my mind is that the Budget has all the appearances of being yours, it smacks throughout of your views and has a fearless courage about it which is characteristic of you. I am reminded that it was the attitude . . . C. B. John Morley and yourself took up 7 or 8 years ago that finally made me, in spite of much opposition, give up . . . official life for politics.

Subsequently, Lloyd George's financial arrangements to provide for eight Dreadnoughts and a program of social reform proved both controversial and painful. Belgravia and the incumbents of the House of Lords would pay. They had clamoured for eight, he had obliged, and they would receive the bill.[38] Andrew

37. Ponsonby to Lloyd George, May 1909, Ponsonby Papers. See also S. Koss, *Sir John Brunner, Radical Plutocrat, 1842–1919*, 235.

38. Speeches, 30 July 1909, and 1 and 8 Jan. 1910, Lloyd George, *Better Times*, 144–56, 256–58, 266–77; *The Times*, 9 and 11 Oct. 1909.

Carnegie responded by describing Lloyd George and Churchill to Morley as "the two coming men who rank with Bright."[39]

Lloyd George felt able to assure the inaugural meeting of the Women's Anglo-German Friendship Union, on 22 July 1909, that Anglo-German relations would follow in the path of Britain's relations with the United States and France.[40] Americans were "blood of our blood, flesh of our flesh, bone of our bone, the same people"; an Anglo-American conflict was now out of the question. Britain and France no longer risked war over African swamps. British and German interests did not really conflict, and both powers desired peace. The new chancellor, Bethmann Hollweg, had sent his son to Oxford, a comforting sign to Lloyd George. He was eloquent on a further source of détente. A vast majority of Englishmen, he said, sprang from German origins; German blood flowed in their veins. German citizens resident in Britain were friends not spies and ultimately sanity would prevail. These assurances, it should be noted, were made precisely one day after the cabinet had authorized the Admiralty to prepare for the construction of the four additional capital ships.

Sanity for Lloyd George meant the resumption of negotiations with Berlin. They were initiated by Bethmann Hollweg in August 1909 and continued, despite several interruptions, to the eve of the Agadir crisis. Bethmann Hollweg sought a nonaggression and neutrality pact, secretly negotiated, prior to an arrangement merely to reduce the tempo of naval construction, and to leave untouched the German Navy Law. Foreign Office officials and the Admiralty were reluctant and pessimistic. Grey was cautious, preferring a more precise and beneficial naval agreement, and being determined to avoid any political arrangement which would jeopardize the Ententes with France and Russia. Lloyd George welcomed Berlin's initiative but supported the cabinet's decision of 1 September 1909 which confirmed Grey's control over the negotiations.[41] Grey broke off the discussions, however, in November and the general election of January 1910 brought

39. Carnegie to Morley, 13 Oct. 1909, Morley Papers, Eur. D.573/66.
40. Lloyd George speech, 22 July 1909, LGP, C/33/2/10. Dame Margaret had convened the meeting; Herbert Samuel, MP, was in the chair.
41. Goschen to Grey, 16 April, BDOW, vi, 174, 265–66, Goschen to Grey, 21 Aug., ibid., 186 and 187, 283–84, Notes by Grey, 31 Aug., ibid., 193, 288, Grey to Goschen, 1 Sept., ibid., 194 and 195, 288–89, and cabinet meeting, 1 Sept. 1909, Cab 41/32/33.

further delay.[42] Lloyd George lamented the impasse but tended to blame German obduracy and evasion rather more than the Foreign Office's reluctance and obstruction. He did not, therefore, collaborate with Lord Loreburn in the attempt to force Grey's hand.[43]

As a result, the debate over the defence estimates for 1910–11 aroused relatively less passion and controversy. Admiral Sir Arthur Wilson had replaced Fisher as first sea lord and the level of intrigue declined. Nevertheless the Admiralty's proposals of December 1909, which Grey supported, for six capital ships to be followed by six more in 1911–12, produced a confrontation in the cabinet.[44] By late January, however, McKenna offered a modified construction program of five capital ships in each of the financial years 1910–11 and 1911–12.[45] The Foreign Office was less than satisfied, but the cabinet agreed to the proposal on 17 February 1910.

Lloyd George had accepted estimates which were increased by £5.5 million and had reached £40,600,000. The cabinet agreed that he should seek ways to spread the cost of naval construction over several years, but nothing came of the proposal.[46] In his second budget speech, in June, he acknowledged the facts and did not offer relief until 1912–13. When Germany reduced her program, as he anticipated she would, the government could return to normal policies.[47] The radical press was understandably dis-

---

42. Goschen to Grey, 15 Oct., *BDOW*, vi, 200, 293–300, Grey to Goschen, 28 Oct., ibid., 202, 303–304, Goschen to Grey, 4 Nov., ibid., 204, 304–309, and Grey to Goschen, 17 Nov. 1909, ibid., 205, 312–13.

43. He had attacked Balfour for introducing the naval question and Anglo-German relations into domestic politics, and had made some capital out of comparing Tory demands for naval security with their obstruction of far-reaching proposals to meet the cost. (Article, 30 Oct. 1909, H. du Parcq, *Lloyd George*, iv, 31–32.) In a speech at Grimsby he praised the strength of the fleet and forecast a rapid victory over the German navy in the event of war. (*Daily News*, 15 Jan. 1910.)

44. Esher to M.V.B., 30 Dec. 1909 and 4 Jan. 1910, *Esher Journals*, ii, 431, 433.

45. Churchill and Board of Trade memoranda, 3 Nov. 1909, Cab 37/101/147 and 148; McKenna memoranda, 11 Dec. 1909 and 14 Feb. 1910, Cab 37/101/157 and Cab 37/102/2. The five capital ships would ensure a margin of twenty-five to seventeen over Germany, or twenty-seven to nineteen if one added two capital ships from the Dominions and two from Austria, as available to Britain and Germany respectively.

46. Esher to Balfour, 31 Jan. 1910, *Esher Journals*, ii, 446.

47. Speech, 30 June 1910. *Parl. Deb.*, H. of C., xviii, 1124–25.

mayed and the chancellor of the exchequer could not evade criticism.[48]

The Anglo-German negotiations were resumed in March 1910, again on German initiative,[49] but the deadlock remained unbroken.[50] Lloyd George's interest in these negotiations was sustained, but he was in sympathy with Grey's position and felt that the foreign secretary genuinely pursued an agreement. The fact that Berlin always took the initiative was as obvious as the reluctance of the Foreign Office to respond. Yet the delay in the negotiations in late August and September resulted, as Asquith assured Lloyd George, from Bethmann Hollweg's reaction and response to the proposals authorized by the cabinet on 29 July.[51] The prime minister noted hopefully that the new German foreign minister, A. von Kiderlen-Wächter, seemed willing to settle with Britain. However, Asquith warned, "there is always the possibility of some fresh outburst from the enfant terrible in the Imperial nursery." Finally, London, not Berlin, was responsible for further interruptions in the negotiations, from October to December 1910, but the second general election within a year provided ample excuse for a generous interpretation of the reasons for the impasse.

This growing disposition to accept Grey's view of the realities governing British foreign policy was also evident in Lloyd George's support of the foreign secretary's handling of the Bosnian crisis of 1908–09, relations with Russia, and the Persian question. In the crucial division of 22 July 1909 over Near Eastern affairs, for instance, he had voted in support of the Foreign Office.

These developments in the realm of foreign policy parallel Lloyd George's proposal for a national government in August

48. The new publication, *Round Table*, defended him, however. (Anon., "Anglo-German Rivalry," *Round Table*, 1, no. 1 (1910), 7–10.)

49. Grey to Goschen, 22 and 31 March, Goschen to Grey, 11 April, and Grey to Goschen, 5 May 1910, BDOW, vi, 336 and 337, 442–43, 344, 454–61, and 361, 478–79.

50. Grey to Goschen, 18 and 29 July, ibid., vi, 382, 496–97, and 387, 501–502, Goschen to Grey, 6, 15, and 19 Aug., ibid., 391, 510–11, 393, 511–12, and 395, 512–13, Grey to Goschen, 11 and 18 Aug., ibid., 392 and 394, 511–12, Goschen to Grey, 12 and 14 Oct., ibid., 399, 400 and 401, 520–29, Goschen to Nicolson, 22 Oct., ibid., 405, 536–37, Grey to Goschen, 26 Oct., 23 Nov., 16 Dec. 1910, ibid., 407, 538–39, 414 and 425, 546–48 and 575–76; cabinet meetings, 20 and 29 July 1910, Cab 41/32/67 and 68; Foreign Office memoranda, 26 and 27 July 1910, Cab 37/103/36 and 37.

51. Asquith to Lloyd George, 24 Sept. 1910, LGP, C/6/11/7.

1910; both themes marked a stage in his education.[52] The fusionist scheme which collapsed in November was not merely the shallow effusion of a politically double-jointed Celt. Lloyd George was, for the first time, exploring how to use power across and beyond party lines. On this occasion, he was tactically inept rather than disingenuous.

In the presence of seemingly intractable constitutional and Irish problems, international complications, and political opportunities, Lloyd George intended to confront antiquated radicals, ambitious socialists, and selfish diehards, and to unite those whom he regarded as political and vital centrists.[53] He sought to establish the leadership of a meritorious and popular élite, dedicated to efficient and progressive government. In this way he could transcend the damaging and ineffective party system, and achieve both national and imperial unity, prosperity, and security. As he explained to F. E. Smith, the Conservative MP and future Lord Birkenhead, in 1913, "You know how anxious I have been for years to work with you and a few others of your side. I have always realised that our differences have been artificial and do not reach the realities."[54] Smith, like Esher and Garvin, concluded that Lloyd George had matured in office and was sick of being wagged by the "Little England" tail.[55]

Lloyd George's famous memorandum of 17 August 1910, prepared at Criccieth with the help of Charles Masterman, undersecretary at the Home Office, was devoted largely to domestic problems; the proposed remedies were those of the New Liberalism.[56] Defence and foreign policy questions received little atten-

52. Lloyd George to Churchill, 25 Sept. 1910, C. Hazlehurst, "Asquith as Prime Minister, 1908–1916," 507, 514; speech, 17 Oct., *The Times*, 18 Oct. 1910; W. Watkin Davies, *Lloyd George*, 358–63; B. B. Gilbert, *The Evolution of National Insurance in Great Britain* (London, 1966), 326–30, and "The British National Insurance Act of 1911 and the Commercial Insurance Lobby," *Journal of British Studies*, 4, no. 2 (1965), 127–48.

53. Crewe to Lloyd George, 21 Oct., LGP, C/4/1/2, and Asquith to Crewe, 27 Oct. 1910, Crewe Papers, C/40.

54. Lloyd George to Smith, 6 Oct. 1913, LGP, C/3/7/2.

55. Smith to Chamberlain, 20 Oct. 1910, V. Bonham Carter, *Winston Churchill As I Knew Him* (London, 1965), 194. Haldane found Lloyd George more appreciative of War Office requirements.

56. Lloyd George memorandum, 17 Aug. 1910, LGP, C/3/14/8; Chamberlain memorandum, 29 Jan. 1915, ibid., and A. Chamberlain Papers, A.C./49/6/1; A. Chamberlain, *Politics From Inside*, 191–93, 283–89; J. T. Davies to E. Evans, n.d., LGP, F/85/8/1; Masterman, C. F. G. Masterman, 170–72.

tion. In his memoirs, however, Lloyd George pointed out that evidence of his concern with these matters had emerged during his conversations with Metternich in July 1908.[57] He had been disturbed, he suggested, by scientific and technological advances relating to air and submarine power which seemed to threaten national security by making Britain more vulnerable to invasion and blockade.

Lloyd George's involvement in the CID and in the debates over strategy preclude a mere dismissal of this claim as one manufactured in retrospect. He offered two solutions in his memorandum: a system of national service to raise a militia force of half-a-million by ballot rather than conscription, to supplement the regular army; and policies to develop the resources of Britain and a more united Empire. He returned to the former in 1931 and advocated the latter in his land campaign, in the interwar years, and finally between 1940 and 1943. Moreover, in January 1915 he brought the whole scheme to the attention of Bonar Law and Chamberlain.

The memorandum made no specific reference to naval supremacy, but Britain's security and international prestige were surely assumptions requiring no elaboration. In the same way Lloyd George did not need to insist either on the merits of multilateral arms limitation or of an Anglo-German naval agreement which upheld essential British interests.

On 22 and 24 December 1910 Lloyd George gave interviews first to Jean Longuet of *Humanité* and then to Jules Hedeman of *Matin*.[58] He was ill-served by both journalists; even *The Times* felt compelled to correct its copy. However, the *amour propre* of various French politicians was aroused and fed the controversy.[59] In fact, Lloyd George had, rather clumsily, courted France. He had referred indelicately, it is true, to Fashoda and the Dreyfus affair, but had pointed out that, in the tradition of Fox and Gladstone, the Liberal party had always admired France as Europe's only great democratic nation. He had come to share this view following

57. Lloyd George, *War Memoirs*, I, 20–24.
58. Bertie to Grey, 25 and 27 Dec. 1910, FO/800/52; and du Parcq, III, 571–73.
59. Premier Aristide Briand, according to S. Pichon, the foreign minister, felt that Lloyd George had slighted the French government and its leader. Pichon attributed the supposed *faux pas* to the fact that Lloyd George was a Celt, not an Englishman. He also suggested that Lloyd George had upset Churchill by references to American heiresses.

the South African war. In other words, regard for France was not a preserve of the Conservative party. Britain was not an unreliable partner because she had a Liberal government dedicated to peace and arms limitation.

The Foreign Office deplored such outbursts, and Grey assured Ambassador Bertie that Lloyd George had caused far more annoyance in London than in Paris.[60] Haldane had complained immediately that Lloyd George was "irritating in the extreme," and wondered why such incidents took place in the midst of negotiations with Germany.[61] Haldane, as concerned as any minister to achieve a naval agreement, obviously disliked what he interpreted as an inopportune wooing of the French.

Lloyd George did not intend, however, to permit the Admiralty to run free. Early in November 1910 he had asked McKenna for his estimates and for information on the state of German naval construction.[62] A cabinet committee investigated the Admiralty's initial proposals for five capital ships in each of the years 1911–12 and 1912–13, but Lloyd George fell ill and retired to the Riviera and then to Folkestone. By February 1911 little had been agreed upon, and Lloyd George, ever concerned with political considerations, consulted a sympathetic Crewe, now at the India Office:

> There is a serious revolt getting up behind us on our armaments policy. I am not at all surprised. Frankly I think our naval expenditure an outrage to Liberal tradition and had it not been that I foresaw the disastrous effect of a split I should not have assented to them in 1909. That we are now committed to, but we are not pledged to repeat that blunder. We must now find all the necessary supply to complete the ships we laid down in that silly (game?), but what about the future? As to that we are free. And I am firmly convinced that if we commit ourselves this year to building in excess of our strict requirements we shall march straight to disruption. I have not yet seen the Admiralty programme—but I have heard something of the new ships it is proposed to lay down. I regret I could not see my way to assent to such a programme. It is quite uncalled for. I think

60. Grey to Bertie, 9 Jan. 1911, FO/800/52.
61. Haldane to Grey, 26 Dec. 1910, FO/800/102.
62. Lloyd George to McKenna, 7 Nov. 1910, LGP, C/5/12/3; memoranda by Churchill, 15 July, by McKenna, 17 Oct., and by the Foreign Office, 10 Nov. 1910, Cab 37/103/32, Cab 37/103/51, and Cab 37/104/61; French chargé (Berlin) to Pichon, 24 Dec. 1910, DDF, 2, xiii, 103.

*I could place some concrete reasons before the committee which might influence them. At any rate as I feel the consequences to the party may be grave I should like my colleagues to give me an opportunity of stating the case before they make a final recommendation. The actual amount of the estimates this year does not matter nearly so much as our commitments. I told McKenna I could face even a large amount this year provided he could assure me of a large reduction— something like a return to the Campbell-Bannerman Estimates—in the immediate future. He undertook to meet me to some extent but the reduction he foreshadowed was not in my judgement at all adequate.*

*A heavy programme this year means little this year as the ships could be laid down late, but it would involve large payments in 1912 and in 1913 when our insurance subsidies arrive at maturity. New taxes would then become inevitable just when the Government will have been seriously weakened by the Home Rule campaign.*[63]

Churchill, now home secretary, brought Lloyd George up to date on the committee's work and explored a variety of ways to secure economies: retention of the "Colonial Dreadnoughts" until 1915, further Dominion naval construction, and strategic fleet redeployments.[64] Lloyd George was naturally sympathetic, "There is an additional reason why postponement of the contingent two could be defended. Everything depends on the disposition of the Colonial two. It might well be contended that this could only be effectively decided when the Premiers of the two Colonies come over for the Conference."[65]

An unyielding McKenna presented his estimates on 16 February 1911.[66] Lloyd George assured C. P. Scott that he would accept only four Dreadnoughts.[67] He described himself, as he was wont to do on such occasions, as virtually isolated in the cabinet, unsure about resignation and Churchill's intentions, and unable to tell whether Asquith would choose him over McKenna. If he

---

63. Lloyd George to Crewe, 13 Feb., Crewe Papers, C/31, Crewe to Lloyd George, 14 Feb., LGP, C/4/1/3, and C. Hobhouse (Treasury) to Lloyd George, 14 Feb. 1911, ibid., C/1/1/2. McKenna had offered to eliminate two cruisers, but the committee felt that Lloyd George's absence precluded a final decision.

64. Churchill to Lloyd George, 14 Feb. 1911, LGP, C/3/15/4; Churchill memorandum, 3 Feb. 1911, Cab 37/105/7.

65. Lloyd George to Elibank, 15 Feb. 1911, Elibank Papers, 8802, f.182/3.

66. McKenna memorandum, 16 Feb. 1911, Cab 37/105/12; Marder, *Dreadnought to Scapa Flow*, I, 218.

67. Scott diary, 16 Feb. 1911, Scott Papers, Add. 50901.

resigned, he would stump the country to defeat the Admiralty. Scott, who was becoming a guardian of Lloyd George's radical conscience, urged him to stand firm, confident that Asquith would not risk his resignation.

Lloyd George met with Asquith later that day and apparently threatened resignation if the cabinet accepted the navy estimates.[68] Lloyd George stood firm and the prime minister presumably informed McKenna that he could not part with the chancellor. Negotiations then ensued between Lloyd George and McKenna.[69] The former accepted estimates of £44,400,500. This constituted an increase of only slightly less than £4 million. McKenna agreed to a reduction in the navy estimates for 1912–13 and to a cut in the combined army and navy estimates for 1913–14 of £4,400,000, as compared with the 1911–12 level. However, he insisted that this proposed saving was conditional on Germany not amending her Naval Law before March 1914. Lloyd George was apparently under the impression that the 1913–14 navy estimates would be reduced to £40 million no matter what the circumstances and irrespective of the response from Haldane at the War Office. Areas for dispute evidently remained.

On 1 March 1911 the cabinet set the navy estimates at £44,400,000. McKenna agreed that if Germany made no alteration to her program he would reduce expenditure on operations in home waters in 1913–14 by £3 million. He would also secure a further reduction of £1.25 million with help from the War Office.[70] The cabinet failed to agree, however, on how the £1.25 million reduction could be made, since Haldane opposed reductions in the overseas garrisons. It was decided, therefore, to create or re-activate a committee comprised of Crewe, Grey, Haldane, Harcourt, now colonial secretary, McKenna, Lloyd George, and Churchill.

Lloyd George pressed McKenna for an assurance that his 1913–14 estimates would return to £40 million.[71] In the last two years, Lloyd George noted, they had laid down at least three

68. Scott diary, 17 Feb. 1911, ibid; Masterman, *C. F. G. Masterman*, 186.

69. McKenna to Lloyd George, 16 Feb., and Lloyd George's reply, 17 Feb. 1911, LGP, C/5/12/8. Lloyd George assured Scott and Masterman that he had won a complete victory but his correspondence with McKenna suggests otherwise.

70. Cabinet meeting, 1 March 1911, Cab 41/33/4.

71. Lloyd George to McKenna, 3 March 1911, LGP, C/5/13/7, and McKenna Papers, 3/20/14.

more Dreadnoughts than McKenna had envisaged in November 1908. The Admiralty exaggerated the speed of German prepared-ness. Anglo-German relations were now greatly improved, he suggested, and Grey was "very sanguine" that he could secure an agreement to reduce the tempo of construction. In addition, Grey seemed hopeful of reducing the forces in foreign waters. Lloyd George assured McKenna that he would hate to launch a "Shylock attack" on him over their agreement, "but I cannot assent to its cancellation. A reduction in Army estimates was no part of the bargain. I agree entirely with you that Haldane ought to contribute, and I shall assist you to the best of my powers in securing a reduction in the Army estimates. You however undertook to 'deliver the goods'."

McKenna held firm; the matter rested on an unsatisfactory and potentially mischievous compromise. Lloyd George, signing as "The mute Chancellor," reported it to Murray of Elibank, the Liberal Chief Whip: "McKenna has sent me another disgusting letter in which he obstinately declines to abide by his bargain. What can I do in face of such conduct? He knows quite well that a reduction in the army was no part of the contract. *He* had to deliver the goods. I must leave the Revenue Bill to my suave lieutenant. Sorry—but the last fortnight has taught me that I cannot defy doctor's orders with impunity. He warned me—politely—to 'shut up' for a month. I refused. Hence my exile every hour of which I grudge."[72]

In his budget statement of May 1911, Lloyd George described the increases in the navy estimates as very considerable, excep-tional, but, he hoped, at their peak.[73] By skilful management and, one might add, increased taxation, Lloyd George claimed that he had financed naval preparedness as well as social reform, reduced the National Debt and produced a budget surplus of between £5 and £8 million. Moreover, in view of the fact that the government would pay the full cost of the four Dreadnoughts begun in April 1910 in the 1911–12 financial year, and because Germany might slow the tempo of her program, Lloyd George forecast reduced

72. Lloyd George to Elibank, 7 March 1911, Elibank Papers, 8802, f.182/3; Marder, *Dreadnought to Scapa Flow*, 1, 218–19. McKenna was pledged to the £3 million reduction in 1913–14. He interpreted the agreement to mean that, should circumstances permit, a further £1,400,000 would be removed from the com-bined army and navy estimates.
73. Speech, 16 May 1911, *Parl. Deb.*, H. of C., xxv, 1853–58, 1868.

expenditures in 1912. It was yet another politically skilful balancing act by the chancellor of the exchequer.

To both McKenna and Parliament Lloyd George had held out the prospect of an Anglo-German naval and political agreement, although negotiations had been suspended in December 1910. On 20 January 1911, the cabinet created a Committee on Foreign Affairs, comprised of Asquith, Grey, Lloyd George, Morley, now lord president of the council, Crewe, and Runciman. Lloyd George welcomed it as a move which would increase the flow of information to the cabinet and permit closer scrutiny of the Foreign Office. Indeed, Arthur Murray, Grey's parliamentary private secretary, suggested (and confirmed as much in 1933) that the committee was created principally to satisfy the chancellor of the exchequer:

> I have had lately to convey to Sir Edward Grey an alleged grievance of Lloyd George's. The latter said that although he was especially interested in Foreign Affairs in that he was called upon to provide money for huge Naval Estimates, he was kept in the dark in regard to essential features of our Foreign policy. He knew nothing, he said, of what was going on, and he demanded that papers should be sent to him. This of course was not feasible in the sense that he desired but the matter has been satisfactorily settled by the setting up of a sub-committee of the Cabinet, of which Lloyd George will be a member, periodically to discuss Foreign Policy.[74]

Obviously Lloyd George was frustrated over the naval estimates and Grey's support of the Admiralty. He carried too much weight to be ignored, but evidently Grey felt that he could be appeased relatively easily.

The Foreign Office chose to regard the committee as having only one specific purpose: to help prepare the promised reply to Berlin on the matter of a naval and political agreement. Sir Arthur Nicolson, now permanent under-secretary, saw it as a threat because some of its members seemed to accept the German view that a political arrangement should precede a naval agreement.[75] They demanded a rapprochement with Germany "at almost any cost."

74. A. C. Murray diary, 27 Jan., Elibank Papers, 8814, f.5, cabinet meeting, 20 Jan., Asquith Papers, file 6, and note by prime minister's office, 25 Jan. 1911, FO/800/100. Hence Murray's comments to E. L. Woodward in 1933.

75. Nicolson to Hardinge, 2 March and 19 April 1911, *BDOW*, vi, 440 and 461, 590–91, and 620–21; J. Cambon to Cruppi, 28 April 1911, *DDF*, 2, xiii, 265.

Lloyd George's illness curtailed his participation in the work of the committee. Unfortunately, moreover, either no minutes were taken or none survive. The committee met probably for the first time on 30 January, and by 17 February arrived at a preliminary draft reply to Bethmann Hollweg.[76] Sir William Tyrrell informed the foreign secretary that Lloyd George could not attend the committee that day because of an engagement in Brighton.[77] He wished to propose several amendments to the reply to Berlin and assumed that he would be able to do so.

Tyrrell's note, however, arrived after the meeting. Grey decided that Asquith must rule on whether the committee should meet again to accommodate Lloyd George, or whether the cabinet should take up the matter. Both the precise nature of Lloyd George's amendments and the resulting discussion remain obscure. On 4 March 1911, the Foreign Office circulated a draft reply[78] to Germany, which the cabinet examined on 8 March.[79] The cabinet emphasized that it must be couched in "unmistakably cordial terms," that a declaration must avoid anything likely to be misinterpreted in France or Russia, and that a general European political agreement would founder on France's refusal to abandon Alsace-Lorraine.

This reply to Germany, presented on 24 March, was undoubtedly a victory for Grey.[80] The cabinet had approved two vital principles: that a naval agreement, maintaining Britain's supremacy, must preface and form the basis of any political settlement, and that any such arrangement must not prejudice Britain's relations with France and Russia. The Ententes were declared inviolable. Moreover, the cabinet had in fact rejected the comprehensive political agreement sought by Germany. They

76. Grey to Goschen, 16 Feb., *BDOW*, VI, 439, 589–90, and Morley to Crewe, 9 Feb. 1911, Crewe Papers, C/37. Grey attributed the delay to the absence from the committee of himself and Lloyd George.

77. Tyrrell to Grey, 17 Feb. 1911, FO/800/100.

78. Foreign Office draft reply, 4 March, Cab 37/105/20, and Grey to Goschen, 8 March 1911, *BDOW*, VI, 444, 598–600. It was based on a compromise between Grey and the committee. It is impossible to determine whether or how Lloyd George's amendments had any effect.

79. Asquith report, 9 March 1911, Cab 41/33/5.

80. Grey to Goschen, 8 March, *BDOW*, VI, 444, 598–600, Goschen to Grey, 11 March, ibid., 445, 600, Nicolson to Goschen, 14 March, ibid., 449, 603–604, Grey to Bertie and Buchanan, 14 March, ibid., 447 and 448, 602–603, and Goschen to Grey, 24 March 1911, ibid., 454, 608–10.

looked to an agreement on specific questions, and suggested piecemeal negotiations on matters such as the Baghdad Railway and Persia. Nevertheless, the cabinet had insisted on the adoption of a significant degree of cordiality toward Germany.

These decisions did not represent a defeat for Lloyd George. He was anxious to secure a satisfactory naval agreement with Germany, which would lead to an Anglo-German and then a European détente. There is no evidence, however, that he had pressed for a rapprochement with Germany at almost any price or on Germany's terms. He was as unlikely as Grey to concede German hegemony in Europe, and he assumed that Grey genuinely desired to improve relations with Berlin and give moral leadership to Europe. Nicolson had not singled him out as unreliable and Asquith gave no indication of any dissatisfaction on Lloyd George's part with the cabinet's formula of 8 March. Lloyd George had never attacked Grey's devotion to the Ententes with France and Russia and his interpretation of their function did not require him to do so. Indeed, loss of the Ententes might result in a demand for increased naval expenditures. Moreover, the cabinet had participated in policy formulation and Lloyd George personally was more fully informed. He and Grey were not divided and in this context their cooperation in the Agadir crisis was neither unpredictable nor an act of apostasy by Lloyd George. The social and intellectual distance between them, however, remained as wide as ever.[81]

Bethmann Hollweg's reply of 9 May was distinctly discouraging and the cabinet accepted the Foreign Office assessment that further negotiations were unlikely to be productive.[82] Grey, with cabinet approval, continued to pursue an agreement to provide for an exchange of naval information, but without success.[83] The negotiations foundered in June and were not resumed until January 1912. Lloyd George agreed that Bethmann Hollweg had delivered the *coup de grâce*.

Foreign Office opinion, however, remained somewhat sceptical of Lloyd George. Cecil Spring-Rice, former minister at Teheran,

81. L. Masterman, "Recollections of David Lloyd George," 160–69, 274–82.

82. Goschen to Grey, 9 and 10 May, *BDOW*, vi, 462 and 464, 621–23, and 625–29, and Asquith report, 17 May 1911, Cab 41/33/15.

83. Asquith report, 31 May, Cab 41/33/17, Grey memorandum, 20 May, *BDOW*, vi, 468, 631–36, and Grey to Goschen, 1 June 1911, ibid., 469, 636–37.

after disparaging the alien Disraeli, had commented, "We are now taking Lloyd George, a Celt from the lower regions, nearly as foreign to our respectable Saxon dam. Germany for years was content with a denationalised mountebank like Bülow. So I suppose we are in the fashion."[84]

Within months a grateful Tyrrell had reason to challenge this view; the Agadir crisis, a crucial test, would, temporarily at least, make Lloyd George *persona grata* at the Foreign Office.

84. Spring-Rice to Lady Helen, 26 Dec. 1910, S. Gwynn, ed., *The Letters and Friendships of Sir Cecil Spring-Rice*, 2 vols. (London, 1929), II, 159–60.

# 7

# Agadir

In that glorious summer of 1911 Grey faced the distressingly difficult situation dramatized by the arrival of the *Panther* at Agadir on 1 July. This provocative German act forced him to support and yet restrain France, even though she had actually precipitated the Moroccan crisis. Grey was bound both to help France resist Berlin's pressure and to seek compensation for Germany. He was also compelled to mediate between France and Spain, and prevent a justifiably irritated Spain from gravitating toward Germany. Above all else Grey sought to preserve Britain's commercial and strategic interests, and secure her representation in any negotiations to replace the Algeciras agreement of 1906. French as well as German policy was therefore a matter of concern. She might connive in negotiations *à deux* or collapse and reach an agreement with Germany which disregarded British interests. Conversely, she might attempt to force on Britain the burden of excluding Germany from Morocco. Finally, Grey dealt with a nervous cabinet and a rather vigorous Foreign Office. His officials and Ambassador Bertie in Paris became convinced that the Entente with France and the balance of power were at issue, not just the future of Morocco. They felt that the situation demanded co-operation with France to resist Germany at all costs.[1]

Lloyd George's involvement continues to be controversial. Supposedly, according to one school of thought, he underwent a dramatic conversion in July 1911. The Germanophile, acting from dubious motives, became the darling of the Foreign Office. Unreliable and naïve, apparently, he did not even understand the import of the Mansion House speech.[2] This thesis misrepresents his position both prior to and after the Moroccan affair.

Others assert that the Mansion House speech was intended not for German consumption but to impress the French or Europe generally, or even to help settle a railway strike at home. This view is generally unacceptable but with regard to relations with France one cannot dismiss it entirely. A third consideration has hitherto escaped adequate attention and, indeed, Lloyd George ignored it in his memoirs. The Mansion House speech was merely the start of his direct involvement. He played an important role well into September.

Lloyd George, in 1924, acknowledged the accuracy of Grey's interpretation of the origins of the Mansion House speech. Lloyd George regarded his own brief comments in his memoirs as mere confirmation.[3] He was concerned to affirm his personal initiative and responsibility, and to deny that he acted as a mere mouthpiece of the cabinet or of Grey and Asquith, scarcely comprehending the significance of his own speech. Indeed, Lloyd George was as

1. Bertie to Grey, 9 July, Asquith to Grey, 11 July, and Grey to Asquith, 13 July 1911, FO/800/100; Nicolson to Hardinge, 5 July, Goschen to Grey, 10 July, minutes on Bertie to Grey, 11 July, Grey to Bertie, 12 July, Bertie to Nicolson, 12 July, Grey to Bertie, 13 July, Bertie to Grey, 14 July, Goschen to Grey, 14 July, Bertie to Nicolson, 16 July, Grey to Bertie, 17 July, Nicolson to Goschen, 18 July, Nicolson to Grey, 21 July 1911, BDOW, vii, 359, 336–38, 367, 345–46, 369, 349, 375 and 376, 358–59, 382, 383 and 384, 362–65, 386 and 387, 366–67, 395, 374–75, 409, 386; Bertie to Grey, 21 and 22 July 1911, FO/800/52.

2. For example, E. T. Raymond, Mr. Lloyd George, 142–45.

3. Grey to Lloyd George, 26 March, and Lloyd George note, 27 March 1924, LGP, G/8/10/1. Grey enclosed an account of the Agadir crisis for the Review of Reviews which he repeated in his memoirs, and Lloyd George minuted that it was "quite accurate." See also Viscount Grey, Twenty-Five Years: 1892–1916, 2 vols. (New York, 1925), i, 215–17; W. S. Churchill, The World Crisis (New York, 1923), 43; G. M. Trevelyan, Grey of Fallodon, 257; Lord Riddell, More Pages from My Diary 1908–1914, 20; Lloyd George, War Memoirs, i, 24–27.

adamant on this point on his eightieth birthday as he was in 1924, and remained convinced that he had helped avert war.[4]

The weeks preceding the crisis are not without significance. On 29 May, when members asked for a statement of official policy on the development of air power, Lloyd George warned the House of Commons that the government must be realistic and single-minded. Britain could not permit any nation to achieve a margin of superiority over her and the government would not initiate negotiations to outlaw the use of air power.[5] Little comfort here for Sir William Byles and his radical supporters. Then in June, at the Imperial Conference, Lloyd George continued to support schemes for closer imperial unity, and for the development of the "All-Red-Route" to link the Empire more effectively together.[6]

Problems of national and imperial security were therefore under review and coincided with the Coronation festivities and the Investiture of the Prince of Wales. Apart from the functions in Wales, Lloyd George was in London for the whole of July, a hot and heady month with temperatures close to 90°. It seems reasonable to suppose that in such an emotional atmosphere Lloyd George's patriotism was aroused.

He left London for Wales on 12 July but was back in the Commons on 17 July, and attended all four crucial cabinet meetings dealing with Morocco. Asquith convened the first of these on 4 July. Ministers agreed that Berlin intended to force acceptance of a revised international agreement on Morocco and secure her share, on the basis of the Bismarckian doctrine of *beati possidentes*.[7] The cabinet decided not to reply in kind and rejected a Foreign Office proposal to dispatch a warship to Agadir. Because of Britain's commercial and strategic interests in Morocco[8] and her treaty obligations to France they could not, however, allow the future of Morocco to be settled in negotiations *à trois*, involving

4. Interview with A. Beverley Baxter for *Sunday Express*, Jan. 1943, LGP, G/3/2/1.

5. Statement, 29 May 1911, *Parl. Deb.*, H. of C., xxvi, 702–703.

6. Imperial Conference, 16 June 1911, Cab 18/13A. Lloyd George attended only this session, devoted to treaties, shipping, and the "All Red Route."

7. Cabinet meeting, 4 July 1911, Cab 41/33/20; Sir A. Fitzroy, *Memoirs*, ii, 453; Nicolson to Grey, Grey to Bertie, Grey to de Salis, 4 July, and Nicolson to Hardinge, 5 July 1911, *BDOW*, vii, 354, 355, 356, and 359, 333–34 and 336–38.

8. British interests were defined as preventing a German port on the Mediterranean shore of Morocco, opposing fortified ports on any part of Morocco's coastline, and securing the Open Door for trade.

only France, Germany, and Spain. The cabinet instructed Grey to inform Ambassador Paul Cambon that while Britain would cooperate with France and honour her treaty obligations, they did not feel that the powers could restore the *status quo ante*. France might even be forced to recognize formally Germany's interest in Morocco. Lloyd George supported these decisions and claimed to have converted Grey away from the scheme to dispatch a warship to Agadir.[9] In any case he had no reason to be dissatisfied with this moderate response.

Grey reported to the cabinet on 8 July in reassuring terms.[10] He hoped that Franco-German conversations would achieve a satisfactory settlement. Germany would recognize France's special position in Morocco as one which permitted virtually complete control. In turn, Germany would receive innocuous compensation, preferably in equatorial Africa and specifically in the French Congo, rather than in Morocco itself.[11] Grey expected that Britain's commercial and strategic interests would be safeguarded, and that a partition of Morocco would be avoided.[12]

As the crisis developed, however, the foreign secretary, under increasing pressure from his officials, became gravely concerned, primarily about German intentions. The disturbing news of her excessive demands for the whole of the French Congo between the Sangha River and the sea,[13] necessitated a further cabinet meeting on 19 July.

The cabinet, while agreeing that Berlin's demands were unacceptable, refused to be stampeded into excessively provocative support for France.[14] Grey's colleagues urged in fact that France submit counter-proposals, offering compensation to Germany in the French Congo. Grey suggested that he propose a conference to

9. Scott diary, 22 July 1911, Scott Papers, Add. 50901.
10. Cabinet meeting, 8 July, Cab 41/33/21, Grey to Knollys, 5 July, FO/800/103, and Burns diary, 11 July 1911, Burns Papers, Add. 46333.
11. Grey to Bertie, 6 July, Bertie to Grey, 9 July, Goschen to Grey, 10 July, Grey to Bertie, 10 July, Bertie to Grey, 11 July, Goschen to Grey, 12 July, and Grey to Bertie, 13 July 1911, *BDOW*, vii, 363, 341–42, 366, 343–45, 367, 345–46, 368, 346–47, 369, 347–49, 373, 353–57, 375, 358, and 377, 359–60.
12. Grey to Bertie, 6 and 10 July, Bertie to Grey, 12 July, and Grey to Bertie, 12 and 13 July 1911, ibid., 363, 341–42, 368, 346–47, 372, 352–53, 375, 358, and 377, 359–60.
13. Bertie to Grey, 17 and 18 July 1911, FO/800/52 and *BDOW*, vii, 391 and 392, 370–73; Asquith to Grey, 18 July 1911, FO/800/100.
14. Cabinet meeting, 19 July 1911, Cab 41/33/22.

Germany, and warn Berlin that Britain would act to protect her interests should Germany refuse. Lord Loreburn vigorously opposed this scheme. He insisted that Britain's direct interests were insignificant and that Grey's proposal could lead to war.

The cabinet decided to delay an approach to Germany and to ascertain whether France would resist to the limit the admission of Germany under any circumstances into Morocco. Grey should point out to France that the cabinet did not regard a German foothold in Morocco as fatal to British interests and certainly not as a *casus belli*. He should also inform Cambon that the government would favour a conference if the Franco-German negotiations failed, and would work in concert with France should that conference convene.[15] Significantly, it was not Lloyd George but Loreburn, supported by Morley, Harcourt, and McKenna, who had opposed the moves which might result in a confrontation with Germany.[16]

Grey was distinctly unhappy. Fifteen days had elapsed, he told Asquith, since his conversation with Ambassador Metternich on 4 July.[17] Yet he had received no indication that Germany recognized Britain's position or was impressed in any way with his communication. Grey feared that Germany, assuming that Britain knew of her demands on France, would feel free to pursue her policy should Britain remain silent. As a result, the Franco-German conversations would collapse, and further developments at Agadir would make it more difficult for Germany ultimately to retract and accept a reasonable settlement. Grey also expressed apprehension about the prospect of embarrassing questions in the House of Commons on 25 July. He insisted that the cabinet, at its meeting on Friday, 21 July, must authorize him to approach Germany afresh unless the situation had clarified itself. It must be impressed upon Berlin that if the negotiations with France failed Britain would have to participate in further discussions. Moreover, unless Germany kept Britain fully informed of the situation at Agadir, Britain must dispatch ships to raise the blockade on

15. Grey to Bertie, 19 July, and Bertie to Grey, 20 July 1911, *BDOW*, vii, 396 and 397, 376, and 403, 380–81.

16. Scott diary, 20 July 1911, Scott Papers, Add. 50901; J. L. Hammond, *C. P. Scott of the Manchester Guardian*, 153–54; Morley to Burns, 14 June 1916, Burns Papers, Add. 46283.

17. Grey to Asquith, 19 July, FO/800/100, *BDOW*, vii, 399, 377–78, Grey to Bertie, 20 July 1911, FO/800/52, and *BDOW*, vii, 402 and 405, 377–80 and 382.

information and safeguard her interests. Meanwhile, he awaited a reply from Paris.

The rather abrupt French response of 20 July denied that the negotiations with Germany had collapsed. France accepted the idea of a conference should these negotiations fail but, while promising to respect the economic rights of all powers, would not concede any territorial concessions to Germany whatsoever in Morocco. On the same day *The Times* published an exaggerated version of Germany's demands on France.

With this information before them the cabinet met on 21 July.[18] The cabinet instructed Grey to inform Metternich, with regret, that seventeen days had passed without a German response to Britain's enquiries of 4 July. Grey should point out that while Britain desired a Franco-German agreement providing Germany with compensation in West Africa or the Congo, they could not permit a settlement awarding Germany compensation in Morocco without British participation in the negotiations.

Grey informed Metternich of these conclusions that same afternoon.[19] He described Germany's demands for the French Congo as unacceptable, and warned that her activities at Agadir were most disturbing. They committed Germany more deeply in Morocco, made her withdrawal more difficult, and might jeopardize British interests. Consequently, should the Franco-German negotiations fail, Britain would not be able to stand by as a disinterested spectator. Her lengthy silence did not imply any indifference. She must become a party to further negotiations and to any ultimate settlement.

Before the cabinet meeting on the morning of 21 July Lloyd George, encouraged by Churchill, decided to attempt to help clarify Britain's position. Churchill described him as wavering up to that point,[20] but Britain had been firm with France and could not be less so with Germany. He attended the cabinet and then consulted Asquith and Grey,[21] probably after Grey's conversation

18. Cabinet meeting 21 July, Asquith Papers, file 6, Bertie to Grey, 20 July, *BDOW*, vii, 401 and 403, 378–81, and Burns diary, 21 July 1911, Burns Papers, Add. 46333. Bertie's dispatch was not printed for the cabinet. Burns's record of the meeting makes no reference to Morocco.

19. Grey to Goschen, 21 July 1911, *BDOW*, vii, 411, 390–91.

20. Churchill, *World Crisis*, 42–43.

21. In his memoirs and in the interview with Beverley Baxter (see note 4), Lloyd George recorded that he consulted Asquith, who approved of his draft

with Metternich, on the text of a statement he had drafted and intended to insert in his speech scheduled for that evening.[22] The foreign secretary and the prime minister saw some value in the government breaking its silence publicly, for both domestic and European consumption.[23] Asquith's statement to the House of Commons on 6 July remained unsupported and the Mansion House banquet was an appropriate forum. Moreover, until Berlin responded officially they could not reveal the content of the cabinet's policy as outlined to Metternich that afternoon. Consequently, Grey and Asquith went over Lloyd George's draft with him, and the three together agreed on the final version. This careful redrafting resulted in Lloyd George arriving more than half an hour late at the Mansion House.

Lloyd George, reading the appropriate sections from a prepared text, made no reference to any specific issue or foreign country with the exception of the United States.[24] He praised Grey for his conduct of Anglo-American relations and for establishing procedures to settle future disputes "with our kinsmen across the Atlantic." Britain, he said, sought only peace and prosperity for herself, the former being the essential precondition of the latter. War was not imminent, but friction existed and all issues should be settled in a peaceful manner. He reminded the European nations of their debt to Britain. She had, in the past, "redeemed Continental nations, who are sometimes too apt to forget the service, from overwhelming disaster and even national extinction."

Lloyd George then warned that where national honour and interests were involved, Britain, whatever party was in power, would not refuse the challenge of war. He would make great

---

and then sent for Grey. The foreign secretary gave his full consent to "every word of my draft." In fact, they "were glad to have me do it," and warned that Germany would protest and attempt to get him dismissed.

22. Arthur Murray was adamant on this point: "it was Lloyd George himself who *of his own accord* drafted his Mansion House speech and then submitted it to Grey and Asquith for their approval." (Murray diary, 17 Jan. 1912, Elibank Papers, 8814, folio 59/60; A. C. Murray, *Master and Brother: Murrays of Elibank*, 84–85.)

23. Riddell, *More Pages from My Diary*, 20–21; O. J. Hale, *Publicity and Diplomacy* (Gloucester, Mass., 1964), 387–90.

24. Notes for Grey's statement to Parliament, Nov. 1911, FO/800/93; Grey's speech, 27 Nov. 1911, *Parl. Deb.*, H. of C., xxxii, 49–50; *Manchester Guardian*, 22 July 1911, LGP, C/35/1/17; Bertie to Grey, 21 Dec. 1911, FO/800/52.

sacrifices to maintain peace and would contemplate war only over questions of "the greatest national moment, but if a situation were to be forced upon us, in which peace would only be preserved by the surrender of the great and benevolent position that Britain has won by centuries of heroism and achievement, by allowing Britain to be treated when her interests were vitally affected as if she were of no account in the Cabinet of nations, then I say emphatically that peace at that price would be a humiliation intolerable for a great country like ours to endure. National honour is no party question. Security of our great international trade is no party question." In conclusion, and to balance these sombre yet stirring phrases, Lloyd George spoke optimistically of a further period of peace and prosperity.

The Mansion House speech represented official policy even though the cabinet as a whole had not given prior approval. Grey had admitted to Asquith on 19 July that he did not relish the prospect of questions in Parliament. He was determined, in the difficult political situation at home, to avert Unionist censure as well as undermine radical criticism,[25] and put an end to Loreburn's opposition in the cabinet. He and Asquith welcomed a declaration which would earn the applause of the press, receive broad support, and maintain the nation's patriotic unity at the level induced by the Coronation festivities in May. A speech delivered by Lloyd George and devoted to nationalist themes, which also reiterated the government's desire for peace, might have the desired effect. The Unionists would applaud and Loreburn, it was hoped, would be deflated.

Lloyd George's intention was to convince the nation that the Liberal government, determined and united, was acutely conscious of its international responsibilities in the current situation. He did not want the Unionists to be able to charge the government with irresponsible weakness, but was also aware that pacific phrases alone were not likely to mollify the radicals and appease Loreburn. He was ready therefore to court, for example, C. P. Scott.

As for Europe, the speech was unquestionably aimed principally at Germany for she had been less cooperative than France. German reactions to the speech, however, carried in the press,

25. Only one observer, Alfred Lyttleton, stated that the government approached the Unionist leaders and secured their support in the event of war with Germany. (Scott diary, 23 Oct. 1914, Scott Papers, Add. 50901.) *The Observer*, 23 July, praised the speech.

gave the impression that it was excessively Germanophobe in tone. Indeed, Grey subsequently used these responses to justify the speech. Yet the evidence is clear; Britain was asserting pressure on Germany publicly to promote a settlement, protect British interests, and preserve peace. If Kiderlen-Wächter came to heel the settlement would be that much more favourable to France and thus strengthen the Entente.[26] Grey had set 21 July as a sort of deadline for a decisive step. The date of Lloyd George's speech was scheduled well in advance. Convenience and necessity coincided.

However, French policy also had given cause for concern; the reliability of her government was questionable. A public statement might both warn and encourage France, by making it clear that she must not deceive and yet could rely on Britain's Liberal administration.

Lloyd George wasted no time in seeing Scott. Arthur Murray recorded on 22 July, "I breakfasted today with Lloyd George. The latter was engaged in an endeavour to inculcate a little commonsense and patriotism in the head of Scott."[27] Britain must, Lloyd George argued, be a party to any Moroccan settlement which changed the status quo. She must also fulfil her treaty obligations to France and protect her rights and interests. While less than clear as to which British rights and interests would justify a war with Germany, Lloyd George insisted that they must prevent the creation of a great naval base across Britain's trade routes. A Franco-German war, Lloyd George suggested, would probably result in a German victory, the levying of a huge indemnity, and the demise of France as a great power. Prussia, he feared, sought European hegemony. The kaiser had behaved "like a cad" and the German chancellor was a "coarse bully." They were mutually delinquent and suitable comrades for each other.

26. P. Cambon to de Selves, 22 and 26 July 1911, *DDF*, 2, xiv, 94, 106; R. A. Cosgrove, "A Note on Lloyd George's speech at the Mansion House, 21 July 1911," 698–701.

27. Murray diary, 22 July 1911, Elibank Papers, 8814, folio 28; H. S. Weinroth, "The British Radicals and the Balance of Power, 1902–1914," 653–82; Scott diary, 22 July 1911, Scott Papers, Add. 50901; Hammond, *Scott*, 154–63. Asquith also met with Scott, and Grey followed up on 25 July. (Grey to Scott, 24 July, Scott Papers, Add. 50908, and Scott diary, 25 July 1911, ibid., Add. 50901.) See also D. Ayerst, *Guardian: Biography of a Newspaper* (London, 1971), 366–68.

As Scott noted, Lloyd George was "not immune from the microbe of Germanophobia."

After assuring Scott that Asquith would resist the anti-German tendencies of the Foreign Office, Lloyd George defended Grey as frank and moderate. The foreign secretary, concerned for British rights and interests, had been firm also with France and expected Germany to receive compensation. Indeed, Lloyd George argued, Grey welcomed Germany playing a greater role in Africa and even in Southern Morocco, providing Britain received compensation in the Near East or Demaraland. It would help divert Germany from Dreadnought construction. Loreburn, in contrast, was petulant, unreasonable, and irritating. The government, Lloyd George suggested, while not now a "Liberal League preserve," must demonstrate that it had stood up to Germany and accepted its responsibilities. It must be a credible as well as a pacific administration.

The *coup d'Agadir* generated a high degree of cooperation between Lloyd George and Grey. The latter welcomed it and Lloyd George positively thrived on it. Along with Asquith, Haldane, and Churchill, they formed a controlling directorate. The cabinet, isolated from vital information, apparently discussed the crisis only twice more and then dispersed on vacation.[28] Grey, explaining policy with more skill than frankness, was able to neutralize criticism. Lord Loreburn made the most persistent attempts to oppose decisions he feared would lead to war, and to remedy the ill effects created at the Mansion House.[29] He could

28. Asquith reports, 1 and 7 Aug., of cabinet meetings, 31 July, 7 Aug. 1911, Cab 41/33/23 and 24. Lloyd George attended both meetings. On 31 July the cabinet discussed a report of Kiderlen-Wächter's uncompromising attitude. They agreed that if the negotiations failed Grey should summon a conference. On 7 August, Grey reported that the Franco-German negotiations seemed more hopeful and that he had rejected the idea of sending a warship to Agadir. Fitzroy, noting the War Office's fear lest Germany attack France and a British counter-stroke be delayed through lack of preparations and respect for constitutional procedures, recorded that a committee of the cabinet, including Lloyd George, Grey, Asquith, and Haldane, handled this problem on 14 August. Asquith, however, disagreed with Haldane's interpretation of their conclusions and preferred the cabinet to decide on the matter. (Fitzroy, *Memoirs*, II, 456, 461–62.) According to *The Times* the cabinet also met on 3 and 22 August with Lloyd George present on both occasions.

29. Morley to Asquith, 27 July, A. J. Marder, *From the Dreadnought to Scapa Flow*, I, 241, and Loreburn to Grey, 27 and 28 July 1911, FO/800/99. Morley likened Lloyd George's speech to that of de Gramont on 6 July 1870.

not, however, undermine the control of those he derided as the "five amateurs." He urged Scott therefore to see Lloyd George and "have it out with him." [30] Tyrrell, on the other hand, was eloquent in his priase:

> Don't ever forget to teach your children to keep alive the memory of Lloyd George who by his timely speech has saved the peace of Europe and our good name. I shall never forget the service rendered by him. His courage was great as he risked his position with the people who have mainly made him. His cooperation with the Chief is delightful to watch. I breakfasted with him last week and I was much struck by his "flair" in foreign politics. From your and my point of view he is as sound as a bell and it hardly needed the Germans to undeceive him. [31]

These were extraordinarily difficult months. The Mansion House speech had clouded the atmosphere rather than cleared the air. [32] The German government, in contrast to the French, regarded it as provocative, menacing, and irresponsibly calculated to produce a deterioration in Anglo-German and Franco-German relations. [33] Both Grey and Kiderlen-Wächter stood firm, and officials in London were unwilling to dismiss the possibility that Admiral Tirpitz might launch a surprise naval attack, "a bolt from the blue," against the fleet. [34] Lloyd George was declared *persona non grata* in Berlin. He expected the German government to

30. Loreburn to Grey, 26 Aug., and Grey to Loreburn, 30 Aug. 1911, FO/800/99; Scott diary, 6–8 Sept. 1911, Scott Papers, Add. 50901.

31. Tyrrell to Spring-Rice, 1 Aug. 1911, S. Gwynn, ed., *The Letters... of Sir Cecil Spring-Rice*, II, 163. Nicolson, describing the Mansion House speech as "no sudden inspiration but a carefully thought out one," gave clear if more reserved approval. (Nicolson to Sir T. Cartwright, 24 July 1911, *BDOW*, VII, 418, 396–97.)

32. Grey to Goschen, 24, 25, and 27 July, *BDOW*, VII, 417, 419 and 430, 394–96, 397–99 and 411–13, Goschen to Grey, 26 and 27 July, 16, 18, 25, and 31 Aug., and 1 Sept. 1911, ibid., 424, 428, 476, 481, 518, 523 and 524, 402–404, 407–10, 450–52, 454–55, 487–88 and 491–93, and note by Sir John French, n.d., ibid., 490, 462–63; Cab 37/107/80–110; P. Cambon to de Selves, 27 July, and P. Cambon to J. Cambon, 27 July 1911, *DDF*, 2, XIV, 113, 117.

33. Goschen to Grey, 16 Aug. 1911, *BDOW*, VII, 476, 450–52, and Cab 37/107/105.

34. Nicolson to Grey, 24 July, FO/800/93, Grey to McKenna, 24 July, *BDOW*, VII, 637, 625, C. L. Ottley to Churchill, 2 Sept., LGP, C/3/15/9, and H. Montgomery to Grey, 16 Sept. 1911, FO/800/93; Churchill, *World Crisis*, 47–48.

attempt to force his resignation, as they had that of Théophile Delcassé, the French foreign minister, in 1905, but he felt secure in the support of his senior colleagues.[35]

The outcome of the Franco-German negotiations remained the central issue; specifically, the extent of German compensation in tropical Africa and elsewhere in return for the recognition of France's exclusive position in Morocco.[36] The status of Tangier, the question of economic concessions, and the problem of satisfaction for Spain[37] helped prolong the crisis through an especially trying phase in mid-September and on into early November. Grey never eliminated the possibility of war, and was concerned that Germany, in the event, be clearly identified as the aggressor.[38] Moreover, the Foreign Office, the War Office, with Lord Kitchener dissenting, and the French seemed reasonably confident of the outcome of a war.

Churchill and Lloyd George were worried, however, because McKenna, at the Admiralty, seemed "as full of cocksureness as his Admiral is deficient in imagination."[39] They chased every rumour: a rise in the price of flour in Germany; the recall of German naval reservists visiting England; Belgian and German troop

35. Lloyd George to his wife, July 1911, Morgan, *Family Letters*, 155–56; P. Cambon to J. Cambon, 30 July 1911, *DDF*, 2, xiv, 129; Bertie to Grey, 21 Dec. 1911, FO/800/52; S. W. Roskill, *Hankey, Man of Secrets*, i, 101; R. S. Churchill, *Winston S. Churchill*, ii, 524–25. Baron Stumm wanted a British leader to visit Berlin, but said that Lloyd George would not be welcome. There is evidence that Lloyd George, embarrassed by this situation, tried to evade responsibility for the speech and show himself free of Germanophobia. (French chargé (Berlin) to de Selves, 10 Nov. 1911, *DDF*, 3, i, 82.)

36. Grey to Bertie, 30 and 31 July, 16, 21, and 23 Aug., and 4 Sept. 1911, *BDOW*, vii, 443, 424, 475, 450, 487, 460, 511 and 512, 483–84, and 531, 503–504; Grey to A. Chamberlain, 17 Aug. 1911, ibid., 477, 452.

37. Knollys to Grey, 31 July, FO/800/103, Grey to Bertie, 11 Sept., *BDOW*, vii, 543, 523, Grey to Carnegie, 30 Oct., ibid., 611, 597, Grey to Bertie, 8 Nov. 1911, FO/800/52 and *BDOW*, vii, 631, 621.

38. Grey to Bertie, 28 July and 4 Sept., FO/800/52, Haldane to Spender, 27 Aug., Spender Papers, Add. 46390, Churchill to Lloyd George, 14 Sept., LGP, C/3/13/11, Nicolson to Buchanan, 12 Sept., *BDOW*, vii, 546, 525, Nicolson to Grey, 2 Nov., ibid., 617, 602, Grey to Bertie, 8 and 20 Sept., FO/800/52, and Bertie to Grey, 31 July 1911, *BDOW*, vii, 447, 426; H. Nicolson, *Sir Arthur Nicolson, First Lord Carnock* (London, 1930), 348.

39. Churchill to Lloyd George, 31 Aug. and 4, 5, and 14 Sept., Churchill to Asquith, 13 Sept., and Churchill to McKenna, 13 Sept. 1911, LGP, C/3/15/8, 9, and 11; Churchill, *Winston S. Churchill*, ii, 525–34; Haldane to Grey, 11 Sept. 1911, FO/800/102; Marder, *Dreadnought to Scapa Flow*, i, 241–45; Buchanan to Grey, 3 Sept. 1911, *BDOW*, vii, 501, 473.

concentrations; and the closing by Germany of the frontier with Belgium. Lloyd George and Churchill questioned whether Belgium was reliable and what the Russian response would be to a German attack on France. They debated strategy, in concert with Henry Wilson, director of military operations, eyed the City, and worried whether food supplies were adequate in the event of war to avert civil unrest. The public temper caused them great concern and not the least of Lloyd George's tasks was to remove the threat of a railway strike late in August. Churchill attributed this menace to German gold and Lloyd George received lavish praise from Asquith and the king.[40]

On 23 August, the ruling quintet, with McKenna and the service experts in attendance, met to review the situation, determine Britain's role in the event of her intervention in a continental war, and resolve the differences between the Admiralty and the War Office.[41] What claims Lloyd George still had to innocence were ended; he had mastered the brief on foreign policy. He was also receiving an education from Asquith in how to circumvent difficult colleagues.

The meeting ruled essentially in favour of the War Office. As the decisive act to defend France against German aggression, launched through Belgian territory, Britain would mobilize on the same day as France and Germany, and dispatch probably six divisions and one cavalry division to France immediately on the outbreak of war. The Admiralty would ensure the safe transportation of the expeditionary force to France and protect Britain against invasion.

40. Fitzroy, *Memoirs*, II, 461–62; Asquith report, 7 Aug. 1911, Cab. 41/33/24; Asquith to Lloyd George, 20 Aug., and the king to Lloyd George, 20 Aug. 1911, LGP, C/6/11/9 and C/5/6/1. Dame Margaret's letters refer exclusively to the railway strike. (Dame Margaret to Lloyd George, 20 and 21 Aug. 1911, LGP, I/1/2/13 and 14.) See also A. Chamberlain, *Politics from Inside*, 330, 346, 353, 360–61.

41. CID, 23 Aug., Cab 38/19/49, Wilson diary, 10 Aug., Sir C. E. Callwell, *Field Marshal Sir Henry Wilson: His Life and Diaries*, 2 vols. (London, 1927), I, 98–100, and Brig.-Gen. Sir G. N. Nicholson memorandum, 6 Nov. 1911, *BDOW*, VII, 639, 626–29. Crewe, Morley, and Harcourt were excluded, presumably because of their predictable support for the Admiralty and opposition to Grey's policy. Perhaps, however, they had already left London. (Hankey to Fisher, 24 Aug. 1911, Marder, *Dreadnought to Scapa Flow*, I, 392–93; Fitzroy, *Memoirs*, II, 461–62; Lord Hankey, *The Supreme Command 1914–1918*, 2 vols. (London, 1961), I, 78–82; Roskill, *Hankey*, I, 101–102; and *Esher Journals*, III, 74.) Esher noted the presence of the CID secretary, "Heaton I think his name." (Scott diary, 4 May 1914, Scott Papers, Add. 50901.)

No one in attendance could possibly have harboured any doubts that, as a result of the Anglo-French staff talks, joint planning was well advanced and in progress. To what precise degree Lloyd George, his colleagues, and perhaps even Henry Wilson himself, understood French strategy, all the implications of the staff talks, and the precise role of the expeditionary force in France remains in doubt.[42] The discussion of France's defensive strategy revealed that much. Moreover, hostility toward McKenna did not help Lloyd George or Churchill to comprehend the nuances of the policy they supported. The basic plan, however, was clear and no words of alarm, criticism, or restraint passed Lloyd George's lips during the whole discussion.

He asked McKenna about the possible cooperation of the French fleet, but concentrated on Henry Wilson's brilliant exposition. The Belgian response to a German attack on France was not predictable, but Lloyd George agreed with Henry Wilson that the Belgian army, even if it did not attack the flank of the German invading force, would be a valuable asset to the French. The Germans would be compelled to make provision against a possible Belgian attack, especially if France repulsed the invasion and Belgium anticipated a German defeat. Henry Wilson assured him that the French staff were excellent, their mobilization plans were perfect,[43] and that, although the Belgians wavered between France and Germany, they would resist the invader.

Lloyd George then turned to Russia's role. Why had she a mere forty divisions concentrated against Germany; was she weak, for example financially; and why, despite forces totalling three to four million men, was Russia so incompetent militarily? Henry Wilson replied that even if Britain provided the necessary shipping Russia would not send a single division to France. Lloyd George's final comment challenged a decision of the 1908

42. Henry Wilson was in Paris on 20 and 21 July. The implications of Joffre's offensive strategy did not become apparent until late August. In so far as Henry Wilson failed to scrutinize French planning, or was misled, he could not instruct the CID with complete accuracy. Alternatively, to the extent that he understood the implications for French strategy of General Michel's dismissal, he was less than frank. (War Office memorandum, 21 Aug., and Bertie to Grey, 25 Aug. and 8 Sept. 1911, *BDOW*, VII, 640, 629–32, 641, 632–34 and 644, 635–37; S. R. Williamson, *The Politics of Grand Strategy*, 126–30, 174–78, 187–93.)

43. Other assessments of the French army were invariably encouraging. (Nicolson to Buchanan, 12 Sept., *BDOW*, VII, 546, 525, and Wilson diary, 11 Sept. 1911, Callwell, *Henry Wilson*, I, 103.)

CID sub-committee; it was not necessary, he suggested, to retain two divisions at home in the early stages of a war, while the Territorial Army grouped itself.

Lloyd George left immediately for Wales.[44] Grey promised to summon him if the situation deteriorated, and he kept in touch with Churchill. Russia's capabilities and Belgium's intentions continued to plague him: "We ought to know what Russia is capable of before we trust the fortunes of Europe to the hazard. We are even now almost at the point whence we cannot recede. 150,000 British troops supporting the Belgian army on the German flank would be a much more formidable proposition than the same number of troops extending the French line. It would force the Germans to detach at least 500,000 men to protect their lines of communication. The Anglo-Belgian army numbering 400,000 men would pivot on the great fort of Antwerp. The command of the sea would make that position impregnable."[45] Could they not, therefore, sound out Belgium and cultivate her fear of Germany as a European and imperial predator?

Lloyd George worried also lest Britain's own preparations should prove inadequate,[46] but on one point he was firm. "People think that because I was a pro-Boer I am anti-war in general; and that I should faint at the mention of a cannon. I am not against war a bit."[47]

It is difficult to assess Lloyd George's calculations about the probability of a German attack on France. At times, in late August and early September, he seemed optimistic. The crisis was "still trembling in the balance" but a settlement was likely and, indeed, he was "prepared for a run on the Continent. Nothing can possibly happen in the next three weeks. The negotiations are safe to drag for some time; and, even if they fail, the resources of diplomacy are not exhausted. I wish we could accidentally find ourselves in Paris."[48] At others, blaming Kiderlen-Wächter, the Junker caste, and German public opinion rather than the kaiser,

44. L. Masterman, *C. F. G. Masterman*, 199–215.

45. Lloyd George to Churchill, 25 Aug., 1911, LGP, C/3/15/6.

46. Lloyd George to Grey, 1 Sept. 1911, FO/800/101, and *BDOW*, vii, 642, 634.

47. Masterman, *C. F. G. Masterman*, 199–215.

48. Lloyd George to Churchill, 3 Sept., Admiralty 116/3474, and Lloyd George to Elibank, 5 Sept. 1911, Elibank Papers, 8802, folio 311. Churchill left for Paris on 5 September.

he seemed to feel that war was "an increasing probability." He found it difficult to follow the debate in Berlin but was sure

> that the Germans mean to squeeze as much out of France as they possibly can. With that object in view, they will keep her in doubt up to the last moment as to their ultimate intentions. They will also seek to weaken her in advance by making it doubtful to her whether Russia will give her material support in the event of a breakdown. But, if France remains firm and declines to give in and shows an evident determination to risk the worst, either alone or with our aid, I have my doubts as to whether the Germans have now quite made up their minds to insist upon their demands up to the point of declaring war. That does not necessarily spell peace. Nations drift into war without any clear conscious intention, by gradually floating into positions from which they cannot withdraw. The odds are in favour of peace, in my judgement. All the same, even if the chances of war were only one out of twenty, the consequences are so great, that we ought to take every precaution that is available to safeguard ourselves against disaster.[49]

Lloyd George regarded Alexander Isvolsky, Russia's ambassador to France, as thoroughly untrustworthy, and confirmed that

> I have been quite unhappy about the position of Russia from the start. . . . I have had serious doubts as to whether they would come in, if they possibly could avoid it. We have substantial interests in Morocco; they have none. Besides, they have just had as much war as they can stand, for some years at least. Their internal situation is not very satisfactory. But, even if they stand out altogether, their abstention would not be necessarily fatal to success. But what might be fatal would be an assurance from Russia to Germany that under no conditions would she intervene. As long as the attitude of Russia is doubtful, the Germans must reserve at least a half a million of men to watch the Russian frontier and prepare for eventualities; but, if Germany knew for certain that in no contingency would Russia take a hand, she might then hurl 20 more Divisions on to the luckless French frontier. This might decide the event. So, if Russian cooperation cannot be secured, it is of the first importance that her attitude should remain in doubt. She would thus serve the double

49. Lloyd George to Churchill, 3 Sept. 1911, Admiralty 116/3474.

*purpose of keeping Austria out of the scrimmage and at the same time remaining as a menace on Germany's eastern frontier.*[50]

Such attitudes won him Unionist approval[51] and caused Arthur Nicolson to describe him, along with Haldane and Churchill, as "perfectly ready—I might almost say eager—to face all possible eventualities. These three have thoroughly grasped the point that it is not merely Morocco which is at stake. In fact, I believe they were a little disappointed that war with Germany did not occur. Winston came to see me every morning and Lloyd George came once, and I was struck by the determination of both of them, not to permit Germany to assume the role of bully and at their belief that the present moment was an exceedingly favourable one to open hostilities."[52]

While Churchill pursued the idea of a triple alliance with France and Russia, to protect the independence of Belgium, Holland, and Denmark,[53] Lloyd George explored the possibility of mediation by President Taft of the United States, who was willing to arbitrate.[54] Grey and his officials were not enthusiastic, however, despite the possible moral and tactical advantages accruing to France from a German refusal to cooperate. They still preferred to see a Franco-German settlement or, failing that, a conference of the Algeciras signatories.

By 8 September Grey realized that the Franco-German negotiations were entering an especially difficult phase. He asked Lloyd George to confer with him on or before 13 September and they agreed to meet in Aberdeen. Lloyd George travelled via London and went over the military situation with Henry Wilson. Ministers

50. Ibid.

51. Curzon to Bonar Law, 28 Nov. 1911, Bonar Law Papers, 24/4/81.

52. Nicolson to Hardinge, 17 Aug. and 14 Sept. 1911, Cosgrove, 698–701; Nicolson, *Carnock*, 347–48.

53. Churchill to Grey, 30 Aug., Churchill to Lloyd George, 31 Aug. and 4 and 5 Sept., and Grey to Churchill, 30 Aug. 1911, LGP, C/3/15/7, 8, and 9, and C/24/2/37; Churchill, *Winston S. Churchill*, II, 529–30; Wilson diary, 28 Aug. and 4 and 5 Sept. 1911, Callwell, *Henry Wilson*, I, 102–103. Churchill saw Belgium's political as well as military value. German violation of her neutrality would provide an unequivocal and popular *casus belli*.

54. Churchill to Lloyd George, and Grey to Lloyd George, 5 Sept., LGP, C/3/15/9, and C/4/14/5, Scott diary, 6–8 Sept., Scott Papers, Add. 50901, Grey to Bertie, 8 Sept., FO/800/52, and Grey to Bertie, 11 and 20 Sept. 1911, *BDOW*, VII, 544 and 561, 523–24 and 542.

and others gathered at Balmoral in what seemed to be a critical atmosphere.[55] The problems discussed were predictable: what were Germany's real intentions; would Russia aid France; and was the fleet ready and the Admiralty in good hands? Arthur Balfour assured the government of his support and Count Benckendorff, the Russian ambassador, confirmed that Russia would aid France in the event of German aggression.[56] Churchill, back from Paris, recorded that "Lloyd George... electrified their majesties by observing that he thought it would be a great pity if war did not come now."[57] Lloyd George reported to Murray of Elibank, "I must be back in town the following Monday morning. Grey is anxious I should be there then. He suggests that I should spend Sunday with him at Fallodon and then travel back by the night express to London. Morocco is dragging painfully, but whether towards peace or war the devil alone can tell—and he means to keep it to himself just awhile."[58] In fact the tension relaxed in late September as a Franco-German settlement appeared likely. The following month, although not devoid of irritants, yielded the anticipated solution.

Asquith and Grey could not, however, escape the political consequences of their conduct.[59] As the evidence filtered in, Grey's

55. Wilson diary, 11 Sept., Callwell, *Henry Wilson*, i, 103, Grey to Lloyd George, 5 Sept., LGP, C/4/14/4, Grey (at Balmoral) to Private Secretary (FO), n.d., FO/800/101, E. Marsh to Lloyd George, 13 Sept., LGP, C/3/15/10, Nicolson to Grey, 12 and 19 Sept., FO/800/93, and Asquith to Harcourt, 10 Sept. 1911, Harcourt Papers, box 27.

56. Nicolson to Grey, 12 Sept. 1911, FO/800/93; Fitzroy, *Memoirs*, ii, 470–71; Lloyd George to Churchill, 15 Sept. 1911, Churchill, *Winston S. Churchill*, ii, 534–35; McKenna to Grey and reply, 15 Sept., and Grey to Nicholson, 17 Sept. 1911, *BDOW*, vii, 645, 646, and 647, 638–39.

57. Churchill to his wife, 24 Sept. 1911, Churchill, *Winston S. Churchill*, ii, 529.

58. Lloyd George to Elibank, 15 Sept. 1911, Elibank Papers, 8802, folio 211. Lloyd George left Balmoral on 18 September, toured with Elibank, met Asquith at Archerfield and Grey at Fallodon on the weekend of 23–24 September, and returned to London on September 26.

59. Hammond, *Scott*, 164–65; T. P. Conwell-Evans, *Foreign Policy From a Back Bench* (London, 1932), 56–82; C. A. Cline, "E. D. Morel and the Crusade against the Foreign Office," *Journal of Modern History*, 39, no. 2 (1967), 126–37; J. A. Murray, "Foreign Policy Debated," in L. P. Wallace and W. C. Askew, *Power, Public Opinion and Diplomacy*, (Durham, N.C., 1959), 140–71; and Weinroth, "Balance of Power," 653–82. Asquith, to some, was already a pathetic figure. "What ails you at poor Asquith. No gossip reached us here. We have not even been told that he was drunk at the Conference." (G. Murray to Russell, 22 Aug. 1911, Bertrand Russell Papers.)

critics charged him with practising dangerous brinkmanship, and irresponsibly straining Anglo-German relations. Furthermore, the hostility of France's premier, Joseph Caillaux, seemed to demonstrate that Grey had actually bungled relations with France even while creating a sinister compact with her. The Ententes with Russia and France were, they suggested, obligatory alliances, encircling Germany and endangering peace. Grey's policy would preface a renewed bout of armaments expenditure.

Grey was indicted on another account; the Ententes were sordid, imperialist bargains intended to deprive Germany of legitimate opportunities, and to oppress the peoples of Egypt, Morocco, and especially Persia. Grey's opponents demanded, therefore, a far greater degree of parliamentary and cabinet control of foreign policy. To this end, two Liberal MPs, Noel Buxton and Arthur Ponsonby, established the Foreign Affairs Committee of the Liberal Party in January 1912.[60] At the height of the campaign some called for Grey's resignation, but only a minority hoped to bring the foreign secretary down.

Obviously Grey would have to mend his ways in cabinet and face an enquiry. Lord Loreburn, Lewis Harcourt, Morley, McKenna, now home secretary, John Burns, and possibly Lord Crewe intended to challenge his conduct.[61] In such a situation, the sustained support of Asquith, Lloyd George, and Haldane was vital.

The confrontation took place during the first two weeks of November 1911. The *enragés* protested specifically that the Anglo-French staff talks were both unconstitutional, having taken place without the prior knowledge and consent of the cabinet, and dangerous.[62] Asquith agreed that at no time had the cabinet either accepted a plan to land troops in Europe or decided whether to render military or naval assistance to France in the event of a war with Germany. He conceded that the cabinet had not

60. Ponsonby Papers, box 1911–14. H. Massingham, C. P. Scott, A. G. Gardiner in the *Daily News*, the *Labour Leader*, and L. Wolf in the *Illustrated Graphic* supported them.

61. Marder, *Dreadnought to Scapa Flow*, I, 249–51.

62. Asquith report, 2 Nov., Cab 41/33/28, Grey to Morley, 3 Nov. 1911, Burns Papers, Add. 46283, and Wilson diary, Nov. 1911, Callwell, *Henry Wilson*, I, 106–107; Fitzroy, *Memoirs*, II, 466–68; Hammond, *Scott*, 144; Scott diary, 3 Nov. 1911 and 23 Oct. 1914, Scott Papers, Add. 50901. Hammond and Fitzroy noted a cabinet meeting on 20 October. Esher recorded that fifteen ministers had challenged Grey. (*Esher Journals*, III, 74.)

been informed until the end of October of the military and naval preparations made that summer to meet the contingency of war.

The group defending Grey, citing Campbell-Bannerman's involvement in 1906, nevertheless insisted that cabinet control of policy remained intact. They denied that France assumed or had any reason to believe the staff talks constituted a binding commitment. The conversations, however, must continue since British policy was not founded on the neutrality and nonintervention principle. The government must plan in order to be able to resist Germany if she broke off negotiations in any dispute and attacked France. On the other hand, if France were in the wrong, refused to negotiate, and attacked Germany, Britain would not intervene.

The cabinet agreed finally that staff talks, envisaging concerted action with a foreign power, could not be entered into without its prior consent, and must not commit Britain in any way to naval or military intervention.[63] Grey's opponents had preserved their political virginity and had apparently affirmed the supremacy of the cabinet. In fact the deed was done, and the Anglo-French staff talks continued until 1914.[64]

Lloyd George was not as prominent as either Haldane or Asquith in the defence of Grey. In the parliamentary and public debate, he remained silent, a prudent if not gallant course. He was also the least embarrassed of the Agadir junta by the cabinet inquiry. His sympathies, however, clearly lay with the foreign secretary. Loreburn assumed that Lloyd George would join Grey if he resigned,[65] and other evidence, while not entirely convincing, points in the same direction. Arthur Murray noted that H. W. Massingham, editor of the *Nation*,

> to succeed in blackening Grey in the eyes of Liberals must
> disassociate him from the pro-Boer element in the Cabinet, and that
> with this object he was endeavouring to make people think that he

63. Burns diary, 15 Nov. 1911, Burns Papers, Add. 46333; Scott diary, 23 Oct. 1914, Scott Papers, Add. 50901; Nicolson to Grey, 20 Nov. 1911, *BDOW*, VII, 617, 602; Harcourt note, 29 Nov. 1911, Burns Papers, Add. 46308.

64. Scott diary, 3 and 4 May and 23 Oct. 1914, Scott Papers, Add. 50901.

65. Scott diary, 1 and 2 Dec. 1911, ibid., Add. 50901. Loreburn speculated on possible successors to Grey: the irresponsible Churchill, Haldane, with his cloudy mind and passion for intrigue, or Birrell? He described Morley as senile, Crewe as hopeless, and Asquith as "putty," a phrase he attributed to Lloyd George.

*(Lloyd George) had been swept along somewhat unwillingly by Grey. "Massingham does not dare attack you", I said, "and therefore his campaign against Grey can only succeed if he gets Grey out by himself and makes him appear to be solely responsible for what he (Massingham) describes as "our anti-Germany policy". Lloyd George, I am glad to say, thoroughly appreciated the situation, though he admitted that hitherto he had not done so. As regards the demand that Grey should resign he said, "If Grey goes, we would go together. I would go and certainly Winston ought to go. I should certainly go if the attempt to hound Grey out were successful."[66]*

Other issues helped cement the relationship with Grey. In March 1912, after the settlement of the coal strike, Lloyd George "spoke in terms of warm admiration of the part played in the negotiations by Edward Grey." Murray noted, "These two are now the very best of friends—and have a deep admiration for each other. It is amusing to read in the Tory press of the alleged attempts being made by Lloyd George to elbow Grey out of the way."[67] The question of women's suffrage brought them together,[68] and only the Marconi affair would cast a shadow over their cooperation.

In so far as Lloyd George had become identified with Grey, he faced an obvious danger: damage to his image in radical circles at a particularly difficult time in his career. Lloyd George did not relish the prospect either of remaining *persona non grata* in Berlin, or of that fact becoming public knowledge. There were also policy questions to be faced which demonstrated that while the Agadir crisis had influenced him markedly, certain venerable considerations retained their validity. Relaxing with his close friend, Rufus Isaacs, the attorney-general, and Arthur Murray at Genoa in January 1912, Lloyd George:

*expounded his views on Anglo-German relations. There were two things, he said, that Germany had to learn. Firstly that we intended to maintain the supremacy of our navy at whatever cost, and secondly that we did not propose to allow her to "bully" whomsoever she pleased on the continent of Europe. After she had thoroughly*

66. Murray diary, 17 Jan. 1912, Elibank Papers, 8814, folio 59/60.
67. Murray diary, 1 March 1912, ibid., folio 68.
68. Churchill to Lloyd George, 16 Dec. 1911, LGP, C/3/15/12.

*realised these two things, then was the time to come to terms to ask
her: "Is there any part of the world, which is not ours, that you would
like?" In his opinion we should allow her almost unrestricted
freedom in Asia Minor right down to the Persian Gulf. This would
open out the region all around Baghdad, thereby giving greater trade
opportunities to ourselves, and in respect of India would permit us
to play off Russia against Germany and vice-versa, thereby lessening
the risks of invasion (such as they are) that we now run.*[69]

He expected Grey to heal the wounds of Agadir, reopen
negotiations for a naval agreement on Britain's terms, and cooperate with Bethmann Hollweg, the German chancellor, over the
Portuguese colonies, the Baghdad railway, and in the Balkans.[70]
Moreover, although Britain must retain the Ententes with France
and Russia, Grey must adopt a firmer line over Russian encroachments in Persia.[71] Lloyd George, therefore, in the relative calm of
1912, looked for fresh initiatives in foreign policy. In broader
fields, he supported cooperation with Japan and the United
States;[72] in Europe he hoped for détente. Clearly he had not
abandoned the concept of synthesis, although the balance of its
component parts could change. Foreign Office officials were to
witness what they would regard as somewhat regressive behaviour
on Lloyd George's part during the last two years of peace.

69. Murray diary, 7 Jan. 1912, Elibank Papers, folio 57/58.
70. Speech, 3 Feb., *Daily News*, 5 Feb. 1912; P. Cambon to Poincaré, 8 Feb.
1912, DDF, 3, II, 7; Riddell diary, 9 Dec. 1911, Riddell, *More Pages from My
Diary*, 32; Chamberlain, *Politics from Inside*, 486. According to Esher, Lloyd
George opposed the appointment of Prince Louis of Battenberg as first sea
lord because of his German origins. (*Esher Journals*, III, 61.)
71. Scott diary, 2 Dec. 1911, and 7, 22, and 24 Jan. 1912, Scott Papers, Add.
50901; French chargé (London) to de Selves, 24 Nov. 1911, DDF, 3, I, 210;
P. Cambon to Poincaré, 18 April 1912, ibid., 3, II, 363.
72. I. H. Nish, *Alliance in Decline: A Study in Anglo-Japanese Relations* (London, 1972), 52, 71, 75, 89. The Anglo-Japanese alliance was renewed in July 1911.

# 8

# Toward an
# Armed Peace

In 1912, Grey's senior aides on the one hand and Harcourt, Burns, and Morley on the other, represented the poles of official opinion on policy toward Europe. Grey and Lloyd George stood between and in a subtle relationship to the extremes and to each other. Colleagues could not decide whether Lloyd George would support government policy or dissent from it. McKenna at least was confident of one thing, the chancellor of the exchequer would never resign. Theodore Roosevelt saw him as "very emotional... but...*the* man of power." Others sensed that somehow England's destiny was tied to his career, but as Waldorf Astor, future proprietor of the *Observer*, told Garvin in January 1913, "Lloyd George's mind is not moving on the right lines, i.e. on the Imperial lines. I dare say he is a jingo but he does not appear to understand the full and big Imperial idea."[1]

Only one foreign policy issue beyond the German question seriously concerned Lloyd George; the fate of the Ottoman Empire. The Italo-Turkish conflict of 1912 passed with little

1. Roosevelt to Gray, 5 Oct. 1911, E. E. Morison, ed., *The Letters of Theodore Roosevelt* (Cambridge, Mass., 1954), vii, 402–403; Astor to Garvin, Jan. 1913, Garvin Papers, box 15.

cabinet scrutiny, but the First Balkan War both aroused his interest and contributed to his understanding of the area.[2] Lloyd George instinctively supported the Balkan states against Turkey and deplored neither the outbreak of war in October 1912[3] not its progress. "The Turk is crumbling. The Lord be praised for that. He is a horrid tramp. I hope the little powers reap full reward for their heroism. I mean to fight for them inside."[4]

He regarded Bulgaria as the most valuable and deserving member of the Balkan League. With Grey's consent, but without any authority to negotiate, he met the Bulgarian minister at Masterman's home at the end of October to discuss the settlement.[5] According to Masterman, Lloyd George showed scant respect for the avaricious Greeks. He insisted that should the Balkan League lapse into mutual hostility after the defeat of Turkey, Bulgaria, the principal contributor to victory, must receive the bulk of the territorial spoils. Greece would be, however, preferable to Italy as a recipient of Turkish territory. Moreover, by January 1914, Lloyd George was sympathetic to the claims put forth by Premier Eleutherios Venizelos and Sir John Stavridi, the Greek consul-general, to Cyprus and Turkey's island possessions.[6] In these exchanges a link of great historical significance had been forged.

Although Lloyd George welcomed the assault on Turkey, he became worried lest Grey's attempt to localize the war failed. Perhaps Austria, supported by Germany, would confront Serbia, and draw Russia, France, and then Britain into a European war.[7] By late December 1912, however, Grey was more optimistic about

2. Lloyd George to N. Buxton, 5 June 1913, N. Buxton Papers.

3. Lloyd George to W. George, 3 and 9 Oct. 1912, W. George, *My Brother and I*, 248; L. Masterman, *C. F. G. Masterman*, 244–48.

4. Lloyd George to W. George, 28 Oct. 1912, W. George, 248.

5. Lloyd George to W. George, 30 Oct. 1912, ibid. He described the Bulgarian minister as anxious to enlist his help, and presumably the government's, to prevent intervention in the war which might rob the Balkan League of the spoils.

6. Scott diary, 21 Jan. 1914, Scott Papers, Add. 50901; J. A. Spender and C. Asquith, *Life of Lord Oxford and Asquith*, II, 77; Lewis diary, 17 Nov. 1912. He doubted, however, whether a Liberal government could dispose of Cyprus.

7. Cabinet meetings, 1 and 21 Nov. 1912, Cab 41/33/66 and 71; Riddell diary, 9 Nov. 1912 and 23 and 24 March 1913, Lord Riddell, *More Pages From My Diary 1908–1914*, 98–99, 134; Scott diary, 9 Oct. 1914, Scott Papers, Add. 50901; Lewis diary, 17 Nov. 1912. In contrast see E. Wrench, *Geoffrey Dawson and Our Times* (London, 1955), 89.

the progress toward a settlement of the ambassadors' conference in London, and did not expect Austria to mobilize against Serbia and defy the powers.[8] He informed Lloyd George that he had advised the Balkan League to remain united and to avoid diffi-culties with the Great Powers. He had also urged Turkey to make concessions and sue for peace.

Lloyd George, approving of the initial settlement of January 1913, applauded Grey for his "brilliant achievement, for it is entirely yours . . . the greatest triumph yet scored for the govern-ment. I shudder to think what would have happened in Europe had you not taken the lead."[9]

The situation in fact remained tense,[10] and in June 1913 the Second Balkan War erupted, ranging an isolated Bulgaria against both her former allies and Turkey. Grey, confident of Lloyd George's support,[11] enlisted his active cooperation.[12] Grey informed him, on 11 July, that the Austrian ambassador had warned about the sensitive state of opinion in the Hapsburg Empire. In reply, he had insisted that he must inform Parliament and that Lloyd George, due to speak that evening at the Mansion House, might also comment. The ambassador was understandably distressed at this prospect; Lloyd George might add to the tension as he had in 1911. Grey had assured him, however, that should Lloyd George refer to the Balkans, he would merely express the hope that none of the participants would act in such a way as to threaten the Concert and the peace of Europe.

Grey proposed, therefore, that Lloyd George comment on the Balkan situation. He enclosed a brief statement which could be amplified with phrases on the efficacy of cooperation between the powers and expressing the hope that the war would quickly end.

8. Grey to Lloyd George, 21 Dec. 1912, LGP, C/4/14/8.

9. Lloyd George to Grey, Jan. 1913, G. M. Trevelyan, *Grey of Fallodon*, 200–201. Lloyd George subsequently dismissed Grey's efforts with contempt. (*War Memoirs*, I, 59.)

10. E. Marsh to Lloyd George, 2 April 1913, LGP, C/3/15/21A.

11. Grey to Lloyd George, 20 June 1913, ibid., C/4/14/9. Grey felt that although the cabinet had laboured for over seven years, their personal relations had survived the strain and had actually improved.

12. Grey to Lloyd George, 11 July 1913, ibid., C/4/14/10. Grey's suggested statement was to the effect that so long as the Balkan States did nothing to defy the Great Powers, e.g. over Albania, Britain hoped that no individual Great Power would act in such a way as to embarrass the Concert. Grey added a phrase in pencil, "fratricidal carnage," which Lloyd George used in his speech.

Lloyd George performed as Grey wished, warning the Balkan States and advising Austria against disruptive behaviour. He did not miss the opportunity to praise the foreign secretary warmly for his role in activating the Concert and for his attempts to cooperate with Germany to settle the problems of the Balkans.

This display of solidarity was logical enough and predictable, but so were the political embarrassments in the light of urgent policy questions. Ponsonby placed the dilemma squarely before Lloyd George:

> *I do not want to embark on a dissertation about Persia. The point. . . is this: the Government have got a stiff task before them during the next two years. Their existence depends not on ship's discipline but on spontaneous party loyalty. To a man practically members are with them in their social and home policy but the disaffection caused by their foreign policy and the consequent expenditure on armaments is fast spreading. . .For myself, I say unhesitatingly that another step towards the partition of Persia and another step towards the further provocation of Germany are matters of infinitely greater importance than Home Rule, Welsh Disestablishment or any other question.*[13]

The strategic balance in the Mediterranean now complicated the problem of naval supremacy and Anglo-German relations. Moreover, the new first lord of the admiralty, Churchill, seemed obsessed with all things naval and ready to place an almost intolerable strain on Lloyd George's personal regard for him.[14] Lloyd George had supported Churchill's promotion in the expectation that he would trim the navy estimates. The latter now appeared to be an ingrate and a turncoat.[15] In fact, the threat of a new Germany Navy Law made economies most unlikely in the 1912–13 navy estimates, unless negotiations produced a naval agreement.

The preliminary discussions in January 1912 had Lloyd George's complete support.[16] The conversations were entirely in line with

13. Ponsonby to Lloyd George, Sept. 1912, Ponsonby Papers, box 1911–14, f.1911–13.

14. Riddell diary, 27 April 1912, Riddell, *More Pages From My Diary*, 54.

15. McKenna to Churchill, 7 Nov. 1911, McKenna Papers, 4/3/1; A. J. Marder, *From the Dreadnought to Scapa Flow*, I, 262; Riddell diary, 17 and 24 April 1912, Riddell, *More Pages From My Diary*, 51, 54.

16. Lloyd George to W. George, 29 Jan. 1912, W. George, 247; Marder, *Dreadnought to Scapa Flow*, I, 275–87; S. R. Williamson, *The Politics of Grand*

his views; they were conducted in secret, through informal channels, and sought to protect Britain's fundamental naval and political interests.[17]

The cabinet met on 2 February to consider the implications of an enlarged German program providing for fifteen rather than twelve Dreadnoughts within six years, a third battle squadron, and increased personnel.[18] The Admiralty suggested that the naval estimates must be increased immediately by between £2.5 and £3 million, but the cabinet was understandably more cautious. Some ministers felt that Germany might bargain and urged that Grey visit Berlin. Finally on 6 February they agreed that Haldane was an appropriate emissary.[19] These developments satisfied Lloyd George. Grey seemed prepared to resist his officials and permit the negotiations to proceed. Moreover, both he and Grey were angered by Churchill's provocative speech at Glasgow on 9 February.

Haldane returned from Berlin on 11 February impressed with the ability and will of Bethmann Hollweg to challenge Tirpitz successfully. He carried with him proposals for a political, colonial, and naval agreement. The cabinet, however, considering Haldane's report on 15 February, was impressed by the Admiralty's alarming deductions.[20] The strategic implications of Germany's naval plans and of the Novelle could not be ignored. It was decided, therefore, that Churchill should circulate counter-proposals.

On 19 February Lloyd George met with Sir Francis Bertie.[21] He justified an Anglo-German agreement on financial and political grounds. Britain would be able to reduce naval expenditures and accomplish the détente which public opinion and patriotic,

---

*Strategy*, 253–57; E. Marsh to Lloyd George, 31 Jan., and Grey to Churchill, 29 Jan. 1912, enclosing telegrams exchanged between Sir E. Cassel and A. Ballin, LGP, C/3/15/4; Grey to Goschen, 20 Dec. 1911, *BDOW*, vi, 480, 650–51.

17. Grey to Churchill, 31 Jan., enclosing Churchill memorandum, n.d., LGP, C/3/15/15, and Churchill to Grey, 31 Jan. 1912, R. S. Churchill, *Winston S. Churchill*, ii, 561–62.

18. Asquith report, 3 Feb. 1912, Cab 41/33/34. Germany would build at the rate of 3, 2, 3, 2, 3, 2, over six years, rather than 2 Dreadnoughts per year. Eventually she would possess thirty-three capital ships; Britain would need forty-one capital ships to preserve the 60 per cent margin.

19. Asquith report, 7 Feb., Cab 41/33/35, and Grey to Goschen, 7 Feb. 1912, *BDOW*, vi, 497, 668–69.

20. Asquith report, 15 Feb., Cab 41/33/36, and Admiralty memorandum, 14 Feb. 1912, Cab 37/109/21; Churchill, *Winston S. Churchill*, ii, 565.

21. Bertie memorandum, 19 Feb. 1912, FO/800/171.

realistic financiers in the City desired. He suggested that Germany might accept restrictions on her naval expenditures in return for colonial territories, excluding Portugal's African possessions, and an arrangement over the Baghdad railway. He conceded that a naval agreement might be temporary while the colonial settlement would be permanent. Against that, Britain might acquire German diplomatic support in the Persian Gulf, so necessary if the Anglo-Russian agreement over Persia lapsed. Moreover, if Germany broke her pledge on naval construction, he assured Bertie that Britain could make up the lost ground, lay down two keels to one, and ensure supremacy. Bertie was not impressed.

Lloyd George expressed concern about France's political stability and public confidence, and Russia's reliability, but on these points Bertie was reassuring. The French, he admitted, were "equally slippery" but Anglo-French interests now coincided. The French were confident, militarily prepared, and devoted to the Entente. They trusted Britain more than Russia and lived in fear of Germany only to the extent that they were unsure of British support. Lloyd George agreed, suggesting that, in the course of the Agadir crisis,

> the French Govt. had thrown away the finest opportunity they had ever had or were ever likely to have again, to try conclusions with Germany. They had the certainty of our armed support. The aid of 150,000 English troops would have had a great moral effect. Our Navy would have cut off Germany commercially from the West, Russia would have put pressure on the Eastern frontier of Germany, and there would have been shortness of food and famine prices in Germany, commercial stagnation and financial disaster. He did not think that France would have crushed Germany as Germany had France in 1870 but it would have brought home to the Germans that they could not ride roughshod over Europe as they appeared to think.

He had, of course, expressed very different views at certain times during the crisis of 1911.

Finally, they discussed the problem of ensuring that public opinion would permit the government to assist France in the event of German aggression. Lloyd George was as clear as Churchill had been in 1911: "to bring the British public to fighting point it would be requisite that Germany should have passed into Belgium for the purpose of attacking France or should have crossed the French frontier."

The cabinet met on 20 February 1912 to consider Churchill's proposals.[22] The Admiralty expected naval expenditures to increase by £14.25 million over the next five years, or by £12 million, if Tirpitz reduced the tempo of his program. The cabinet instructed Grey and Haldane to warn Ambassador Metternich of the consequences of a naval race, and suggest that Germany amend her plans.[23]

Whatever optimism Grey and Haldane retained rested in part on the assumption, cultivated by Metternich and the beleaguered German chancellor himself, that Bethmann Hollweg would challenge Tirpitz.[24] Berlin apparently harboured its moderate and extreme factions, its doves and hawks. Indeed, Harcourt and Morley had not resigned in 1912 with Loreburn in order to avoid taking any step which would strengthen the military faction in Berlin. They wanted to demonstrate that those in Britain who favoured an agreement had not lost power.

The Anglo-German conversations followed the familiar pattern of attempting to reconcile a naval agreement satisfactory to London, with a political arrangement which met Berlin's needs.[25] The cabinet refused, however, to guarantee unconditionally British neutrality in the event of a European war.[26] Bethmann Hollweg could not accept any formula that offered less.[27] On 10 April Berlin broke off the negotiations.[28]

The Foreign Office[29] and the Unionists welcomed the collapse;[30] Harcourt and radical opinion outside the cabinet were deeply

22. Asquith report, 21 Feb. 1912, Cab 41/33/37.

23. Grey memorandum, 22 Feb. 1912, BDOW, vi, 523, 696–97.

24. Goschen to Nicolson, 15 March 1912, ibid., 541, 716–17.

25. Haldane memorandum, 12 March, ibid., 533, 710–11, Asquith report, 14 March, Cab 41/33/40, Nicolson to Goschen, 13 March, and Grey to Nicolson, 13 March 1912, BDOW, vi, 534, and 535, 711–12.

26. Grey to Goschen, 14 March 1912, BDOW, vi, 537, 713–14.

27. Metternich to Grey, and Grey to Goschen, 15 March, ibid., 538 and 539, 714–15, Asquith report, 16 March, Cab 41/33/41, and Grey to Goschen, 16, 19 March 1912, BDOW, vi, 544, and 545, 718–21. The cabinet accepted the spirit of Bethmann Hollweg's proposed preface to a defensive alliance. They also added an amendment to the effect that Britain would neither make "nor join in" any unprovoked attack on Germany. Bethmann Hollweg hinted that he might be replaced as chancellor unless Grey accepted his demands.

28. Asquith report, 30 March, Cab 41/33/45, and Grey to Bertie, 29 March 1912, BDOW, vi, 559, 731.

29. Grey to Bertie, 9 April, Asquith to Grey, 10 April, and Grey to Goschen, 10 April 1912, BDOW, vi, 569, 571, and 573, 745–46.

30. Maxse to Bonar Law, 20 May 1912, Bonar Law Papers, 26/3/32.

disturbed. Lloyd George stood apart from both these responses. Grey had drafted the nonaggression or conditional neutrality formula of 14 March. Lloyd George regarded this as a genuine offer. It demonstrated that Grey was not a captive of his officials. The foreign secretary would not go further; he would not offer an unconditional neutrality agreement, but Lloyd George accepted Grey's conclusion that "although we cannot bind ourselves under all circumstances to go to war with France against Germany, we shall also certainly not bind ourselves to Germany not to assist France."[31] Moreover, Grey continued to support a colonial agreement with Germany.[32]

Germany's record, in contrast, seemed less commendable. Her government was unaccommodating on the political formula and unyielding on her naval program. Furthermore, Bethmann Hollweg had actually broken off the negotiations. Lloyd George regarded Germany as responsible for the breakdown. In addition, he regretted the recall of Metternich in May 1912, whatever his views of Baron Adolf Marschall, the new German ambassador.[33] Lloyd George braced himself, therefore, to face the consequences.

The Admiralty demanded a margin of 60 per cent over Germany in Dreadnoughts. The estimates would approach £45 million. Britain must lay down four capital ships as a routine measure in 1912–13 and match the three projected German Dreadnoughts by constructing six additional ships over a six-year period. Churchill looked also for a significant contribution from the Dominions.[34]

Lloyd George, in his budget speech of 2 April 1912, did not question the Admiralty's program; all ships would be completed as planned.[35] Embarrassed by the contrast with Asquith's record of parsimony as chancellor of the exchequer, Lloyd George

31. Grey to Nicolson, 21 April 1912, BDOW, vi, 580, 751.

32. Crewe report, 4 June 1912, Cab 41/33/51; P. H. S. Hatton, "Harcourt and Solf: the search for an Anglo-German understanding through Africa 1912–1914," European Studies Review, 1, no. 2 (1971), 123–45.

33. He described Marschall as anxious to come to terms with Britain. (Lloyd George to W. George, 1 July 1912, W. George, 247.)

34. Asquith report, 20 June 1912, Cab 41/33/54; Churchill memoranda, 15 March, Cab 37/105/27, 18 April and 2 and 20 July 1912, Cab 37/110/65, and Cab 37/111/84 and 92; Marder, Dreadnought to Scapa Flow, i, 283–84; D. C. Gordon, "The Admiralty and Dominion Navies, 1902–14," Journal of Modern History, 33, no. 4 (1961), 414–22. For Lloyd George's involvement see Tyrrell to Gowers, 29 March and 3 April 1912, LGP, C/4/14/6 and 7.

35. Statements, 2, 17, and 29 April 1912, Parl. Deb., H. of C., xxxvi, 1057–68, and xxxvii, 360–62, 1622–24.

deplored the waste on armaments. He had hoped to reduce the estimates, but he could not gamble with naval supremacy. Social reform might suffer and taxation would increase, but the demands of national security permitted no other course.

Tirpitz's program became law in May 1912. Lloyd George told the House of Commons, on 24 June, that in view of Germany's planned increases in naval expenditure of £10 million over the next six years, they must draw on reserve funds, table supplementary estimates of up to £1 million, and prepare to face heavy commitments in subsequent years.[36] He faced Churchill's new demands, informing him in the cabinet on 16 July that "Bankruptcy stares me in the face."[37] Churchill's laconic reply was little comfort and Lloyd George's optimism in public was not convincing.[38]

The complicating problem of Mediterranean strategy brought Churchill into confrontation with a group in which McKenna, the home secretary, was most prominent. The Admiralty preferred to withdraw in part from the Mediterranean, concentrate in the North Sea against Germany and develop closer naval and even political cooperation with France. Churchill's critics wanted to preserve the status quo in the North Sea and avoid a withdrawal from the Mediterranean.[39] They were ready to accept increased naval expenditures and, if necessary, face the whole Triple Alliance because they abhorred the prospect of an alliance with France.[40]

---

36. Speech, 24 June, *Parl. Deb.*, H. of C., XL, 49, and P. Cambon to Poincaré, 27 June 1912, *DDF*, 3, III, 145.

37. Churchill to Lloyd George, 12 July, Asquith Papers, file 24, and Lloyd George–Churchill exchange, 16 July 1912, LGP, Cabinet notes 1908–1915, C/12.

38. Speech, 12 July 1912, LGP, C/35/2/17.

39. Churchill to Haldane, 6 May 1912, and Esher to Churchill, n.d., Churchill, *Winston S. Churchill*, II, 588, 595–96; Nicolson to Bertie, 6 May, Nicolson to Grey, 6 May, Crowe memorandum, 8 May, Grey to Kitchener, 8 May, Kitchener to Grey, 19 May 1912, *BDOW*, X, II, 384, 385, 386, and 387, 583–90, and 390, 592; Williamson, *Grand Strategy*, 264–83.

40. Admiralty memoranda, 15, 20, 22, 25, and 28 June and 2 and 6 July 1912, Cab 37/111/76, 77, 78, 80, 83, 85, and 89; McKenna memoranda, 24 June and 3 July 1912, Cab 37/111/79 and 86; Marder, *Dreadnought to Scapa Flow*, I, 287–311. It was possible to envisage a partial withdrawal from the Mediterranean without involving tighter political as opposed to naval links with France, or increased naval construction. Alternatively one could argue that Britain must not abandon her position in the Mediterranean, but still needed to secure either an alliance with France or a larger fleet, or both.

The cabinet began to weigh the critical variables on 16 May, one of which was French pressure for naval staff talks.[41] Churchill, Asquith, and Lord Kitchener, consul-general in Egypt, reached their celebrated compromise at Malta on 2 June 1912.[42] The cabinet assessed it in bitter tones and inconclusive manner on 19 and 27 June, and agreed that a meeting of the CID was necessary.[43]

The CID convened on 4 July 1912. The Admiralty planned to rely on a force of two or three battle cruisers and the cruiser squadron stationed at Malta, in conjunction with the French fleet, to ensure an adequate presence and even supremacy in the Mediterranean. They also proposed to maintain the Fourth Battle Squadron at Gibraltar ready for service in either home waters or the Mediterranean.[44]

For comparative purposes, Churchill also used the standard of a ten per cent margin over the next two naval powers, calculating in terms of Germany and the United States. Lloyd George, however, insisted that he omit all reference to America; it was hardly "serviceable" to calculate in relation to the United States. Lloyd George and Asquith suggested that they might make a more useful calculation with regard to Austria and Italy. Churchill proposed a margin of sixty per cent over Germany, a two-power standard in relation to other European fleets, and a degree of superiority over "any reasonable combination of powers." In response to the last point Lloyd George denied that Britain would either face the Triple Alliance single-handed, or be friendless in the event of a war in the Mediterranean. He did not regard as necessary, therefore, a British Mediterranean fleet equal to the

41. Nicolson to Grey, 4 May, Bertie to Nicolson, 9 May, and Grey to Churchill, 11 May 1912, BDOW, x, II, 383, 388 and 389, 582–83 and 590–92; Asquith report, 17 May 1912, Cab 41/33/50.

42. Kitchener to Grey, 2 June 1912, BDOW, x, II, 392, 594–95. The Malta agreement assumed that an Anglo-French naval arrangement was necessary, providing for British defence of France's northern coasts, and that France would maintain a Mediterranean fleet which, in combination with the British force, would match the naval power of Austria and Italy. As a permanent force, the Admiralty would retain two and preferably three battlecruisers and four armoured cruisers in the Mediterranean at Malta. The Fourth Battle Squadron, consisting of eight battleships based at Gibraltar by the end of 1913, would patrol the Mediterranean, but would be available for active service elsewhere.

43. Asquith reports, 20 and 28 June 1912, Cab 41/33/54 and 55; Crewe to Selborne, 28 June 1912, Crewe Papers, C/45; Churchill to Lloyd George, June 1912, Lloyd George Papers (National Library of Wales), 20462 C.

44. CID, 4 and 11 July 1912, Cab 38/21/26 and 27.

combined forces of Austria and Italy. Lloyd George conceded that a surprise attack by Germany was "perhaps conceivable," but he was reluctant to accept the hypothesis that Germany would manufacture a crisis in order to justify a strike at the British fleet. Grey assured him that Germany could use any diplomatic crisis as a *casus belli*. Lloyd George, however, dismissed the possibility of an attack by the Triple Alliance, secretly planned and organized by Berlin.

Admiral Sir Francis Bridgeman, A. K. Wilson's successor as first sea lord, insisted that Britain must retain a twenty-four to sixteen margin in Dreadnoughts over Germany. Lloyd George felt that a three to two ratio was unnecessary. He was also sceptical of Churchill's forecast that Germany would commit all her naval forces in one great battle. He asked the Admiralty to ponder the impact of the recreation of Russian naval power on German strategic thinking.

The CID decided on a compromise arrangement. They would ensure a reasonable margin of superiority in home waters over Germany, and also retain a battle fleet at Malta equal in strength to that of the next Mediterranean naval power, excluding France. By inference, France was accepted as the prospective ally in a war against the Triple Alliance. Churchill protested, for he had failed apparently to secure in full his strategic redistribution, and a more substantial force than he had envisaged would remain at Malta. On the other hand the CID had confirmed the primacy of the North Sea theatre.

McKenna was not satisfied and Grey in fact had the best of most worlds: naval superiority over Germany; a continued, impressive naval presence in the Mediterranean for diplomatic and other purposes; and the probability of a closer alignment with France short of an actual alliance. Whether Lloyd George would applaud and the Treasury benefit depended on the impact on Anglo-German relations and the navy estimates. Even though Esher described him as standing with McKenna and Harcourt,[45] the debate was so diffuse and the long-term results sufficiently inscrutable that Lloyd George had avoided taking a firm position. He had expressed greater faith in the German élite than Grey, but he could only have meant France when he suggested that Britain would not be isolated and friendless in a war with the Triple Alliance.

45. Esher to the king, 4 July 1912, Marder, *Dreadnought to Scapa Flow*, I, 294.

The cabinet discussed the CID recommendations and Churchill's proposals to evade as much as to implement them, on 5, 12, 15, and 16 July.[46] The Admiralty planned to constitute a Mediterranean battle fleet of initially only four battle cruisers and the four armoured cruisers stationed at Malta. Churchill told the cabinet that the Admiralty would station eight battle cruisers in the Mediterranean by 1915, and retain four of them at Malta even in the event of war with Germany, thus reassuring his colleagues that both the Mediterranean and the North Sea were or would be secure. Actually Churchill had not provided for a one-power Mediterranean standard, as he admitted in January 1914.

He could, however, present the bill to Lloyd George. The 1912–13 estimates would approach £50 million. They authorized construction of four capital ships, as part of a five-year program providing for twenty-one rather than seventeen Dreadnoughts. Despite expectations of aid from the Dominions, the burden would be heavy.[47]

On 16 July the cabinet agreed that military and naval staff talks with France should proceed, but that they would not prejudice Britain's freedom of action in the event of a European war.[48] Clearly it was also necessary to construct a formula to express the essence of Britain's relationship with France in the light of the staff conversations.[49] As a result, Grey and Paul Cambon, the French ambassador, exchanged the letters of 22 and 23 November 1912 which attempted to define and regularize Anglo-French relations, while avoiding precise commitments.[50]

The cabinet played a significant and detailed role, deciding on the content and wording of the notes, but Lloyd George was not prominent.[51] In all probability he accepted the Grey-Cambon

46. Asquith reports, 5, 12, 15, and 16 July, Cab 41/33/56, 57, and 58, and Grey to Carnegie, 11 July 1912, BDOW, x ii, 398, 600.

47. Churchill to Lloyd George, 12 July 1912, LGP, C/24/3/9 and Cab 37/111/92.

48. Churchill, *Winston S. Churchill*, ii, 596–97; Churchill memorandum, 17 July 1912, BDOW, x, ii, 399, 600–601.

49. Marder, *Dreadnought to Scapa Flow*, i, 299–308; Williamson, *Grand Strategy*, 320–25; Grey to Carnegie, 22 July 1912; BDOW, x, ii, 400, 601.

50. Grey to Bertie, 30 Oct. and 7 and 21 Nov., Grey to Cambon, 22 Nov., and Cambon to Grey, 23 Nov. 1912, BDOW, x, ii, 413, 414, 415, 416 and 417, 612–15.

51. Bertie to Grey, 30 July, Nicolson to Grey, 4 Aug., Bertie to Grey, 13 Aug., Grey to Bertie, 19 Sept., and Asquith to Grey, 11 Oct. 1912, BDOW, x, ii, 404,

formula only a little less easily than the foreign secretary, but with far fewer misgivings than Lewis Harcourt and other critics of Grey.[52] The cabinet would decide on the question of involvement in war and Lloyd George did not take exception to the soothing and ambiguous public utterances of Grey and Asquith.

Lloyd George was bound, however, to attempt to impose as tight a financial restraint as possible. At the CID meeting on 1 August 1912 he clashed briefly with John Seely, who had inherited the War Office from Haldane in June 1912.[53] Seely insisted that certain powers had made significant strides in the development of bombers. Lloyd George replied that such dangers had not impressed the original sub-committee on which he had sat, and that the *Morning Post* had reported that the Turks had ridiculed Italian bombing efforts in the recent war. He was therefore reluctant to spend vast sums on the development of air power.

Lloyd George also demanded adequate Treasury representation on all sub-committees which reported on naval base construction. He wanted in fact a full enquiry into the development of naval bases on the east coast, citing Rosyth as an example of a project approved by experts who were now suspect. He won the CID's approval for subjecting the whole policy to cabinet scrutiny before committing the government to an expensive program. As Lloyd George told the CID on 6 December 1912, he did not oppose the fortifying of Cromarty and Scapa Flow as such, but he objected to the assumption that the Admiralty and the War Office could proceed without reference to the cabinet.[54] As a result he was able, for instance in August 1913, to defeat Churchill's proposals for installations in the Shetland Isles and balk at the cost of providing defences for west coast ports.[55]

Of necessity, and from conviction, he fulfilled the role of the concerned chancellor of the exchequer, although there exists evidence pointing in another direction.[56] At the CID on 6 December 1912, he explored certain implications of a war between the

---

405, 407, 409, 410, 411, 605–12; Asquith reports, 1 and 21 Nov. 1912, Cab 41/33/66 and 71.

52. C. P. Trevelyan to Morel, 20 Feb. 1913, Morel Papers, file F.8; P. Cambon to Jonnert, 23 Jan. 1913, *DDF*, 3, v, 248.

53. CID, 1 Aug. 1912, Cab 38/22/33.

54. CID, 6 Dec. 1912, Cab 38/22/42.

55. CID, 5 Aug. 1913, Cab 38/24/33.

56. Report of the sub-committee on trading with the enemy, 30 July 1912, Cab 38/21/31.

Triple Entente and the Triple Alliance. Lloyd George argued that if Belgium and Holland asserted their neutral rights, they could deprive Britain of the vital weapon of blockade. They could prevent her from asserting effective economic pressure on Germany. Britain could not, he insisted, permit this to happen. They must reject the claim that exporters could distinguish between commodities destined for neutral as opposed to enemy consumption. Resale to the enemy by the neutrals would inevitably take place. Consequently, Britain must curb imports into Belgium and Holland beyond their average domestic consumption levels. She could not afford to wait and see whether Belgium and Holland entered the war against Germany. The first six weeks would be vital, and Britain must clamp a tight blockade on Northwestern Europe to help ensure victory.

The government must, Lloyd George argued, develop a plan which in the event of war would demonstrate Britain's friendliness towards the neutral states, but would impose a blockade immediately and without exception. To defeat Germany, Britain must destroy her industrial base and cut off her imports of food. The General Staff, however, expected Germany to violate Belgian and possibly Dutch neutrality in the event of war with France. Churchill pointed out that if Belgium and Holland remained neutral and accepted Britain's blockade regulations Germany would invade them. The problem was either academic or temporary. Lloyd George insisted, nevertheless, that should Belgium and Holland remain neutral, Britain must permit them to import commodities to meet average consumption needs plus a reasonable margin, but no more. The meeting concluded that Holland and Belgium must be either neutral and friendly toward Britain, severely limiting their trade with Germany and receiving a subsidy for loss of transit trade, or face a tight blockade. Lloyd George added that a subsidy must be very limited.

Lloyd George also participated in the CID sub-committee established on 13 January 1913 to examine the threat of invasion in the light of fresh circumstances.[57] Lloyd George submitted no memoranda and attended only five of its twenty-one meetings between 18 March 1913 and 19 February 1914. He signed the

---

57. Sub-committee on "Attack on the British Isles from Oversea," Cab 16/28A and 28B, and Cab 38/26/13; Hankey to Balfour, 21 Jan. 1913, Balfour Papers, Add. 49703; Williamson, *Grand Strategy*, 306–11.

final report, however, which essentially confirmed the conclusions of 1908 and 1911. The recommendation that two regular divisions remain at home if the expeditionary force were dispatched to Europe was more in line with the conclusions of October 1908 than with those of August 1911, but did not challenge fundamentally the role of the expeditionary force.

Lloyd George doubted, as he had in August 1911, the feasibility of a German invasion. He distinguished between a treacherous and surprise German attack and one launched simultaneously with a declaration of war. He denied that Germany could launch a "bolt from the blue" without detection and therefore without prior warning. Balfour and Churchill were less confident, and Henry Wilson suggested that Germany could achieve an element of surprise for twenty-four hours. Lloyd George, as in July 1912 over a German attack on the fleet, remained sceptical both of the practicability of and the will to risk such a manoeuvre.

In the final months of 1912 Lloyd George faced Churchill's alarms, analyses, and blandishments.[58] Seely's estimates, below £28 million, were far less controversial.[59] The implications of the German and Austrian naval programs and demands to raise the navy's pay scales, for which Churchill requested £750,000 in November, constituted an almost irresistible case. Qualitatively Britain's capital ships must match those of Germany and Austria, and inflation was an evil with which the government must live.[60] Lloyd George, despite the possible embarrassment to himself, did oppose Churchill in November on the question of increased pay scales. In the cabinet on 10 December he insisted that he would not raise taxes to provide revenue for increased defence estimates.[61] Crewe and others supported him. Haldane, now lord chancellor, Churchill, and Seely maintained, however, that the estimates were at the lowest level consistent with national security.

58. Churchill to Lloyd George, 18 Oct. 1912, enclosing Cartwright to Grey, 1 Oct. 1912, LGP, C/3/15/16. Churchill emphasized the report that Austria intended to build three new super-Dreadnoughts.

59. Seely to Lloyd George, 29 Nov. 1912, and 29 Jan. 1913, Mottistone Papers, xx, f 39 and f 76–9.

60. Churchill to Lloyd George, 3 Nov., Churchill, *Winston S. Churchill*, II, 601–602, Churchill memoranda, 17 Oct., 11 and 23 Nov., Cab 37/112/114, 124, and 127, Riddell diary, Nov., Riddell, *More Pages From My Diary*, 103–106, and Churchill to Lloyd George, 18 Nov. 1912, LGP, C/12. Lloyd George persuaded the cabinet to reduce the £750,000 to £350,000.

61. Asquith report, 11 Dec., Cab 41/33/74, and Churchill to Lloyd George, 9 Dec. 1912, Churchill, *Winston S. Churchill*, II, 606–607.

They must be accepted even at the cost of additional taxation. The cabinet decided that Lloyd George, Churchill, Seely, and Asquith should meet in order to reach a *modus vivendi*.

Whatever the precise nature of these discussions *à quatre*, Lloyd George was unable to resist the Admiralty demands. On 22 January 1913 the cabinet discussed Churchill's estimates which showed an increase of over £1 million.[62] Exchanges with Tirpitz in early February were not productive and in March Churchill published estimates of £46,309,000, representing an increase of £1,233,900 over the 1912 figures. Britain would construct five Dreadnoughts and a significant number of auxiliary vessels.

Lloyd George, in his budget speech of 22 April 1913, explained the predicament.[63] The German Navy Law had necessitated a supplementary estimate of almost £1 million. £3.5 million would be spent on naval works, and the Admiralty required £1 million to establish oil fuel reserves. The international situation, Lloyd George lamented, resembled that following the Crimean War. Professional demands for increased defence expenditure fed on rumours of invasion. He could not offer Parliament any hope of arresting the trend unless the powers altered their policies and prevented "this strangulation of civilisation." Dismissing once again the policy of unilateral disarmament, he called for a multi-lateral agreement. Europe's financial giants had prevented war over Morocco in 1911, he suggested, and they could also check the growing expenditure on armaments. This was the last great and dangerous problem facing Europe; this was the task facing Grey and the Concert. Lloyd George, of course, needed Grey's support if he were to challenge the Admiralty.

The realities of the situation, however, continued to favour Churchill. Naval assistance from Canada did not materialize. Germany rejected the scheme for a one-year pause in construction, and Italy, in September, announced plans to build four Dreadnoughts. The cabinet agreed, therefore, that the Admiralty could accelerate construction of three of the five projected capital ships at an additional initial cost of £500,000.[64]

62. Asquith report, 22 Jan. 1913, Cab 41/34/3; Admiralty memoranda, 11 Jan. and 10 Feb. 1913, Cab 37/114/11 and 15; Marder, *Dreadnought to Scapa Flow*, I, 311–12.

63. Speeches, 22 and 29 April 1913, *Parl. Deb.*, H. of C., LII, 262–68, 1128.

64. Asquith report, 5 June, Cab 41/34/18, and Admiralty memorandum, 9 June 1913, Cab 37/115/37.

For Lloyd George the issue became one of timing. How long could he delay a confrontation with Churchill and at what point could he charge him with being reckless and irresponsible? In August 1913 Lloyd George served notice on the Admiralty.[65] He warned the House of Commons that the government must reduce defence expenditures and not shirk that duty for fear of being branded as an unpatriotic, "Little Englander" administration. He insisted, however, on a reciprocal response from Europe. That sick and suspicion-ridden society might yet plunge into war. Trade and social reform languished while menacing qualitative and quantitative rearmament programs paralysed the very forces which created wealth.

In preparation for a contest with Churchill where else would Lloyd George reach but back to the convictions of his youth? They had not lost their appeal; contacts with rising politicians such as Sir John Simon, the new attorney-general, revealed that to be so. The Liberal party was restless and demanding retrenchment, and an election could not be long delayed.[66] Lloyd George, however, could not break with Grey, and indeed, he was developing political intimacies with certain Unionists who would oppose any threat to the navy.[67]

On 12 November 1913, two days after Churchill had given notice publicly of the increased financial requirements of the navy, Lloyd George dined with Asquith, Grey, Crewe, and Haldane.[68] He forecast a deficit of £10 million. The navy estimates for 1914–15 would reach £52,300,000 with additional charges of £2 million for construction left over from the preceding financial

65. Speeches, 13 and 14 Aug. 1913, *Parl. Deb.*, H. of C., LVI, 2545–49, 2739–40.

66. The N.L.F. meetings at Leeds on 26 and 27 November 1913 revealed how restless Liberals were over increased defence expenditure. The meeting called on the government to initiate negotiations for arms limitation, and to endorse the freedom of the seas. (H. du Parcq, *Lloyd George*, IV, 76–77; P. A. Molteno, "Liberalism and Naval Expenditures," *Contemporary Review*, 105 (Feb. 1914), 153–64.)

67. Lloyd George to Bonar Law, 13 Nov. 1911, Bonar Law Papers, 24/3/27; Lloyd George to Asquith, 28 Dec. 1912, Asquith Papers, file 13; Scott diary, 16 Jan. 1913, Scott Papers, Add. 50901; Lloyd George to F. E. Smith, 6 Oct., and Smith to Lloyd George, 9 Oct. 1913, Lloyd George to Garvin, 31 Dec. 1913, and Garvin to Lloyd George, 1 Jan. 1914, LGP, C/3/7/2 and 3, and C/4/13/1 and 2; A. Chamberlain, *Politics from Inside*, 522.

68. Notes of a discussion, 12 Nov., LGP, C/14/1/10, and Margot Asquith to Lloyd George, 17 Nov. 1913, ibid., C/6/12/6.

year. Lloyd George's colleagues agreed unanimously to postpone payment of the £2 million until 1915. They would urge Churchill to pare his estimates by at least £1.5 million, and ruled against an increase in taxation before the next election. Whereas Asquith and Grey favoured going to the polls in 1914, Lloyd George counselled delay. He duly warned the cabinet on 17 November.[69] Departmental estimates, with particularly heavy demands from the Admiralty, the Post Office, and the Board of Education, showed an increase of £10 million. The Treasury could provide only an additional £6 million without imposing new taxation.

Churchill presented formidable estimates on 5 December.[70] He asked for £50,694,800, an increase of approximately £3 million over the combined 1913 and supplementary estimate figures. He attributed the increase to inflation, additional personnel, higher pay scales, qualitative improvements in armaments, costlier maintenance of a larger fleet, and the growing requirement for oil fuel reserves.[71] The Admiralty requested four new capital ships and twelve destroyers as necessary to retain the 60 per cent margin over Germany in the next three years, and to increase the margin by 1920. Churchill made one gesture to the Treasury; the Admiralty would undertake no further construction of airships until the CID, as Lloyd George advised, reviewed the whole future of air power.

Tactically speaking, Lloyd George had every reason to let others challenge Churchill. Simon, Herbert Samuel, the postmaster-general, J. A. Pease, president of the board of education, McKenna, and Lewis Harcourt, from a variety of motives would not disappoint him. Moreover, despite the strain, Lloyd George was personally less hostile toward Churchill, and the distance between them on what constituted an acceptable financial outlay on the navy was less than between Churchill and these other opponents.[72]

69. Asquith report, 18 Nov. 1913, Cab 41/34/35. The deficit would be £4 million, not £10 million.
70. Churchill memorandum, 5 Dec. 1913, Cab 37/117/86.
71. Lloyd George placed minimal administrative obstacles in the path of the scheme to purchase 51 per cent of the shares of the Anglo-Persian Oil Company. (M. Jack, "The Purchase of the British Government's Shares in the British Petroleum Company, 1912–1914," *Past and Present*, 39 (1968), 139–68.)
72. Churchill memorandum, 13 Dec., Cab 37/117/93, Riddell diary, 14 and 18 Dec., Riddell, *More Pages From My Diary*, 190–92, Lloyd George–Churchill exchanges, 16 Dec., LGP, Cabinet notes, C/12, and Churchill to Lloyd George,

The controversy was fought out initially at a series of cabinet meetings between 8 and 19 December.[73] Churchill's critics insisted that two capital ships would suffice to preserve the 60 per cent margin over Germany. They deplored the cost of the oil fuel reserves, and were also reluctant to accept the number of ships in commission as justifiable. Lloyd George reaffirmed that the Treasury could not meet all the demands made on it without a most unwelcome increase in taxation. Even if he rejected the requests of the Board of Education he would still need an additional £1.5 million over the 1913 figures, and might still face a deficit of over £1 million. He therefore insisted that the Admiralty reexamine its proposals and produce substantial reductions.

In response, Churchill offered estimates of £49,970,000 by effecting economies in the expenditures on oil fuel reserves and aircraft. Despite the increase over the 1913 figures, Lloyd George seemed willing to accept this offer as the lowest possible consistent with national security. Samuel and the others, however, were still not satisfied and the cabinet dispersed for the holidays without ruling on this difference. The tactical question facing Lloyd George was how far he should support the dissenting group of ministers.

Lloyd George circulated a lengthy memorandum and a covering letter on Christmas Eve, 1913.[74] As he has been charged, unjustifiably, with seeking to abandon the 60 per cent margin over Germany, with endangering national security, and with violating government policy, his letter merits quotation. The Treasury suggested:

> that the proposals put forward by the Admiralty are greatly in excess of the necessities. . . more especially in battleships, cruisers and men. If the programme of new construction be adopted by the Government in its entirety not merely will the 60% superiority over Germany be more than attained, but it will be exceeded by a figure which is

---

18 Dec. 1913, LGP, C/3/15/30; Churchill, *Winston S. Churchill*, II, 661–63. Lloyd George charged Churchill with violating an agreement made when Churchill went to the Admiralty in 1911; Churchill seemed to suggest that Lloyd George had broken a more recent agreement to support the 1914 estimates.

73. Asquith report, 20 Dec. 1913, Cab 41/34/39. The cabinet met on 8, 15, 16, 17, and 19 December. Asquith put the navy estimates at £50,700,000, an increase of £3 million.

74. Lloyd George covering letter and Treasury memorandum, 24 Dec. 1913, Cab 37/117/97, and LGP, C/24/3/26 and C/243.

*distinctly provocative. It would be construed as a direct challenge
to Germany, and such a policy, at a time when our relations with
that country are better than they have been for ten years, is, to say the
least of it, highly inopportune. To commit the country to a new
expenditure of millions unless it is abundantly clear that it is
necessary in order to maintain the security of our shores would . . . lay
the Government open to a serious charge of extravagant folly,
and to do so now, when trade is on the decline, when we are confronted
by a political crisis of the gravest possible character, and when there
is a widespread revolt not merely in this country, but throughout the
whole of Europe, against the grievous burden imposed by increased
armaments, would be not merely to invite but to deserve disaster for
the party and the Government responsible for such a proceeding.*

Churchill interpreted this letter to mean that Lloyd George had
joined Samuel in the campaign to limit construction to two capital
ships. In fact the Treasury memorandum deserves further comment. The difference between the Admiralty and the Treasury was
to some degree one of semantics compounded by their use of
statistics. The former demanded "the minimum programme
necessary" to ensure the 60 per cent margin; the latter insisted on
proposals which met that requirement. In consequence, the
question could reduce itself to one of merely delaying two of the
projected four capital ships for six months.

The Treasury identified Germany as the probable enemy and
specifically accepted the 60 per cent standard as "adequate for all
purposes." They argued, however, that when existing programs
were completed by early 1917, excluding the 1914–15 program,
Britain would be "numerically well above the 60 per cent standard." In terms of Dreadnoughts and battle cruisers Britain would
have forty-three to Germany's twenty-six, a margin of 65.4 per
cent. The Treasury gladly accepted the hypothesis that qualitative
factors, demonstrating the "margin of power," were more valid
than a mere numerical comparison. They concluded that whereas
the latter calculation provided the margin of 65.4 per cent, the
former tabulation indicated that Britain enjoyed tentatively a
margin of 84.4 per cent. Both standards exceeded the 60 per cent
level. Therefore, as Germany would lay down only two capital
ships in 1914–15, the Admiralty should do no more than match
the Germans. Four capital ships laid down in 1914 would raise the
numerical margin to 68 per cent.

An analysis of the balance in pre-Dreadnoughts pointed in the same direction and here the Treasury luxuriated skilfully in the statistical game. Categories where Britain enjoyed a quantitative and probably a qualitative superiority, as in armoured cruisers and submarines, were duly noted; classes in which Germany enjoyed a margin, as in unarmoured cruisers, were dismissed as inconsequential. Where, as in the case of destroyers, the German quantitative and qualitative lead was acknowledged as disturbing, the Treasury counted on the massive British lead in torpedo boats to produce a safe quantitative margin of 69 per cent, which qualitative factors could not reduce below 60 per cent. After such calculations the Treasury had little difficulty in labelling the Admiralty's construction program excessive and unjustifiable.

The Treasury also insisted that Britain had forced the pace; she led the world in naval research and development, as the Dreadnought and more recently the oil-burning *Queen Elizabeth* demonstrated. She bore a large measure of responsibility for the notoriously inflated expenditures on naval construction and operation. The Admiralty's excessive demands for personnel illustrated the last point. Perhaps the moment had come to pause, reassess, and possibly reverse the trend. Britain could halt the qualitative race, whatever the cost in prestige. Indeed to combine qualitative improvements with quantitative preponderance was simply unnecessary. In the Treasury's opinion, the European powers, all beset with financial problems, would reciprocate and acquiesce in the current numerical balance.

Before Churchill could reply, Lloyd George, from Criccieth, gave the celebrated interview published in the *Daily Chronicle* on New Year's Day, 1914,[75] and then left for North Africa. He offered reasons why the time was now favourable to reduce armament expenditures. In the first place, the strain and tension in Anglo-German relations had been largely dissipated by Grey's "wise and patient" diplomacy and Berlin's response. The Agadir crisis in fact had served as a salutory lesson, restoring sanity on both sides of the North Sea. Secondly, the European states were bent on developing their military power in order to safeguard against invasion. Germany preferred therefore to avoid a naval competition with

---

75. LGP, C/36/2/1. The headlines read: "Arms and the Nation, Lloyd George's bold indictment. The Chancellor and Germany. Arrest this 'organised insanity' and 'work for peace'."

Britain. In turn Britain should merely retain the present margin of naval superiority and maintain the fleet at peak efficiency. However, the two great democracies, Britain and France, should preserve the friendly relations established over the last ten years. Finally, Lloyd George pointed to a public revolt in Britain and Europe against militarism. The government must turn to different policies and remain faithful to the glorious traditions of Liberalism.

This controversial step, revealing the essence of the Treasury memorandum, was an expression of Lloyd George's convictions as well as a tactical move.[76] He had praised Grey and challenged Churchill. He had made a gesture to Germany, but had attempted to avoid upsetting the French. In fact many of his colleagues, with Churchill to the fore, regarded the interview as indiscreet, and even as provocative and disloyal. Others including Balfour, denounced it as a shameless political ploy.[77]

French responses mixed contempt with irritation. Unlike the French press, Prime Minister Gaston Doumergue, dismissed the interview as mere electioneering. Bertie assured him that Lloyd George would not carry the cabinet in any attempt to deplete the navy. Unfortunately, Georges Clemenceau, in *L'Homme Libre*, attacked Lloyd George, and the British press translated his *"prime sauteur Gallois"* as "Welsh mountebank." Bertie discreetly assured Grey that Clemenceau's phrase was inoffensive and meant merely "impulsive Welshman."[78]

The German press and the American ambassador to Britain described Asquith's vacation visit to France as undertaken to explain away the *Daily Chronicle* interview and soothe the French. The *Vossische Zeitung*, however, claimed that Lloyd George had elsewhere admitted that while France was Britain's insurance against Germany, the cabinet would show France the door should they secure a rapprochement with Germany. Grey assured Lloyd

---

76. French chargé to Doumergue, 2 Jan. 1914, *DDF*, 3, ix, 5. Lloyd George told Riddell that he had said nothing new and only gave the interview to help a reporter. (Riddell diary, 17 Jan. 1914, Riddell, *More Pages From My Diary*, 196.)

77. Asquith to Venetia Stanley, 6 Jan., Churchill, *Winston S. Churchill*, ii, 666, and Riddell diary, 6 Jan. 1914, Riddell, *More Pages From My Diary*, 192–93; Sir A. Fitzroy, *Memoirs*, ii, 532; Balfour to Selborne, 7 Jan. 1914, Marder, *Dreadnought to Scapa Flow*, i, 319; *Esher Journals*, iii, 151.

78. Bertie to Grey, 8 and 9 Jan. 1914, FO/800/55. Clemenceau meant what he said. *Sauteur* is a derogatory term in this context, meaning a politician who trims his conduct shamelessly.

George that he regarded that report as an absurd, childish, and even malicious invention. Lloyd George categorically denied its authenticity and left Grey to decide whether or not he should make a public denial.[79] The matter was let rest, but Grey obviously deplored any suggestion that the cabinet was divided over naval policy or was wavering in its determination to ensure supremacy. He felt that such impressions had a dangerous effect on military and naval opinion in Germany, and would serve both to injure Anglo-German relations and undermine the prospects for peace. Clearly the *Daily Chronicle* interview could not have pleased Grey.

A confrontation with Churchill and his flood of unyielding memoranda was virtually unavoidable once the first lord returned, as Asquith put it, from "his Paris fleshpots."[80] Asquith hoped that C. P. Scott, for example, would not excite Lloyd George's radical conscience to excess. On 15 January 1914 Lloyd George reviewed the problem with Scott and Simon.[81] He was less hostile than Simon toward Churchill, and told Scott that he would not insist on limiting construction to two Dreadnoughts if Churchill offered reductions elsewhere and kept the estimates below £50 million. They failed, however, to reach an understanding,[82] and on 18 January Simon suggested that Churchill intended actually to procure between £55 and £56 million for 1914–15. Lloyd George, McKenna, and Samuel agreed with Simon that Churchill must be forced to resign, and Scott urged Lloyd George to stand firm even to the point of his own resignation. Amid this bitterness, however, there always existed room for compromise, especially as Lloyd George failed to influence Grey.[83]

79. Goschen to Nicolson, 15 Jan., Grey to Lloyd George, 23 Jan., and Lloyd George to Grey, 26 Jan. 1914, LGP, C/4/14/12 and 13, and FO/800/101; B. J. Hendrick, *The Life and Letters of Walter Hines Page 1855–1918*, 2 vols. (New York, 1927), I, 283–84. Asquith and Lloyd George were both in Paris on 13 January, but Asquith did not leave the train.

80. Admiralty memoranda, 10, 14, 16, 21, 28, 30, and 31 Jan. 1914, Cab 37/118/6, 8, 9, 13, 15, 17, and 18; Churchill, *Winston S. Churchill*, II, 669.

81. Lloyd George to his wife, 15 Jan., Morgan, *Family Letters*, 165–66, P. Illingworth to Scott, 15 Jan., and Scott diary, 15 Jan. 1914, Scott Papers, Add. 50908 and 50901. Illingworth's note from Asquith, delivered to Scott at Lloyd George's breakfast table, said "Much will turn on the nature of the advice you give this morning. Weigh your words."

82. Scott diary, 16 Jan. 1914, Scott Papers, Add. 50901.

83. Riddell diary, 17 and 18 Jan., Riddell, *More Pages From My Diary*, 196–97, and Asquith to Lloyd George, 29 Jan. 1914, LGP, C/6/11/14; Spender and

On 19 January Lloyd George began to explore an accommodation in which he would concede 1914–15 estimates of approximately £51 million, if Churchill offered 1915–16 estimates of £49 million.[84] The first lord was neither receptive nor sanguine; he could offer no guarantees for 1915. The next day, in Asquith's presence, Lloyd George offered to accept all current obligations, the four new capital ships, and estimates of £53 million. In return he expected a full disclosure to Parliament and Churchill's guarantee, backed by Asquith's pledge, of 1915 estimates of £46 or £47 million.[85] Churchill remained obdurate, offering only minor concessions.[86] Asquith, expressing complete confidence in Churchill's integrity, threatened an immediate dissolution.

Lloyd George did not relish the consequences of a breach with Churchill and the prime minister, and an immediate dissolution. At the cabinet on 22 January he informed Asquith that a compromise was still possible, and asked the prime minister to postpone the cabinet scheduled for the following day.[87] That evening, and at breakfast on the following day, Lloyd George, Scott, Simon, and Masterman weighed the consequences; would the Liberal party accept navy estimates now of £54 million in return merely for a promise to reduce the 1915 estimates?[88] Scott and Simon demanded immediate economies. They also regarded Churchill's promises as valueless; he must commit himself to reduce the estimates to £46 or £47 million in 1915. Lloyd George finally admitted that he would accept 1914 estimates of £54 million and chided Simon, "a kind of Robespierre," and his supporters for their vendetta against Churchill.

After this breakfast, on 23 January, Lloyd George held further

Asquith, *Asquith*, I, 76–77; Scott diary, 17 and 18 Jan., Scott Papers, Add. 50901, and C. Hobhouse to Harcourt, 15 Jan. 1914, Harcourt Papers, box 29.

84. Churchill to Lloyd George, 19 Jan., LGP, C/3/16/3, and Asquith Papers, file 25, Hawtrey (Treasury) to Masterman-Smith (Admiralty) and reply, 20 Jan., LGP, C/3/14/3, and Asquith to Lloyd George, 20 Jan. 1914, ibid., C/6/11/14.

85. Scott diary, 21 Jan. 1914, Scott Papers, Add. 50901; Spender and Asquith, *Asquith*, II, 76.

86. Lloyd George to McKenna, 22 Jan. 1914, McKenna Papers, 4/4/241. Churchill's letter, he said, "puts an end to all my efforts for peace."

87. Lloyd George to Asquith, 22 Jan. 1914, LGP, Cabinet notes, C/12. Asquith's letters to his wife between 20 and 29 January suggested that Lloyd George had sought an accommodation with Churchill.

88. Scott diary, 22 and 23 Jan. 1914, Scott Papers, Add. 50901. Seebohm Rowntree was also present.

conversations with Churchill and Asquith.[89] The Admiralty still demanded its full construction program and 1914 estimates of £54 million. Churchill offered 1915 estimates, however, of £48,850,000, and 1916 estimates of £48 million or less. Lloyd George preferred 1915 estimates of £47 million, but he recognized that a point would emerge at which he must accept a figure or wreck the government, the party, and the future of Liberalism.

Scott, R. G. Hawtrey of the Treasury, and McKenna advised rejection of Churchill's proposal, but Lloyd George, tired and despondent, seemed anxious to avoid prolonging the struggle.[90] Only the prompting of McKenna and Scott persuaded him to call a meeting of those ministers who were strongly opposed to the Admiralty.[91]

Churchill informed Lloyd George on 26 January that while he would attempt to hold to his forecast for 1915, he could not be bound by any bargain or any commitment.[92] He now offered, however, 1914 estimates of £52,850,000. Urged on by Charles Hobhouse, chancellor of the Duchy of Lancaster, and Simon, Lloyd George ignored the reduction just offered in the 1914 estimates and charged that:

> *Your letter warns me—in time—that you can no more be held bound by your latest figures than you were by your original figure of £49,966,000. This intimation completely alters the situation. I now thoroughly appreciate your idea of a bargain: it is an agreement which binds the Treasury not even to attempt any further economies in the interest of the taxpayer, whilst it does not in the least impose any obligation on the Admiralty not to incur fresh liabilities.*
>
> *In one vital respect the task of the Cabinet is simplified by your letter, for it demonstrates that you and your critics are in complete agreement as to the real value of your last proposals. The only certainty about them is that the Exchequer would this year have to*

89. Churchill to Asquith, 23 Jan. and Lloyd George to Scott, 23 Jan. 1914, LGP, C/3/16/6, C/8/1/14 and G/244.

90. Scott to Lloyd George, 24 and 25 Jan., LGP, C/8/1/14 and 16, and Scott diary, 25 Jan. 1914, Scott Papers, Add. 50901.

91. The meeting at the Treasury was a bitter disappointment to McKenna, Simon, and Hobhouse. McKenna described Lloyd George as "unwilling to act," "as bad or worse," and as a defector. (Scott diary, 6 Feb. 1914, Scott Papers, Add. 50901.)

92. Churchill to Lloyd George, 26 Jan., LGP, C/3/16/7 and 8; Asquith Papers, file 25, and Riddell diary, 25 Jan. 1914, Riddell, *More Pages From My Diary,* 199–200.

*find 56 millions—supplementaries included—for the Navy, whilst*
*the reductions promised for 15/16 do not bind either the Board of*
*Admiralty or the First Lord. Therein you and your critics agree.*
*I have been repeatedly told that I was being made a fool of; I declined*
*to believe it. Your candour now forces me to acknowledge the justice*
*of the taunt. You proposed before Christmas to take 50 millions.*
*As a compromise on that you proposed Friday last to take four*
*millions more this year on condition of coming down 1½ millions next*
*year. Not a sumptuous offer at best. Now you qualify that!*

*I have laboured these last few days—not to favour you or to save*
*myself—but to rescue Liberalism from the greatest tragedy which has*
*yet befallen it. I have a deep and abiding attachment for Liberal*
*causes, and for the old Party, and the prospect of wrecking them*
*afflicts me with deep distress. That is why I have been prepared to*
*risk the confidence of my friends and to face the gibes and sneers from*
*friend and foe alike with which I foresaw the publication of the*
*figures would be greeted. I know too well that every paper would*
*gloat over my humiliation. That I did not mind if the ship and its*
*precious cargo could be saved. You decreed otherwise, and the*
*responsibility is yours and yours alone.*[93]

Lloyd George confessed to Asquith that his efforts to effect a
compromise and spare the cabinet a disastrous controversy had
"utterly failed." Churchill must shoulder the responsibility; his
figures were misleading and he seemed determined to secure £54
million in 1914 without honoring his promise to effect reductions
in 1915. Consequently Lloyd George now accepted the view of the
"economists."

Churchill's reply scarcely improved the situation, but when the
cabinet met on 28 January, Asquith appealed for an accommodation.[94] He was able to report to the king that the cabinet accepted
a construction program of four capital ships, 1913 expenditures of
£48,800,000, 1914 estimates of £52,800,000, and 1915 estimates of

93. Simon to Lloyd George, and Hobhouse to Lloyd George, 26 Jan., LGP,
C/8/3/6 and C/5/2/1, Lloyd George to Churchill, and Lloyd George to Asquith,
27 Jan. 1914, ibid., C/3/16/9, and Asquith papers, file 25. Lloyd George seemed
to accept Simon's analysis that Churchill had gone back on his offer for 1914,
and again demanded £54 million.

94. Churchill to Lloyd George, 27 Jan., LGP, C/3/16/10, Lloyd George,
cabinet notes, 28 Jan., ibid., C/12, and Asquith report, 29 Jan. 1914, Asquith
Papers, file 25. Asquith recorded meetings on 27, 28, and 29 January. (Spender
and Asquith, *Asquith*, II, 77.)

£49,500,000. Lloyd George, Simon, Samuel, and Lord Beauchamp, first commissioner of works, had registered strong protests against the inflated costs of fleet maintenance rather than the construction program. Lloyd George personally had demanded substantial and definite reductions in 1915. He had warned of a £9 million deficit in 1914–15, necessitating increased taxation, and forecast that the House of Commons would expect a substantial portion of increased revenues to be diverted to education and the relief of local rates. Churchill had therefore consented to review the costs of fleet maintenance and the cabinet awaited his report.

Clearly, Churchill had gained a substantial victory. On 6 February, as a result of his review of costs, he proposed certain reductions which the cabinet readily accepted.[95] The revised 1914 estimates then stood at £51,580,000. Churchill also agreed that the government should announce anticipated economies in the order of £2 million in the 1915 naval estimates. They would not, therefore, fall back to £47 million.[96]

Churchill had offered estimates around £50 million in December, while demanding four capital ships. During the last week of January he asked for £54 million and then for £52,850,000. On 28 January he accepted £52,800,000 and then, on 11 February, he enabled the cabinet to agree on estimates of £51,580,000. The economists had demanded estimates below £50 million and the construction of only two capital ships. Very reluctantly, they acquiesced in the decisions of 28 January and 11 February, which accepted estimates above their original expectations and granted four new capital ships.

Lloyd George, in November 1913, had hoped for estimates close to or even below £50 million. He had urged a construction program to meet but not exceed the 60 per cent margin over Germany, but he did not seriously attempt to limit new construction to only two capital ships. Between 19 and 23 January, moreover, he wavered and seemed ready to accept estimates of £51, £53, and even £54 million. Churchill, however, reduced his demands and Lloyd George accepted the lower sum arrived at on 11 February.[97]

95. Asquith to Churchill, 1 Feb., Churchill, *Winston S. Churchill*, ii, 678, and Asquith report, 11 Feb. 1914, Cab 41/35/3.

96. Canada's failure to assist Britain by building Dreadnoughts was an important factor. The cabinet permitted the Admiralty to accelerate the construction of the first two battleships of the 1915–16 program, although they refused to authorize three additional ships.

97. Lloyd George to Sir J. Bradbury (Treasury), 13 Feb., and Treasury notes

Throughout the greater part of the controversy he had sought a compromise, but had been guilty of tactical ineptness and indecision. He did not join the economists in their final protest[98] and to them he seemed irresponsibly unreliable. McKenna contemptuously dismissed him as "Churchill's man," the most degrading of epithets. Lloyd George had suggested that Churchill's enemies were impotent unless he led them; McKenna insisted that they had rejected the lead of the devious and treacherous chancellor.[99] As if that were not enough, Grey had stood resolutely by Churchill, and the Admiralty's victory had cut across the policy of seeking a détente with Germany. Little wonder that Scott described Lloyd George as not his buoyant self.

In his budget speech Lloyd George implied that the European situation had forced him to accept naval estimates which showed an increase of £2,717,000 and army estimates which had risen by £539,000.[100] He offered one tenuous ray of hope: the forecast reductions for 1915 and the anticipated diversion of resources to the social services. Elsewhere, he claimed to have strengthened the nation's defences against every *possible* foreign enemy, and was now poised to tackle the social and economic problems at home.[101] He had done his duty by the Admiralty and the War Office. If he diagnosed the international scene accurately, however, he would be able in the future to serve the Liberal party and the nation. If Grey's settlement of the Balkan Wars was not an isolated event and if the powers built on that foundation to check the arms race, peace would prevail.

In other words, Britain was secure, the naval race was won, and Lloyd George was not averse to receiving some of the credit.

---

on the navy estimates, 23, 24, and 26 Jan. 1914, LGP, C/24/3/34 and C/24/3/30A, 31, and 32.

98. Beauchamp, Hobhouse, McKenna, Runciman, and Simon to Asquith, 29 Jan. 1914, Asquith Papers, file 25.

99. Scott diary, 6 Feb. 1914, Scott Papers, Add. 50901. McKenna dissolved in laughter when Scott reported that Lloyd George had threatened to resign, and speculated that all along Lloyd George had been attempting to remove obstacles from Churchill's path. See also P. Cambon to Doumergue, 5 Feb. 1914, *DDF*, 3, IX, 224, and Churchill to Lloyd George, 13 May 1914, LGP, Cabinet notes, C/12. Perhaps Lloyd George felt indebted to Churchill for his support in the Marconi affair.

100. Speeches, 4 and 11 May and 9 June 1914, *Parl. Deb.*, H. of C., LXII, 58–85, 799, and LXIII, 160.

101. Speeches, 20 June and 17 July 1914, LGP, C/36/2/23 and 27.

Grey's diplomacy had brought Europe through a period of crisis, from a cold war, where defence expenditures and qualitative, scientific developments provoked conflict, to an armed peace. Citing the Duke of Wellington's defence of Sir Robert Peel's decision to revive the income tax in 1842, Lloyd George observed to Parliament, during the third reading of the Finance Bill on 23 July 1914, "We have been engaged in something which is as like war as you could imagine and there is the description by a man who knew war."[102]

A thaw had occurred, however, and England's relations with "a neighbour of ours" had improved. Financial interests and the industrial classes were in revolt against folly, and where political machinations and humanitarian motives had failed, their cosmopolitan pressure would succeed. Lloyd George never actually referred to Germany in this celebrated speech of 23 July, but no one could mistake the inference.

Contemporary and later observers, noting that Austria presented her ultimatum to Serbia that very day, have derided Lloyd George's lack of prescience. The historical significance of the speech does not lie, however, in its faulty prognostications. It both reflected Lloyd George's political predicament and expressed in a premeditated way the state of his thoughts on the international situation as they had evolved since 1906; the results of the education which came from holding office and attempting to construct an unconventional policy synthesis. Significantly, it praised Grey without reservation.

---

102. Speech, 23 July 1914, *Parl. Deb.*, H. of C., lxv, 726–29. Wellington had said, "I will not say . . . that we have been at war but I believe we have been at something as like war, if it be not war, as anything could well be."

# 9

# Understandable Emotions, Predictable Decisions

No member of Asquith's government joined lightly in the decision to involve the nation in war on 4 August 1914. Hesitation, fear, and self-deception permeated the twelve days of discussion from 24 July. Flawed memoirs and faltering memories, indictment and apologia, of men hurt by the reopening of old wounds and distracted by new conflicts, complicate the process of understanding. Lloyd George's own memoirs, in addition to the analytical inadequacies, were a patent attempt to discredit Grey.[1] Lloyd George minimized the degree of his support for Grey's policies before 1914 and built on that dubious foundation to interpret the final crisis. He accused the foreign secretary of bungling the mediation attempts in July, failing to activate the Concert or inform and guide the cabinet, and, finally, mishandling

1. Lloyd George, *War Memoirs*, I, 32–49, 128–32; H. B. Needham, "Mr. Lloyd George on the War," 258–67. He indicted only Berchtold, the Austrian foreign minister, with responsibility beyond that stemming from weakness and confusion. Rather, he rediscovered the militarist conspiracy. His memoirs were intended to warn against armaments and militarism. In a letter to *The Times* of 1 April 1936 he attacked Eden's policy of permitting military conversations with France, on the grounds that similar agreements had undermined negotiations, permitted escalation, and helped produce war in 1914. (LGP, G/214.)

the Belgian question. Grey, in fact, "might have averted war altogether."

Lloyd George, at fifty-one years of age, was in his prime; a senior minister with an impressive record of reform, beloved in Wales despite blemishes on his conduct, and popular in the country at large. He was indispensable to the Liberal party, and his resignation would be pivotal, second in importance only to that of Asquith. The first six months of 1914, however, had brought a series of reverses in addition to the problems raised by Churchill's naval program, and Lloyd George was bent on mending his political fences. As Masterman recorded, "L.G. is jumpy, irritable, overworked and unhappy; disturbed at the unpopularity of Insurance, at the failure of the Land Campaign to bring up a great emotional wave...; now at the failure of his Budget to command any measure of enthusiasm. Also he is very disturbed about the Irish question...the most difficult problem ahead is Labour."[2]

In any crucial discussion of foreign policy, therefore, Lloyd George would act cautiously. He would neither join those who challenged Grey nor seek to reactivate the governing quintet of 1911. If the issue became that of war or peace, the Liberal and radical press, led by C. P. Scott and Robertson Nicoll, editor of the British Weekly, would demand neutrality.[3] Garvin would expect Lloyd George to do his duty. Sheer political realism dictated that Lloyd George should neither lead those most reluctant to risk war, nor trail behind those who concluded that Britain must intervene in Europe. War was the political as well as the strategic unknown, the unexplored. It might destroy the party, or Liberals might wage war successfully, organize the peace, and initiate an era of reconstruction. The government was, ironically, damned whether it accepted or evaded its responsibilities. In August 1914, however, rather than relinquish power in whole or in part to the Unionists, Liberals did not recoil. For Lloyd George

2. Masterman to Ponsonby, 30 May 1914, Ponsonby Papers; C. Hazlehurst, *Politicians at War, July 1914 to May 1915*, 104–11. Robertson Nicoll, however, thought Lloyd George's stock was rising. (Robertson Nicoll to Lloyd George, 14 March 1914, T. H. Darlow, *William Robertson Nicoll: Life and Letters* [London, 1925], 381–82.)

3. Lord Riddell, *Lord Riddell's War Diary* (London, 1933), 6, 11; Darlow, *Robertson Nicoll*, 236–42. On 3 August Robertson Nicoll agreed that Britain must support France, and Riddell so informed Lloyd George through Masterman.

*184*

neither resignation nor fresh political alignments were attractive. His political instincts served him well; charges of bewildering inconsistency are irrelevant.

Convictions and perceptions about foreign policy reinforced this position. Lloyd George regarded Grey as constructive and pacific. His hesitations in 1914 did not reflect any hostility toward the foreign secretary.[4] Lloyd George identified the European balance of power, the preservation of France, and the prevention of German hegemony with the nation's security. He understood the significant relationship of Belgian neutrality to the question of a *casus belli* which British public opinion would accept. He also realized that the appeal of a small nation raped by Germany would touch responsive chords in Wales.

Yet the group in which John Simon was prominent could touch responsive chords in Lloyd George when men in crisis discussed war, the role of experts, and the debate between rational doves and irresponsible hawks which supposedly took place in Berlin. Lloyd George also knew how his family would respond, and war threatened the lives of his two sons. Almost inevitably then, the 1914 crisis was a monumentally emotional experience for Lloyd George. In the course of it he weighed evidence and yet grasped at improbabilities; he temporized and then acted decisively. Finally, he joined in the cabinet consensus and explained his reasons to C. P. Scott. Conviction was laced with embarrassment, but Lloyd George expected the nation to follow his example in facing what he described as a justifiable and ultimately unavoidable war.

The reports of the ten cabinet meetings between 24 July and 4 August never refer specifically to Lloyd George. Frances Stevenson recorded an initial reaction: the assassination at Sarajevo would result in a local Balkan war.[5] Apart from that, the first significant record was made by Scott on Monday, 27 July.[6] By then Lloyd

4. L. Masterman, "David Lloyd George," 160–69; W. George, *My Brother and I*, 234–43.

5. Frances Lloyd George, *The Years that are Past*, 70–71. Her evidence is inconsistent on the larger question of Lloyd George's attitude toward British involvement in a European war, and appears to have confused others.

6. Scott diary, 27 July 1914, Scott Papers, Add. 50901; J. L. Hammond, *C. P. Scott of the Manchester Guardian*, 177–78; Lloyd George to his wife, 27 July 1914, Morgan, *Family Letters*, 166. His cabinet notes contain only one earlier comment: "Slav and Teuton = Arranging assassination of Archduke." (Cabinet notes, 1908/1915, LGP, C/13.) He claimed subsequently to have no

George had attended two cabinet meetings, on 24 and 27 July,[7] and had heard Grey report on Austrian intransigence and his proposals for four-power mediation in the Austro-Serbian dispute.[8] He was aware that Grey expected Bethmann Hollweg to restrain Vienna,[9] but that Germany might reject the four-power conference scheme[10] and had asked for a declaration of British neutrality to help restrain Russia. France like Italy appeared more willing to cooperate in a mediation attempt. Grey, moreover, had already broached the subject of whether Britain would support France in the event of a European war.[11]

Lloyd George told Scott that there could be no question of British involvement "in any war in the first instance." No minister would support such involvement and the editorial in *The Times* that day, with its disturbing reference to the balance of power, did not represent the views even of Grey's officials. A Franco-German naval clash in the Channel, however, would present a difficult problem for the cabinet.

Lloyd George regarded Austria as determined on war with Serbia and he was in favour of exerting joint diplomatic pressure on the Hapsburg Monarchy, in cooperation with France and Russia, in order to localize and minimize the conflict. He hoped

---

personal recollection of a cabinet discussion on the European situation before that of 31 July.

7. Asquith reports, 25 and 28 July 1914, Cab 41/35/20 and 21; Z. S. Steiner, *The Foreign Office and Foreign Policy 1898–1914*, 155–56; M. Bonham Carter to J. A. Spender, 7 Aug. 1929, Spender Papers, Add. 46386; J. A. Spender and C. Asquith, *Life of Lord Oxford and Asquith*, II, 79–83. Spender regretted the unavailability of Harcourt's diary which supposedly contained a full record of the cabinet debate. (Spender to Samuel, 9 and 20 Nov. 1941, Samuel Papers, A/45.)

8. M. Ekstein-Frankl, "The Development of British War Aims, 1914–1915," (Ph.D. thesis, University of London, 1969), and "Sir Edward Grey and Imperial Germany in 1914," *Journal of Contemporary History*, 6, no. 3 (1971), 121–31; House diary, 20 July 1914; K. Robbins, *Sir Edward Grey*, 286–89; Bertie to Tyrrell, 22 July 1914, FO/800/55.

9. Sir F. Maurice, *Haldane, 1856–1915, The Life of Viscount Haldane of Cloan*, 2 vols. (London, 1937), I, 348–53; F. R. Bridge, "The British Declaration of War on Austria-Hungary in 1914," *The Slavonic and East European Review*, 47, no. 109 (1969), 401–22; R. B. Haldane, *An Autobiography* (London, 1929), 270–73.

10. Berlin rejected the proposal later that day. (Goschen to Grey, 27 July 1914, BDOW, XI, 185, 128; J. Bowle, *Viscount Samuel* [London, 1957], 118.)

11. Samuel to his wife, 27 July 1914, Samuel Papers, A157/689; Viscount Morley, *Memorandum on Resignation*, 1–3; Burns diary, 27 July 1914, Burns Papers, Add. 46308.

also to prevent Italy from joining the Central Powers should a European war develop. An offer of British neutrality might detach Italy and in this way Britain would render service to France. A European as opposed to a local war would, of course, range Austria and a reluctant but obligated Germany against Serbia, Russia, and France. He demonstrated how Germany might conduct the war. She would, Lloyd George suggested, strike first at France "across Belgium" and then at Russia, combining these moves with joint naval and military operations in the Channel intended to land a force at the rear of the French army. In addition, in combination with the Austrian fleet, Germany would launch a naval attack in the Mediterranean to sever France's communications and supply lines with Algiers.

Certain features of this *tour d'horizon* merit comment. Lloyd George, like Herbert Samuel, realized that Austrian intransigence could result in a European war from which only Italy and Britain might escape. If war erupted he expected Germany to violate Belgian neutrality, at least to some extent, and to conduct other military and naval operations, the significance of which Britain could hardly ignore. He contemplated joint diplomatic action with France and Russia and an independent move to neutralize Italy. France would likely benefit, and Lloyd George's significant concluding remark to Scott was, "You know I am more pro-French than you are." Realism and a desire for peace existed side by side. As Lloyd George told his wife, "War trembling in the balance. No one can tell what will or will not happen. I still believe peace will be preserved."[12]

The sharply deteriorating European situation strained Grey's ingenuity to the limit.[13] He retained only faint hopes of the four-power conference and brief expectations of Austro-Russian conversations producing restraint. Consequently, he was reduced to attempting to influence events and force moderation on Austria almost solely through Berlin. To accomplish that task Grey must convince Bethmann Hollweg of the possibility of a disastrous war and warn him of the consequences of irresponsibility.[14]

12. Lloyd George to his wife, 28 July 1914, Morgan, *Family Letters*, 167.
13. Samuel to his wife, 28 July 1914, Samuel Papers, A157/689; Crewe to Hardinge, 30 July 1914, Crewe Papers, C/24.
14. Grey to Buchanan, and Grey to Goschen, 28 and 29 July 1914, *BDOW*, xi, 203, 141–42, 218, 149, 223, 150, 263, 170–71, and 266, 173. Haldane was

Meanwhile, as a final move, Grey refused to commit Britain to any course of action; in this way he attempted to spread an efficacious uncertainty in Europe and keep the powers guessing about Britain's intentions.

A "very grave" cabinet endorsed this policy on Wednesday, 29 July.[15] Because of Russia's expected mobilization Samuel speculated on, "whether or not Germany, regarding war as inevitable, will then at once strike at France. There is a slight hope that, under the influence of the Emperor and Bethmann Hollweg, the Chancellor, she may not do so." Berlin's doves were supposedly at work. In view of her obligations to Austria and the military benefits accruing to Germany from rapid mobilization and an attack on France, however, Samuel was not very optimistic.

Of necessity the cabinet investigated the implications of a European war. Asquith, according to J. A. Pease, indicated to the cabinet that day that Germany's invasion route lay through Belgium.[16] The Foreign Office had circulated copies of the relevant treaties, but the cabinet decided that Britain's commitments to Belgium were questionable if the other signatories abstained from or refused to accept their obligations. They made no effort to discuss the attitude of France and face up to the inevitable: that France would accept her obligations in the face of German aggression against Belgium. Consequently, the cabinet concluded, if the question of Belgian neutrality arose, they would decide the matter as an issue of policy rather than one of legal duty. British national interests would be the decisive factor and all alternatives theoretically remained open. Finally, the cabinet agreed that the "precautionary stage" had arrived and that the "warning telegrams" to the fleet should be dispatched immediately.[17]

Lloyd George's response, in a note to Churchill, was, "This means we ought *at once* to have a meeting of the CID." The situation resembled Agadir. Lloyd George, as Miss Stevenson recorded, was concerned lest Britain's preparations for war were inadequate, and the phrase "ready to defend ourselves" appears twice in his

---

already pessimistic: "The German General Staff is in the saddle." (Maurice, *Haldane*, 353, and Haldane, *Autobiography*, 274.)

15. Asquith report, 29 July, Cab 41/35/22, and Spender Papers, Add. 46386, Samuel to his wife, 29 July, Samuel Papers, A157/691, and Lloyd George to his wife, 29 July 1914, Morgan, *Family Letters*, 167.

16. Hazlehurst, *Politicians at War*, 73.

17. Lord Hankey, *The Supreme Command*, I, 154–57.

cabinet notes.[18] Lloyd George suggested a further interpretation in his memoirs. He insisted that his was not an attitude of " passive non-intervention." Rather he urged the cabinet to make full military preparations so that Britain could ultimately mediate in a war in which the belligerents had become exhausted and dis-illusioned. That evening, to a London-Welsh audience, Grey praised Lloyd George as patient and wise, and as a contributor to cabinet unity.[19]

During the interval before the next cabinet meeting Grey pursued the tactic of noncommitment and cunctation.[20] On 30 July he angrily dismissed Berlin's ominous attempt to secure British neutrality, while offering, in a way that revealed how desperation and hope were enmeshed, a future political agreement, in order to secure Germany's cooperation in the current crisis.[21] In addition, Grey watched renewed Austro-Russian contacts and German representations at Vienna and St. Petersburg, and produced his own "halt at Belgrade" formula to localize the conflict.[22]

When the cabinet convened on Friday morning, 31 July, the fateful decisions and divisive debate feared by Samuel did not materialize. The cabinet decided merely to endorse Grey's rebuff to Berlin.[23] Should Germany attack France and violate Belgium the cabinet would reevaluate the situation.[24] Later that afternoon Grey asked both France and Germany to agree to respect Belgian

---

18. Lloyd George to Churchill, 29 July 1914, LGP, cabinet notes, 1908–15, C/13. Randolph Churchill printed the cabinet notes to demonstrate how his father won over Lloyd George—an unacceptable interpretation. (R. S. Churchill, *Winston S. Churchill*, II, 717–19.)

19. Lewis diary, 29 July 1914. Lloyd George was indisposed and did not attend.

20. Grey to Bertie, and Grey to Goschen, 29 July 1914, BDOW, XI, 283 and 286, 180 and 182–83.

21. Goschen to Grey, and Grey to Goschen, 30 July 1914, ibid., 293, 185–86, and 303, 193–94.

22. Grey to Buchanan, and Grey to Goschen, 30 and 31 July, ibid., 309, 196–97 and 340, 215–16, and Samuel to his wife, 30 July 1914, Samuel Papers, A157/689.

23. Samuel to his wife, 31 July 1914, Samuel Papers, A157/694; Earl of Oxford and Asquith, *Memories and Reflections, 1852–1927*, 2 vols. (Boston, 1938), II, 10; Burns diary, 31 July 1914, Burns Papers, Add. 46308.

24. Grey to Buchanan, Goschen to Grey, Nicolson to Grey, and Grey to Goschen and Bertie, 31 July 1914, BDOW, XI, 335, 213, 337, 214, 339, 215, 340, 215–16 and 352, 220; Hazlehurst, *Politicians at War*, 84–85.

neutrality.[25] Samuel indicated that at least one reason for very guarded optimism remained; Germany had declared martial law but had not yet mobilized, and the kaiser, despite Austrian intransigence, was working to preserve peace.

Arthur Nicolson, on the other hand, was distressed by the cabinet's apparent unwillingness to stand by France. Certain ministers were suggesting that while France was bound by treaty to Russia, Britain was not. They were arguing that:

> as we were free from any obligations to any party and as British interests were not for the present involved we should stand out and hold ourselves free to act as circumstances might demand. Cambon declined to communicate this message to his government. I was appalled by this outlook—this was on Friday, July 31st—and I wrote to Grey in as strong language as possible in regard to our deserting our friends. The Cabinet was at sixes and sevens over the matter but the majority was in favour of standing aside—and with the exception of Winston the minority was weak-kneed.[26]

Asquith was more revealing in a conversation that day with his friend, the Archbishop of Canterbury.[27] He described Britain as the only power with diplomatic weight, precisely because she was not committed and retained her freedom of action. She held the balance and Grey intended to keep Europe in suspense about British intentions. In that way, Asquith explained, the foreign secretary hoped to deter and restrain all the potential belligerents. He urged the archbishop to try and prevent public demonstrations against intervention. They might delude Europe into thinking that Britain had already decided on neutrality and that public opinion was already committed to non-intervention. None of the Great Powers, and especially Germany, wanted war, but they were

25. Tyrrell note, Buchanan to Grey, and Grey to Bertie, 31 July 1914, *BDOW*, xi, 344, 347 and 348, 217–18, and 367, 226–27. News that Berlin would proclaim "Kriegsgefahr" arrived after Grey had made his request for a declaration of respect for Belgian neutrality. (Goschen to Grey, 31 July 1914, ibid., 349, 219.)

26. Nicolson to Hardinge, 5 Sept. 1914, FO/800/375. Hardinge's response was revealing: "war had to come, and we were probably in a better position at its outbreak than we have ever been before or shall be again. It would have been a universal misfortune if we had been unable to profit by the miscalculation of Germany and had allowed her to choose a more favourable moment." (Hardinge to Nicolson, 8 Oct. 1914, FO/800/375.)

27. G. K. A. Bell, *Randall Davidson: Archbishop of Canterbury*, 2 vols. (London, 1935), ii, 733–35.

trapped by their commitments. It could, Asquith concluded, "be most mischievous were the military party in Germany to be able to point out that England had shown such an expression of public opinion against intervention that it would clearly stand aloof, and, therefore, Germany need have no fear that its shipping would be interfered with in the North Sea."

Asquith also expressed utter contempt for the Serbs. They were responsible for the crisis and "deserved a thorough thrashing." Austria seemed determined on stern measures, but Russia could not permit Serbia to be humiliated.

The cabinet which met on the morning of 1 August feared the worst and yet resisted Churchill's attempts to prepare for intervention in war. They grasped, understandably if unrealistically, at straws, in the face of what appears to be, in retrospect, conclusive evidence that Germany would attack France through Belgium in the event of war.[28] Germany, in contrast to France, had not given a formal pledge to respect Belgian neutrality. However, what seems unrealistic now was unavoidable then in order to preserve governmental unity. Asquith seemed convinced that the bulk of the party preferred a policy of unconditional neutrality.[29]

Ministers prayed that diplomacy would yet foil military preparations.[30] Even Churchill confirmed that lingering grounds for optimism still existed. He informed Lord Robert Cecil of the possibility of Austro-Russian negotiations based on a formula proposed by Grey.[31] He feared the worst, of course, and warned that Britain's interests and honour would suffer if they allowed Germany to trample on Belgian neutrality and did not come to the aid of France. Samuel explained to his wife that "We may be brought in under certain eventualities. A suggestion of mine was adopted by the Cabinet which may a good deal affect the issue. Much depends on Germany's attitude to the neutrality of Belgium. I am less hopeful than yesterday of our being able to keep out of it. Italy's neutrality is an important fact."[32]

---

28. Bertie to Grey, and Goschen to Grey, 31 July 1914, BDOW, xi, 382 and 383, 234–35.

29. Asquith, Memories, ii, 11; Steiner, The Foreign Office, 159; Hazlehurst, Politicians at War, 33–40.

30. Grey to Goschen, and Grey to Buchanan, 1 Aug. 1914, BDOW, xi, 411, 246, 417, 249, and 422, 251.

31. Churchill to Cecil, 1 Aug. 1914, Cecil Papers, Add. 51073.

32. Samuel to his wife, 1 Aug. 1914, Samuel Papers, A157/696; note from

The cabinet parted "in a fairly amicable mood" and still united.[33] Grey proceeded to lecture Ambassador Lichnowsky on Germany's obligations toward Belgium, warning him of the probable consequences of a violation of her neutrality and refusing to guarantee Britain's non-intervention no matter what the circumstances.[34] He could not, however, give a commitment to Paul Cambon, the French ambassador, and speculated with both ambassadors on the possibility of a limited Austro-Russian war and British and French neutrality in a war between Russia and the Central Powers.[35] Such hypotheses defied political and military realities. Nevertheless, Grey insisted that Britain had no obligation to assist Russia, and as for aid to France, "we could not propose to Parliament at this moment to send an expeditionary military force to the continent. Such a step had always been regarded here as very dangerous and doubtful. It was one that we could not propose, and Parliament could not authorise, unless our interests and obligations were deeply and desperately involved."

Obviously the cabinet preferred to avoid intervention, but it was less divisive and surely less traumatic to contemplate limited naval participation in circumstances that were judged unavoidable. As Churchill observed to Lloyd George after a long exhortation to remain united, "The naval war will be cheap—not more than 25 millions a year."[36]

Pressed by Nicolson and Cambon, Grey, with Asquith's support, agreed to raise the question of Britain's responsibility to protect France's northern and western coasts at the cabinet on the following day.[37] He would see whether he could extract a guarantee of British assistance.

German embassy, 31 July 1914, BDOW, xi, 372, 229–30; Goschen to Grey, 1 Aug. 1914, ibid., 385, 236.

33. Burns diary, 1 Aug. 1914, Burns Papers, Add. 46336.

34. Grey to Goschen, 1 Aug. 1914, BDOW, xi, 448, 260–61.

35. Grey to Bertie, 1 and 2 Aug., ibid., 419, 250, 426, 253, 440, 256, and 447, 260, Bertie to Grey, 1 Aug., and Grey to Bertie, 2 Aug. 1914, ibid., 453, 263, and 460, 266.

36. Churchill to Lloyd George, n.d. [1 Aug. 1914?], LGP, C/13. Asquith told the C.I.G.S. that they were not committed to send the B.E.F. to France. (Sir C. E. Callwell, Field Marshal Sir Henry Wilson, i, 154.)

37. Nicolson to Hardinge, 5 Sept. 1914, FO/800/375; Nicolson to Grey, 1 and 2 Aug., and Grey to Bertie, 1 Aug. 1914, BDOW, 424, 252, 446, 259, 426, 253, and 447, 260. Grey told Professor Temperley in 1929 that Cambon never pressed him on the subject of a pledge of honour to France, an observation not

Lloyd George, by 1 August, had acquiesced in decisions which had tested the resources of diplomacy to the full, preserved cabinet unity, and sought to avoid, delay, or limit Britain's involvement in a European war. Pusillanimity, genuine caution, self-deception, and realism were all present. No evidence exists that he had adopted any extreme position. Ponsonby's Foreign Affairs Committee operated without his support. Harcourt took the lead in organizing unofficial gatherings,[38] and Lord Morley did not include Lloyd George in the peace group of eight or nine ministers, which supposedly emerged in the last days of July. Indeed, Morley did not even count Lloyd George as a member of the expanded neutralist faction of ten or eleven ministers he saw coalescing by 2 August.[39] Hence his criticism that Lloyd George

> *informed us that he had been consulting the Governor and Deputy Governor of the Bank of England, other men of light and leading in the City, also cotton men, and steel and coal men etc., in the North of England, in Glasgow, etc., and they were all aghast at the bare idea of our plunging into the European conflict; how it would break down the whole system of credit with London as its centre, how it would cut up commerce and manufacture—how it would hit labour and wages and prices, and, when the winter came, would inevitably produce violence and tumult. When I pressed this all-important prospect in a later debate, the Chancellor of the Exchequer said rather tartly that he had never said he believed it all.*[40]

Asquith described Lloyd George at the 1 August cabinet meeting as "all for peace...more sensible and statesmanlike for

---

irrelevant to his claim that the proposal to police the Channel came from the peace group (see note 87). See also Austen Chamberlain diary notes, 31 July and 1 and 2 Aug., A. Chamberlain Papers, AC/14/2/1–12, Bonar Law to Asquith, 2 Aug., LGP, C/6/11/29, and Nicolson to Balfour, 2 Aug. 1914, Balfour Papers, Add. 49748.

38. Conversation in 1929 between Grey and Professor Temperley; Austen Chamberlain to Lansdowne, 2 Aug. 1914, A. Chamberlain Papers, AC/2/14/1–12.

39. Morley, *Memorandum*, 4–7, 11. Neither Crewe nor Samuel accepted Morley's *Memorandum* as either fair or accurate. (Crewe to Samuel, 26 Nov. 1928, Samuel Papers, A/45.)

40. See also F. Owen, *Tempestuous Journey*, 263; Riddell, *War Diary*, 2. Owen noted Lloyd George's meeting with a gloomy Sir Walter Cunliffe, the governor of the Bank of England, on 1 August.

keeping the position still open."[41] Churchill was evidently concerned lest Lloyd George defect.[42] He urged him to stand firm with
his senior colleagues and not to forfeit the opportunity to shape
the future of Britain and Europe. Churchill understood, however,
that Lloyd George was not acting irresponsibly, even though he
was known to be in close contact with Robert Donald, editor of
the *Daily Chronicle*, and Labour's Ramsay MacDonald.[43]

Lloyd George, in fact, was deeply involved in the cabinet
committee dealing with financial, commercial, and maritime
insurance matters, which met for six hours after the cabinet
meeting on 1 August.[44] It met again in the evening, but Lloyd
George spent Saturday night neither in earnest consultation nor in
drawing up contingency plans for war. Instead, he went to the
opera with Mr. Baring and Lord Lucas, parliamentary secretary to
the Board of Agriculture, and on to Baring's house to hear Sir
John Barrie sing Russian folk songs until the small hours. He
walked home with Barrie at dawn.[45] Meanwhile, the Foreign Office
had received word of Germany's declaration of war on Russia, and
that she had mobilized and invaded Luxemburg.[46]

The cabinet met at 11 a.m. on Sunday, 2 August. Within hours
came the news that German forces had penetrated across the
French border and might invade Belgium south of the Meuse and
Sambre rivers.[47] Before the meeting, Lloyd George, Harcourt,
Lord Beauchamp, Simon, and Pease agreed that "we are not
prepared to go into war now, but that in certain events we might
reconsider our position, such as the invasion wholesale of
Belgium."[48] Harcourt felt sure, according to Morley, that ten or
eleven ministers would oppose Grey if he contended that Britain

41. Asquith, *Memories*, II, 11.

42. Churchill to Lloyd George, n.d. [1 Aug. 1914?], LGP, C/13.

43. H. A. Taylor, *Robert Donald*, 23.

44. Lloyd George to his wife, 30 July, Morgan, *Family Letters*, 167, Samuel to
his wife, 2 Aug., Samuel Papers, A157/697, and Buchanan to Grey, and Bertie
to Grey, 1 Aug. 1914, BDOW, XI, 445, 259, 451 and 452, 262–63; Hankey,
*Supreme Command*, I, 160–61.

45. Frances Stevenson to D. Mackail, 7 Nov. 1939, LGP, G/48/1/74.

46. Morley, *Memorandum*, 7–8; Churchill to Cecil, 1:00 a.m., 2 Aug. 1914,
Cecil Papers, Add. 51073. Churchill felt that an attack on France could not long
be delayed and Belgium therefore faced a serious situation.

47. Goschen to Grey, 1 Aug., Sir F. Villiers to Grey, 2 Aug., Crowe note,
2 Aug., Cambon note, 2 Aug. 1914, BDOW, XI, 457, 264, 465, 268, 471 and 473,
269–70.

48. Hazlehurst, *Politicians at War*, 66.

had obligations of honour, and commitments resulting from policy, toward France.[49] Lloyd George waited for Grey's analysis both of the situation in Berlin and of the implications of Germany's military actions.

The foreign secretary took the lead and brought the cabinet closer to disruption than at any other time in the whole crisis. As Samuel testified, "The morning Cabinet almost resulted in a political crisis....Grey expressed a view which was unacceptable to most of us. He is outraged by the way in which Germany and Austria have played with the most vital interests of civilisation, have put aside all attempts at accommodation made by himself and others, and while continuing to negotiate have marched steadily to war."[50]

Grey was angered, full of righteous indignation, and sensitive to Paul Cambon's expectations: an irresistible combination. Lichnowsky's tears could not eradicate Grey's feeling that he had been deceived. The reason seemed obvious: the hawks had defeated the doves in Berlin. As Grey confirmed, "There were two sets of people in Germany: people like the German Chancellor, Herr von Bethmann-Hollweg, and the German Ambassador here, Prince Lichnowsky, who dealt with all these things as we deal with them; on the other hand, there was the military party of force, who had no respect at all for these things."[51]

Momentarily, Grey was attempting to drive the cabinet faster and further than the majority would permit. Under threat of his resignation and therefore of Asquith's, the cabinet must acknowledge obligations to France and the balance of power.[52] Specifically, they must undertake to protect the Channel, and France's coasts and shipping. Such demands prompted Harcourt to implore Lloyd George, "You must now speak for us. Grey wishes to go to war without any violation of Belgium."[53] Churchill's counsel was

49. Morley, *Memorandum*, 11.
50. Samuel to his wife, 2 Aug. 1914, Samuel Papers, A157/697; Asquith, *Memories*, II, 11–12.
51. Grey to Barclay, 4 Aug. 1914, *BDOW*, XI, 638, 328. Grey told J. A. Spender that while those who sought to indict Germany solely for responsibility for the war did not serve the cause of future peace, they substantially served the truth. Those who sought to blame Britain for the war did a disservice both to the cause of peace and the truth. (Grey to Spender, 21 May 1927, and 5 Aug. 1928, Spender Papers, Add. 46389.)
52. Hazlehurst, *Politicians at War*, 95.
53. Harcourt to Lloyd George, n.d. [2 Aug., morning cabinet], LGP, C/13.

"At the present moment I would act in such a way as to impress Germany with our intention to preserve the neutrality of Belgium. So much is still unknown as to the definite purpose of Germany that I would not go beyond this. Moreover public opinion might veer round at any moment if Belgium is invaded and we must be ready to meet this opinion." [54]

Samuel probably represented the majority view, which contained various degrees of emphasis, when he concluded:

> we were not entitled to carry England into war for the sake of our good-will for France or for the sake of maintaining the strength of France and Russia against that of Germany and Austria. . . . we should be justified in joining in the war either for the protection of the northern coasts of France . . . or for the maintenance of the independence of Belgium, which we were bound by treaty to protect and which again we could not afford to see subordinated to Germany. We sanctioned a statement being made by Grey to the French Ambassador this afternoon, to be followed by a statement in Parliament tomorrow, that we should take action if the German fleet came down the Channel to attack France (Almost the whole of the French fleet is in the Mediterranean).

Despite continued hopes that avenues of escape or limited involvement still existed, the cabinet had begun to emerge from the amber light of uncertainty and unrealism. John Burns, now at the Board of Trade, Morley, and Harcourt found the most difficulty in accepting the position reached, which Asquith and others summarized as follows.[55] Britain was under no obligation to France or Russia to afford them military or naval assistance. They could not, however, ignore "the ties created by our long-standing and intimate friendship with France." Britain could not permit the elimination of France as a Great Power and Germany must not be

54. Churchill to Lloyd George, n.d. [2 Aug.?], LGP, C/13.
55. Asquith to Bonar Law, 2 Aug., and A. Chamberlain to Lansdowne, 2 Aug. 1914, A. Chamberlain Papers, AC/14/2/1–12; Nicolson to Hardinge, 5 Sept. 1914, FO/800/375; Grey to Bertie, 2 Aug., BDOW, xi, 487, 274–75, and Crewe report, 2 Aug. 1914, Cab 41/35/23. Before the morning cabinet on 3 August, Grey told Cambon that Britain's policing of the North Sea as well as the Channel implied protection of France's coasts and shipping in the Eastern Atlantic and the Channel, and if implemented would mean "that from that moment Great Britain and Germany would be in a state of war." (Cambon to Viviani, DDF, 3, xi, 661.)

allowed to use the Channel as a hostile base. Britain, moreover, had obligations to Belgium to "prevent it being utilised and absorbed by Germany." However, "the despatch of the Expeditionary force to help France at this moment is out of the question and would serve no object." In any case Parliament must approve any decisive steps.

The phrase "utilised and absorbed" pertaining to Belgium left room for manoeuvre. Those anxious to limit British involvement, should it become unavoidable, welcomed continued restraints on military as opposed to naval intervention. Policing the Channel and ensuring that the fleet would act only in response to actual German naval moves were acceptable propositions. Defensive naval operations were not in the same category as dispatching the expeditionary force, and perhaps Germany might yet refrain from criminal folly. Lloyd George accepted this policy and as late as 11 August still seemed to envisage Britain fighting a limited war. "We are keeping the sea for France—that ought to suffice here for the moment especially as we are sending 100,000 men to help her to bear the first brunt of the attack. That is all that counts for Russia will come in soon." [56]

Despite the reaction to Grey's tactical error in cabinet on 2 August, the fissures seemingly threatening unity were in reality less menacing. After the cabinet Lloyd George lunched at Beauchamp's, and talked on into the afternoon with Morley, Simon, Harcourt, Samuel, MacKinnon Wood, the secretary for Scotland, and Pease, a late arrival.[57] Lloyd George had attempted to arrange a luncheon himself, including at least Harcourt, Simon, and Runciman, president of the board of agriculture. Harcourt, however, was already "engaged to lunch with Beauchamp" and asked his host whether "he could entertain others." He replied to Lloyd George that "Beauchamp would be glad to see you and Simon. Perhaps the food would not run to more." [58]

The discussion was almost as superficial as the food was sparse. Morley described himself, Simon, and Lloyd George as "all three

56. Lloyd George to his wife, 11 Aug. 1914, Lloyd George Papers (National Library of Wales), 20434C; Taylor, *Robert Donald*, 25.
57. Morley, *Memorandum*, 14–20; Samuel to his wife, 2 Aug. 1914, Samuel Papers, A157/697; Runciman to Samuel, 14 Jan. 1942, ibid., A/45.
58. Harcourt–Lloyd George exchanges, n.d. [2 Aug.], LGP, C/13; Sir A. Fitzroy, *Memoirs*, II, 559. Beauchamp was one of the few ministers to keep his London house open.

*197*

for resignation." Simon seemed "pretty sure of decisive influence over Lloyd George," but the gathering was "a very shallow affair." Their earnest talk of avoiding a "Russian or Central European quarrel" and not permitting the Ententes to drag England into war, spurious applause for Burns, who had resigned, distaste for what the cabinet had just permitted Grey to tell Cambon, and concern for the future of Liberalism were understandable, but were as unimpressive as Morley's conclusion that "if I, or anybody else, could only have brought home to them that the compound and mixed argument of French liability and Belgian liability must end in expeditionary force, and active part in a vast and long-continued European war, the Cabinet would undoubtedly have perished that very evening, Lloyd George and Simon heading the schism." Yet Morley also wrote, "what exactly brought Lloyd George among us and what the passing computations for the hour inside his lively brain I could not make out. The motives of Lloyd George were a riddle. He knew that his 'stock' had sunk dangerously low."

The group, in fact, lacked purpose, cohesion, and leadership. Resignation would be at best an unpredictable and possibly a fatal step. There were responsibilities to Asquith, the government, the party, the nation, and themselves, not necessarily in that order, and could they merely relinquish power to the Unionists? Samuel understood the situation much more clearly than Morley. There was a good deal of emotional heart-searching, but cabinet unity was being preserved. It depended for its final cement on the question of Belgian neutrality, and as Samuel noted, "they all agreed with my formula except Morley who is now so old that the views he expresses are sadly inconsequent and inconsistent. I went from there to see McKenna, whom I found in bed, tired out. He concurred. After an hour at the LGB...I went to Downing Street and saw the PM and told him the situation. At 6 several of us, including Crewe, met again at Lloyd George's." This gathering also included Augustine Birrell, chief secretary for Ireland, and clearly was mixed in attitude.

Lloyd George assumed, according to Runciman, that his guests at tea were all opposed to a declaration of war at that time and were prepared to resign. He himself still seemed uncertain and speculated on various courses of action should he be forced to leave the government. He would not campaign against a war as he had against the Boer War, but he would not assist in its prosecution. He would retire to Criccieth for the time being for "there appears to be nothing for a Liberal to do but to look on while the hurricane rages."[59] After tea Lloyd George insisted, to the point of sending a car, that Ramsay MacDonald leave Robert Donald's house and come up to London.[60] At the same time Garvin attempted to rally him to the interventionist cause. He must not fail the nation, for "if we leave our friends to fall we are done as a people. Your democracy is solely shielded by the sea. Oh Agadir, Agadir, and your courage then!"[61]

Runciman identified Lloyd George with those who contemplated resignation. Like McKenna he had no deep regard for the chancellor of the exchequer and probably attributed his hesitation to the basest motives. Lloyd George's expressed concern over the implications and consequences of resignation at that point in the crisis is nevertheless most revealing. He sent for MacDonald, as he did for Scott on the following day, as much to explain why he had not resigned as to consult and to test reactions. Political considerations dictated such steps, but the vacillation and the indeterminate attitude were genuine. They were predictable responses as he contemplated the results of policy decisions made in London and Berlin, and an indication of his personal anguish as he faced the probable outcome.

The information received from Europe late in the afternoon and on into the evening served to deepen the distress and yet force a decision.[62] Germany was undertaking further military operations which threatened Belgium, and indulging in transparently feeble attempts to label France as the aggressor. These developments simultaneously solidified the cabinet consensus and yet tore at Lloyd George's emotions. Anger at Berlin joined with apprehension about the consequences of war.

The cabinet met at 6:30 p.m. and Samuel described the situation as easier:

---

59. Runciman memorandum, 4 Nov. 1929, Spender Papers, Add. 46386; Samuel to his wife, 2 Aug. 1914, Samuel Papers, A157/697. Lloyd George had invited Runciman, Reading, Beauchamp, McKinnon Wood, Samuel, Hobhouse, and Simon. Simon included Crewe.

60. Taylor, *Robert Donald*, 23.

61. Garvin to Lloyd George, 2 Aug. 1914, LGP, C/4/13/3.

62. French embassy note, Grey to Bertie, and Bertie to Grey, 2 Aug. 1914, *BDOW*, XI, 486, 274, 505, 506, and 507, 281.

> *the point of contention was not pressed and with the exception of the two I have mentioned (Burns and Morley) we remain solid. Had the matter come to an issue Asquith would have stood by Grey in any event and three others would have remained. I think all the rest of us would have resigned. The consequences would have been either a Coalition Government or a Unionist Government, either of which would certainly have been a war ministry. Moreover, the division or resignation of the Government in a moment of utmost peril for the country would have been in every way lamentable.[63]*

They delayed discussion of Grey's statement to Parliament and agreed:

> *that no communication as regards restrictions on the employment of the German fleet should be made to Germany beforehand, and that when the announcement is made it would be clear that the practical protection of the French coasts that would be involved is not only a recognition of our friendship with France, but is also imperatively required to preserve British interests. As regards Belgium it was agreed, without any attempts to state a formula, that it should be made evident that a substantial violation of the neutrality of that country would place us in the situation contemplated as possible by Mr. Gladstone in 1870, when interference with Belgian independence was held to compel us to take action.*

Although the German army was poised in Luxemburg, however, the cabinet had no news of an actual invasion of Belgium.

Samuel explained in what sense the group, embracing neither the small and dispensable faction which resigned, on the one hand, nor Grey, Asquith, Churchill, and Haldane, on the other, was emerging as a somewhat coherent body:

> *I still have hopes that Germany will neither send her fleet down the Channel nor invade Belgium and that we shall be able to keep England at peace while rendering France the greatest of all services— the protection of her northern coasts from the sea and the protection of her 150 miles of frontier with Belgium. If we can achieve this without firing a shot we shall have accomplished a brilliant stroke of policy. For this object I have been working incessantly all week.*

63. Crewe report, 2 Aug., Cab 41/35/23 and Spender Papers, Add. 46388, and Samuel to his wife, 2 Aug. 1914, Samuel Papers, A157/697. This letter was postmarked 3 August at 12:15 a.m.

*If we do not accomplish it, it will be an action of Germany's and not of ours which will cause the failure, and my conscience will be easy in embarking on the war. The guarantee of the neutrality of Luxemburg is collective and England is not separately responsible. It is different in the Belgian case. If Germany chooses to tear up that treaty too she must bear the blame for the consequences. Nor is it possible for us to tolerate great naval conflicts at our own doors with grave risk of permanent national disadvantage as a consequence. The fleet is mobilised. It is probable that tomorrow we shall mobilise the army also.*[64]

Lloyd George would not have taken exception to Samuel's analysis which makes understandable the crucial decisions of 2 August. From 30 July Grey had become convinced, in the face of German diplomatic initiatives, evasions, and military moves, that Britain must act to ensure assistance to France. This conviction was in accord with the logic of his policy. Strategic factors would determine the *casus belli* and Grey saw the decision of 2 August as an essential if inadequate step towards intervention.

Burns and Morley regarded this policy as deliberately provocative and damnably warlike because it threatened Berlin with British involvement. Lloyd George and the colleagues with whom he associated viewed the situation differently. The decision to police the Channel, but not to embark on military operations, could be a move to avoid or at least to limit involvement in a European war; it could be a step away from intervention rather than toward it. At the same time, however, as the decision on Belgian neutrality confirmed, he realized full well that the risk of involvement was present and that such decisions might induce intervention. Indeed, if the deterrent value of British policy proved ineffective, involvement was unavoidable. A terrible prospect, genuinely heart-rending for Lloyd George, but not only was it a matter of policy that Berlin should decide the outcome, but also one of emotional necessity. In any case, would Germany, in the final analysis, actually risk war with the British Empire?

The balancing involved was demonstrated at Riddell's dinner table on 2 August. Lloyd George said "that as a compromise the

64. Samuel to his wife, 2 Aug. 1914, Samuel Papers, A157/657. See also Burns diary, 2 Aug., Burns Papers, Add. 46336, Burns to Asquith, 2 Aug., and Burns to a friend, 3 Aug. 1914, ibid., Add. 46282; Morley, *Memorandum*, 21–23; Charles Trevelyan to Burns, 3 Aug. 1914, Burns Papers, Add. 46303.

Government had determined to tell Germany that England would remain neutral if Germany undertook not to attack the coast of France or to enter the English Channel with a view to attacking French shipping. He said that if the Germans gave this undertaking in an unqualified manner and observed the neutrality of Belgium, he would not agree to war but would rather resign. He spoke very strongly, however, regarding the observance of Belgian neutrality." [65] Ramsay MacDonald agreed with him on Belgium, and Lloyd George balked when Masterman and Riddell insisted that the crucial issue was the defence of France against Germany, irrespective of the benefits accruing to Russia.

Only at this stage did the Russian factor emerge clearly. Riddell recorded that

> Lloyd George strongly insisted on the danger of aggrandising Russia and on the future problem that would arise if Russia and France were successful. How would you feel if you saw Germany overrun and annihilated by Russia. . . . in 1916 Russia would have a larger army than Germany, France and Austria together. The French have been lending the Russians millions of money for the purpose of constructing strategical railways to carry their armies to the German frontier. They will be completed by 1916. The French papers have been boasting that in that year France and Russia will be able to smash Germany. No doubt the Germans think they must strike before their enemies are ready to annihilate them.

Subsequently, Lloyd George wrote, "I am dead against carrying on a war of conquest to crush Germany for the benefit of Russia. Beat the German Junker but not war on the German people." [66]

Lloyd George had made no actual move toward resignation for in the final analysis he could face the consequences of war. No one has surpassed Ramsay MacDonald's picture of him on that evening. "Lloyd George, with a map of the Franco-German frontiers, marked with red and blue blotches, like sausage balloons, which had been circulated to the cabinet, propped up in front of him. As he munched his cutlets Lloyd George kept talking and pointing to the map, 'dabbing at it' with his fork—as Napoleon is said to have done." In fact, Riddell's dinner guests seemed to conclude, perhaps for the benefit of Sir John French, chief of the Imperial

65. Riddell, *War Diary*, 4–6; Hankey, *Supreme Command*, i, 161–62.
66. Lloyd George to his wife, 11 Aug. 1914, Morgan, *Family Letters*, 169.

General Staff, that Britain would be involved in war and that the British Expeditionary Force would go to Europe under French's command. Lloyd George told French to "be at Downing St. tomorrow at ten o'clock sharp."

Lloyd George could see every alternative in terms of national interests. Peace if sanity prevailed; if not, limited naval involvement,[67] and, should Germany violate Belgium, no doubt more than that. He must pray for peace and yet contemplate war, for the cabinet had prescribed the specific conditions under which Britain would be involved.[68] The alternatives were stark, and the emotional content was not reduced because political considerations were fused with conviction. Lloyd George had made contacts with or was subject to pressure from all parts of the political spectrum; this was the inevitable result of his quest for a policy synthesis, of seeking the best of all worlds, and of his concern for unity.

The information received on Monday, 3 August, despite Germany's encouraging reply to the request for the neutralizing of the Channel, showed that moderation did not prevail in Berlin.[69] The cabinet, when it assembled at 11 a.m., knew or was rapidly informed of Germany's ultimatum to Belgium, thinly disguised as an offer of an entente and requesting permission to cross her territory in order to attack France, and Belgium's rejection of that démarche.[70] They were finally at the brink of involvement.

Morley wrestled with Lloyd George even before the cabinet met. Lloyd George, he recorded:

*seemed astonished. "But if you go it will put us who don't go in a great hole"... He asked if I had considered the news of Germany*

67. In a note of 3 August, Lloyd George seemed to envisage blockade action, a view perhaps based on the German offer to respect the neutrality of the Channel. He wrote, "Whilst others fighting our business confined to starving the women and children including our own. What will be the effect on Italy, Belgium and Holland." (LGP, C/13.) See also Hankey to Blake, 3 Sept. 1928, S. W. Roskill, *Hankey, Man of Secrets*, 134–35; S. R. Williamson, *The Politics of Grand Strategy*, 362–67; Hankey, *Supreme Command*, I, 157. The cabinet authorized mobilization on 4 August, and agreed to dispatch the B.E.F. on 6 August.

68. Lloyd George to Masterman, and Masterman to Lloyd George, n.d. [2 Aug.?], LGP, C/13. Masterman warned against precipitate decisions and argued for cabinet unity.

69. German note, 3 Aug. 1914, BDOW, XI, 531, 291; Morley, *Memorandum*, 11; Needham, 264.

70. Asquith report, 3 Aug., Cab 41/35/24, Villiers to Grey, 3 Aug., BDOW, XI, 521, 288, and 514, 286, Burns diary, 3 and 5 Aug., and Burns to Margot Asquith, 15 Aug. 1914, Burns Papers, Add. 46336 and 46282.

*bullying Belgium etc. . . . He told me that it had changed Runciman's line and his own.*

*My impression is that he must have begun the day with one of his customary morning talks with the splendid* condottiere *at the Admiralty, had revised his calculations, as he had a perfect right to do, had made up his mind to swing around, as he had done about the Panther in 1911, to the politics of adventure, and found in the German ultimatum to Belgium a sufficiently plausible excuse.*[71]

Morley had recorded only one fact: Lloyd George's concern not to move out of step politically. The rest is misrepresentation and speculation, and surely exaggerates Lloyd George's reaction to Morley's impending departure. The resignation of three other ministers, including Simon, would be more serious, and Asquith recorded that in the cabinet Lloyd George made "a strong appeal to them (the four) not to go, or at least to delay it."[72] Moreover, Lloyd George now admitted that Germany would in all probability fulfil the most fateful alternative and violate Belgium.[73] He asked Churchill, and received a categorical "No" in reply, "Would you commit yourself in public *now* [Monday] to war if Belgium is invaded whether Belgium asks for our protection or not?" He then cautioned the first lord, "If patience prevails and you do not press us too hard tonight we (personally) might come together."[74] He still grasped at the final reservations and the last hopes of peace.

To his wife Lloyd George wrote: "I am moving through a nightmare world these days. I have fought hard for peace and succeeded so far in keeping the Cabinet out of it but I am driven to

71. Morley, *Memorandum*, 23–24; Scott diary, 27 Nov. 1914, Scott Papers, Add. 50901; Morley to Bertrand Russell, 7 Aug., Bertrand Russell Papers, and Morley to Crewe, 7 Aug. 1914, Crewe Papers, C/37.

72. Asquith, *Memories*, II, 24; Morley, *Memorandum*, 24–27. Morley's comment was "Lloyd George earnestly expostulated especially to my address." See also A. Chamberlain diary, 3 and 4 Aug., A. Chamberlain Papers, AC/14/2/1–12, and Neville to Austen Chamberlain, 15 Aug. 1914, ibid.; Sir A. Chamberlain, *Down the Years* (London, 1935), 92–106.

73. The Foreign Office heard at 12:30 that Germany had violated Belgian and Dutch territory. (Sir C. Hertslet to Grey, and Grey to Villiers, 3 Aug. 1914, *BDOW*, XI, 523 and 525, 288–89.)

74. Lloyd George–Churchill exchanges, n.d. [3 Aug.], LGP, C/13. Churchill replied: "Please God—it is our whole future—comrades—or opponents. The march of events will be dominating." See also Riddell, *War Diary*, 6.

the conclusion that if the small nationality of Belgium is attacked by Germany all my traditions and even prejudices will be engaged on the side of war. I am filled with horror at the prospect. I am even more horrified that I should ever appear to have a share in it but I must bear my share of the ghastly burden though it scorches my flesh to do so." [75]

After the morning cabinet Lloyd George lunched with Samuel and went on to the House of Commons. "He was warmly cheered by the excited people waving little Union Jacks. 'This is not my crowd', he said, 'I never want to be cheered by a war crowd'." [76] C. P. Scott, in contrast to Robertson Nicoll, telegraphed a warning against involvement in war, but Lloyd George sat with Grey as the foreign secretary prepared to deliver his authorized statement to the Commons. [77]

The cabinet reassembled briefly at 6 p.m. As the evening unfolded the uncertainties of the military situation and those surrounding Belgium's responses largely evaporated. [78] Samuel condemned those colleagues who had resigned for their craven behaviour. [79] Churchill, Robert Donald, and Riddell, who were close to Lloyd George, knew that he was committed, would not waver, and would face the consequences of the cabinet's decisions on 4 August. [80]

Scott was in the garden of No. 11 immediately after the morning cabinet. [81] A worn and disillusioned Simon declared himself entirely deceived about Germany. The war party, the crown prince, Tirpitz, and the rest, dictated policy and "had

75. Lloyd George to his wife, 3 Aug. 1914, Morgan, *Family Letters*, 167.

76. Samuel to his wife, 3 Aug. 1914, Samuel Papers, A157/699.

77. Asquith, *Memories*, II, 25; Asquith to the king, 3 Aug., Cab. 41/35/24, and Nicolson to Hardinge, 5 Sept. 1914, FO/800/375; Hazlehurst, *Politicians at War*, 43–48; Riddell, *War Diary*, 7; see also note 3.

78. Chilton to Grey, Villiers to Grey, Goschen to Grey, Bertie to Grey, and Hertslet to Grey, 3 Aug. 1914, *BDOW*, XI, 547, 551, 553, 556, 557 and 558, 297–301, and 561 and 562, 301–302.

79. Samuel to his wife, 2 [3?] Aug. 1914, Samuel Papers, A157/698. The letter is postmarked 3 August at 7:45 p.m. and could not have been written on the previous day.

80. Churchill to Lloyd George, 3 Aug. 1914, Churchill, *Winston S. Churchill*, II, 719; Taylor, *Donald*, 26–28; *Esher Journals*, III, 174; Grey to Goschen, 4 Aug. 1914, *BDOW*, XI, 573, 306 and 594, 314.

81. Scott diary, 3 Aug. 1914, Scott Papers, Add. 50901. Scott came to London at Lloyd George's request on 4 (not 3) August. The date in the diary is incorrect.

deliberately played for and provoked the war." The kaiser was impotent and the hawks had pushed the crisis beyond control, refusing to restrain Austria. Lloyd George, according to Scott,

> confirmed all that Simon had said about the provocative attitude of German diplomacy and said the despatches when they were published would prove it up to the hilt. Up to last Sunday only 2 members of the Cabinet had been in favour of our intervention in the War, but the violation of Belgian territory had completely altered the situation. He had gone so far however as to urge that if Germany would consent to limit her occupation of Belgian territory to the extreme southerly point of Belgium, the sort of nose of land running out by Luxemburg, he would resign rather than make this a casus belli.... [82] At the same time he said he could not have tolerated attacks on the French coast of the Channel and had the government done so public opinion would have swept them out of power in a week. He had done his utmost for peace but events had been too strong for him. [83]

He also explained his position to D. R. Daniel: "I would not be in it at all if it were not for Belgium. 'He (the Kaiser) doesn't want war now either,' said G., 'but it's the war party in Germany that has won the day'." [84] In this way Lloyd George justified his position to a powerful and respected radical and to an estranged Welsh friend.

Lloyd George never deviated from this interpretation and enshrined it in his memoirs. Belgium was the honourable pivot of conversion; the tragic and treacherous actions of the German militarists had governed the situation. It had become merely academic that "Grey had, under pressure, agreed that if Germany would respect Belgian neutrality he would not insist on supporting

---

82. Owen, 266. He wrote that Lloyd George demonstrated this idea to the cabinet with the aid of a map; Germany might cross a narrow portion of Belgium, evacuate it later and pay compensation. See also Scott diary, 23 Oct. 1914, Scott Papers, Add. 50901, and R. Lloyd George, *My Father, Lloyd George*, 141–43.

83. Simon was apparently the only minister to argue that Britain could not dispatch a force to France, because all troops were needed to meet the crisis in Ulster. Masterman shared Lloyd George's perception of the German élite. He praised Grey's sincere concern, condemned Churchill for "light-hearted irresponsibility," and defended Lloyd George's struggle to preserve peace.

84. Daniel memorandum, D. R. Daniel Papers, 2914.

France; (perhaps, G. said, he knew she wouldn't), but he admitted that these terms had never been presented to Germany."[85]

Asquith's ministers had worked under a significant degree of strain in a crisis with diplomatic, strategic, and financial dimensions. From the end of July a sense of diminishing time to resolve the situation pressed upon them. Perhaps they faced an overload of information which caused them to reject sources which did not conform to their expectations. Certainly, their information rarely pointed consistently in one direction and, more significantly, was not uniformly discouraging until 2 August. Nevertheless, it would be an exaggeration to suggest that the crisis overwhelmed Asquith's government, causing it to flounder or drift, and this notwithstanding the troubled domestic scene.

The cabinet shared Grey's belief that hawks and doves functioned in Berlin and that faith in Bethmann Hollweg's will and ability to prevent escalation was justified. These false perceptions were not relinquished until the cabinet meeting on the morning of 2 August, despite the mounting evidence to the contrary from 30 July. Indeed, the longer ministers clung to these perceptions after 30 July the greater the degree of credulity and self-deception. Ultimately this trend resulted in irrational behaviour; tears were shed, nerves torn, and fists shaken at the perfidy in Berlin. D. R. Daniel recorded, citing John Burns and others, "that G. for days was thundering about almost tearing his hair out in the Cabinet against...going to war."[86]

The cabinet favoured the maintenance of the policy of a free hand; they intended to secure all possible advantages from the grey area of indeterminate action, and to keep Europe guessing. Cabinet unity was at a premium and policies which threatened disruption were shunned. Resignation was a drastic and perhaps a permanently debilitating step, and ministers preferred conscious and deliberate delay to divisive and premature decisions. When decisions were unavoidable, as on the function of the BEF., they opted for the cautious, even pusillanimous alternative. Legitimate hesitations shaded into desperate hypothesizing as they sought justification to stay united and formulae to preserve peace or avoid involvement in war.

85. Scott diary, 3–4 Sept. 1914, Scott Papers, Add. 50901.
86. Daniel memorandum, Daniel Papers, 2914.

As the situation deteriorated the government turned to the concept of limited involvement in a European war to assist France, and defined, on 2 August, the dual conditions under which Britain would become involved. While they abandoned their preconceptions about the Berlin élite they continued to assume that Germany possessed a full range of alternatives and freedom of choice. Indeed, the decisions taken and the measures planned to aid the French might avert British intervention in so far as they deterred Germany. Conversely, Britain's alternatives were seen to be narrowing dramatically. In this way the cabinet became convinced that the question of war and peace could not be decided anywhere else than in Berlin. In fact, they saw their responsibility for involving Britain in war as a declining factor, to the point where they felt sure that no other choice but intervention remained. Resignation from the cabinet therefore became condemnable defection. Germany was responsible for the catastrophe.

Viewed from a different perspective, the onus was on Grey to demonstrate that circumstances in Europe permitted no other course of action but to assist France and preserve the balance of power. In fact, divisions within the cabinet were not as deep and unyielding as many have supposed. The careful definition on 2 August of the conditions under which Britain would intervene in a war was possible, however, only because ministers accepted it from differing assumptions, motives, and expectations. They could act from that point with tolerably clear consciences, avoid resignation, and, with varying degrees of realism, still pray fervently for peace.[87]

Personal and political considerations were obviously critical and were constantly in play. This was particularly true of Lloyd George. Caution was at a premium for him and affected his response to policy considerations. He was reluctant to accept the argument

87. Professor Temperley prepared a paper containing thirteen questions for J. A. Spender to submit to the surviving cabinet members in January 1929. Crewe, Samuel, McKenna, Runciman, and one unidentified minister, but not Lloyd George, replied. McKenna did not answer Temperley's questions, which he regarded as of little value, but said that he agreed generally with Crewe. (McKenna to Spender, 8 May 1929, Spender Papers, Add. 46386.) See also Spender's notes of Temperley's conversation with Grey in 1929, ibid., Crewe to Samuel, 26 Nov. 1928, Runciman to Samuel, 14 Jan. 1942, Samuel Papers, A/45. Spender told Samuel that Temperley posed unimportant questions and "really did not know how cabinets work." (Spender to Samuel, 9 and 20 Nov. 1941, Samuel Papers, A/45.)

that Britain had undertaken automatic and binding military obligations to France, and should respond to the situation solely from that basis. Nevertheless, the discussion of France's predicament and Britain's relationship to it demonstrated that he was not insensitive to Grey's arguments. Britain's prestige and security were involved and inescapably so over Belgian neutrality. The dogma of the independence of northwestern Europe retained its credibility, and he recognized that France's strategic problems would be severely compounded should the German fleet and army have free rein. Moreover, in contrast to Germany, France had conducted herself with such moderation as to appear virtually blameless in the escalating crisis.

This view gained strength from Grey's concealment of Cambon's pressure and from Germany's indulgence in spurious explanations and transparently frail charges of French aggression. If war came, Lloyd George, who had indicated both a concern for France and fear lest Britain's preparations were inadequate, was at least confident that the fleet was ready. Limited naval involvement, in response to German action in the Channel, was therefore acceptable. As war became probable, and cabinet unity was maintained effectively, a sense of stoicism, relief, and even anticipation may have overtaken him.

Crewe's letter to Hardinge of 6 August provides an entrée to the problems surrounding Belgium which exercised Lloyd George. "Not a few thought that Germany would accept the conditions of neutrality of Belgium and abstention from attack on the French coast, which would have been so advantageous to France as to offer almost complete payment of our debt to her."[88] Issues that seem clear in retrospect were not necessarily so at the time, and no minister would easily discount the deterrent power of Britain. In the event of a European war would Germany violate Belgium? The evidence from 29 July pointed to the fact that Belgium would share the fate of Luxemburg rather than Holland. Both Samuel and Crewe, the latter with reservations, confirmed that the cabinet understood and expected this development, should diplomacy and deterrence fail. Only one slim piece of information challenged this perception: Belgium insisted, as late as 2 August, that she expected all the powers to respect her neutrality. She preferred not to

88. Crewe to Hardinge, 6 Aug. 1914, Crewe Papers, C/24.

question Germany's intentions and maintained this posture until she faced the German ultimatum on 3 August.[89]

Conversely, the cabinet assumed that France would not violate Belgium. France's military preparations seemed justifiable, limited, and innocent of aggressive intent.[90] The only possible reason for deviating from this conclusion was Belgium's own impartial military preparations, technically against both France and Germany, but made in fact for diplomatic rather than strategic reasons.

More remarkably, the cabinet actually ignored the evidence that France would assist Belgium in the event of German aggression and presumably at the invitation of the Belgian government. On 29 July they concluded that it was doubtful whether a unilateral obligation to Belgium existed; on 2 August they accepted that such an obligation to Belgium did exist. The latter decision swept aside the former, but both were superfluous exercises for they defied the critical evidence about French intentions. Ministers obviously were reluctant to attach the question of Belgium to that of France. Grey, realistically, was willing for the most part to let the trend of events rule; Britain would escape assisting France if the probable did not occur.

The extent of any German violation of Belgian territory was also an issue. The War Office assumed that Germany would attack France and invade that part of Belgium to the south of the Sambre and Meuse Rivers. Such operations would activate Britain's treaty obligations and require the dispatch of the expeditionary force. Asquith, Grey, Churchill, and Haldane led the cabinet toward acceptance of the War Office's position. At the evening cabinet meeting on 2 August the government decided that "a substantial violation" of Belgian neutrality would necessitate British intervention. Clearly, operations conducted to the south of the Sambre and Meuse Rivers would constitute a "substantial violation."

Since becoming chancellor of the exchequer, and certainly from August 1911, Lloyd George had been aware of the War Office's strategic plans and their assumptions about German strategy. He indicated this to Scott on 27 July. On 1 August Churchill instructed Maj.-Gen. A. H. Ollivant of the General Staff to confirm these

89. Grey to Villiers, 31 July, and Villiers to Grey, 1, 2, and 3 Aug. 1914, BDOW, XI, 351, 220, 395, 240, 476, 271, and 521, 288.

90. Bertie to Grey, and Villiers to Grey, 30 and 31 July, and 1 and 3 Aug. 1914, ibid., 318, 200–201, 353, 220–21, 382, 234, and 562, 302.

strategic realities for Lloyd George.[91] He obviously read the Ollivant paper (it contains his marginalia), of which the fundamental premise was that Germany would attack France in a war embracing all the six European great powers. Ollivant estimated that eighty-four German divisions would seek a decision in Eastern France, the attack being launched, "Westwards into France and Southwestward through Belgium into France." Consequently, Britain must dispatch the expeditionary force which would determine the action of the Belgian army and "will very probably decide the fate of France." Henry Wilson's influence was unmistakable and had never been irrelevant to Lloyd George's education in strategy.

Nevertheless, Lloyd George, on 4 August, set out the proposition that an insubstantial German violation of Belgium, involving only a small area of territory in the south, need not necessarily be regarded as a reason for war. In other words, if Germany's violation were merely a technical one and if she promised to evacuate the area as soon as possible, annex no Belgian territory, and pay due compensation Lloyd George might opt for noninvolvement. In retrospect the proposition was totally lacking in realism and Lloyd George can hardly have pursued it at the time without a measure of self-deception or worse. Indeed, he told Scott that he had raised the idea in cabinet on 4 August only after he had been informed that Germany had already violated Belgian territory in force. On the other hand, it could be argued, that was the time for such a proposition. Crewe, moreover, testified subsequently that the cabinet had not eliminated the possibility of alternative or improvised German military operations. They assumed that Germany would probably violate Belgium, but speculated on a possible frontal attack on France along a broad front between Luxemburg and Switzerland. Such speculation obviously was more likely to occur in the absence of a meeting of the CID and because of the failure to include military experts in the cabinet's deliberations. However, on the evening of 3 August, Sir Francis Villiers, the ambassador in Brussels, reported that Belgium would not seek military assistance "so long as Belgian soil is not violated by formidable bodies of German troops. At present it appears that there are only German patrols on Belgian soil."[92]

91. Ollivant memorandum, 1 Aug. 1914, "A Short Survey of the Present Military Situation in Europe," LGP, C/14/1/14.
92. Villiers to Grey, 3 Aug. 1914, BDOW, xi, 562, 302.

Belgian reactions had for years been unpredictable, and, in view of her military deployments in 1914, the cabinet had reason perhaps to question her policy.[93] They could not eliminate entirely, until 3 August, the possibility that Belgium would acquiesce in a German advance south of the Meuse. Obviously, if Belgium did not intend to resist she would not call on her guarantors in the face of aggression. She refused to seek prematurely military assistance, and, as a political exercise to avoid taking sides, imprudently delayed a request for aid from France and Britain until 4 p.m. on 4 August.[94]

The cabinet did not ignore these elements of uncertainty. The evidence from Brussels suggested that Belgium would defend herself. Samuel recorded subsequently that he had expected a vigorous resistance to Germany, and Crewe agreed. So did Runciman, although he felt it necessary to insist that while no uniform opinion existed on this question, it was incorrect to suggest that the whole cabinet did not expect Belgium to resist.

D. R. Daniel, however, suggested to Lloyd George that until the afternoon of 1 August the cabinet believed that Belgium would not resist Germany. Lloyd George agreed, relating, as he did more dramatically to Miss Stevenson, "Only two in the government of Belgium wanted to go to war. The King and Vandervelde, the Socialist leader.... Vandervelde told them that if they did not resist he would shake the dust from his feet."[95] Villiers explained that

> in official and purely Conservative circles the proclivities were decidedly German. This feeling induced confidence which proved to be wholly misplaced.... As recently as the 2nd instant... M. Davignon declared to me that there was no reason whatever to suspect

93. J. E. Helmreich, "Belgian concern over neutrality and British intentions, 1900–1914," *Journal of Modern History*, 36, no. 4 (1964), 416–27; a rumour to this effect had circulated in 1911. (Loreburn to McKenna, 2 Jan. 1912, McKenna Papers, 4/4/12.)

94. Villiers to Grey, 28 and 31 July, and 2, 3, and 4 Aug., *BDOW*, xi, 243, 160, 345, 217, 377, 233, 476, 271, 521, 288, 551, 298, 562, 302, and 654, 338; Bertie to Grey, 3 Aug., ibid., 556, 300, Chilton to Grey, 3 Aug., ibid., 547, 297, and Belgian note, 4 Aug. 1914, ibid., 581, 309.

95. Daniel memorandum, Daniel Papers, 2914; A. J. P. Taylor, ed., *Lloyd George: A Diary by Frances Stevenson*, 2–3. United States ambassador Willard told Colonel House, however, that the King of Spain informed him in August 1914 that King Albert had agreed to permit German troops to cross Belgian territory. (House diary, 29 Dec. 1916.)

> *that Germany intended to violate the neutrality of Belgium. The Government had consequently not even considered the question of an appeal to the guaranteeing Powers, more especially as they considered themselves in a position to resist aggression from whatever quarter it might come. This last attitude was not so much due to reliance on their own forces as to a desire not to commit themselves irrevocably on either side.*[96]

The government in Brussels, in spite of its knowledge of the Schlieffen Plan, obviously could or would not accept until the last moment the probability that Germany would invade in force.

Lloyd George discussed the ultimate refinement with Daniel. A moral question was involved which also emerged in the First and Second World Wars with regard to the Balkans and the Baltic states respectively. Could a Great Power, as an act of deliverance, compel a small nation to involve itself and accept the prospect of large-scale military operations on its soil? Grey and the War Office might assert that irrespective of Belgium's wishes Britain must fulfil her obligations to Belgium and France, but would the whole cabinet have agreed? Daniel asked Lloyd George, "If Belgium had opened the door to Germany would our government have declared war on Belgium at the start of the week and landed an army there." "Yes," said G., "but he would not be with them."[97] Daniel believed him.

The problems relating to Belgium had permitted the most reluctant and the least realistic to recoil as long as possible from the prospect of involvement in war. Lloyd George had weighed both policy options and political calculations. In the final analysis, however, he had sat too long with Asquith and Grey to walk away from responsibility and power.

---

96. Villiers to Grey and Nicolson, 12 Aug. 1914, *BDOW*, xi, 670, 349–50.

97. Daniel memorandum, Daniel Papers, 2914. See also Maurice, *Haldane*, 354.

# IO

# The Promise and the Cost of Victory

Three sets of factors, emotional, intellectual, and political, contributed to Lloyd George's conduct in the 1914 crisis. The war presented fresh challenges and opportunities, and exercised its own influence, but it also confirmed that the assumptions, ideas, and convictions he had developed about foreign policy constituted a mature and resilient, if unconventional, synthesis. This was evident in Lloyd George's response to policy problems involving the United States and Turkey, and in his contributions to the debates on sea power, the freedom of the seas, war aims, imperial security, the balance of power, disarmament, and war itself as an instrument of social change.

Asquith, Grey, Lord Kitchener at the War Office until the spring of 1916, and initially Churchill exercised oligarchic powers during the first two years of the war, and did so inadequately. Lloyd George, was not, however, a mere frustrated spectator, and must bear a greater degree of responsibility for policy than he acknowledged subsequently. His were not insubstantial and trivial activities. He played a complex role at the Treasury until May 1915, as minister of munitions until July 1916, and at the War

Office, and his record, by many standards, was mixed and uneven.[1] Even the celebrated metaphor, the knock-out blow, does not capture fully the way he conceived of and pursued victory.

Lloyd George was involved in the response to the United States initiative to bring about a negotiated peace with Germany in 1916, conducted by President Wilson's egotistical confidant, Col. Edward House.[2] In the course of his conversations with House, the record of which does not always provide satisfactory evidence, Lloyd George explored several themes. Radicals had long regarded with favour the political and social experiment attempted in the United States, and Lloyd George was able to identify with what he had regarded since his youth as a great and energetic democracy. He had, as a senior minister before the war, refused to accept the validity of weighing American sea power when calculating Britain's naval requirements, had proposed arbitration by the United States as a solution to the Moroccan crisis of 1911, and had supported Grey's conduct of Anglo-American relations. During the war he sought United States assistance, on British terms, and was willing to explore certain scenarios of future cooperation between the Atlantic powers, to the satisfaction of C. P. Scott, Grey, and H. A. L. Fisher, the historian and future Liberal minister.

On the other hand, Lloyd George displayed firmness toward the United States, and a stern realism which grew in intensity, especially after he went to the War Office and as Wilson's conduct became more exasperating and suspect. The evidence of a certain

1. The records of the cabinet and the CID are of little value. (Cab 41/35, Cab 37/123–161, Cab 38/28, and Cab 27/2.) The minutes of the nineteen meetings of the War Council are more revealing but do not document adequately the conduct of the war. (Aug. 1914 and 25 Nov. 1914–14 May 1915, Cab 22/1 and 2, and Cab 42/1 and 2.) Lloyd George, as munitions minister, did not attend seven of the twenty-four sessions of the Dardanelles Committee. (7 June–30 Oct. 1915, Cab 42/3 and 4.) The minutes of the 101 meetings of the War Committee are, however, far more valuable. Lloyd George missed only twelve sessions and that body did achieve a degree of detailed control over the conduct of the war. (3 Nov. 1915 to 1 Dec. 1916, Cab 42/5–26.) See also the records of allied conferences, the Treasury, the Munitions Ministry, the War and the Foreign Offices, and the Dardanelles Commission of Enquiry. (Cab 28/1, Cab 37/145/39, Treasury Papers, 1908–15, files T2, 3, 5, 6, 7, 12, 27, 108, and 170, Munitions Ministry Papers, 1915–16, Mun 2, 3, 4, 5, 7, and 8, War Office Papers, WO 32, 106, 107, 158, and 159, FO 800 and 371, and Cab 19/29 and 33.)

2. Historians should not rely on the published version of the House Papers and diary in C. Seymour, *The Intimate Papers of Colonel House*, 2 vols. (Boston, 1926).

contempt for American politicians, and of his expressed views on the freedom of the seas, naval supremacy, and an independently-timed United States mediation attempt illustrate the trend, and further demonstrate the subtle relationship existing between Lloyd George and Grey. Radicals would have applauded Lloyd George's response to House's disarmament scheme, but would have deplored his observations on the efficacy of war, just as they reacted angrily to his escalating belligerency.

Lloyd George had no part in the initial exchanges from December 1914 to March 1915. Grey responded sufficiently to encourage and yet mislead House.[3] He then retreated, pleading the reluctance of both his colleagues and Britain's allies, and lamenting the irritations in Anglo-American relations brought on by the blockade. House was led on rather than frustrated, and began both to exaggerate the willingness of the British government to respond and to deceive himself.[4] He warmed to Arthur Balfour, although he feared the Unionists, looked on Grey as a kindred spirit, and concluded that German intransigence over Belgium was the major obstacle to peace negotiations.[5]

Lloyd George had not impressed House in June 1914.[6] They met again at lunch on 17 May 1915, though the encounter proved unrewarding, largely because of Lord Cowdray's obsession with Mexican oil, and again on 2 June.[7] At both meetings Lloyd George invited American assistance, either directly or inferentially. Murray of Elibank recorded, on 17 May:

> *Lloyd George said that . . . if German arms were to succeed her next enterprize would be to seize Brazil for the overflow of her own population. . . . Supposing Germany were successful in this war, her fleet is as great—if not greater—than the American fleet—and the*

3. Grey insisted to his colleagues that they must preserve allied unity and avoid divisive peace negotiations. (War Council, 10 March 1915, Cab 42/2/5.)

4. House diary, vols. 5 and 6; Seymour, *Intimate Papers*, I, 341–49; Grey to Bertie, 4 Dec. 1914 and 11 Jan. 1915, FO/800/56 and 75.

5. House to Wilson, 23 Feb. 1915, Seymour, *Intimate Papers*, I, 380–83.

6. House diary, 26 June 1914. He had found Lloyd George an agreeable personality, but not well informed on the United States. Sir Horace Plunkett and Sir Edgar Speyer sought to disparage Lloyd George, describing him as ineffective, shifty, without integrity, and a brilliant but cheap opportunist who would do virtually anything for personal advancement. (House diary, 3 March and 1 June 1915, and 22 Dec. 1916.)

7. House diary, 17 May and 2 June 1915; Elibank note, 17 May 1915, Elibank Papers, 8803, f. 155.

*lessons of the war will have taught the Americans that although the States possess a mighty population she could not expect to train and equip sufficient men to fight the German armies under a year . . . it might even be behind their present policy (i.e. Germany's) to exasperate the Americans. Lloyd George told the Ambassador and Colonel House that America must not miss this opportunity of using her striking influence to settle the affairs of humanity for the next 500 years.*

On 2 June Lloyd George discussed problems of munitions production and voiced his distrust of the War Office. House did not respond favourably to his proposal that the allies might purchase rifles for Russia in the United States, but felt that Lloyd George was more "the virile, aggressive type of American politician than any member of the cabinet. He lacks the learning, the culture and the trustworthiness of his governmental associates. But he had something dynamic within him which his colleagues have not and which is badly needed in this great hour." Clearly, House recognized the importance of establishing a closer relationship with the minister of munitions, and did not regard him as an alien force.[8]

On 5 January 1916 House returned to England to convince the government that an attempt to secure a moderate and negotiated peace through President Wilson's mediation was more attractive than prolonged warfare without the assistance of the United States. Moreover, he could offer the probability of American intervention should Germany wreck the mediation attempt. House expected to succeed, despite Ambassador W. H. Page's scepticism, largely by appealing to the moderation, common sense, and Atlanticist sentiments of Grey and Balfour, now first lord of the admiralty.[9]

Lloyd George, House, and Lord Reading, lord chief justice, dined at the Savoy on 14 January.[10] House had asked Grey to

8. House diary, 16 Oct. 1915. They agreed to correspond directly should the United States enter the war. Indeed, as a result of the 1916 exchanges, House disliked Curzon more and trusted the king less than he did Lloyd George.

9. House diary, 6, 10, and 11 Jan. 1916; Seymour, *Intimate Papers*, II, 116–21. "Atlanticist" is used to describe those who sought intimate Anglo-American cooperation to the point of creating a pax Anglo-Americana. See Michael G. Fry, *Illusions of Security, North Atlantic Diplomacy 1918–1922* (Toronto, 1972).

10. House diary, 14 Jan. 1916; House to Wilson, 14 and 15 Jan. 1916, House Papers, Wilson file; Seymour, *Intimate Papers*, II, 126, 128–29. They had met on

consult only Balfour and noted that "George did not know the purpose of my visit nor that I had talked with Grey and Balfour, although he must have had some inkling of it." Lloyd George seemed as ignorant as ever about the United States, but "it was pleasant to find George able to look at this ghastly war in an impartial way. His view of what may happen during the spring and summer largely coincides with mine."

Lloyd George seemed confident, House recorded, that the allies would soon secure a clear advantage. Then, "around September first," President Wilson should intervene, whatever the state of the American election campaign, and dictate peace terms. Meanwhile, the president should initiate a program of naval and military preparedness to support his diplomacy.[11] Furthermore, House reported to Wilson, Lloyd George "believes unless you do this your intervention might fail. . . . He has a fantastic idea of the power the President may exert at the peace conference. He thinks the economic force of the United States is so great that no nation at war could withstand its power if exerted against it."

After expressing equally remarkable views on the benefits of war to a decadent and indolent Britain,[12] Lloyd George suggested that "if the United States would stand by Great Britain the entire world could not shake the combined mastery we would hold over the seas. If the President should propose mediation George thought each belligerent government would object but would soon be brought to accept by public opinion." To House's satisfaction, Lloyd George was proving himself a democrat and an Atlanticist rather than a warlord, although his version of an Anglo-American entente which would police the postwar world and create a joint hegemony surely envisaged British leadership and pre-eminence. They found a further area of agreement when House suggested that the peace terms must prohibit the manufacture of armaments and munitions for a specified period, and provide for a government takeover of munitions plants. Lloyd George, in response,

---

11 January with Page, McKenna, and Austen Chamberlain present. Recruiting on the east coast, Lloyd George had observed, ran ahead of any other area and noticeably ahead of Clydeside. A Zeppelin raid or two would suffice; "we might have large electric signs saying, 'This way to the Clyde!'"

11. House advocated this policy himself and subsequently deplored Wilson's inaction.

12. He argued that a fitter, more productive, and potentially richer Britain would emerge from the war. The United States, he suggested, had set the pace for extravagant living.

"seized upon this as a practical idea and one which would better meet the requirements of the situation than any he had heard proposed." One might ask who was flattering whom, but arms limitation was one of the radical themes which continued to flourish in Lloyd George's armoury of assumptions.

One issue clearly separated them: the threat to the freedom of the seas posed by the spread of militarism and deplored by the United States, although House was confident both that Britain and the United States could adjust the problems created by the blockade, and that he had influenced Lloyd George's views.[13] They then discussed the generalities of a peace settlement and longer-term prospects, with Lloyd George listening courteously to House's plans for Britain's withdrawal from Asia.[14]

Subsequently, House ridiculed Lloyd George's proposal for Wilson's intervention. He distinguished it sharply from his own, and suggested that Asquith, Grey, and Balfour had found it "grotesque."[15] C. P. Scott also tended to dismiss similar comments as the product of Lloyd George's delightful irresponsibility. Even Scott, however, could not quite be sure how far Lloyd George was serious or merely groping "in the air." At breakfast on 15 December 1915, Lloyd George had rejected the idea of destroying Germany. He suggested that deadlock and mutual exhaustion were preferable so that the United States could intervene and impose peace terms, and concluded, "There, I think I have talked enough treason."[16] Lloyd George speculated in this way because the audience was appropriate, but such "treason" had a genuine basis. It also reflected his frustration with the War Committee's decisions on strategic policy.

On 14 January 1916 Grey had urged his colleagues to confirm their decision of 28 December 1915 to mount a spring offensive on

13. Lloyd George expected Britain to retain the supremacy of and obstruct the freedom of the seas while destroying German militarism, an assumption which House found absurd. When, however, House pointed out that Washington not Berlin proposed the freedom of the seas, Lloyd George "seemed to think better of it." Reading later claimed to have taken Lloyd George to task "for acquiescing in my (i.e. House's) view that navalism should go and that the freedom of the seas was a debateable question." (House diary, 15 Jan. 1916.)

14. House to Wilson, 15 Jan. 1916, House Papers, Wilson file. House suggested that Britain devote her energies to Africa and the Dominions, rather than Asia.

15. House diary, 19 Jan., and House to Wilson, 9 and 29 Dec. 1916, ibid.

16. Scott diary, 15 Dec. 1915, Scott Papers, Add. 50901.

the Western Front.[17] He challenged Balfour and Lloyd George, both of whom preferred operations in Syria and the Balkans, for, "I am still more impressed by the fact that all military opinion is united in favour of it and that nothing else is suggested as possible, except a prolonged defensive, to end in the exhaustion of Germany. I believe that the only chance of victory is to hammer the Germans hard in the first eight months of this year. If this is impossible we had better make up our minds to an inconclusive peace." Despite these differences over strategy, Lloyd George became part of the inner group which handled the question of United States mediation.

On January 15, House reported to Grey and Balfour the substance of his conversation with Lloyd George and Reading.[18] Both denied that they had discussed the matter with Lloyd George and, House informed the president, suggested that "he has probably thought the thing out and seized upon your being in London to discuss it with you."

> Grey and Balfour look upon George as brilliant and unstable. He jumps to conclusions quickly but as quickly forms another. I asked how trustworthy he was and how well he could keep a matter of this nature to himself. They thought he would be inclined to talk to his newspaper friends and give them an inkling of what was passing in his mind. This they thought was the danger with him. I told them I had not been altogether open with him and had not informed him of the conferences the three of us have been having upon the same subject. I had asked George to talk with them and with Asquith.

Four days later Grey and House agreed that, "Lloyd George was likely to talk and yet was essential. He must have talked to McKenna already or to someone who has told him, since McKenna has expressed about the same views as to a settlement as Lloyd George has."[19]

17. Grey memorandum, 14 Jan. 1916, Cab 42/7/8.
18. House diary, 15 Jan. 1916; Seymour, *Intimate Papers*, II, 129–31. House was disappointed with Asquith and began to speculate on Lloyd George becoming leader, with Grey as foreign secretary, to produce a combination of boldness and moderation. (House diary, 19 Jan. and 11 Feb. 1916; House to Wilson, 16 Jan. 1916, House Papers, Wilson file.)
19. House diary, 19 Jan. 1916; and S. W. Roskill, *Hankey, Man of Secrets*, 245–46.

House's negotiations with Grey were interrupted by his visit to Europe and were not resumed until 10 February.[20] Grey urged that the United States use the Lusitania incident as the *casus belli*. Once in the war, she could bring about peace negotiations by threatening a separate peace. House disagreed; if the United States became a belligerent she would be committed to the end. He preferred Wilson to call a peace conference "within a very short time." Grey acquiesced; Wilson would mediate and seek an end to the hostilities. The allies would accept the conference proposal, House assured Wilson, but should Germany refuse, the United States would "throw in all our weight in order to bring her to terms."

Asquith and Balfour were more cautious than Grey, but House felt able to report to Wilson, on 11 February, that by the time he left England he would have a complete understanding to secure a peace conference through American mediation.[21] He should have weighed the reservations more carefully. The attitude of Aristide Briand, the French prime minister, was unclear, the timing of American mediation was at issue, and Grey was particularly concerned to avoid differences with the allies.[22] Asquith was not especially impressed with House's warnings about the defection of France or Russia, and felt that premature peace discussions might provoke that very development. Moreover, Grey, Asquith, and Balfour could not accept House's pessimistic analysis of the Entente's military prospects. Finally, they simply did not share House's priorities.

Asquith's government had reached a certain order of preferences which reflected the belief that the allied military position was not so desperate as to require a rescue operation from across the Atlantic. First, victory without American military intervention but with her economic assistance, since, as Lloyd George told the War Committee, the United States at heart was committed to the allies.[23] Secondly, victory after American military intervention

---

20. House diary, 7, 8, 9, 10, and 17 Feb. 1916; Seymour, *Intimate Papers*, II, 163–65; House to Wilson, 10 Feb. 1916, House Papers, Wilson file.

21. House to Wilson, 11 Feb. 1916, House Papers, Wilson file; House diary, 11 Feb. 1916.

22. The conversations between House and Briand had become a source of confusion. House insisted that Briand understood that the allies must not permit their military fortunes to wane to the point where mediation would be hopeless.

23. War Committee, 3 Feb. 1916, Cab 42/8/1.

caused for example by German submarine warfare, and, a relatively unattractive third alternative, American mediation requested by the allies in order to escape the consequences of defeat. Needless to say, a mediation attempt made without allied consent, and at an unpropitious time, for example to enhance Wilson's election prospects or as a result of his reelection, was utterly unacceptable. The same consideration, the presidential election, also made less credible the assumption that the United States would enter the war in 1916 should mediation collapse, even if Germany were responsible for the failure.

Two vital factors permeated the debate in London. First, American involvement in the war would lead inevitably to an increase in her naval power. The United States would therefore be able to challenge Britain's use of the weapon of maritime blockade, and even her naval hegemony. When Sir Maurice Hankey, secretary to the CID and the War Committee, reviewed Wilson's controversial speech of 27 May 1916 for Asquith, he emphasized "that what President Wilson aims at is the Freedom of the Seas in time of war. If this were adopted the American peace would be more dangerous to the British Empire than the German war.... Mr. Balfour... gives a pretty strong hint that the whittling down of sea power is quite incompatible with President Wilson's desire to create some form of international machinery for the maintenance of peace, but it would really seem better to indicate that we should not allow America, under any circumstances, in peace or war, to whittle down the value of sea power once war has begun."[24]

Secondly, United States participation in the peacemaking was unwelcome and would increase in its effectiveness the lower down the scale of policy alternatives Britain was forced to go. In agreement with her allies and Dominions, she did not wish to be bound by Wilson's moderate peace terms. Britain aimed to improve on the status quo ante bellum, territorially, militarily, and commercially. The prewar situation had not provided security and would be an unacceptable basis from which to conduct postwar diplomacy.[25] If the United States entered the war over the sub-

24. Hankey to Asquith, 29 May 1916, Hankey Papers, Cab 63/14/2. Wilson had attempted to establish a relationship between the freedom of the seas and the creation of a league of nations.

25. Grey was not prepared to make peace "at once" on terms accepting "the status quo," as Frances Stevenson charged. (Stevenson diary, 23 Feb. 1916, A. J. P. Taylor, ed., Lloyd George: A Diary, 101.)

marine question the allies must seek as free a hand as possible from Washington to dictate peace terms. The degree of freedom, however, was not likely to match that achieved by defeating Germany without American belligerency, but with her sympathetic neutrality. Yet, allied to the United States in common cause against Germany, and still powerful, the Entente could expect to influence the peace. If Wilson mediated, however, he would protect Germany's interests.

On the other hand the War Committee might oscillate between the first and second major policy priorities because, while the latter would bring Wilson's involvement in the peace, it would also enable the Entente to achieve victory with considerably less strain than if the United States remained neutral. Moments of pessimism could make American intervention even seem indispensable.[26] In fact, in a presidential election year, Asquith's government was realistically debating the alternatives of continued warfare to secure victory and American mediation, with its unacceptable political and its unpredictable military consequences.

House possessed one lever: the United States would not salvage the Entente on the very eve of its collapse. Instead, America would withdraw into isolation and launch a policy of military and naval preparedness. House could offer, as a douceur, a postwar alliance embracing the United States, Britain, France, and Italy.

On 11 February, House dined with Lloyd George and Reading.[27] He felt their discussions were productive but noted, "It is evident that Lloyd George is somewhat distrustful of the Prime Minister, Grey and Balfour, and they are equally so of him. Neither group wants the other to have the advantage and both are afraid to go as far in the direction I am pushing as their inclination would lead them for fear capital might be made of it by the others. Both Reading and George assured me that a peace proposal would be the most unpopular move that could be thought of in England."

Lloyd George had reversed his earlier assessment of the attitude of the public toward peace negotiations, but at least he was consistent on the question of the efficacy of war. "George said England was now aroused for the first time. John Bull had grown

26. Stevenson diary, 21 and 23 Feb. 1916, ibid., 101–102.
27. House diary, 11 Feb. 1916. On the following day Lloyd George told his brother that he did not expect Germany to relinquish her conquered territories; peace was not in sight (Lloyd George to W. George, 12 Feb., W. George, *My Brother and I*, 248.)

fat and lazy but he was working off his flesh and getting as lean and fit as an athlete and had no fear of the result. George believes the war had done the nation good—greater good than harm; that it had aroused the best in people and that they will come out of it rejuvenated with better impulses and purposes." It seemed probable, however, that calculations about political advantage would also obstruct House. Clearly he was the victim of equivocation in London and again guilty of self-deception. He dissented when Lloyd George admitted, as had Grey, that he preferred United States intervention over the Lusitania question, or over "another such issue which is alive and burning" to mediation, and recorded that "Reading agreed with me and so also did George after I had stated the position."[28]

Grey, in House's view, was least concerned with personal and political considerations, and remained the key to the situation. On 14 February the inner group met at Reading's for dinner.[29] They agreed that "the President should at some time, to be later agreed upon, call a halt and demand a conference," which Wilson would attend and which might convene at The Hague. Moreover House noted, "I drew George out upon this subject and thoroughly committed him to the idea that the President should act in this capacity." The problem of timing was left unresolved. It depended on selecting the critical moment when Germany was sufficiently discouraged and Entente opinion was not yet intoxicated by military success. Grey seemed to favour prompt action; Lloyd George and Balfour preferred delay until the allies secured an undisputed military advantage.

Lloyd George seemed more concerned than any of his colleagues to secure an agreement with the United States on minimum peace terms before and in the event that Wilson intervened. House discouraged this idea but Asquith pursued the matter. What, he asked, would Wilson do if he found the allies' proposed peace terms unacceptable? Alternatively, how would the president react if he regarded Germany's offer as unjust? In the former case, House replied, Wilson would withdraw from the conference and leave the allies to their own devices. In the latter situation the United States would join the Entente and enter the war so as to secure a just and reasonable settlement and an end to war as such. A more

28. House to Wilson, 13 Feb. 1916, House Papers, Wilson file.
29. House diary, 14 Feb. 1916.

*225*

perceptive man than House would have probed further; a realist would have faced the attendant difficulties.[30]

House reported to Wilson, however, that only the timing of mediation was at issue.[31] A hostile cabal might emerge within the cabinet, but Grey was enthusiastic, Balfour seemed content, and Asquith's reluctance appeared to be only temporary.[32] None of them would seek political advantage; all seemed committed to what was acknowledged to be an unpopular policy.[33] House noted that both Balfour and Grey applauded Lloyd George's "breadth of vision and courage...they had not believed it was in him." Howard Whitehouse, a Liberal MP who supported a peace move, expected Lloyd George to oppose mediation as vigorously as Lord Curzon, lord privy seal in the coalition government from May 1915, but House felt "he must be wrong. I was surprised because Whitehouse was at one time Lloyd George's parliamentary secretary."

On 17 February Grey and House, unattended, drafted a memorandum.[34] To House, and incorrectly, it reflected their mutual concern that Wilson should intervene immediately to negotiate a peace. They seemed to have agreed that to end the slaughter and secure Anglo-American cooperation was more vital than a military success achieved even within a year. Moreover,

30. Seymour recorded that House seemed to have secured acceptance of the terms on which Wilson would insist at the peace conference, or would enforce if the United States entered the war after the conference failed. (Seymour, *Intimate Papers*, II, 170.) Lloyd George stated that he took the lead to set down minimum terms and that they were agreed to at the 14 February dinner. (Lloyd George, *War Memoirs*, I, 411–13, 523.) Both interpretations are unacceptable, but Lloyd George's minimum terms, to be secured only if the allies were forced to call for United States mediation, were virtually identical to those envisaged by House. The powers would restore Belgium, award Alsace-Lorraine to France, reconstitute Serbia, and establish an independent Poland. Italy would secure the Italian-speaking areas of the Hapsburg Monarchy. The Turkish Empire would be dismembered, Germany receiving compensation in Asia Minor, and Russia securing an outlet to the sea at Constantinople, or at a port in Asia Minor. In addition, the powers would attempt to establish guarantees against future wars.

31. House to Wilson, 15 Feb., House Papers, Wilson file, and House diary, 15 and 16 Feb. 1916. Grey seemed to agree. He would secure cabinet approval, and then they would "button up the details."

32. Balfour criticized Asquith's failure to control the negotiations, but Asquith did not relish being committed at first hand, while Wilson could repudiate House.

33. House diary, 17 Feb. 1916.

34. Ibid.

House was confident that Grey realized how vital a factor Wilson was, at that time and for constructing such postwar arrangements as a Pan-American pact to guarantee the integrity of the Western Hemisphere. Vice-President Marshall was unsympathetic toward involvement in Europe. A Republican victory would be equivalent to the reactionaries securing power in Britain, for the United States would regress into jingoist imperialism.

The final version of the agreement, drawn up by Grey and dated 22 February, was confirmed on the following day, and accepted by Asquith, Balfour, Lloyd George, and the French ambassador, Paul Cambon.[35] Subject to Wilson's right of amendment or veto, Grey understood that, at the allies' request, the president would propose a peace conference. Should the Entente accept and Germany refuse, the United States would probably enter the war. Should the conference fail to secure terms of peace favourable to the allies, because of the unreasonable attitude of Germany, the United States would "probably" leave the conference as a belligerent on the Entente side. If, however, the allies delayed excessively and their military fortunes waned sufficiently to render United States diplomatic intervention ineffective, America would disinterest herself in Europe and look to her own defences. Wilson inserted the second "probably," but House dismissed its significance almost immediately, and Grey agreed with him. The word "was merely overlooked in our original draft as it occurs in the sentence above and with the same meaning."[36]

Grey insisted on informing the War Committee but agreed not to circulate the actual document. He maintained, however, that the allied military advisers must retain the right to decide on the timing of Wilson's mediation. If they demanded a few months' grace they must have it. In effect, the Entente retained the initiative. The length of the delay was left indefinite, and Reading described Lloyd George to House as "cordial in his support of the understanding though he does not believe with Asquith and Grey that the time will be as auspicious as soon as they think."[37]

Grey had taken the matter to the War Committee on 22 February.[38] He was cool toward the idea at that time; mediation was a pale substitute for victory and "would result in the status quo

35. House diary, 21 and 23 February 1916.
36. House to Grey, 8 and 10 March 1916, House Papers, Grey file.
37. House diary, 22 Feb. 1916.
38. War Committee, 22 Feb. 1916, Cab 42/9/3.

ante." For the moment they should merely avoid friction with the United States. Yet Grey expressed faith in Wilson's sincerity; they must neither assume that America would never enter the war nor prematurely discard "a great opportunity."

Kitchener actually sought assurances that, should Wilson intervene, Berlin would reject mediation.[39] Asquith was con-vinced the United States would not enter the war and he did not see how Wilson could coerce the belligerents. Lloyd George agreed, in defiance of his own comments to House. Wilson would possess no coercive power that year. The United States might enter the war later, but at this stage "it would be far better to leave the United States alone." Everyone supported the contention of McKenna, chancellor of the exchequer since May 1915, that Wilson preferred the war to end in a stalemate rather than a victory. They could not tolerate this outcome, for, as Asquith observed, "to the Allies a draw was much the same as defeat." In any case United States policy seemed governed by the fact that 1916 was an election year, and Bonar Law, Tory leader and colonial secretary in Asquith's coalition, would interpret any diplomatic initiative by Wilson as a quest for domestic political advantage.[40]

Grey did not dissent from Lloyd George's conclusion that "nothing should be done at present," and made no mention of this discussion to House in their final meeting on 23 February. Wilson's envoy understood the situation in only one respect; should any senior member of the War Committee champion the scheme it would be Grey. In order to define their position more clearly before Grey met with Briand, the War Committee reviewed these conclusions on 15 and 21 March.[41] Grey put the best possible interpretation on the scheme but proposed, with Hankey, that they be guided largely by expert analysis of the military situation.[42] If

39. In an interview with American financial leaders on 24 March 1916, the details of which were passed on to House, Kitchener spoke strongly against a premature peace. (House Papers, 34, file 18.)

40. A month earlier he had circulated a Canadian intelligence report on the growing Anglophobia in the United States and the impact of the election. It suggested that Wilson would win if he maintained neutrality. (Borden to Bonar Law, 28 Jan., and Christie memorandum, 27 Jan. 1916, Cab 42/8/9.)

41. Grey to the War Committee, 15 March 1916, Asquith Papers, file 29; Addendum to the Proceedings of the War Committee, 21 March 1916, Cab 42/11/6. The minutes, labelled "Most Secret," were sealed separately and were opened by Hankey on 26 July 1922 for Sir Julian Corbett.

42. Hankey, who gave the subject of "Peace Kites" only three pages in his memoirs, was very sceptical. (Lord Hankey, *The Supreme Command*, II, 478–80.)

in the next six months they could achieve victory and dictate terms to Germany, or so improve their military situation as to be able to secure a more rewarding settlement, they should ignore mediation. Alternatively, if they faced military deadlock and diminished economic and financial resources, the defeat of Russia, or allied exhaustion, they should explore the expedient of United States diplomatic intervention.

Gen. Sir William Robertson, chief of the Imperial General Staff from 1915, refused to predict the outcome of the approaching campaigns in France but opposed House's plan. Asquith, with Bonar Law's support and reiterating that neither the government nor the public would be content with a return to the prewar status quo, counselled delay. He doubted whether Wilson could carry through a policy of mediation. Balfour actually ridiculed House's proposal as "not worth five minutes thought" and as an obvious attempt to extricate Wilson from political difficulties. He called instead for a realistic appreciation of allied weaknesses, beyond the obvious areas of finance and shipping. Lloyd George expressed apprehension about the Eastern Front but Robertson and Kitchener assured him that Russia would hold firm. McKenna reported that the financial situation was safe until July and that careful management should eventually permit them to overcome shortages of credit and labour. He even paid a tribute to Lloyd George's "inestimable service" in stimulating production through the use of female labour.

A cable from Grey would have activated House's scheme but, clearly, the War Committee was in no mood to resort to a policy which they did not regard as best serving British interests.[43] They were not committed to the plan as House understood it and Grey resorted to evasion. He offered the most convenient explanation to House; Britain could not entertain peace negotiations except in concert with her allies, who were opposed while the prospect of victory remained.[44] A German peace offensive, moreover, launched to escape a deteriorating military situation, would merely

43. G. Locock (FO) to J. T. Davies, 11 May 1916, LGP, D/16/17/9. Cecil sent documents showing what he had done to demonstrate to the American public that Britain could not discuss peace at that time.

44. Grey to House, 24 March, 7 April, and 12 and 29 May 1916, House Papers, Grey file; Grey to Bertie, 24 Aug., Cab 37/154/18, and Grey to House, 28 Aug. 1916, House Papers, Grey file. Grey also pointed out that British public opinion expected military successes to precede mediation, and that Berlin's terms, for example on the freedom of the seas, were unacceptable. Frederick

strengthen the resolve of those allies who were unmoved by the charge that the Entente was responsible for prolonging the war.

Understandably, House felt rebuffed and warned of the dire consequences of delay.[45] He also developed an understanding of British policy.[46] Anglo-American relations deteriorated perceptibly during the summer, but as Eric Drummond, Grey's private secretary, explained to Ambassador Spring-Rice, the government would not accept United States mediation unless France was on the verge of collapse.[47] Lloyd George tackled the Irish question, recognizing that, apart from other considerations, they could not invite further United States antagonism while "victory is still in the mist," but offered little comfort to House: "I wish it had been possible to carry out the programme we sketched out at those momentous little dinners, but I fear it is premature. The allies are winning at last but they have not yet won; and although Germany must now be getting anxious her rulers are not quite convinced as yet that the game is up."[48]

The War Committee did not discuss American mediation again until 10 August 1916.[49] Lloyd George, now secretary of state for war, and aware not only that he would be held directly responsible for any lack of military success but also that some of his colleagues would be delighted to so indict him, was in a most belligerent

---

Dixon, editor of the *Christian Science Monitor*, warned House that Grey, Balfour, Lloyd George, and Cecil opposed a premature peace.

45. House to Grey, 11, 19, and 23 May 1916, House Papers, Grey file.

46. House to Plunkett, 3 and 11 May 1916, ibid., Plunkett file. Grey's actions, House wrote, were utterly discouraging and suggested three possible interpretations. Either he was gambling on a rupture between Berlin and Washington or was in fact opposed to or at best indifferent to American entry into the war at that stage. Britain seemed to prefer victory without American intervention, and with France and Russia bearing the military burden. Perhaps Britain was concerned lest United States involvement in the war stimulate the development of her naval power. Alternatively British policy might simply be hesitant and lacking in design.

47. The blockade, British interference with mail services, Ireland, naval rivalry, and commercial competition were the principal irritants. (Spring-Rice to Grey, 19 and 30 May, 2 June, 24 Nov., and 1 Dec., Spring-Rice to Drummond, 14 July, Grey to Spring-Rice 29 July, and Drummond to Spring-Rice, 25 July 1916, FO/800/86; Hankey to Balfour, 5 May, Balfour Papers, Add. 49704, and Balfour draft, 24 May 1916, Cab 37/148/28.)

48. Lloyd George to R. J. Lynn, 5 June, and to J. Dillon, 10 June 1916, LGP, D/14/2/13 and 24; Lloyd George to House, 31 July 1916, House Papers, Lloyd George file.

49. War Committee, 10 Aug. 1916, Cab 42/17/5.

mood. Should peace negotiations prove unavoidable, the Entente must not relax the blockade and afford Germany a breathing space. Full stomachs, Lloyd George warned, meant military recovery. McKenna now expressed concern lest Wilson deny the allies economic and financial assistance if they obstructed peace talks, but Lloyd George doubted whether Germany would negotiate that year. He declared, moreover, that an American embargo on cotton shipments would be tantamount to a declaration of war. Bonar Law supported him in this irresponsibility, but Lord Robert Cecil, under-secretary of state at the Foreign Office from May 1915, and Asquith suggested that at least they must give some thought to the implications of eventual negotiations and therefore to actual peace terms.

The prime minister was surely correct. Briand's pressure, Robertson's fear that France was better prepared for negotiations than Britain,[50] the possibility of a Central Powers' declaration on Polish independence or a Russo-German deal consummated over Poland, and the prospect of an American or German peace move all pointed to the need for a study of war aims. Asquith therefore elicited memoranda on 30 August.[51]

Lloyd George was not at the War Committee on 30 August and never wrote a memorandum on peace terms. However, he agreed with H. A. L. Fisher that France might reduce her claims, and that the United States was vital to a global settlement.[52] Lloyd George declared himself opposed to a public discussion of peace terms at that time; the insane spirit of war prevailed and the government must avoid definite pledges and platforms.

The memoranda produced in response to Asquith's request or as a result of departmental studies, demanded, without exception, that the Entente dictate peace to Germany. They deplored the prospect of inconclusive, moderate, and unsatisfactory terms arrived at through the mediation of the electioneering Wilson.[53] Edwin Montagu, now minister of munitions, was as extreme as

50. Robertson to Lloyd George, 17 Aug. 1916, K. J. Calder, "National Self-Determination in British Government Policy during the First World War," (Ph.D. thesis, University of London, 1971), 147; *Esher Journals*, IV, 47–48.

51. War Committee, 30 Aug. 1916, Cab 42/18/7.

52. Fisher's notes of a conversation, 27 Aug. 1916, H. A. L. Fisher Papers, box 27. David Davies was also present and this may have affected Lloyd George's comments.

53. Memoranda by Montagu, 29 Aug., Cab 42/18/7, by the General Staff, 31 Aug., Cab 42/18/10, by Lord Crawford and Balcarres, 17 Sept., Cab 42/20/2,

anyone. "It is horrible to allow oneself to think even for a moment that the fruits of victory may be spoiled for us by unsatisfactory terms of peace." He feared transatlantic influences, for, "so contemptible and untrustworthy does the American politician of all parties seem to me that I hope this question will be answered in the negative—for we can rely on no solution from America which considers civilisation, merits, or the future security of peace, but only the immediate political interests of either party." Germany must, Montagu insisted, pay the full price of defeat, receive no compensation, and be deprived of a negotiated peace which Berlin would celebrate as victory. These were sentiments with which the Foreign Office, the War Office, and the Admiralty were in accord and which the War Committee endorsed completely.

They were buoyed, temporarily, by the German failure at Verdun, and by the Somme and Russian offensives. Lloyd George, cultivated by Lord Northcliffe, jumped to the fore and in public. At the War Committee on 20 September he dismissed Wilson's angry representations over the blockade with laconic contempt; they should send the president a lengthy legal note to occupy him until 4 November.[54] At the same time Northcliffe, unalterably opposed to a compromise settlement, urged Lloyd George to meet Roy Howard, head of United Press of America, who had reported "certain disquieting things."[55] Within two days Lloyd George talked with Howard. Northcliffe read over the record of their conversation and strongly recommended its immediate publication.[56] He had heard, he said, from a "leading member" of

---

by Admiral Sir H. Jackson, 12 Oct., Cab 42/21/8, by Balfour, 4 Oct., Cab 37/157/7, and by Foreign Office, 7 Aug., 1916, Cab 42/17/4. Sir Ralph Paget and Sir William Tyrrell wanted to discredit the German militarists, secure a revolution in German policy, and not leave Germany as an even more formidable rival in Europe and the Near East. In a negotiated peace, however, Britain would be forced to return Germany's colonies or award Germany certain Belgian, French, or Portuguese colonies. Germany would refuse to pay reparations to Belgium. Britain would be saddled, therefore, with the costs of Belgian recovery, and France might not secure Alsace-Lorraine or an indemnity. Russia would be tempted to offer Germany economic concessions in the Near East in order to retain Constantinople and to secure the evacuation of Poland and Courland. Finally, Austria and Bulgaria would insist on territorial gains at Serbia's expense and in the Balkans.

54. War Committee, 20 Sept. 1916, Cab 42/20/6.
55. Northcliffe to Lloyd George, 25 Sept. 1916, LGP, E/2/21/2.
56. Northcliffe to Lloyd George, 27 Sept. 1916, ibid., E/2/21/3; Riddell diary, 1 Oct. 1916, Lord Riddell, *War Diary, 1914–1918*, 212.

the American Embassy that "a peace squeal" to arouse world sympathy was imminent; they must prevent it. Consequently, Northcliffe advised Lloyd George to publish the interview world-wide and without alteration, and avoid the bungling interference of the official propaganda machine. Lloyd George followed North-cliffe's advice; consulting neither the Foreign Office nor the War Committee, he released the text of the interview on 28 September. It appeared in *The Times* on the following day. The message rang out: fight to a decisive finish, to a knockout; destroy Prussian military despotism, save civilization, and reject interference from neutral states. "The whole world—including neutrals of the highest purposes and humanitarians with the best of motives—must know that there can be no outside interference at this stage. Britain asked no intervention when she was unprepared to fight. She will tolerate none now that she is prepared . . ."

Lloyd George suggested in his memoirs that he had intended also to counter defeatism within the government, and unjustly charged Grey with that sin.[57] Obviously, Grey did not share the delight of Lord Hardinge, his permanent under-secretary from June 1916, and Ambassador Bertie.[58] While lamenting the lack of prior consultation and the flagrant disregard of the Foreign Office, Grey and McKenna objected to the deleterious effect the interview would have on Anglo-American relations and the opportunities it would present to Berlin.[59] In any case, Grey argued, the attitude of the French government made pressure on Wilson superfluous.[60]

57. *War Memoirs*, I, 508–10. He made no mention of Northcliffe and sugges-ted that he met Howard on 28 September for a routine press interview. Lloyd George insisted elsewhere in his memoirs, to show that he had acted correctly, that the War Committee were united in their opposition to a negotiated peace. Howard told House that "Lloyd George gave the interview of not long ago under the impression that it would help you in holding Germany off concerning mediation until after the election." (House to Wilson, 6 Nov. 1916, House Papers, Wilson file.)

58. Riddell diary, 1 Oct. 1916, *War Diary*, 212; Bertie to Lloyd George, 2 Oct. 1916, LGP, E/3/14/15. See also A. Gordon Lennox, *The Diary of Lord Bertie of Thame 1914–1918*, 2 vols. (London, 1924), I, 337, and II, 10–11, 34–35, 44–46.

59. Grey to Lloyd George, 29 Sept. 1916, LGP, E/2/13/5. McKenna regarded the interview as "an affront to Washington which would injure British credit." His hostility to Lloyd George had reached chronic proportions. (Scott diary, 2–3 Oct. 1916, Scott Papers, Add. 50902.)

60. Lloyd George knew that France would rebuff any peace offer (LeRoy Lewis to Lloyd George, 12, 20, and 29 Sept. and 2 Oct. 1916, LGP, E/3/14/10, 12, 13, and 14.)

Britain would now be held responsible, Grey feared, for warning Wilson off and the president might use the interview as an excuse for inaction in the future. German-American relations would improve, Germany had a further reason to intensify submarine warfare, and, finally, Grey pointed out, the United States would feel free to increase pressure on Britain to ease the blockade. He concluded, "It has always been my view that until the allies were sure of victory the door should be kept open for Wilson's mediation. It is now closed for ever as far as we are concerned.... I hope you won't think me captious in questioning one point in your interview of which the rest not only draws my assent but also my admiration."

Grey's response was not that of a defeatist. In his opinion, Lloyd George had erred. He had gone too far and had destroyed a policy alternative, United States mediation, which, while not to be implemented at that time, was to be held in reserve in the event of a deterioration in the Entente's position. In fact, the policy alternative which Grey still seemed to cherish had evaporated, and his own tactics throughout the summer had contributed to its demise. As Ambassador Spring-Rice had predicted since May, Wilson was determined on an independent mediation attempt once the election was behind him, in order to avoid United States belligerency despite the submarine warfare.

Lloyd George, pointing to his favourable reviews,[61] understood this to be the case and invited Grey to retract.[62] His interview, he claimed, had offset the influence of the Germans and the Irish in Washington; Wilson would not now attempt a unilateral act of mediation. The allies were saved therefore from a premature cessation of hostilities. Britain would not have to face the predicament of either refusing to negotiate, or negotiating in bad faith by offering impossible peace terms. Indeed, Lloyd George suggested, he had performed this vital service, committed this "serviceable indiscretion," because Grey could not have done so himself except formally and at the risk of political ruin. He on the other hand

61. The information received from Washington was generally favourable to the interview. Commentators saw it as a deterrent to a mediation attempt which Germany was thought to be urging on Wilson, and to which the president might respond. (Dixon to Cecil, 1, 13, and 18 Oct., and 20 and 27 Nov., Cecil Papers, Add. 51092, and Spring-Rice to Grey, 4 and 6 Oct. 1916, LGP, E/3/28/1 and 2.)

62. Lloyd George to Grey, 2 Oct. 1916, LGP, E/2/13/6; Taylor, *Lloyd George: A Diary*, 114.

was immune from such a fate. In any case, Lloyd George assured Grey, his fears were unfounded for the interview would have beneficial results. The American politician had no international conscience, thought only of the ticket, and did not care about European opinion.

Lloyd George's reply was an attempt to refute Grey's accusation of endangering official policy by pointing out, quite rightly, that the option offered by House had disappeared. It had been replaced by the prospect of mediation activated unilaterally and brought on, in Lloyd George's opinion, by hostile influences close to Wilson in the critical last weeks of an election campaign. Whether the outburst would deter Wilson from unilateral action was, however, questionable. Perhaps Lloyd George, as Scott and McKenna suggested, was also concerned to boost his reputation with the army, now that he ruled at the War Office.

Public reaction to the interview reflected the broad process which was altering Lloyd George's position politically. The Liberal and left wing press were hostile; the *Labour Leader*, on 5 October 1916, described it as "the wickedest thing which has been done by any politician during the war."[63] The Unionist press were delighted; not surprisingly, *The Times* praised the interview as "apposite in form, excellent in substance and most opportune in season."[64] Other more sensitive minds were distressed at the style of the interview.[65] Lloyd George defended his actions to an outraged C. P. Scott:

> He said he had positive and documentary evidence that Gerard, the United States ambassador at Berlin, had gone to America with a proposal to Wilson that he should propose mediation and Wilson would be under very strong temptation to do this in order to conciliate German-American opposition to his re-election which would probably turn the scale. Once mediation was proposed, it would have been very difficult to refuse and once the war was stopped it would have been impossible to resume it. But the time for a

63. R. O. Davis, "British policy and opinion on war aims and peace proposals, 1914–1918" (Ph.D. thesis, Duke University, 1950).

64. *The Times* and the *Daily Mail*, 29 Sept. 1916.

65. Esher to Haig, 29 Sept. 1916, Haig Papers, vol. 214: "Lloyd George suffers from a swollen head. Also he cannot shake off his hopelessly 'common' outlook on men and things . . . he said things that were right in the main, but he said them in a fashion that makes one blush for one's country."

*235*

*settlement was for us extremely unfavourable and for the Germans favourable.*[66]

In Parliament, Lloyd George maintained that his statement to the press represented the views of the War Committee, their military advisers, and the allies.[67] Subverting the truth, he stated that he had consulted his colleagues. Beyond that he insisted on his right to speak out on military and diplomatic issues, and not to confine himself to routine departmental matters, "and how they make breeches in Pimlico." He was unrepentant, charging that those who now clamoured for peace actually favoured the German cause and had said nothing about negotiations when the Central Powers held the initiative militarily. He also pointed out that Grey had anticipated President Wilson's call for a league of nations. The creation of a league in the postwar era, however, did not require premature American diplomatic intervention during the war.

The War Committee were brought rapidly to a more sober mood in early October and explored two critical variables: would Wilson, if re-elected, assert sufficient economic and financial pressure on the Entente to force them to a conference, and would a re-evaluation of the military situation compel a change of policy?[68] Lloyd George, dismissing the views of McKenna and Montagu, did not anticipate a confrontation with Wilson. They would be able to utilize American resources to the full and must not permit financial conservatism to hinder the war effort. They must continue, he argued, to place orders with American firms, for this very policy exasperated the enemy, and also gave Britain considerable influence in the United States. The Entente must, he insisted, achieve victory independently and largely through Britain's exertions. When France was exhausted Britain would lead the allies and dominate the peace settlement.

The War Committee decided to resume the study of war aims, and to create a sub-committee to review all aspects of the war situation. In effect it would analyse stamina. This process produced a flurry of papers which suggested two apparently contradictory

66. Scott diary, 20–22 Nov. 1916, Scott Papers, Add. 50902. The *Manchester Guardian* attacked the interview as detrimental to Anglo-American relations and as defiant of Grey and Asquith.
67. Speech, 11 Oct. 1916, *Parl. Deb.*, H. of C., LXXXVI, 134–36, 150–51.
68. War Committee, 5 Oct. 1916, Cab 42/21/2.

conclusions. Lord Lansdowne, minister without portfolio, in his memoranda of 13 and 27 November, effectively summarized the principal one; the allied military, economic, and financial position had deteriorated to a dangerous point.[69] Therefore, he asked, was it wise to pursue victory in a prolonged war, inviting exhaustion, a crippling financial burden, and staggering casualty lists.

The evidence was impressive; to the accumulated strains of the first two years were added fresh burdens. The Board of Trade feared a merchant shipping crisis by June 1917, food shortages were likely, and Admiral Sir John Jellicoe, commander of the Grand Fleet, warned that a resumption of unrestricted submarine warfare could force Britain to negotiate peace. The Admiralty was pessimistic about naval construction, and the Manpower Distribution Board expressed unease about the supply of labour. Sir William Robertson could offer only continued attrition on the Western Front despite the meagre results of the Somme offensive.[70] Meanwhile, neither Italy nor Russia prospered militarily, both might defect, and Rumania faced defeat.

Only Lansdowne, however, dissented from the second conclusion, that Britain must fight on. Why not, he asked, explore the peace terms publicly endorsed by Asquith and Grey? Why discount the idea of mediation in tones which made the Entente seem vindictive and selfish?

Grey was the only member of the War Committee not to deride Lansdowne's hypothesis, and to raise the idea of United States mediation, should peace negotiations become necessary. He refused, however, to challenge the War Committee's military and naval advisers, even as he answered Robertson's attack on the Foreign Office.[71] Grey was gravely concerned over shipping losses

69. Lansdowne memoranda, 13 and 27 Nov. 1916, Cab 37/159/32 and Cab 37/160/22; Loreburn to Lloyd George, 29 Nov. 1916, ibid., E/4/2/30; C. R. Buxton, *Peace this Winter* (London, 1916), Milner Papers, file 116.

70. Memoranda by Board of Trade, 24 Oct., Cab 37/158/10, by Lord Crawford and Balcarres, 30 Oct. and 9 Nov., Cab 37/158/21 and Cab 37/159/22, by Balfour, 14 Oct., Cab 37/157/31, by Robertson, Oct. and 3 Nov., Cab 42/22/15, and Lloyd George, *War Memoirs*, I, 536–41, by War Office, 28 Nov., Cab 37/160/25, and report by Manpower Distribution Board, 19 Nov. 1916, Cab 42/23/12; Buchanan to Hardinge, 17 and 28 Oct., LGP, E/3/23/1 and 3, and Jellicoe to Asquith, 30 Oct. 1916, Hankey, *Supreme Command*, II, 553–54.

71. Grey memorandum, 27 Nov. 1916, Cab 37/160/20, and memorandum on Russia, n.d., Viscount Grey, *Twenty-Five Years*, II, 131–33. He attached a copy of the House scheme to his paper on Russia. Robertson charged that the Foreign Office had bungled the negotiations with Turkey and Bulgaria, and that foreign

and advocated more effective policies to combat the submarine menace, accompanied perhaps by changes at the Admiralty, and greater sacrifices at home. Germany seemed more confident and was probably less interested in peace negotiations, but Grey could not rule out the possibility that the Central Powers might propose mediation while they held the initiative.[72] Provided the Entente could campaign vigorously for the next eight or twelve months, however, and as long as the experts remained sanguine, they must avoid mediation, Grey argued, even though they might not ultimately achieve the complete defeat of Germany. Only if a further year's campaigning seemed unlikely to enhance their bargaining position would Grey advocate negotiations. Even then, he would support continuing the war in order to weaken Germany further and delay her postwar recovery. He would therefore activate peace negotiations through "the medium of not unsympathetic mediation" to secure minimum terms, only if the military situation continued to deteriorate and defeat seemed probable. Grey still debated the issues as if the Entente could decide whether and when the United States would attempt mediation; he spoke as if the policy option which he said Lloyd George had destroyed in September was still open.

In fact, Grey had left the initiative to the War Office. Robertson, prompted by Lloyd George, indulged in a vulgar and bitter attack on Lansdowne, denouncing "cranks, cowards and philosophers," and describing Germanophiles as "those miserable members of society."[73] He declared himself convinced that sound planning, correct strategy, the application of the nation's resources to the

---

policy and military preparations had been out of step before 1914. (Robertson to Grey, 29 Nov. 1916, FO/800/102.)

72. Drummond to Grey and Grey minute, 14 Oct., and Grey to Balfour, Nov. 1916, Balfour Papers, Add. 49731; Spring-Rice to Grey, 24 Nov. and 1 and 5 Dec. 1916, ibid., and FO/800/86. Grey told Spring-Rice that Britain could neither encourage American mediation without being prepared to accept it, nor risk the odium of being responsible for rejecting mediation in advance. Britain should therefore urge her allies to state the minimum conditions on which they could accept mediation or become involved in negotiations. (Grey to Spring-Rice, 26 Nov. 1916, FO/800/86.)

73. Robertson memorandum and appendix by Haig, 24 Nov. 1916, Cab 37/160/15; Sir W. Robertson, *Soldiers and Statesmen, 1914–1918*, 2 vols. (New York, 1926), I, 280. The journalist H. Wickham Steed warned Lloyd George of Germanophil intrigue in Italy, involving politicians T. Tittoni, G. Giolitti, and the Vatican, which was synchronized with the German peace campaign in the United States. (Steed to J. T. Davies, 29 Nov. 1916, LGP, E/2/21/4.)

war effort, assistance from the diplomats, and wise policies would bring victory. The war, Robertson predicted, would be long and the strain great, but they must fight on and dictate peace, leaving neither Prussian militarism intact nor the Dominions and the allies estranged and betrayed. Robertson concluded with rather terminal advice: "We shall win if we deserve to win."

Hankey, Cecil, and Walter Long, president of the local government board, agreed, and Asquith, on 11 October, had already opposed publicly a precarious and dishonourable compromise, masquerading as peace.[74] He was sufficiently convinced of the policy and mistakenly confident that the consensus in opposition to Lansdowne was conducive to governmental unity. Lloyd George's position required little elaboration. He feared the impact on public morale of continued defeats and new burdens, and warned, "Efforts will be made perhaps by powerful neutrals to patch up peace on what would appear to be specious terms, and there is a real danger that large masses of people, worn out by the constant strain, may listen to well intentioned but mistaken pacificators." He did not seek, however, "debatable victory, but unchallengeable victory, not victory won here countered by disaster there."[75]

McKenna, still alarmed lest Wilson withhold financial support from the Entente, asked the War Committee, on 28 November, to contemplate the consequences of escalating expenditures, increased levels of borrowing, and an inability to purchase sufficient wheat and munitions.[76] Grey, Balfour, Asquith, and Montagu were impressed with the seriousness of the situation. Grey explained that President Wilson, convinced that neither side could achieve victory, planned to assert pressure on both sets of belligerents. The president "believed that the War could be wound up now on reasonable terms, but those terms we should regard as unsatisfactory and inconclusive." Grey concluded, however, that unless they could combat the submarine menace, they "might have to consider the question of terms." Bonar Law and Lord Curzon were most aggressive in their opposition and the War Committee did not change its policy, preferring to risk the

74. Hankey memorandum, 31 Oct., Cab 42/22/14, Cecil memorandum, 27 Nov., Cab 37/160/21, and Long memorandum, 29 Nov. 1916, Cab 37/160/27.
75. War Committee, 13 Nov. 1916, Cab 37/159/33; Lloyd George's draft of Asquith's statement for the Paris Conference, 15 Nov. 1916, Cab 28/1.
76. War Committee, 28 Nov. 1916, Cab 42/26/2.

consequences of prolonged warfare rather than peace negotiations through American mediation.

Why had the attempt to secure a negotiated peace in 1916 failed? In the first place, perceptions of the relationship between military developments and diplomatic policies, in London and Berlin, did not favour mediation. Asquith's government never regarded any point of time in the military situation as an appropriate moment for negotiations. The optimism and expectations of June and September pulled the Entente away from mediation; the gloom of November was Germany's joy, and the War Committee would not parley in the shadow of escalating submarine warfare. They could not concede Britain's vulnerability to the submarine, and admit that sea power had turned on the island race. Grey led House to believe that he would call for mediation after the allies had achieved a certain level of military success. In fact London would approachWashington only if the Entente faced defeat.

Neither House's threats nor his blandishments had moved the War Committee. He represented a seemingly perfidious president and ignored Ambassador Page. House courted Grey and yet consulted those, like Lord Loreburn, who publicly excoriated the foreign secretary. Wilson's "probably" was not the issue. The United States was primarily, in British calculations, an invaluable source of material assistance. She might, in certain circumstances, become a desirable and even necessary ally, but Wilson, on the hustings, preferred moral leadership to belligerency. Moreover, as Lloyd George feared in September, Wilson was likely to attempt mediation unilaterally rather than at the bidding of the allies. Who could ignore, in this regard, the evidence of improved German–American relations and the irritants existing between London and Washington. A peace conference under Wilson's guidance was at best an inscrutable proposition. Its proceedings would be unpredictable and might endanger both allied morale and unity. Hostilities once ended would be difficult to resume. Rightly or not the War Committee assumed that public opinion opposed peace negotiations. They feared, with perhaps more justification, that to accept them would injure governmental unity.

Asquith's administration preferred the pursuit of victory to peace on moderate terms. The allies and the Dominions shared this view, and Britain could risk jeopardizing neither Entente solidarity nor the future security of the Empire. Reasonable terms were only minimum expectations to be salvaged through mediation. In the final analysis the British government, despite the presence of Atlanticist sentiments, was unsure about the development of American naval power. Britain was not at war to achieve anything less than future security, as the investigation of war aims revealed, and Lloyd George approved thoroughly of that objective.

# II

# What Constitutes Victory?

On 30 August 1916, Asquith asked the members of the War Committee to prepare memoranda on war aims. Up until then the Foreign Office and those departments concerned with specific areas and problems had virtually monopolized a sparse and limited investigation of and negotiations on war aims.[1] Grey, enjoying Asquith's complete support, had discouraged discussion of the question, as being mischievously divisive and premature. Lord Hardinge, then viceroy of India, had welcomed the allied agreement of 5 September 1914 to make war and peace in common, partly because he did not trust a "radical Government" which harboured "Haldane and others with German sympathies and peace at any price ideas."[2]

As the territorial scope and the intensity of the war increased it became more difficult to reconcile national, imperial, and allied

1. Only one interdepartmental committee, that under de Bunsen, functioned in 1915. On 27 August 1916 a CID sub-committee to study territorial changes outside Europe was created. It met between September 1916 and February 1917. (Cab 16/36; *Esher Journals*, iv, 4–8; E. T. S. Dugdale, *Maurice de Bunsen, Diplomat and Friend* [London, 1934], 316.) In general see V. H. Rothwell, *British War Aims and Peace Diplomacy 1914–1918* (Oxford, 1971), 1–58.

2. Hardinge to Nicolson, 8 Oct. 1914, FO/800/375.

interests. When the government made increasing demands on the nation, public opinion, élite publicists, and pressure groups could influence policy more effectively. An emotional as well as an analytical escalation took place. Victory was the goal, yet members of the government explored, for instance during and after the House mission, what adjustment of war aims would be necessary should the costs of prolonged warfare prove excessive, victory itself be unattainable, or popular enthusiasm for the war falter.

The fact that Lloyd George became prime minister and conducted Britain's case at the Paris Peace Conference with almost supreme control, makes necessary an examination of his views on war aims. Like the majority of his colleagues he was involved in little long-term planning about the peace settlement before 1917. He tended to accept the commitments and arrangements which masqueraded as a policy, and resided comfortably enough within the official consensus. This role did not reflect a lack of interest or concern. War aims were not a mere side issue for Lloyd George, as the conversations with House revealed. Apart from utilizing the sparse set of memoranda and Foreign Office material which circulated before August 1916, he examined ideas through conversation and explored policy alternatives in executive debate. On the other hand, he agreed with Grey that they must impose a moratorium on public discussion of war aims, at a time when reason and sanity did not flourish, and he violated that rule only in his speeches on the future of the Ottoman Empire.

What comprised reason and sanity for Lloyd George was clearly the middle ground between hysterical Germanophobia and unnecessarily feeble and unwisely modest demands. If any trend developed, it was that he became more sternly insistent in his expectations of what the Empire should secure from the war. National and imperial security and a postwar balance of power which served Britain's interests were his principal concern. The Foreign Office, in inter-allied negotiations, must specify and defend those interests, particularly in the face of Russia's demands. Indeed, Lloyd George seemed as determined as any minister to ensure that, by making her war effort the key to victory, Britain would dominate the peace settlement. Neither France nor Russia, nor the United States for that matter, could be permitted to disregard her vital interests.[3] At home, after accepting the need for

3. War Committee, 5 Oct. 1916, Cab 42/21/2.

the government to exercise powers of compulsion, he denounced those who would not fight for nation and Empire.

On the other hand, he was reasonable, enlightened, and even prescient in his attitude toward Germany. This was consistent with his prewar views and genuinely based, even though he was less generous by the fall of 1916. Moreover, he sought a higher purpose for the war, the eradication of militarism, and was able to indulge his radical sentiments in the denunciation of the Turk. Nevertheless, a unity of ideas was maintained; the destruction of the Ottoman Empire would serve Britain's imperial interests, and a reduced but viable and even cooperative Germany would function in the balance of power in such a way as to safeguard British security. In a similar way, Lloyd George's response to the wartime proselytizing of the Zionists demonstrated how nonconformist and imperialist themes could function in unison.

Asquith's governments assumed that Europe would never enjoy peace and security unless the allies defeated Germany sufficiently to dictate peace terms. They must humiliate and punish those whom they felt to be criminally responsible for the catastrophe and likely to make a further bid for armed supremacy. The allies must cleanse and reform Germany, and exorcise Prussian militarism. Presumably the emergence of a chastened Germany would make an excessively harsh peace unnecessary. In any case Britain did not intend to reduce her to a subservient status. Under Asquith, Britain was determined to limit Germany's potential for aggression, destroy her naval power, and remove the Kiel canal and possibly Heligoland from her control, but not to make her feeble.[4] She would be essential to a more self-regulating postwar balance of power where Russia flourished and France made excessive demands.[5] Britain must seek to create a secure, indemni-

4. Page to Bryan, 10 Sept. 1914, Page Papers, Wilson file II; Grey to Bertie, 16 Sept. 1914, FO/800/56A, and 24 Aug. 1916, Cab 37/154/18; Grey to Buchanan, 15 May 1916, Cab 37/147/40; Grey to House, 29 May 1916, House Papers, Grey file; Kitchener memoranda, 16 and 21 April 1915, FO/800/102 and Cab 37/127/34; Haldane memorandum, 8 April 1915, Cab 37/127/17; Foreign Office memorandum, 7 Aug. 1916, Cab 42/17/4; Robertson memorandum, 31 Aug. 1916, Cab 42/18/10; Admiralty memorandum, 12 Oct. 1916, Cab 42/21/8. Hence the support for proposals to unit Catholic, pacific Austria with Germany. Grey and the Foreign Office were more moderate than the Admiralty and the War Office. Lloyd George was willing to see Denmark secure the Kiel Canal if she entered the war. (Scott diary, 27 Nov. 1914, Scott Papers, Add. 50901.)

5. War Council, 10 and 19 March 1915, Cab 42/2/5 and 14; Kitchener memorandum, 21 April 1915, Cab 37/127/34; Balfour draft reply to the United

fied, and even enlarged Belgium, restore Alsace-Lorraine to France, and make other territorial adjustments at Germany's expense, favouring, for example, Denmark.[6] A less than complete victory would mean compensating Germany for her losses to France and for the costs of restoring Belgium. Ministers discussed whether territory in Asia Minor or East Africa as opposed to Eastern Europe would be acceptable for that purpose. The French, however, were not sure of Britain's determination to drive Germany from their soil, and Lloyd George's interest in theatres beyond the Western Front and his insistence that Germany's attack on Belgium was the sole cause of Britain's intervention fed French apprehensions.[7]

Lloyd George entertained no reservations about the basic policy. The Prussian military caste was "the road-hog of Europe." They must smash this aggressor, this "hectoring bully."[8] But, wary of Russia, he regarded a united Germany as essential to future stability. He told the War Council in March 1915 that "We

States, 24 May 1916, Cab 37/148/28; Balfour memorandum 4 Oct. 1916, Cab 37/157/7; Foreign Office memorandum 7 Aug. 1916, Cab 42/17/4; Grey to Buchanan, 15 May 1916, Cab 37/147/40; Robertson memorandum, 31 Aug. 1916, Cab 29/1/4; and Montagu memorandum, 29 Aug. 1916, Cab 42/18/7. Kitchener's scenario envisaged a war between Russia and the Slavs, and Germany, Austria, France, and Italy. The victors would turn on the British Empire. Grey and Lloyd George expected France to make demands on Germany beyond Alsace-Lorraine in the peacemaking. (Grey to Bertie, 24 Aug. 1916, Cab 37/154/18, and Lloyd George–Fisher–Davies conversation, 27 Aug. 1916, Fisher Papers, box 27.)

6. Grey to Bertie, 5 Jan. and 24 Aug. 1916, Cab 37/140/10 and Cab 37/154/18; Grey to Buchanan, 15 May 1916, Cab 37/147/40; Foreign Office memorandum, 7 Aug. 1916, Cab 42/17/4; Balfour memorandum, 4 Oct. 1916, Cab 37/157/7; Robertson memorandum, 31 Aug. 1916, Cab 42/18/10. The General Staff were less reserved than the Foreign Office on the future of Schleswig-Holstein. All expected partition and a reversion to Denmark of part of the duchies. An Anglo-French-Belgian alliance might replace the prewar neutrality treaty. The Scheldt must be open to British forces in wartime in order that they could defend Antwerp. The Foreign Office and the General Staff wanted to provide for British assistance to Belgium in the event of German aggression, and favoured the incorporation of Luxemburg into Belgium.

7. Hankey to Grey, 21 Jan. 1915, FO/800/90; Cecil to Asquith, 2 March 1915, Cecil Papers, Add. 51073; A. Gordon Lennox, The Diary of Lord Bertie of Thame 1914–1918, I, 120. Lloyd George's article in the Methodist Times of 17 December 1914 had escaped such criticism. He told Scott that France could not formally claim even Alsace-Lorraine until Germany was driven back to the Rhine. (Scott diary, 11 March 1915, Scott Papers, Add. 50901.)

8. Riddell diary, 19 Aug. and 6 Dec. 1914, Lord Riddell, War Diary, 1914–1918, 14, 45.

ought not to rule out the possibility of giving Germany a bone of some sort. She would always be a very powerful nation and it might eventually even be desirable to have her in a position to prevent Russia becoming too predominant."[9] In February 1916 Lloyd George commented to Riddell, "For my part I still say we must beat the Germans, and when they are beaten I would endeavour to make the peace real and lasting. A great nation like Germany must live."[10] He accepted the possibility of Anschluss and, in the event of military stalemate, extra-European compensation for Germany. As he told C. P. Scott and T. P. O'Connor, the Irish MP, he would have much greater pleasure in smashing Turkey than in smashing Germany. Indeed, after the allies were satisfied at Turkey's expense, leaving a rump in Asia Minor, Lloyd George thought that it "would be a good plan to give it to Germany as a solatium."[11] Despite the problems anticipated over Germany's colonies and the Baghdad Railway, he returned to a prewar theme: an Anglo-German détente might follow on victory and on the moral and political rehabilitation of Germany.[12]

Asquith's oratory elevated these issues to an ideological level and gave the war a seemingly higher purpose. Lloyd George joined Asquith, invoking Gladstone's name in the process.[13] The immorality of Germany's position equalled that of Britain during the Boer War. This struggle, therefore, was just and righteous. "It is a great war for the emancipation of Europe from the thraldom of a military caste." Britain, in an act of Christian chivalry, defended the weak, and protected Europe against the "Turk of the West." In phrases which marked his maturity Lloyd George insisted that

9. War Council, 19 March 1915, Cab 42/2/14.

10. Riddell diary, 26 Feb. 1916, Riddell, *War Diary*, 157.

11. Scott diary, 27 Nov. 1914, 11 March, and 15 Dec. 1915, Scott Papers, Add. 50901 and 50902; Lloyd George–Fisher–Davies conversation, 27 Aug. 1916, Fisher Papers, box 27.

12. House to Wilson, 15 Jan. 1916, House Papers, Wilson file; speeches in London, 10 Nov. 1914, LGP, C/23, and at Bangor, 28 Feb. 1915, P. Guedalla, ed., *Slings and Arrows*, 227–35; Lloyd George, preface to *Through Terror to Triumph*.

13. Riddell diary, 19 Aug. and 18–19 Sept. 1914, Riddell, *War Diary*, 14, 32; speeches at Queen's Hall, 19 Sept., Guedalla, *Slings and Arrows*, 223–24, Caernarvon and Cardiff, 24 and 29 Sept. 1914, LGP, C/36/2/30 and 31, in London, 7 May 1915, ibid., C/36/2/42, and *Parl. Deb.*, H. of C., June 1915, lxxii, 1183–206, 28 Oct. 1915, lxxv, 347–48, and 28 Nov. 1916, lxxxviii, 295–97; article, *Methodist Times*, 17 Dec. 1914, LGP, C/36/2/34; H. B. Needham, "Mr. Lloyd George on the War," 265; Viscount Simon, *Retrospect* (London, 1952), 97–99; A. J. P. Taylor, ed., *Lloyd George: A Diary*, 2, 11.

power alone underwrote justice and nations forfeited their rights unless they could enforce them. British military preparedness was not Prussian militarism. Lloyd George took pride in the fact that he had found larger sums of money for the defence of England and the Empire than any chancellor of the exchequer before him! Atrocity stories fed such oratory and Lloyd George warned Berlin that Britain would exact a terrible but just reckoning; "the long account must be settled to the last farthing."[14]

Haldane, lord chancellor until May 1915, Lord Robert Cecil, under-secretary of state for foreign affairs, Grey, and to some extent Balfour began to envisage the problem of postwar security in terms of a league of nations.[15] Lloyd George was not unsympathetic to the idea of attempting to create guarantees against aggression and was cognizant of the work of Lowes Dickinson, a member of the League to Abolish War, and of Lord Bryce and others.[16] He seemed more interested, however, in Atlanticist solutions to postwar security problems and in arms limitation, although he avoided any collusion with left wing and dissenting opinion.[17] For the most part, Asquith's administration debated the fundamental concern, national security, in terms of traditional dogma which were not alien to Lloyd George: naval hegemony, the independence of northwestern Europe, and the balance of power.

Imperial security was viewed in terms of consolidation rather than expansion. It meant protecting existing territories, lines of communication, trade and commerce, and adjusting outer frontiers. Sweeping annexations, as opposed to selective advances, would invite both diplomatic and strategic problems, as Grey well

14. Speeches, 15 Feb. 1915, *Parl. Deb.*, H. of C., LXIV, 912, and at Conway, 6 May 1916, LGP, D/27/2/23; War Committee, 1 Aug. 1916, Cab 42/17/1.

15. Haldane memorandum, 8 April 1915, Cab 37/127/17; Grey to Buchanan, 15 May 1916, Cab 37/147/40; Balfour draft reply to the United States, 24 May 1916, Cab 37/148/28; Cecil memorandum, May 1916, Cab 29/1/18. Kitchener, Hankey, and Crowe were particularly opposed to the idea. (Kitchener memorandum, 21 April 1915, Cab 37/127/34; Hankey to Balfour, 25 May 1916, Balfour Papers, Add. 49704; Crowe memorandum, 12 Oct. 1916, Cab 29/1/19.)

16. Lloyd George, *War Memoirs*, I, 411–12; E. R. Cross to Lloyd George, n.d., [Feb. 1915?], LGP, C/1/2/8; Bryce memorandum, 24 Feb. 1915, ibid.; Needham, 267.

17. House to Wilson, 15 Jan. 1916, House Papers, Wilson file; speech, 17 Nov. 1914, *Parl. Deb.*, H. of C., LXVIII, 353–57; War Council, 10 March 1915, Cab 42/2/5.

understood. Considerations of naval strategy, Japan's involvement, and the territorial expectations of the Pacific Dominions and South Africa, however, placed Germany's empire in the Pacific and Africa in jeopardy.[18] Generally, Lloyd George shared Grey's apprehension but accepted the arguments for seizing Germany's colonies, although he was more concerned with the Middle East than Africa and the Pacific. In the debates on strategy he demonstrated beyond question his awareness of the significance for the Empire of the area between the eastern Mediterranean and India.

The strains produced by coalition warfare demanded that Grey cement the Entente, prevent defections, and lure fresh allies into the field. Russia, both because of the dimensions of her appetite and her vulnerability to German overtures, was the Foreign Office's principal concern.[19] Militarily, Grey sought to ensure that Russia concentrated her effort against Germany, rather than in the Balkans or against Turkey. He worried lest Russia seize spoils at Turkey's expense and then leave Britain and France to face the Central Powers. Politically, Grey was concerned to moderate and to render Russia's ambitions as innocuous as possible. She must threaten neither the European balance of power nor British interests in the Middle East and Persia.

The answer was clear enough to Grey by November 1914. The allies must offer Russia control of Constantinople, the Straits, and perhaps less sensitive areas in Asiatic Turkey.[20] C. P. Scott realized

18. War Council, 10 March 1915, Cab 42/2/5. Kitchener, Grey, and Churchill opposed the retention at will of German colonies. Robertson feared lest Germany attempt to regain her colonies via negotiations with France and Russia. Harcourt demanded the retention of German East Africa, and envisaged elaborate adjustments in Africa to check Germany and forestall France and Belgium. (Harcourt memorandum, 25 March 1915, Cab 37/126/27; Jackson memorandum, 12 Oct. 1916, Cab 42/21/8; Robertson memorandum, 31 Aug. 1916, Cab 42/18/10; W. R. Louis, *Great Britain and Germany's Lost Colonies, 1914–1919* [Oxford, 1967].)

19. Nicolson to Hardinge, 5 Sept., and Hardinge to Nicolson, 8 Oct. 1914, FO/800/375. Nicolson wrote, however, "I put my faith in the Russians who to my mind will continually save the situation," and "the result (i.e. victory) will be largely due to Russia in my opinion." Hardinge agreed. "The determination of Russia to settle scores with Germany once and for all time is a very reassuring and encouraging symptom." He argued that if the allies infringed on Turkish or Persian neutrality they would play into Germany's hands. He preferred that the Turks attack the oil facilities at Abadan and violate Persian neutrality; such an act would justify a British reprisal.

20. Cabinet meetings, 23 Sept., 2 and 30 Oct. and 2, 15, and 17 Nov. 1914, Cab 41/35/47, 55, and 56 and Asquith Papers; C. Jay Smith, Jr., "Great Britain

that this policy raised enormous questions, but concluded that the cabinet had given the matter "only the most cursory consideration." Lloyd George, however, accepted Grey's analysis and added that Britain must take Mesopotamia.[21]

The military and political factors necessitating a formal treaty with Russia did not mature until March 1915.[22] Lloyd George argued that Russia would not be satisfied with a mere general declaration of mutual support. She expected a specific treaty, granting her control of the Straits and accepting her other territorial demands.

Lloyd George was correct, and Grey placed Russia's explicit demands before the cabinet and the War Council on 9 and 10 March.[23] In order to neutralize Russia's fear that Britain, Italy, or a Balkan power would obstruct her aims, and to commit her permanently to the Entente, Grey asked his colleagues to accept his policy. Asquith, speaking also for the Admiralty and the War Office, and Bonar Law were in complete agreement.[24] Despite Balfour's fears and Lansdowne's reservations, the War Council concurred; providing British interests were protected Russia would secure her demands.[25]

---

and the 1914–1915 Straits Agreement with Russia; the British promise of November 1914," *American Historical Review*, 70, no. 4 (1965), 1015–34; W. A. Renzi, "Great Britain, Russia and the Straits, 1914–1915," *Journal of Modern History*, 42, no. 1 (1970), 1–20; and M. Ekstein-Frankl, "The Development of British War Aims, 1914–1915," 201–54.

21. Scott diary, 27 Nov. 1914, Scott Papers, Add. 50901.

22. War Council, 3 March 1915, Cab 22/1. Balfour preferred international control of the Straits. Haldane called for neutralization, with Russia enjoying a position similar to that of Britain at Suez. Kitchener suggested Greek control of the Gallipoli peninsula. Crewe looked to Rumanian involvement, while Admiral Fisher, seeing Lemnos as the key, urged Grey to trade Cyprus for it.

23. Buchanan to Foreign Office, 4 March, and cabinet meeting, 9 March 1915, Cab 37/125/28 and 29; War Council, 10 March 1915, Cab 42/2/5. Russia claimed Constantinople, the Straits, and European Turkey to the Enos-Midia line.

24. By October 1916 the Admiralty seemed less confident. The first sea lord argued that Russian control of the Straits meant that the route to India was not safe, even though Britain retained Gibraltar, Malta, and Egypt. Britain must therefore obtain certain islands between Crete and the mainland, and retain Cyprus. (Jackson memorandum, 12 Oct. 1916, Cab 42/21/8.)

25. Subsequently, Grey assured the Japanese ambassador that the secret treaty with Russia did not relate to areas east of Asia Minor, and that until victory was achieved, all such agreements remained provisional. (Grey to Greene, 6 Aug. 1915, Cab 37/132/10.)

Lloyd George, however, wanted at the same time to stake out British war aims lest she be left empty-handed. Russia, he argued, was now inclined to be generous, and they should not be satisfied merely with a general statement that she would support British aims. He proposed a foreign ministers' conference, at Salonika, Lemnos, or on a British warship in the eastern Mediterranean, prior to which the Entente should warn those powers interested in sharing the spoils and settling the future of Asia Minor that they must participate. Grey, Asquith, and Bonar Law, however, were opposed.

Grey carried his policy on every count; war aims were left unspecified, Persia was made more secure, Russia's demands were canalized and limited, and her rulers more firmly committed to the war against Germany.[26]

By February 1916 both Balfour and Lloyd George appeared less certain than either Grey or Asquith of the wisdom of these decisions. Lloyd George still felt not that the price paid to Russia was excessive but that Britain's own interests were not clearly enough delineated. As the most persistent advocate of military assistance to Russia, he now saw the problem as one of keeping a faltering and incompetent ally in the war, and linking her to his Balkan schemes. He was more impressed with Russia's vulnerability than her power. She might defect from exhaustion rather than from machiavellian design, but he expected Germany to attempt to defeat rather than to negotiate with her.[27] Britain had therefore less cause to be so free-handed.

At the same time Lloyd George had not lost sight of the post-war significance of improved Anglo-Russian relations.[28] He argued that as British capital flowed into Russia and as British investors became more familiar with Russian securities, a new era of cooperation would ensue. Lloyd George was aware of the immediate and long-term dangers should Germany control Russia's resources, and his plea that the allies assist Russia did not reflect merely the desire to ensure an effective war effort. He saw

26. Foreign Office memoranda, 11 and 13 March 1915, Cab 37/126/3 and 5.
27. Lloyd George, *War Memoirs*, I, 411–12; Riddell diary, 12 Feb. and 19 Nov. 1916, Riddell, *War Diary*, 155, 220–21. They were also divided on the idea of Russia receiving a warm water port in Asia Minor, in the event of the neutralizing of Constantinople.
28. Lloyd George to H. Llewellyn Smith (Board of Trade), 13 April 1915, E. Vandervelde to Lloyd George, 20 Aug. 1915, and Lloyd George to Asquith, 26 Sept. 1916, LGP, C/7/5/14, D/19/1/2, and E/21/23/5.

military aid as a way to secure Russia's confidence, improve their relations in a more permanent manner, and avoid disruptive confrontations at the peace conference. At the same time, as I have shown, he recognized the danger of Russia emerging from the war with her power greatly enhanced.

Italy stood next to Russia in Grey's concern.[29] He regarded her intervention both as militarily vital and as the key to the formation of a Balkan League. He hoped that a victory at the Dardanelles in 1915 or even an allied military presence at Salonika would impress Rome sufficiently. Moreover, he preferred Italian to either south Slav or Russian naval control of the Adriatic. Dalmatia of course was Italy's contentious price; Serbia must concede, and her champion, Russia, must compromise. A connection was thereby established; Britain's acceptance of Russia's claims might persuade Sergei Sazonov, the Russian foreign minister, to agree to Italy's demands.

Grey placed these considerations before the War Council on 19 March 1915.[30] Again he convinced his colleagues, with Asquith's help, and the Treaty of London followed on 26 April.[31] The south Slavs and their spokesmen protested, but the bargain retained its validity throughout the war and the peacemaking.[32]

Lloyd George had not been prominent in these exchanges and preferred to create a Balkan League by other means, but he raised no opposition to the Treaty of London. From the beginning of the war he had looked for Italian intervention on the Entente side, but feared lest Italy, "the most contemptible nation," play the jackal

29. C. J. Lowe, "Britain and Italian Intervention 1914–1915," *The Historical Journal*, 12, no. 3 (1969), 533–48.

30. War Council, 19 March 1915, Cab 42/2/14; Cabinet meetings, 23, 26, and 30 March, and 7 and 27 April 1915, Cab 37/126/21, 31 and 39, and Cab 37/127/14 and 40. Grey suggested that Italy could not expect to receive all she demanded, and raised the problem of her defection should she be frustrated and should the war go badly.

31. Italy would secure the northern Dalmatian coast from Zara to Cape Planca and enjoy unrestricted use of it and of the islands awarded to her, i.e., they would not be neutralized. She would also receive the Tyrol, the Trentino, and most of Istria.

32. Eustace Percy memorandum, 2 May 1915, FO/800/95. Paget and Tyrrell recognised that the treaty violated the nationality principle, but they, along with the Admiralty and the War Office, regarded it as a commitment. (Foreign Office memorandum, 7 Aug., Cab 42/17/4, Robertson memorandum, 31 Aug., Cab 42/18/10, Balfour memorandum, 4 Oct., Cab 37/157/7, and Jackson memorandum, 12 Oct. 1916, Cab 42/21/8.)

and wait for others to kill her meat.[33] The fact that Sydney Sonnino, San Giuliano's successor at the Italian Foreign Office in November 1914, was born of a Welsh mother, could hardly be expected to alter this assessment. Nor could the fact that Garibaldi's own progeny looked to him to provide £40,000 to raise a force of "Redshirts."[34] If Italy joined the allies, however, she would receive her reward. In his memorandum of 1 January 1915 on strategic questions, Lloyd George argued that Italian public opinion would not tolerate intervention on the side of Austria, "if we made it clear that the whole of this littoral (i.e. the Dalmatian coast) would become Italian territory if Italy helped conquer it."[35]

These negotiations with Italy also demonstrated that Lloyd George regarded the nationality principle as a negotiable factor.[36] His attitude toward the Hapsburg Monarchy confirmed that this was so. In wartime, realists accepted the demands of small powers where necessary, but they were forfeit to the military requirements of the great powers. Lloyd George's eloquent support in public for the submerged nations of Europe and the fact that his strategic preferences seemed to envisage the liberation of the subject peoples of the Hapsburg Monarchy should not mislead. Asquith and he agreed that Britain did not set out to free Eastern Europe; this was "not a war of liberation for oppressed races." They blamed Prussian militarism for the war, not the pre-1914 failure to apply the nationality principle. Asquith's government was concerned to provide security for states already legally constituted; for Serbia and Belgium, and, until her treachery, for Montenegro.[37]

33. Riddell diary, 9 Aug. 1914, Riddell, *War Diary*, 11; Scott diary, 27 Nov. 1914, Scott Papers, Add. 50901; A. Ribot, *Journal d'Alexandre Ribot et correspondances inédites, 1914–1922* (Paris, 1936), 243.

34. Rodd to Grey and Lloyd George, 31 March 1915, LGP, C/4/14/32.

35. Lloyd George memorandum, 1 Jan. 1915, Cab 42/1/8. Subsequently, Lloyd George defended the Treaty of London but still attacked Grey, and both he and Hankey indicted Grey and Asquith for deceiving Italy over the Near East. (Lloyd George, *Truth about the Peace Treaties* [London, 1938], I, 27–29, and II, 761–68, 771–72, and Hankey to Chamberlain, 10 Oct., and Hankey memorandum, 12 Oct. 1922, Hankey Papers, Cab 63/33.)

36. War Council, 8 Jan. and 3 Mar. 1915, Cab 22/1; War Committee, 28 July 1916, Cab 42/16/11; Lloyd George testimony, Dardanelles Committee of Enquiry, 30 Oct. 1916 and 2 April 1917, Cab 19/33.

37. Scott diary, 27 Nov. 1916, Scott Papers, Add. 50901; Lloyd George, *Truth about the Peace Treaties*, II, 752–53; statement, 2 March 1916, *Parl. Deb.*, H. of C., LXXX, 1192; Needham, 267.

Poland was perhaps the single exception. By May 1916 Grey, Balfour, Asquith, and Lloyd George looked with favour on the Polish cause. They could not, however, risk a disagreement with Russia. A united and autonomous Poland in Russia's embrace was the limit of their support.[38]

Clearly, despite his concern for the Balkan theatre, Lloyd George had not thought through any long-term policy for eastern Europe.[39] The government simply kept all alternatives open as military considerations dominated policy. In the first optimistic months Grey was quite cavalier with Hapsburg territory. He seemed willing to accept the destruction of the Empire, or contemplate its survival in various stages of repair and in a variety of rump territorial forms. The nationality principle was an attractive enough formula; it could provide a moral and even realistic guideline for the political regeneration of eastern Europe and the Balkans.[40] Certainly it did not lack advocates; emigrés, academics, and publicists infiltrated officialdom with varying degrees of success. Moreover, the subject races offered actual and potential benefits to the allies. They had a role in espionage and propaganda, they provided information, they helped counteract German activities in the United States, and they seemed to offer immediate military benefits. However, as the war progressed, allied demands, British interests, the nationality principle, and the balance of power competed with each other for attention.

As late as August 1916 Lloyd George seemed somewhat ill-informed about the Slavs.[41] He suggested to H. A. L. Fisher that they should separate Hungary from Austria, and establish the former as an independent kingdom deprived of its Slav peoples. Bohemia, he thought, would present a difficult problem. When

38. Grey to Buchanan, 15 May 1916, Cab 37/147/40; Balfour draft reply to the United States, 24 May 1916, Cab 37/148/28. However, Lloyd George spoke to House of recreating Poland as an independent nation, and House also seems to have referred to an independent Poland. See also Scott diary, 11 March 1915, Scott Papers, Add. 50901; War Committee, 20 Sept. 1916, Cab 42/20/6; Hankey memorandum, 31 Oct. 1916, Cab 24/2/92.

39. David Davies to Fisher, 2 Sept. 1916, Fisher Papers, box 1. He said that Lloyd George retained an open mind on the future of the Hapsburg Monarchy.

40. Grey to Buchanan 15 May 1916, Cab 37/147/40; Foreign Office memorandum, 7 Aug. 1916, Cab 42/17/4.

41. Lloyd George–Fisher–Davies conversation, 27 Aug. 1916, Fisher Papers, box 27, Fisher memoirs, box 14; H. A. L. Fisher, An Unfinished Autobiography (London, 1940), 89–90. Fisher, a Germanophile who distrusted the Poles, began to influence Lloyd George's views. They had met in Oxford before 1916.

Fisher included the Slovaks, he replied, "Who are the Slovaks?" Fisher: "Well they are Slavs, peasants, and about 2 million strong." Lloyd George: "Where are they? I don't seem to place them." Fisher: "On the west of Hungary." Lloyd George: "And where are the Ruthenians?" Fisher: "On the north."

Lloyd George declared himself in favour of a Yugo-Slav state, embracing both Serbs and Croats, despite their religious differences. He was opposed, however, to a federal solution for the Hapsburg Empire, insisting that the Germans and Magyars would never risk Slav preponderance. The Austrian Empire must be dissolved. Fisher concluded subsequently that Lloyd George regarded the dismemberment of the Hapsburg Monarchy as a necessary step towards the democratization of Europe. He was eloquent, Fisher recalled, on the grievances of the Slavs. Yet Fisher, perhaps understandably, had missed the nuances. Military factors had dictated the Treaty of London and might yet earn a reprieve for the Hapsburg Monarchy. Moreover, although Lloyd George insisted that he was attracted to the Serbs, who seemed to him to resemble the Welsh, he gave preference to Bulgaria's claims.

Neither Grey nor Lloyd George eliminated one other strategy: the negotiation of a separate peace with Austria. Such a policy was difficult enough even prior to the Treaty of London; Italy's intervention made it virtually impossible. Rumours of Austria's disenchantment with the war had begun to filter through Switzerland and Spain in December 1914, and Murray of Elibank informed Lloyd George, who "thought the memorandum so important that he showed it to the Prime Minister and sent it to Grey."[42] The foreign minister held secret conversations with Théophile Delcassé, the French foreign minister, in January 1915, but nothing came of their discussions.

In the east the integrity of the Ottoman Empire was in jeopardy.[43] Grey, Asquith, Kitchener, Churchill, Crewe, and Lloyd

42. Elibank to Bertie, 23 Dec. 1914, and Elibank memorandum, 21 Dec. 1914, FO/800/161; Lennox, *Bertie*, I, 78–82. Noel Buxton's claim that Lloyd George was interested neither in the political reorganization of nor a separate peace with the Hapsburg Monarchy is unjustified. (M. Anderson, *Noel Buxton: A Life* [London, 1952], 80.)

43. I. Friedman, "The McMahon–Hussein correspondence and the question of Palestine," and A. Toynbee and I. Friedman, "The McMahon–Hussein correspondence," *Journal of Contemporary History*, 5, no. 2 (1970), 83–122 and 5, no. 4 (1970), 185–201; A. S. Klieman, "Britain's War Aims in the Middle East, in 1915," ibid., 3, no. 3 (1968), 237–51; E. Kedourie, *England and the Middle*

George, whatever their various motives, contemplated revolutionary changes. All were sensitive to one consideration: they must avoid insult to Moslem opinion, particularly in India. Lloyd George had unwittingly violated this rule on one occasion and had required guidance from Crewe.[44]

The War Council first debated the future of the Middle East on 10 March 1915.[45] Churchill, Admiral Fisher, and Kitchener argued that, on strategic and political grounds, Britain must secure Alexandretta, a railway link to Basra and the Persian Gulf, and the Mediterranean terminus of the Baghdad Railway. The security of Egypt, India, and Mesopotamia, the need to balance the anticipated Russian, French, and Italian acquisitions, the demand for a naval base to offset French and Russian power in the Mediterranean, and the desirability of an oil export terminal pointed to this policy. McKenna, Balfour initially, and Lewis Harcourt, were sceptical. Lloyd George tended to agree with them in part. Furthermore, he preferred to occupy Palestine and develop the port of Haifa in order to avoid a quarrel with France over Alexandretta. Grey shared this last sentiment but Kitchener brutally rebuffed them; Alexandretta not Palestine was vital if they intended to annex Mesopotamia.[46]

Grey posed two other basic questions: would significant territorial acquisitions contribute to imperial security; and should they grant Mohammedanism a political as well as a religious existence?[47] He was opposed to such territorial aggrandisement; Haldane, McKenna, and Asquith supported him, although Asquith and

*East: The Destruction of the Ottoman Empire 1914–21* (London, 1956), and "Sir Mark Sykes and Palestine, 1915–16," *Middle Eastern Studies*, 6 (1970), 340–45; V. H. Rothwell, "Mesopotamia in British War Aims," *The Historical Journal*, 13, no. 2 (1970), 273–94; J. Nevakivi, *Britain, France and the Arab Middle East 1914–1920* (London, 1968), 13–44; I. Friedman, *The Question of Palestine, 1914–1918* (London, 1973), 1–118.

44. Crewe to Lloyd George, 2 Oct. 1914, LGP, C/4/1/13 and 14. In a 19 September speech, Lloyd George described the kaiser's blasphemous claims as like those of Mohammed. Crewe asked him to explain to the Aga Khan that he meant the Mohammed of Western legend, and to refrain from making public statements likely to offend Moslem opinion.

45. War Council, 10 March 1915, Cab 42/2/5.

46. Kitchener memorandum, 16 March 1915, Cab 42/2/10; J. Nevakivi, "Lord Kitchener and the partition of the Ottoman Empire, 1915–1916," K. Bourne and D. C. Watt, *Studies in International History* (London, 1967), 316–29.

47. War Council, 19 March 1915, Cab 42/2/14.

Balfour felt that allied claims would force their hand. Britain could neither stand aloof from the scramble for Turkey nor invite French control of the Middle East. With Russian and Italian interests confined to the north and Arab expectations undefined at that stage, France was the principal source of concern. She must not be allowed to secure the whole coastline from Syria to Suez, Kitchener's view notwithstanding, and she must not encroach on the Arabian Peninsula and the Persian Gulf. She was a vital ally but also a postwar rival in the Middle East and Britain must negotiate a *modus vivendi* with her. Lloyd George preferred to exclude her from Palestine and to satisfy her elsewhere. The War Council concluded, on 19 March, in regard to Grey's second question, that Britain should seek to establish a Moslem political entity. That state would include Arabia, but its precise boundaries and status were left undecided. Moreover, Grey would inform the allies, as Churchill preferred, that negotiations on the partition of Turkey were felt to be premature at that stage. The War Council obviously required expert guidance. On 9 April Asquith set up an inter-departmental committee under Sir Maurice de Bunsen, former ambassador in Vienna.

This was the level of policy debate at which Lloyd George functioned. He was more interested in the Balkans and the Near East than in any other theatre outside the Western Front, and his papers contain the vital memoranda on Mesopotamia.[48] Lloyd George's attitude toward the Ottoman Empire reflected perfectly his fusion of Gladstonian radicalism and devotion to imperial security. Oratorically, for instance in his speech of 10 November 1914 to a Free Church Demonstration, he ridiculed and threatened Germany's newest ally.[49] The incompetent but predatory and treacherous Turk had insulted Britain. The Ottoman Empire was, "a human cancer, a creeping agony in the flesh of the lands which they misgovern, rotting every fibre of life." The British Empire, he declared, had no quarrel with the Arabs and with Mohammedanism. They intended, however, to punish the Turk for his record of infamy against humanity.

It followed that there was no question of an honourable peace with Turkey. Lloyd George agreed with an old acquaintance, P. P. Graves, then with the War Office Intelligence Department in

48. These memoranda are in the G. Series. See also J. Wedgewood note, 22 April 1915, circulated by Harcourt, LGP, C/10/2/12.
49. Speech at the City Temple, 10 Nov. 1914, LGP, C/23.

Cairo, that the Turk believed in a concept of racial superiority and worshipped the mysticism of violence.[50] Pan-Turkism or Turkish inspired Pan-Islamism was as dangerous as Pan-Germanism. Defeat by a Teuton–Turk axis meant the loss of Britain's eastern empire and the triumph of injustice. In February 1916, therefore, Lloyd George opposed negotiations for a separate peace with the Ottoman Empire.[51] Partition seemed justified, and in any such redistribution of territory Greece should acquire Smyrna, as the de Bunsen committee had recommended.

Clearly, Lloyd George accepted the basic policy premise; any allied arrangement governing the Middle East must further the immediate war effort, and any partition scheme must serve the future interests of the British Empire. Whether territorial acquisitions would constitute an advance or a liability depended on their extent and location, and he saw rather more merit in Grey's assumptions than in the claims of the Admiralty and the War Office. Nevertheless, with his index finger moving due north from Aden on one of Stanford's maps, Lloyd George could trace the vital area, as he envisaged the disintegration of the Ottoman Empire. Britain must secure some form of control or influence over the crescent of territory and its communication facilities stretching from the Mediterranean to Mesopotamia and the Persian Gulf. They must explore ways to safeguard British interests from Egypt to Basra without taking on unmanageable responsibilities.

His contributions to the debates of 10 and 19 March 1915 were confined essentially to the future of Palestine. Three complementary theses were present: a romantic, even spiritual, sympathy with Zionism, sterner wartime considerations of strategy and allied unity, and a concern for the prestige and security of the Empire. Lloyd George would in fact seek Britain's advantage and God's purpose, in that order. At the same time he was ambivalent in his attitude toward Jews, both individually and as a race, but then only the Celts escaped censure.[52]

50. Graves to Lloyd George, 15 Sept., and Lloyd George notes, 1 Oct. 1915, ibid., D/20/2/18. Graves was a former *Times* correspondent in Constantinople and had met Lloyd George at Criccieth in 1913.

51. War Committee, 22 Feb. 1916, Cab 42/9/3; Lloyd George–Fisher–Davies conversation, 27 Aug. 1916, Fisher Papers, box 27.

52. In November 1916, for instance, he described Montagu as nervous, rattled, hollow-cheeked and seeking cover like a Jew. (Scott diary, 20–27 Nov. 1916, Scott Papers, Add. 50903.)

His contacts with Zionism went back over a decade. In 1903 he had assisted Theodor Herzl's endeavour to establish a Jewish colony in Uganda. A year later Lloyd George declared himself publicly in favour of offering land to the Zionists in East Africa, providing they could avoid a confrontation with the native people.[53] In March 1906 he had acted as an intermediary between L. J. Greenberg, a British-born Jew, and Grey on a scheme to establish a Jewish settlement in the Sinai Peninsula. The proposal foundered on Egyptian objections and Grey's lack of interest.[54] Lloyd George had done enough, however, to be recognized as an early and even valuable supporter of Zionism.

The evidence that the war rekindled this interest in Zionism, born of fundamentalist religious feelings, an attraction to the Jewish mystique, and personal involvement is, by reason of its origin, elusive. Lloyd George could not speak of such things easily in the War Council. Evidence of his romanticism in this regard comes from later speeches and from impressions recorded infrequently in letters, such as that from Reading to Herbert Samuel in February 1915. "I had a talk to Lloyd George about the matter before his departure for Paris. He is certainly inclined to the sympathetic side. Your proposal appeals to the poetic and imaginative as well as to the romantic and religious qualities of his mind."[55]

However, Lloyd George's exchanges with Samuel, from November 1914, point to other conclusions. Samuel's advocacy of a Jewish state in Palestine implied a British presence, at least a sphere of influence or protectorate, whatever the precise arrangement.

---

53. Dr. T. Nussenblatt to Lloyd George, 16 Feb. and 28 March 1931, and Secretary to Nussenblatt, n.d., LGP, G/33/1/13. Nussenblatt, writing a biography of Herzl, discovered a document by Lloyd George dated 1 July 1903, dealing with Herzl's negotiations on Uganda with Chamberlain, Lansdowne, and Cromer. Lloyd George's secretary replied that they had no record of any letters before March 1906, when Lloyd George wrote to Grey on the Sinai Peninsular scheme. See also L. Stein, *The Balfour Declaration* (New York, 1961), 28, 137–38.

54. Unsigned letter to L. J. Greenberg, 6 April 1906, LGP, G/33/1/16. Lloyd George urged Greenberg not to press Grey at that time because unrest involving Egypt and the Sinai would result in a rebuff from the Foreign Office. Grey had rejected the scheme in a memorandum of 20 March 1906. Stein also notes a sympathetic message sent by Lloyd George to a Zionist meeting in Cardiff in 1906.

55. Reading to Samuel, 5 Feb. 1915, Viscount Samuel, *Memoirs* (London, 1955), 143. For other romantic flights of imagination see Taylor, *Lloyd George: A Diary*, 31, 125.

Lloyd George, in his concern for Palestine's "ultimate des-tiny," spoke sympathetically about a Jewish state, within the embrace of the British Empire, but to Scott he talked in terms of "a partly Jewish buffer state," the dimensions of which were not particularly clear. He was concerned with French and Russian reactions. France, he surmised, would object to a buffer state, but Russia might prefer Jewish to Catholic control of the Holy Places.[56]

Scott and Samuel arranged for Lloyd George to meet Chaim Weizmann, the Zionist leader, in January 1915. Scott, while not dismissing rather esoteric considerations about "the Jews of Judea as a possible link between East and West...and as a channel of ideas and of enterprise in the Arabian Peninsula," recorded Lloyd George's concern over "much more concrete matters than these— the present strength of the Jewish element in Palestine and the possibility of its rapid expansion; its relation to the local Arab population which so greatly outnumbers it; the potential value of Palestine as a 'buffer State' and the means of evading for ourselves an undesirable extension of military responsibility; the best way of allaying Catholic and Orthodox jealousy in regard to the custody of the Holy Places."[57] Nevertheless, Asquith's frequently quoted condemnation, that Lloyd George "does not care a damn for the Jews or their past or their future but thinks it will be an outrage to let the Holy Places...pass into the possession or under the protection of 'agnostic, atheistic France'," is quite unacceptable.[58] On the other hand, Lloyd George was neither indifferent nor hostile to Arab aspirations and rights.

There are no grounds for emphasizing Weizmann's influence at this stage on Lloyd George, despite his personal regard for the Zionist leader. Indeed, in November 1915, Scott felt it necessary actually to ask Lloyd George whether he distrusted Weizmann as a security risk.[59] Their November 1915 conversations, including

56. Samuel–Lloyd George conversation, 9 Nov. 1914, Samuel, *Memoirs*, 142; Scott diary, 27 Nov. 1914, Scott Papers, Add. 50901.

57. Samuel to Lloyd George, 13 Jan. 1915, LGP, C/7/9/6; Samuel memoranda, 21 Jan. and 11 March 1915, Cab 37/123/43 and Cab 37/126/1; Scott to Weiz-mann, 14 Jan. 1915, Stein, *Balfour Declaration*, 139–40; Riddell diary, 17 Jan. 1915, Riddell, *War Diary*, 52; C. Weizmann, *Trial and Error* (New York, 1966), 194.

58. Asquith diary, 13 March 1915, Asquith, *Memories and Reflections*, II, 78.

59. Scott diary, 14 and 26 Nov. 1915, Scott Papers, Add. 50902. Scott asked whether Lloyd George feared that Weizmann would leak information to the

Scott and Samuel, confirmed that while Lloyd George seemed as determined as ever to liberate the non-Turkish areas of the Ottoman Empire, Palestine was for him a problem of logistics, railway construction, and the defence of Egypt. Samuel argued for a state in Palestine under British protection, but Lloyd George feared both that "France would probably object and wanted Palestine for herself...[and that] there would be an objection in this country to such an extension of our responsibilities." He speculated on the possibility of a condominium for Palestine, involving Britain, France, and Russia. When Samuel and Weizmann objected he showed himself, if anything, somewhat sceptical of Zionist hopes. Lloyd George was not impressed by Weizmann's projections of the number of Jewish colonists likely to settle in Palestine—half a million in fifty years at great cost. In turn Weizmann did not encourage Lloyd George's idea that Russian Jews might increase the flow of immigrants.[60]

Within months Lloyd George faced more tangible evidence: the conclusions of the de Bunsen committee about theoretical alternatives,[61] the exchanges between Sir Henry McMahon, high commissioner in Egypt, and Sharif Hussein of the Hejaz in October and December 1915,[62] and the agreement negotiated by Sir Mark Sykes, for the Foreign Office, and François-Georges Picot, for the Quai d'Orsay, between October 1915 and March 1916.[63] The

---

enemy if he were allowed to travel abroad. Lloyd George insisted that he trusted Weizmann fully. The Lloyd George–Weizmann correspondence in the Lloyd George Papers refers only to scientific matters. See also Lloyd George, *War Memoirs*, I, 348–49.

60. Scott diary, 11–15 Dec. 1915, 27–29 Jan., 22–23 Feb., and 13–20 April 1916, Scott Papers, Add. 50902; Lloyd George, *Truth about the Peace Treaties*, II, 1116–17.

61. Report of the Committee on British Desiderata in Turkey in Asia, 30 June 1915, Cab 27/1.

62. Grey to Kitchener, 4 Nov. 1915, FO/800/102; Foreign Office memoranda, 2, and 4 Feb. 1916, Cab 37/142/6 and 10; McMahon to Hardinge, 13 Oct. and 21 Nov. 1916, LGP, E/3/12/1 and 2; Islington to Lloyd George, 5 Nov. 1916, ibid., E/2/8/1; Grey to Lloyd George, 2 Nov. 1916, ibid., E/2/13/12.

63. Foreign Office memorandum, 8–23 May 1916, Cab 37/147/18; working map, LGP, F 205/3/24; Grey to Buchanan, 15 May 1916, Cab 37/147/40; War Committee, 23 March 1916, Cab 42/11/9; E. L. Woodward and R. Butler, *Documents on British Foreign Policy 1919–1939* (London, 1952), 1st ser., IV, 241–51; Foreign Office memoranda, 21, 22, and 28 Sept. and 4 Oct. 1916, Cab 37/155/33 and 35, Cab 37/156/3, and Cab 37/157/6. Lloyd George subsequently denounced the agreement as egregiously foolish, and lamented its mutilation of Palestine (*Truth about the Peace Treaties*, II, 1022–26, 1115.)

Sykes–Picot agreement achieved a certain precedence, making Arab aspirations forfeit to Anglo-French interests, particularly if the Arab revolt proved ineffective.

The War Committee reached a preliminary consensus in 1916. They worked from two assumptions, whatever the inner reservations: that victory, if attained, must serve to eliminate German influence from the Near East, and that, in the absence of a separate peace with Turkey, annexations or the creation of spheres of influence were preferable to the maintenance of a reformed Ottoman Empire in Asia. The reluctance to accept further significant obligations, however, had not evaporated. The strategic considerations were essentially unchanged from 1915. Britain would attempt to prevent French and Russian penetration toward the south, erect a French barrier between the British and Russian spheres, and create an Arab buffer between the British and French zones. Arab aspirations pointed to the creation of an independent Arabia, where British influence would be paramount and her treaties with independent Arab rulers on the Persian Gulf remain intact. Britain's economic and commercial interests were easily defined or manufactured: the oil of Mosul, the mineral and agricultural products of Mesopotamia, markets, port, transit, and communication facilities, irrigation resources, navigation rights, and an outlet for Indian immigration.

In the unpropitious military circumstances of 1916 Britain failed to secure her desiderata in three ways. In the first place her influence was limited to the southern part (B zone) of a designated Arab State or Confederation of States, and did not include the Mosul vilayet. Existing British rights and concessions were protected, but the Admiralty deplored the inclusion of Mosul in the French sphere (A zone). Secondly, while the Sykes–Picot agreement envisaged exclusive British control of the Acre–Haifa enclave and the vilayets of Baghdad and Basra (Red zones), the Hussein–McMahon correspondence suggested merely special administrative arrangements for the two Mesopotamian vilayets. While London and Delhi would acquiesce in the inclusion of the Baghdad vilayet in the B zone of the Arab state, unrestricted British control of Basra was not negotiable.

Finally, the status of Palestine was not satisfactory. Ideally it should reside in Britain's sphere of influence. An international administration, as envisaged for the Brown zone in the Sykes–Picot agreement, would permit France's involvement and was therefore less attractive. However, it was more acceptable than either outright French or Arab control. The concept of an international jurisdiction offered, moreover, two obvious advantages: it enabled Britain to deny to Hussein that she was free to award Palestine to the Arab State, and, secondly, it was imprecise. Campaigns and diplomacy would create further opportunities. Reduced to its essentials the problem would become how to get France to accept amendment of the Sykes–Picot agreement and to acquiesce in British control of Palestine, without endangering the Entente and the war effort.[64]

An element of continuity in policy existed, therefore, between the Asquith and Lloyd George governments. The former recoiled from accepting sweeping new imperial commitments, but identified those Middle Eastern areas crucial to British interests. Lloyd George, like Sir Mark Sykes himself and elements in the Foreign Office, became eager to redress the deficiencies of the Sykes–Picot agreement. While attributing President Wilson's December 1916 peace note to the influence of Germanophil Jews, Lloyd George, as prime minister, was determined that Gen. Sir A. J. Murray's campaign should result in British control of Palestine. When Neil Primrose, the chief whip, posed the question directly, "What about Palestine?", Lloyd George replied, "Oh, we must grab that; we have made a beginning."[65] Yet again an element of the romantic emerged. In a letter to his brother, in which he also insisted that as a "renegade Radical in a Tory camp" he would not permit reactionary policies, he described the news from Palestine as "thoroughly cheerful. I am looking forward to my Government achieving something which generations of the chivalry of Europe failed to attain."[66]

64. Scott diary, 26–30 Jan. 1917, Scott Papers, Add. 50903; D. Barzilai, "On the Genesis of the Balfour Declaration," *Zion*, 33, no. 3–4 (1968), 190–202; M. Vereté, "The Balfour Declaration and its Makers," *Middle Eastern Studies*, 1 (1970), 48–76. An allied declaration of support for Zionism offered immediate and long-term benefits. In the short run it would rally Jewish support, especially in the United States, for the Entente, thus assisting the war effort and thereby being attractive to France and Russia. In the long run, as the Zionist leaders already leaned towards a British protectorate, Britain's aims would be satisfied. Montagu dissented. (Montagu memorandum, 16 March 1915, LGP, C/25/14/1; Montagu to Drummond, 3 Aug. 1916, FO/800/99.)

65. Scott diary, 26–30 Jan. and 22–23 Feb. 1917, Scott Papers, Add. 50903. Lloyd George stated that the government had "positive evidence" that Wilson's peace note was sent to fulfil a promise made in return for Jewish election funds.

66. Lloyd George to W. George, 30 March 1917, LGP, I/2/2/70.

Charges of excessive Francophobia levelled against him are clearly unjustified. In February and again in the final discussions of November 1916, Lloyd George actually advocated a somewhat generous attitude toward France.[67] Britain should, he argued, encourage military operations against the Turks and permit France to assist the Arab revolt even in the politically sensitive Hejaz, as Britain herself could not apparently do so. He urged the War Committee to avoid a narrowly contriving attitude, merely to deprive France of a possible future advantage in the Arab world.

Equally unacceptable are suggestions that Lloyd George was particularly sceptical about the Arab revolt. From December 1914 he had supported operations against Turkey from Syria, Egypt, or Basra.[68] He evidently agreed with P. P. Graves that Arab "Pan-islamism" and Arab nationalism did not constitute a threat to the British Empire. The Arab, he knew, had no love for the Turk. The War Committee first debated the Arab uprising seriously, weighing its costs and France's uncertain reaction, in December 1915.[69] Lloyd George offered simple advice: if the Syrian campaign was militarily necessary they should launch it on a scale large enough to ensure its success. The War Committee, however, should not act unless they were committed fully to the Middle Eastern theatre; he would not support a mere bridgehead as at Salonika. He contributed neither to the June 1916 discussions on the Arab revolt nor to the debate of 6 July, which decided on the measures necessary to support that uprising.[70] Yet, once established as minister of war, Lloyd George made a bid to secure War Office control over India and the Mesopotamian theatre. Moreover, along with Lord Curzon and others, he advocated vigorous military support for the Arabs.

This question finally came down to the problem of the dispatch of reinforcements to Rabegh, to prevent a Turkish advance on Mecca and relieve pressure on the Arab revolt. Robertson, as devoted as ever to the Western Front, and the government of India, as concerned as ever with Moslem opinion, opposed the

67. War Committee, 22 Feb. and 20 Nov. 1916, Cab 42/9/3 and Cab 42/24/13.

68. Lloyd George memorandum, 1 Jan. 1915, Cab 42/1/8; Dardanelles Committee, 14 Oct. 1915, Cab 42/4/9; War Committee, 28 Dec. 1915 and 13 Jan. 1916, Cab 42/6/14 and Cab 42/7/5; Lloyd George testimony to the Dardanelles Commission, 2 April 1917, Cab 19/33.

69. War Committee, 16 Dec. 1915, Cab 42/6/9 and 10.

70. War Committee, 22 and 30 June, Cab 42/15/11 and 15, and 6 July 1916, Cab 42/16/1.

sending of reinforcements. They wrestled with a variety of opponents in London and Cairo. Lloyd George was not as prominent as some but, in the last two weeks of September 1916, he urged the General Staff to decide on means to assist the Arab revolt.[71] He regarded operations in the Red Sea theatre as important both for political and military reasons. They would enhance British prestige in the Arab world and, whether the Arabs defeated the Turkish forces or forced the Turks to embroil themselves more completely in Arabia, the allies would benefit. Robertson was unmoved. The same simple reasoning led Lloyd George, in November, to support the idea of France's military involvement in the Hejaz. The Foreign and India Offices feared for the future of the Arabian peninsula and pressed Robertson to dispatch British reinforcements to Rabegh. The CIGS refused and, ironically, he and Lloyd George found themselves in agreement; France could assist the Sharif. The War Committee on 20 November, however, failed to rule on the matter.

Very little of a decisive nature was settled in 1916. Military considerations governed, interim allied arrangements were made, the Arabs had an opportunity to prove themselves, and Zionist expectations were aroused. Lloyd George was not satisfied but understood the limiting factors. Complications with Italy, opportunities in Palestine, Russia's defection, and the attraction of a separate peace with Turkey would test him as prime minister.

71. War Committee, 18 Aug. and 1, 18, and 25 Sept. 1916, Cab 42/16/8, Cab 42/19/1, and Cab 42/20/3 and 8.

# 12

# A Ring of Flame

When Lloyd George examined complex and interacting political and military problems, and the means by which diplomacy as well as strategy could contribute to victory, he put into operation in the clearest way his fusionist approach. On the one hand he thought in terms of immediate military success and the future security of the Empire, demonstrating a taste for strategy and a detached, pragmatic, and even ruthless attitude toward the small powers, even as he attempted to protect Serbia and Rumania. Indeed, he was very free with contested territory as he searched for allies. On the other hand, he spoke of liberating subject races from Hapsburg rule, albeit as a by-product, and, as the discussion of war aims demonstrated, he welcomed the assault on the Turk, even though he regarded the Balkan theatre as the key to the Near East.

During the brief period of Turkish neutrality until November 1914, Grey did not encourage the belligerency of any individual Balkan state. The cabinet rejected Greece's offer of military and naval assistance in August because it might provoke Turkey or even Bulgaria to join the enemy.[1] At the same time Britain would

1. Cabinet meetings, 20 Aug. and 2 Sept. 1914, Cab 41/35/34 and 40; Erskine (Athens) to Grey, 19 Aug. 1914, LGP, C/4/14/15; Headlam-Morley to Asquith, 18 Dec. 1922, Asquith Papers, file 29; A. J. P. Taylor, ed., *Lloyd George: A Diary*, 20–23, 28–30, 32, 66–68, 70–71, 82–86, 116–19; Asquith, *Memories and Reflections*, II, 68–74; Viscount Grey, *Twenty-Five Years*, II, 157–232.

assist the formation of a Balkan league, embracing Serbia, Greece, Bulgaria, and Rumania, to enable the Balkan states to resist the approaches of the Central Powers, and to reduce the risk of inter-Balkan conflicts.[2] Once Turkey had entered the war any credible military combination was sufficiently attractive to warrant an energetic Balkan policy.[3] Bulgaria appeared to many, and particularly to Lloyd George, to be the key to the situation.

Implementation of a successful policy, however, proved beyond Britain's resources and capabilities. In the first place, while Kitchener and Field-Marshal Joffre, commander-in-chief of the French army, ruled, the Entente's military presence in the Near East was never so impressive as that of the Central Powers. Events on the Russian front, failure at the Dardanelles, the futile Salonika expedition, and Germany's victories in the main theatres provided apparently incontestable evidence that the Entente would be defeated. Bulgaria demonstrated a reasonable preference for the winning side. Rumania waited for the defeat of either the Turks or the Austrians, or at least for large-scale allied operations in the Balkans. Greece, particularly after the eclipse of Prime Minister Venizelos in March 1915 and despite Lloyd George's exhortations, was reluctant to assist Serbia. As Lloyd George remarked to Scott, after his offers of British financial and military aid if Greece assisted Serbia had failed to impress Athens, it took a man of imagination and insight like Venizelos to discern in 1915 that over the long haul Britain would triumph.[4] Meanwhile, diplomacy and financial inducements of various kinds, not excluding outright bribery of Bulgaria's leaders, failed to bridge the chasm of military credibility.[5]

On the other hand, there were strategic and logistic difficulties of sufficient magnitude to suggest that it would be unwise for the

2. Cabinet meetings, 11 and 20 Aug. 1914, Cab 41/35/27 and 34; Grey to Bertie and Buchanan, 20 Aug. 1914, LGP, C/4/14/15, and FO/800/55; Drummond memorandum, 26 Oct. 1915, FO/800/100. Britain deferred to Russia over Rumania. Kitchener, however, argued that Russia should cede Bessarabia to Rumania to secure her intervention, if Turkey entered the war.

3. Lloyd George blamed Churchill and the naval attack on Akaba as being finally responsible for Turkey's entry into the war. (Scott diary, 11 March 1915, Scott Papers, Add. 50901.)

4. Cabinet meeting, 20 Jan. 1915, Cab 37/123/33; Asquith to Grey, 21 Jan. 1915, FO/800/100; Greek minister (London) to Venizelos, 20 Jan. 1915, LGP, C/8/7/1; Scott diary, 11 March 1915, Scott Papers, Add. 50901.

5. War Council, 16 Dec. 1914, Cab 22/1. Lloyd George seemed to expect that a loan of £5 million would attract Rumania.

Entente to commit a large force to a Balkan front. Intractable problems resulted. Without the presence of such a force the Entente could not secure allies. While victories were necessary to attract military support in the Balkans, such local aid was a prerequisite of military success. Serbia might survive with Greek, Rumanian, and Bulgarian assistance, but the allies must demonstrate that they could save Serbia before such aid would be forthcoming. Again, after the fall of 1915, the Entente must defeat Bulgaria before Greece would risk belligerency and yet Greek intervention seemed necessary to ensure Bulgaria's defeat.

The Entente, moreover, never secured a sufficiently impressive ally to convince the Balkan states that they should intervene against the Central Powers. Grey, in March 1915, argued that Italy would be just such an acquisition, but Italy's entry into the war did not appear to tip the military balance toward the allies.

Politically the problems were just as baffling. Endemic rivalries and disputes over the future of Macedonia, Thrace, and Kavalla undermined the policy of forming a Balkan league through Serb and Greek concessions to Bulgaria. Germany had the easier task of promoting discord and being free with Serb and Greek territory in her negotiations with Bulgaria. The allies, on the other hand, were committed to Serbia. She seemed either sadly unrealistic to the point of self-destruction or simply inept. She refused to commit herself to surrender territory to Bulgaria in return for immediate military advantages, whatever the impact on the war.[6] Greece was equally obdurate and Rumania would not act prematurely. Ironically, Grey's attempts at territorial readjustments meant that Bulgaria received offers which enabled her to ask more of the Central Powers. Conversely, excessive, unofficial offers from London indicated to Bulgaria that either insincerity or confusion reigned there.

A domino theory situation existed but was thoroughly unpredictable. That is to say, some argued that if Britain secured Bulgarian belligerency, Rumania and Greece would follow. Others insisted that the price demanded by Bulgaria would so alienate Greece and Rumania as to destroy the project entirely. Once Bulgaria had joined the Central Powers the problem was complicated further. Grey feared lest they fail either to detach Bulgaria or to secure Rumanian intervention. The War Committee decided,

6. Drummond memorandum, 26 Oct. 1915, FO/800/100.

therefore, to suspend discussions with Sofia until the Bucharest government had committed itself.[7] This decision favoured Grey over Lloyd George.

The need to secure a coordinated allied policy brought additional complications. The Russo-Rumanian agreement of October 1914, the secret treaty with Russia, and the Treaty of London were all counter-productive in terms of inducing Balkan unity.[8] On specific issues, for instance Russia's refusal to permit Greek involvement in the Dardanelles campaign, British policy as advocated by Lloyd George and Churchill, was frustrated.[9] Furthermore, Britain and France could not agree on whether the Entente should coerce Serbia and Greece into accepting Bulgaria's claims. In the critical negotiations between June and September 1915 Paris was more willing than London to adopt a hard line, but, viewed from Sofia, the allies seemed merely dilatory and disunited.

Perceptions of the political situation in various Balkan capitals affected calculations about the prospects for a military league. Official and other informed opinion conflicted, and convinced some in London that the Entente could not purchase Bulgarian support. Others, including Lloyd George, believed that a pro-allied faction in Sofia could amend Bulgaria's policy. Lloyd George, primed by Sir John Stavridi, saw Venizelos as the key to the situation in Athens. When the latter temporarily regained power, in September 1915, Lloyd George hoped that Greek, Rumanian, and allied forces operating from Salonika would assist Serbia.[10] Venizelos was ousted again, however, Greece hesitated, and Lloyd George therefore argued that the allies should dispatch a force to

7. Grey to Lloyd George, 4 Aug., FO/800/102, and LGP, E/2/13/1, Robertson memorandum, 4 Aug., Cab 42/17/2, and War Committee, 10, 18 Aug. 1916, Cab 42/17/5 and 11.

8. Lloyd George testified that while Delcassé's policy and the negotiations with Italy presented difficulties, Grey could have surmounted them at a foreign ministers' conference which he had proposed in March 1915. He argued, unjustifiably, that Russia's claim to Constantinople was not an insuperable obstacle to securing a Balkan league in February 1915. (Dardanelles Commission of Enquiry, 2 April 1917, Cab 19/33.)

9. Asquith to Grey, 1 March 1915, FO/800/100.

10. Dardanelles Committee, 23, 24, 29, and 30 Sept., and 4 and 6 Oct. 1915, Cab 42/3/28, 30, 34, and 35, and Cab 42/4/2 and 3. Lloyd George explained away Venizelos's hesitations and equivocations as resulting from a legitimate fear of Bulgaria. (Erskine to Foreign Office, 30 Oct. 1915, LGP, D/19/8/4; Crawford Price (Times correspondent in Constantinople) to Lloyd George, 23 Sept. 1915, ibid., D/20/2/26; Sir John Stavridi report, 26 Nov. 1915, ibid., D/25/3/1.)

Salonika large enough to convince the new regime in Athens. Indeed, he was ready to coerce Greece by military and naval action, despite the fact of Greek neutrality and a disturbing parallel with Germany's attack on Belgium. Coercion, he felt, might restore Venizelos's fortunes and thereby secure Greek intervention.[11] There was, however, always the danger that such action would work against Venizelos and Lloyd George wavered.

When, from December 1915, the possibility arose that Greece would connive with Germany and actually menace the Entente position at Salonika, Lloyd George preferred sterner measures: an ultimatum, a naval demonstration, and even the shelling of Athens. This was war and the liberties of one small nation must not stand in the way of victory. In the fall of 1916 he looked to Greece to help save Rumania. With Bonar Law he advocated coercion to restore Venizelos, the "strongest man in Greece" and "the wisest and sanest man in the Balkans," and depose the treacherous king, who had made a laughing-stock of the Entente.[12] They could not convince the War Committee.

Grey, blaming Greek and Serb intransigence, tended to reduce these problems to a simple formula: diplomacy alone was impotent; military success must preface negotiations and provide the Foreign Office with a credible base.[13] The War Office was equally categorical; the diplomats must secure new allies and assist the successful conduct of the war.

Lloyd George provided a synthesis; a grand schema. The Entente must activate a Balkan juggernaut, "a ring of flame," by a creative diplomatic and military thrust into southeast Europe. Diplomacy and firepower must reinforce each other in an irresistible onslaught and induce continued United States investment

11. War Committee, 5–29 Nov. 1915, 1–28 Dec. 1915, and 13 Jan. 1916, Cab 42/5/2, 4, 5, 8, 10, 12, 14, 17, 20, 22, and 24, Cab 42/6/1, 4, 6, 7, 8, 13, and 14, and Cab 42/7/5; cabinet meetings, 24 Nov. and 3 and 17 Dec. 1915, Cab 37/138/7, and Cab 37/139/7 and 17.

12. War Committee, 21 and 22 June, Cab 42/15/10, and 11, 23 Aug., Cab 42/18/6, 1, 5, 18, 20, 25 and 28 Sept., Cab 42/20/3, 4, 6, 8, and 9, and 9 Oct. 1916, Cab 42/21/3; Robertson to Balfour, 26 Aug. 1916, Balfour Papers, Add. 49726; Lee to Lloyd George, 25 Sept. 1916, LGP, E/1/2/1; Lloyd George to A. Thomas, 21 Sept. 1916, Lee Papers, Lloyd George file. Balfour, Grey, and Robertson opposed coercion, fearing the American response. Briand was also opposed and Lloyd George charged him with deceit, and with being under the influence of a lady. (War Committee, 28 Sept. 1916, Cab 42/30/9.)

13. Grey to Lloyd George, 13 Oct. 1915, LGP, D/16/17/7; Grey memorandum, 13 Oct. 1915, Cab 37/136/6.

in a successful allied cause. He was ultimately frustrated and indicted the Foreign and War Offices for incompetence.

Lloyd George drew on many sources for inspiration and information: military history,[14] serving officers including Gen. Sir Arthur Paget and Gen. P. Howell,[15] and those who became disenchanted with Asquith, such as Admirals Fisher and Beresford, Sir John French, Gen. Sir Henry Rawlinson, and Henry Wilson.[16] He regarded Maj.-Gen. A. W. F. Knox as an authority on Russia,[17] and accepted the arguments on the Balkans of Noel and Charles Buxton, and the Rumanian diplomat, Také Jonescu.[18] Bonar Law, Sir Edward Carson, attorney-general from May to October 1915, and the Milnerites shared many of Lloyd George's ideas. He had never discounted Esher,[19] and Hankey[20] and particularly Arthur Lee became valuable aides.[21] Lloyd George employed Lee, a

14. He consulted Jean de Bloch's work when preparing his memorandum of 1 January 1915. (LGP, C/16/1/3 and 7.)

15. Paget to Kitchener, 9 Feb. 1915, ibid., C/5/7/15. This letter helped Lloyd George prepare his 22 February 1915 memorandum. Howell to Lloyd George, 7 Nov. 1915, ibid., D/20/2/56.

16. Beresford to Lloyd George, 16 Oct. 1915 and 24 Nov. 1916, ibid., D/20/2/5 and E/4/2/30; Fisher to Lloyd George, 6 Jan. 1916, ibid., D/16/15/1; Taylor, *Lloyd George: A Diary*, 71–72; Wilson to Milner, 11 April 1916, Milner Papers, 142; A. M. Gollin, *Proconsul in Politics*, 335–42; Lloyd George to Hankey, 2 March 1916, LGP, D/17/3/21.

17. Knox dispatches, July 1915 to Oct. 1916, for example, LGP, E/5/1/9 and 10. Ian Malcolm and B. Pares provided additional information on Russia. (Malcolm to Lloyd George, 27 Oct. 1915, ibid., D/19/16/8.)

18. N. Buxton to Lloyd George, 21 and 28 Jan. and 16 Feb. 1915, and N. and C. Buxton, "Notes on the Balkan States, Nos. I and II," LGP, C/6/7/2, 3, and 4; Jonescu to Lloyd George, 30 Aug., 24 Sept., n.d., and 14 Oct. 1915, ibid., D/19/13/3, 4, 5, and 7; Lloyd George to Asquith, Grey, and Kitchener, Oct. 1915, ibid., D/19/13/6; Jonescu to Lloyd George, 2 Sept. 1916, ibid., E/3/20/1; War Committee, 9 and 17 Oct. 1916, Cab 42/21/3 and Cab 42/22/1.

19. Esher note, 12 Oct. 1915, Cab 37/136/4; Esher to Lloyd George, 5 Aug. 1916, LGP, E/2/11/1.

20. Hankey to Lloyd George, 2 Jan. 1915 and 28 June and 9 Nov. 1916, ibid., C/4/19/2, D/17/3/40, and E/2/15/3; Hankey to Lee, 24 and 29 Nov. 1916, E/2/15/4 and 5; Hankey memorandum, 28 Dec. 1914, Cab 37/122/194; Hankey–Balfour correspondence, 29 Dec. 1914–5 Jan. 1915, Balfour Papers, Add. 49703.

21. Lee to Lloyd George, 28 Dec. 1915 and 2 April, 18 June, 1 July, and 25 Sept. 1916, LGP, D/1/1/11, 13, 21, and 22 and E/1/2/1; Lee memoranda, 28 Feb., 27 Nov. and 2 Dec. 1916, ibid., D/2/2/22, E/5/2/6 and E/5/1/3; Lloyd George to Lee, 1 and 17 July 1916, ibid., D/1/1/23 and Lee Papers, Lloyd George file; Davies to Lee, 24 Nov. 1916, LGP, E/5/1/3. Lloyd George minuted the 28 Feb. 1916 memorandum, "A most admirable memorandum—Very helpful to a poor civilian member of a War Council groping in the dark and crying for guidance."

Conservative MP and defence critic, when he became munitions minister. Lee became a bitter opponent of Asquith, insisting that intrigue against him was virtue, and loyalty, perversion. He described his government as "an irrational union, a sexless apathy, a static neurasthenia." Lloyd George valued his opinion on strategy, Russia, and the Balkans, and Lee provided him with crucial position papers. He even shared Lloyd George's interest in phrenology.[22]

The principles underlying the military component of the Balkan juggernaut were heretical, but were not the mere proclivities of an "Easterner." Lloyd George argued that the allies must develop a coordinated strategy which embraced theatres beyond the Western Front and acknowledged other priorities. His was a thesis of strategic pluralism which demanded attention to but not pre-eminence for the Balkans. He virtually ignored the African and Pacific theatres, but the Middle East remained an important if secondary area. There was, however, no question of neglecting the Western or the Russian fronts. He looked for victories anywhere, whatever the locale. His design involved the maintenance of at least a firm defensive grip in France,[23] an ever more vigorous blockade, and the securing of a mighty Russian war effort, as well as the opening of a Balkan front. Russia became a logistics problem of the first order, and Lloyd George, as munitions and then war minister, consistently advocated supplying her with war material on a large scale.[24] Russia could then hold Germany, eventually attack the Hapsburg Empire, and ultimately play a decisive role in

22. Lee to Lloyd George, 30 Sept. 1916, LGP, E/1/2/2. He described L. Bissolati as having a small, narrow head and resembling a blend of Milner, Prime Minister W. Hughes of Australia, and Sir F. Milner.

23. In September 1915 he was temporarily enthusiastic about the Western Front and the potential of the flame-thrower. Lloyd George shared responsibility for the Somme offensive in 1916, and for allowing Balkan operations to wait on its outcome and on the verdict at Verdun. He stood with the "Westerners" against Lansdowne. (Dardanelles Committee, 23 Sept. 1915, Cab 42/3/28; War Committee, 7 June 1916, Cab 42/15/6; Lloyd George to Hankey, 8 June 1916, LGP, D/17/3/37; Scott diary, 5–8 June 1916, Scott Papers, Add. 50903.)

24. Dardanelles Committee, 27 Oct. 1915, Cab 42/4/18; War Committee, 13 Nov. 1915, Cab 42/5/10; Scott diary, 26 Nov. 1915 and 27–29 Jan. 1916, Scott Papers, Add. 50902; Lloyd George memoranda, 29 June and 21 Aug. 1916, Asquith Papers, file 30 and Cab 42/18/3; Lloyd George to A. Thomas, 3 June and 1 July 1916, LGP, D/19/6/31 and 34; Lloyd George, note, 1 July 1916, FO/800/101; Lloyd George to Asquith, 26 Sept. 1916, LGP, E/2/23/5; allied conferences, July and Nov. 1916, WO 32/5089 and 106/397, and Cab 28/1.

the Balkans.[25] He aimed at encircling Germany and presenting the Central Powers with all the predicaments of a multi-front war. The allies must prevent German superiority in any sector and sever her lines of supply from all vital sources, in order to ensure ultimate victory in a prolonged conflict. Lloyd George drew comfort from the theory of the long haul, which envisaged the triumph of the allies after a lengthy war.[26]

Lloyd George's heresies on strategy led him to argue that the vision of politicians must neutralize the obscurantism of military experts.[27] Both considerations led to his virtual isolation by October 1915. He was also opposed to French control of allied strategy, but he was willing to amend his attitude in so far as the French supported operations in the Balkans.[28] He became an exponent of conference diplomacy to produce a coordinated strategy, ensure political control over the military, and help convert his colleagues to his own policies.[29] This theme matured to the point where Lloyd George, Briand, Albert Thomas, the French munitions minister, and even Joffre confronted the Dardanelles

25. Lloyd George to Asquith, 18 Feb. 1915 and 29 Sept. 1916, Lloyd George, *War Memoirs*, I, 264–65 and Asquith Papers, file 30; cabinet meeting, 18 Feb. 1915, Cab 37/124/34; War Committee, 8 Nov. 1915, 28 April, and 5 and 10 Aug. 1916, Cab 42/5/5, Cab 42/12/12, and Cab 42/17/3 and 5.

26. Statements, 13 and 15 July 1916, WO 32/5089, and LGP, E/10/4/1; Lloyd George to W. George, 26 Sept. 1916, ibid., I/2/2/53; Riddell diary, 19 Sept. 1916, Lord Riddell, *War Diary, 1914–18*, 210–11.

27. War Committee, 21 and 23 March, Cab 42/11/6 and 9, 7 April, Cab 42/12/5, and 3, 7, and 9 Nov. 1916, Cab 42/23/4, 9 and 11; Lloyd George draft of Asquith's statement for the Paris Conference, 15 Nov. 1916, Cab 28/1. He described the commander at Ypres in June 1916 as a "slobbering dotard."

28. Lloyd George to Grey, 23 Jan., and Lloyd George to Churchill, 29 Jan. 1915, LGP, C/4/14/22 and C/3/16/17; War Council, 28 Jan. 1915, Cab 22/1. The War Council decided that Lloyd George should approach the French to secure a coordinated strategy and open up the Salonika front. In Paris he worked to convert Poincaré, Briand, and Delcassé away from the baleful influence of Joffre and Millerand. (Memorandum of interview with Poincaré, 3 Feb., and note to Briand, 4 Feb. 1915, LGP, C/3/6/2.) Lloyd George met with only limited success, but exaggerated his impact in Paris to Grey (Lloyd George to Grey, 7 Feb. 1915, ibid., C/4/1/16). Bertie sent Grey "the correct card of the races." (Bertie to Grey, 7 Feb., enclosing memorandum, 3 Feb. 1915, FO/800/75; Grey to Lloyd George, 8 Feb. 1915, LGP, C/4/14/27.) See also Scott diary, 26 Oct. and 1–2 Nov. 1915, Scott Papers, Add. 50902; conversation between Lloyd George, Millerand, and Joffre, 19 Oct. 1915, Lloyd George, *War Memoirs*, I, 305; Dardanelles Committee, 25 Oct. 1915, Cab 42/4/17.

29. Scott diary, 11–15 Dec. 1915, Scott Papers, Add. 50902; War Committee 27 Feb. and 21 March 1916, Cab 42/9/3 and Cab 42/11/6.

and the War Committees. The French connection, however, brought distressingly few advantages[30] and the allied conferences were either indecisive or barren.[31]

In January and February 1915, Lloyd George proposed an assault on the vulnerable and racially divided Hapsburg Empire, preferably from Salonika or some point on the Adriatic.[32] Slav confronted Teuton under Hapsburg rule and the subject races might welcome a liberating Entente army. If the allies opened up a front at Salonika, he argued, a Balkan league would take the field. Italy and Rumania would offer assistance in order to share in the spoils. Lloyd George spoke freely of a force of at least one-and-a-half million men. Consequently, Germany would either over-extend her resources in an effort to save her ally, or risk Austria's collapse. In either case, he contended, Germany would face defeat.[33] However, he succeeded in inducing his colleagues merely to

30. War Committee, 6 Dec. 1915, Cab 42/6/4, 22 Feb., 3, 17, and 26 May, 16 June, 5, 10, and 22 Aug., and 24 Oct. 1916, Cab 42/9/3, Cab 42/13/2, Cab 42/14/1 and 11, Cab 42/15/8, Cab 42/17/3 and 5, Cab 42/18/4, and Cab 42/22/5; Joffre to Robertson, 25 April 1916, LGP, D/18/8/11; Grey to Robertson and reply, 12 and 17 June 1916, FO/800/102; Grey to Lloyd George, 21 Aug. 1916, LGP, E/2/13/4.

31. London Conference, 29–30 Oct. 1915, Paris Conference, 17 Nov. 1915, Cab 28/1 and Cab 37/137/34; Calais conference, 4 Dec. 1915, Cab 37/139/15; Grey note, 6 Dec. 1915, LGP, D/23/5/10; Paris Conference, 9–11 Dec. 1915, Cab 37/139/24; London conference, 19 Jan. 1916, Cab 37/141/10; London conference, 9 June 1916, Cab 21/16 and Cab 28/1; Grey memorandum, 10 June 1916, Cab 37/149/28; Grey to Lloyd George, 4 and 7 Aug., and Lloyd George to Grey, 4 Aug. 1916, LGP, E/2/13/1 and 3 and FO/800/102; Lloyd George–Briand meeting, Paris, 11 Aug., and War Office memorandum, 11 Aug. 1916, Cab 42/17/6; Boulogne conference, 20 Oct. 1916, Cab 28/1 and Cab 42/22/4.

32. Lloyd George to Asquith, 31 Dec. 1914, Asquith Papers, file 133; Lloyd George memorandum, 1 Jan. 1915, Cab 42/1/8; War Council, 7, 8, 13, and 28 Jan. 1915, Cab 22/1 and Cab 37/123/33; G. Trevelyan to F. Acland, 15 Jan. 1915, LGP, C/4/14/9; Lloyd George note, 13 Jan. 1915, ibid., C/16/1/4. The General Staff reported unfavourably on the feasibility of an attack from the Adriatic with Italian support, and from Salonika with Serb assistance. Lloyd George also proposed a landing at Dedeagatch to encourage Bulgaria to attack Adrianople, and to ensure that Bulgaria would not aid an Austrian assault on Serbia.

33. War Council, 9 Feb. 1915, Cab 22/1; Hankey to Balfour, 10 and 17 Feb. 1915, Balfour Papers, Add. 49703; Lloyd George–Kitchener correspondence, 29 Jan. 1915, LGP, C/5/7/12, 13, and 14; Lloyd George, War Memoirs, I, 217–18, 238–40; Lord Hankey, The Supreme Command, I, 272–73. Churchill supported Lloyd George and Lloyd George backed the Admiralty's proposals to some extent for naval action at the Straits. (M. Gilbert, Winston S. Churchill [London, 1971], III, 228–311.)

begin preparatory measures and to make a political rather than a military gesture in the Balkans. Crewe's applause was of little comfort and Serbia's vulnerability increased.[34]

In the following months, Lloyd George attempted to exploit the interrelationship between the various Near Eastern theatres. He described the Dardanelles campaign to Scott as "a mad enterprise," and was sceptical of its success, but was in fact more cooperative and open-minded in the War Council and the Dardanelles Committee.[35] Britain must dispatch a substantial and well-supplied force to the Levant, he argued in support of Churchill against Kitchener, to prepare for two eventualities. Victory at the Straits would enable the army to occupy vital areas of the Ottoman Empire. If, however, the navy failed at the Dardanelles, the army must not attempt a salvage operation. In each case they must then turn to the Balkan theatre, attack the Hapsburg Monarchy, and remove what he began to fear was intolerable German pressure on Russia.

Deteriorating circumstances, Lloyd George believed, demanded a considerable readjustment of goals; the Entente must save Serbia from disaster, prevent Bulgaria orientating toward Germany, and secure a military convention with Rumania and Greece by sending a special diplomatic mission. They must not, he warned, rely on men "in inferior diplomatic berths" who were "not of the first order."

Imperialist considerations were never absent from Lloyd George's calculations. Not only must the Entente cut Germany off from the resources of southeast Europe, they must also prevent the creation of a Berlin–Constantinople axis. Germany must not be allowed to establish direct links with Turkey, and thereby threaten imperial security. To eliminate this menace and destroy Turkey the allies should operate from the Balkans rather than at the Dardanelles or Alexandretta. His colleagues, however, wanted neither special missions sent to the Balkans nor commitments to alternate theatres should the Dardanelles attack fail. Grey, from whatever motive, would concede only that perhaps Lloyd George himself might accomplish something in Athens and Bucharest.[36]

34. Crewe to Lloyd George, 9 Feb. 1915, LGP, C/4/1/16.
35. War Council, 14 May 1915, Cab 22/1; Scott diary, 16 June 1915, Scott Papers, Add. 50901.
36. Lloyd George to Asquith, 18 Feb., Lloyd George, *War Memoirs*, I, 264–65, cabinet meeting, 18 Feb., Cab 37/124/34, and War Council, 19, 24, and

Mounting pessimism permeated these months and matured during September and October of 1915 as disaster loomed at the Dardanelles.[37] Urged on by Také Jonescu, Lloyd George advocated forward planning rather than a simple evacuation from Gallipoli. Indeed, in order to secure the dispatch of an allied force to the Levant, he would support further military involvement at Gallipoli, at least in preference to a further offensive in France.[38] The allies might tie down the Turks, but ideally they should prepare for a large-scale offensive from Salonika in which Italy would participate and which a Balkan league would assist.

The imperial theme in Lloyd George's argument became even more pronounced. Germany intended to smash through Serbia to Constantinople and mobilize the Turks. As a result a force of two million men would threaten Egypt, the Middle East, Persia, and India, and rally Moslem support against the allies.[39]

When Bulgaria joined the Central Powers on 11 October 1915 Lloyd George pressed even more vigorously for the creation of a Balkan front. He also advocated, with some reluctance, evacuation from Gallipoli. Initially, Asquith ruled against him on both counts.[40] The Anglo-French conference in London and Kitchener's eventual support for evacuation from the Dardanelles, provided only fleeting encouragement between November 1915 and

---

26 Feb. 1915, Cab 22/1; Lloyd George, cabinet notes, n.d., LGP, C/13; Lloyd George memorandum, 22 Feb., Cab 42/1/39, and Kitchener memorandum, 25 Feb. 1915, Cab 42/1/45.

37. Dardanelles Committee, 7 July, 31 Aug., and 3 and 23 Sept. 1915, Cab 42/3/7, 20, 23, and 28; Admiralty and General Staff memorandum, 9 Oct. 1915, LGP, D/23/4/16; Elliot (Athens) to Foreign Office, 6 Sept. 1915, ibid., D/19/8/1; Hankey memorandum, 30 Aug. 1915, Cab 42/3/19.

38. Dardanelles Committee, 29 and 30 Sept. 1915, Cab 42/3/34 and 35; O'Beirne (Sofia) to Foreign Office, 20 Aug. and 15 Sept. 1915, LGP, D/12/3/15 and D/19/2/2; Churchill notes, 21 Aug. and 15 Sept. 1915, ibid., D/23/4/12. Kitchener was able, however, to launch an offensive on the Western Front in September.

39. Lloyd George to War Office (Petrograd), 11 Sept. 1915, LGP, D/19/15/1; Scott diary, 3 Sept. 1915, Scott Papers, Add. 50901; Dardanelles Committee, 7 and 11 Oct. 1915, Cab 42/4/4 and 6; Reading to Lloyd George, 1 Sept., and McMahon to Grey, 14 Nov. and 14 Dec. 1915, LGP, D/18/5/3 and D/19/4/2 and 3.

40. Cabinet meeting, 2 Oct., Cab 37/135/1, Dardanelles Committee, 4, 6, 11, and 14 Oct., Cab 42/4/2, 3, 6, and 9, Lloyd George memorandum, 12 Oct., Cab 37/136/9, Grey memorandum, 13 Oct., Cab 37/136/6, Grey to Lloyd George, 13 Oct., LGP, D/16/17/7, and Grey to Bonar Law, 20 Oct. 1915, Bonar Law Papers, 51/4/23; Scott diary, 11–15 Dec. 1915, Scott Papers, Add. 50902.

January 1916.[41] Indeed, Kitchener also wanted to evacuate Salonika and to retire all forces to Egypt. Lloyd George was compelled to fight for the maintenance and the reinforcement of the Entente position to ensure that the enemy did not seize Salonika itself. Evacuation was effected from the Dardanelles in January 1916, though not from Salonika, but Serbia collapsed and Greek assistance did not materialize. Rumania remained neutral as Russia floundered and the Turks triumphed.[42] Meanwhile the Munitions Ministry produced shells to serve Kitchener's strategic priorities. Lloyd George's humiliating frustration was complete. He acknowledged the brutal facts; the inadequate Salonika force neither threatened the Central Powers nor impressed Bulgaria and Greece.[43]

Rumania became the culminating issue in the summer of 1916.[44] Initially, Lloyd George suggested that the allies should supply Rumania with military aid, tempt her with territorial spoils, and prepare adequately for an offensive from Salonika. His matured

41. Dardanelles Committee, 25 and 27 Oct., Cab 42/4/17 and 18, and Lloyd George to Asquith, 31 Oct. 1915, Lloyd George, *War Memoirs*, I, 307–309. Lloyd George described Churchill, Curzon, and Lord Selborne as most committed to the Dardanelles campaign, Grey as leaning toward the Serbian alternative, and Balfour as undecided. (Scott diary, 26 Oct. 1915, Scott Papers, Add. 50902.) Curzon and Balfour were bitterly opposed to evacuation from the Dardanelles (Curzon memoranda, 25 and 30 Nov., ibid., D/23/5/8, and Balfour memorandum, 19 Nov. 1915, ibid., D/23/5/6). However, Balfour, for a brief period in December 1915 and January 1916, supported Lloyd George on strategic questions. (War Committee, 28 Dec. 1915 and 13 Jan. 1916, Cab 42/6/14 and Cab 42/7/5; Balfour memoranda, 27 Dec. 1915, and 18, 20, and 25 Jan. 1916, Balfour Papers, Add. 49726, Cab 42/6/13 and Cab 42/7/12.)

42. War Committee, 5–29 Nov. 1915, 1–28 Dec. 1915, and 13 Jan. 1916, Cab 42/5/2, 4, 5, 8, 10, 12, 14, 17, 20, 22, 24, Cab 42/6/1, 4, 6, 7, 8, 13 and 14, and Cab 42/7/5; Cabinet meetings, 24 Nov. and 3 and 17 Dec. 1915, Cab 37/138/7 and Cab 37/139/7 and 17.

43. War Committee, 22 Feb. 1916, Cab 42/9/3; Lloyd George to Hankey, 23 Feb. and 8 June, and Hankey to Lloyd George, 23 and 25 Feb. 1916, LGP, D/17/3/18, 19, 20, and 37; Joffre to Robertson, 25 April 1916, ibid., D/18/8/11; Robertson memoranda, 22 March and 14 June, 1916, ibid., D/23/5/12 and 13; Robertson to Grey, 29 July and 1 Aug. 1916, FO/800/102.

44. War Committee, 23 March, 3, 17, and 26 May, 6, 7, 16, 21, and 22 June, 6, 18, and 28 July 1916, Cab 42/11/9, Cab 42/13/2, Cab 42/14/1 and 11, Cab 42/15/4, 6, 8, 10, and 11, and Cab 42/16/1, 8, and 11; Hankey to Lloyd George, 1 May 1916, LGP, D/17/3/28; Esher notes of conversations with Briand, Poincaré, and Gallieni, 5 and 23 May 1916, ibid., D/25/1/1; cabinet meeting, 8 June 1916, Cab 37/149/13; Grey memoranda, 10 and 14 July 1916, Cab 37/149/27 and 36; Scott diary, 5–8 June 1916, Scott Papers, Add. 50903; Lloyd George to Asquith, 30 May 1916, LGP, D/18/2/11.

plan envisaged a joint Russo-Rumanian attack on Bulgaria from the north, to coincide with a thrust from Salonika. The offensive would, of course, isolate Turkey and preface decisive operations against the Ottoman Empire. Grey would leak the plan to Sofia and Lloyd George would convince the French. He expected Bulgaria to capitulate and Rumania to permit the presence of Russian troops on her soil.

Rumania joined the Entente in August 1916 but by October Lloyd George's arguments were of necessity reversed. The allies must launch an offensive to forestall a German–Bulgarian assault on Rumania and to ensure that her food and oil resources did not fall into the hands of the Central Powers. Failure to protect Rumania, Lloyd George insisted, would mean a lengthy extension of the war with all the attendant risks and dangers.[45] The allies must therefore offer Rumania all possible assistance, including the dispatch of troops from France and Egypt, and the sending of aircraft. Lloyd George contended that workers in cities such as Sheffield would accept the risk of increased Zeppelin raids, realizing that Rumania's survival was more vital than the protection of their own homes. The War Committee, however, ruled that a major offensive from Salonika would be both futile and dangerous. Robertson would commit only one additional division, as a political move to strengthen Entente morale.

On 1 December Lloyd George delivered a funereal address.[46] Blundering military advisers had led the allies astray. The Entente was unable to save any of the small nations which had joined its cause. They had failed Rumania just as they had sacrificed the Serbs, by egregious neglect of the Balkan front.

The diplomatic component of Lloyd George's Balkan policy aligned him with Churchill and Noel and Charles Buxton against Grey. Both Lloyd George and Grey favoured the creation of a Balkan league, but Lloyd George was more sanguine and expected the allies to secure significant military advantages. Grey preferred

45. Lloyd George to D.M.O., 4 Sept. 1916, LGP, E/1/5/6; War Committee, 3, 9, 12, 26, and 31 Oct. and 3 Nov. 1916, Cab 42/21/1, 3, and 6, Cab 42/22/8 and 13, and Cab 42/23/4; Jonescu to Lloyd George, 30 Oct. and 3, 7, and 9 Nov. 1916, LGP, E/3/21/1 and 2; Lloyd George to W. George, 26 Nov. 1916, W. George, My Brother and I, 256; Montagu to Grey, 13 Oct. 1916, FO/800/99.

46. Lloyd George to Robertson and the cabinet, 29 Nov., and Robertson to Lloyd George, 3 Dec. 1916, LGP, E/5/1/2 and 4; War Committee, 1 Dec. 1916, Cab 42/26/6.

Kitchener's assessment. Lloyd George coupled his emotional praise of small nations with a willingness to coerce them; Grey disparaged the Balkan states to the point of contempt but insisted on a less forceful policy. While the foreign secretary preferred to keep Russia out of the Balkans, Lloyd George increasingly saw Russia's military presence there as an advantage, and even, by the fall of 1916, as vital.

Apart from the proposition that victory at the Dardanelles would help secure the creation of a Balkan league, two other approaches were seriously considered during 1915. The Entente could either encourage Serbian and Greek concessions to Bulgaria or purchase Italian intervention in the war and trust that the Balkan states would follow. Grey and Lloyd George were willing to pursue both policies, but on balance the foreign secretary preferred the latter and Lloyd George the former.

Here lay the link with Charles and Noel Buxton, high-minded Gladstonians driven by religious zeal to an unyielding opposition to the Turk and the tsar. Obsessed with the future of Macedonia, the Buxtons were original members of the Balkan Committee, and were decidedly pro-Bulgarian. Lloyd George agreed with them that the strategic and political value of Bulgaria exceeded that of any other Balkan power. She was the key to Serbian and Rumanian security, and to a Balkan league. Both Lloyd George and Noel Buxton were prepared to sacrifice Balkan manhood to those ends. They agreed that diplomacy and military operations must reinforce each other. However, whereas the Buxtons were concerned to liberate Macedonia, champion the Bulgars, and assault Turkey, Lloyd George regarded Bulgaria's intervention more exclusively as a war measure aimed primarily and initially at Austria. The Buxtons' hostility to the Turk, and their nonconformist, humanitarian aims, however, clearly appealed to him.[47]

Churchill, Lloyd George, and perhaps Charles Masterman, then chancellor of the Duchy of Lancaster, had proposed an active Balkan policy at the time of Venizelos's initiative in August 1914. As Lord Emmott recorded:

47. H. N. Fieldhouse, "Noel Buxton and A. J. P. Taylor's 'The Trouble Makers'," in M. Gilbert, ed., A Century of Conflict 1850–1950, 182–86; M. Anderson, Noel Buxton: A Life (London, 1952), 62–64; T. P. Conwell-Evans, Foreign Policy from a Back Bench, 89–90. Buxton submitted Conwell-Evans's chapter to Lloyd George, who accepted it as accurate. (Lloyd George to Buxton, 22 April 1931, Buxton Papers.)

*Churchill . . . launched out with great fervour in support of an anti-Austrian Balkan Federation. Lloyd George's imagination began to take fire. He said it was not enough to back them up with words. If they could bring Bulgaria in we must find them money to fight for us and let them help themselves out of Austria (as suggested by Venizelos) at the finish. Also Italy was to have something. I wonder if she would not come in against Austria if the rest do. . . . When Lloyd George talked of finding money for the Balkan Federation he mentioned £20 or £30 million. Kitchener immediately said, "But whatever you do, offer in francs. It sounds better.*[48]

Grey, anxious to preserve Foreign Office control, was not particularly cooperative. Indeed, Lloyd George's guarantee to Noel Buxton that "Any Balkan State that decides to throw in its lot with the Triple Entente . . . may depend upon the support of British Credit in raising the necessary funds to equip and maintain its army. I authorize you to make such arrangements on my behalf as you may deem desirable to guarantee British financial assistance under these conditions," earned the notation "Suppressed by Grey."[49]

The brothers Buxton were anything but modest about the scheme and their own accomplishments once they, Lloyd George, and Churchill had persuaded a sceptical Grey to acquiesce in their mission to the Balkans.[50] Bulgaria, they suggested, was now less likely to attack Serbia, Greece, or Rumania; the allies could purchase her benevolent neutrality. They had provided a focus for the "floating Anglo-philism" in Sofia, and had induced a sympathetic outburst in the press. Although the Bulgarian government and King Ferdinand still favoured Austria, the Anglophile and Russophile groups were greatly encouraged. Furthermore, the Buxtons suggested, "even a modicum of definite English policy"

48. Emmott diary, 11 Aug. 1914, Emmott Papers, F 103/4; cabinet meetings, 10 Aug., Cab 41/35/27, and 23 Sept. 1914, Cab 41/35/47; Asquith, *Memories*, II, 34; Taylor, *Lloyd George: A Diary*, 18.

49. Lloyd George to Buxton, 22 Aug. 1914, Buxton Papers.

50. Grey to Churchill, 26 Aug. 1914, LGP, C/3/16/13; N. Buxton to Lloyd George, 26 Aug. 1914, ibid., C/6/7/1; Grey to Buxton, 31 Aug. 1914, ibid., C/6/7/1A; C. R. Buxton to Churchill, 1 Oct., and N. Buxton to Lloyd George and Grey, 5 Oct. 1914, LGP, C/25/9/2 and C/6/7/1A. Grey suggested that George Trevelyan might accompany the Buxtons. Churchill minuted for Lloyd George, "it is important to grasp this as it brings in Grey." Noel Buxton noted that Grey had accepted Churchill's proposal for a mission to the Balkans, and that he should consult Grey on how best to use Lloyd George's letter.

would secure Bulgaria's military intervention initially against Turkey should she enter the war, and ultimately against the Hapsburgs. Rumania would then intervene and a Balkan league would be forged, if the allies acted vigorously and refused to be swayed by Greek and Turkish representations.

The Buxtons did not regard Bulgaria's territorial demands as excessive. If Serbia received Bosnia, Hercegovina, and part of Dalmatia, Bulgaria, as the price of her neutrality, should secure that area of Macedonia ascribed to her in the Serb–Bulgarian treaty of 1912 and, they argued subsequently, Monastir. Should Serbia receive only part of those territories, Bulgaria would secure proportionately less of Macedonia. If Rumania obtained part of Transylvania, Bulgaria must take part of the Dobrudja. Should Turkey enter the war, Bulgaria would attack her in return for allied recognition of her claims in Thrace up to the Enos-Midia line, and to Kavalla. Greece would receive compensation in Asia Minor. Finally, the Buxtons suggested, Bulgaria might assist Rumania against Austria if the allies were sufficiently generous, united, and firm in their support of territorial adjustments, and secured the consent of all the Balkan powers.[51]

Sir Henry Bax-Ironside, minister at Sofia, described by the Buxtons as depressed, incompetent, and in error, Bertie in Paris, Sir Rennell Rodd in Rome, Foreign Office officials, and Grey were not impressed.[52] In fact the Buxtons had become an intolerable nuisance, troublesome and even dangerous. They were afforded a decidedly cool reception on their return to London in January 1915, and Asquith did not contest Grey's assessment.[53] Where the Buxtons offered facile solutions, the Foreign Office dwelt on

51. Buxton to Grey, 22 Oct. 1914, Anderson, *Noel Buxton*, 65, 70; Conwell-Evans, *Foreign Policy*, 93–94, 101–102, 108.

52. Bax-Ironside to Grey, 18 Nov. 1914, and 27, 28, and 29 Jan. 1915, FO/800/43, and LGP, C/25/9/3 and G/244; Bax-Ironside to Nicolson, 8 March 1915, LGP, C/4/14/30; Rodd to Grey, 26 Jan. 1915, ibid., C/4/14/23. Bax-Ironside contended that King Ferdinand, a Russophobe, would join the allies only if they captured Constantinople or demonstrated that they could win the war. Bertie poured contempt and ridicule on the Buxtons. (Bertie to Grey, 7 Jan. 1915, FO/800/57.) Clerk, Nicolson, and Tyrrell deplored the scheme and Grey promised to deal with Churchill (Foreign Office minutes, 23 Oct., on Buxton to Churchill, Oct. 1914, FO/371/1901/62507; Grey to Bax-Ironside, 4 and 19 Nov. 1914, and 21 Feb. 1915, FO/800/43 and Cab 37/123/30.)

53. Asquith to Grey, 17 Jan. 1915, FO/800/100; Grey to Buchanan, 1 Feb. 1915, LGP, C/4/14/24. The Buxtons had expressed views contravening official policy and Buchanan must disavow them in St. Petersburg.

complex problems and a multitude of repercussions. Bulgaria's demands seemed excessive rather than reasonable, and Grey would not coerce Serbia or Greece into accepting them, especially after Serbia had bowed to Italy over Dalmatia. Nor would Grey permit the immediate implementation of Bulgaria's demands while Serbia's claims waited on victory. Realistically cautious, Grey expected neither King Ferdinand to be converted to the Entente cause nor the opposition in Sofia to achieve power. He agreed with Bax-Ironside that only military successes would induce Bulgaria to join the allies, and that they could not outmatch the Central Powers in territorial *douceurs*. Moreover, the Foreign Office worried lest the consequences of Bulgaria's demands offend France as well as Russia. The Buxtons would have provided compensation all round, a well-lubricated chain of mutually satisfying responses, but they underestimated the problems involved. France, for instance, was reluctant to see Greece compensated at Smyrna for the loss of Kavalla, and Russia was scarcely uninterested in the various territorial adjustments.

In turn the Buxtons denounced Grey and sought support elsewhere. Asquith, like Grey, favoured the Italian tactic. Kitchener was more impressed with the Serb than the Bulgarian army, and Churchill immersed himself in the Dardanelles campaign. Others canvassed lacked sympathy or influence.[54] Lloyd George remained, therefore, the most promising and willing advocate who could bypass Grey and provide an entrée to the War Council.[55] Tactically they were in tune and Lloyd George seemed quite willing to sweep aside objections, dispense with caution, and accept risks. The Buxtons possessed a certain fervour, and were not the last publicists to conclude that Lloyd George was a receptive medium. They could use Lloyd George, and he seemed necessary to the success of their policy.

Consequently, Lloyd George and Noel Buxton, in contact with P. H. Mischev, the Bulgarian minister in London, became

54. N. Buxton to Garvin, 28 and 30 Jan. and 24 Feb. 1915, Garvin Papers, box 55; N. Buxton to Balfour, 4 Feb. and 7 July, and Balfour to Grey, 20 July 1915, Balfour Papers, Add. 49748 and 49731; N. Buxton to A. Chamberlain, 27 and 30 July 1915, A. Chamberlain Papers, AC/13/3/1–106. Others approached included Bonar Law, Carson, Simon, Hankey, Bryce, Sykes, and St. Loe Strachey.

55. Lloyd George to Grey, 23 Feb. 1915, FO/800/101. Grey agreed with Lloyd George that they must eliminate interfering interlopers from the Balkans, but he included the Buxtons in that category.

embroiled with Grey in the spring of 1915.[56] The future of Kavalla became the territorial point of contention, as the Foreign Office came to accept Bulgaria's claims in Macedonia and Thrace. Grey's other reservations remained intact. After his initial reluctance, Lloyd George was willing to promise Kavalla to Bulgaria. He insisted that Venizelos was willing to cooperate. Grey would not yield. He controlled the line to Sofia, represented the government, and did not intend to relinquish his authority to Lloyd George. The dissenters were left, therefore, with only two alternatives. They could either circumvent the Foreign Office and use *The Times* cypher, or convince Sofia through Mischev or the Bulgarian minister in Paris that Grey misrepresented official policy. They attempted the latter tactic but Grey denied Lloyd George's unwarranted assertion that "You may take Kavalla when you like." The issue then degenerated into a dispute between Lloyd George and Grey over the cabinet's ruling on Kavalla. The Bulgarian government was aware of the disagreement, which inevitably reduced Britain's credibility. All attempts by Lloyd George and Noel Buxton in April 1915 to convince Sofia that Grey was either in error or merely confused, and now endorsed the award of Kavalla, failed.[57]

Undoubtedly Grey was fully justified in discrediting Lloyd George. The cabinet had not authorized an unreserved offer of Kavalla or a more attractive inducement to Bulgaria. On the other hand, Grey was forced to admit that he had made no progress whatsoever toward the formation of a Balkan league. He was barren of achievement, and yet he would try no other tactic or concede any error on his part.[58] Buxton was correct at least in that assessment. Grey was dogmatic and stubborn, even arrogant, and such attitudes did not sit well with inaction. Noel Buxton concluded that tainted information from Sofia, dislike of Mischev, Foreign Office

56. Buxton to Lloyd George, 13 and 22 March 1915, LGP, C/6/7/5 and 6; conversations between Buxton, Lloyd George, and Mischev, 2, 3, and 21[?] March 1915, Anderson, *Noel Buxton*, 75–77; Conwell-Evans, *Foreign Policy*, 110–11; Foreign Office memorandum, 7 Aug. 1916, Cab 42/17/4.

57. Lloyd George to Churchill, 17 April, LGP, C/3/16/30, and Buxton to Lloyd George, 20 and 21 April 1915, ibid., C/6/7/8 and 9.

58. Cabinet meetings, 4 May and 4 June 1915, Cab 37/128/1 and Cab 37/129/9; Grey to Bax-Ironside, 15 May, FO/800/43, Grey to Spender, 15 May, Spender Papers, Add. 46389, and Grey to Stamfordham, 28 June 1915, FO/800/103.

conservatism and incompetence, and a fatal unwillingness to take risks had combined to cripple legitimate initiatives in the Balkans.[59]

In the summer and early fall of 1915, as Serbia's predicament became more acute but Serbian and Greek obstruction did not waver, Asquith's coalition government grappled again with the problem of securing Bulgarian intervention. Briefly, in late June and early July, with Grey ill and Crewe at the Foreign Office, there seemed reason even to threaten as well as to court Sofia.[60] Bulgaria's leaders must be made to realize that the value of her assistance would decline if the Entente forced the Dardanelles. They must therefore accept the somewhat enlarged territorial offer and a bribe of £2.5 million, and attack Turkey before the end of July. If not, Britain would reduce or even withdraw the offer which again stopped short, however, of an unconditional award of Kavalla. Moreover, the allies still refused either to coerce Serbia and Greece or to countenance Bulgaria's immediate occupation of the areas awarded to her. Greece remained obdurate, and Serbia's final concessions over Macedonia and further diplomatic manoeuvres in August and September failed to impress Sofia.[61]

Later in September Lloyd George and Buxton made a last attempt to convert Grey. Lloyd George urged him to make an official approach to Sofia, through Hugh O'Beirne. The Entente should also launch an offensive from Salonika and demonstrate that they could guarantee Bulgaria's territorial gains.[62] Such manoeuvres, however, proved futile. In October, an unrepentant Grey admitted that little had been accomplished, but further

59. Buxton to Lloyd George, 28 May 1915, and "Notes on the Balkan States, No. III," May 1915, LGP, C/6/7/10.

60. Churchill to Lloyd George, 25 June 1915, LGP, D/16/8/1; N. Buxton to Lloyd George, 1 and 6 July 1915, ibid., D/17/19/1 and 2; Grey to Bax-Ironside, 26 June 1915, FO/800/43; Balfour to Cecil, 26 June, Cecil Papers, Add. 51093, Cecil to Balfour, 26 June, and Cecil minute, 28 June 1915, Balfour Papers, Add. 49737; cabinet meetings, 30 June and 6 July 1915, Cab 37/130/29 and Cab 37/131/7.

61. Cecil to Balfour, 14 Aug., Balfour Papers, Add. 49737, and Cecil to Drummond, 27 Aug. 1915, FO/800/383; Cecil to Grey, 23 Sept., FO/800/195, Cecil to Bonar Law, 16 Oct., Bonar Law Papers, 51/4/15, and Cecil to Asquith, 22 Oct. 1915, FO/800/196; Grey to Lloyd George, 7 Aug. 1915, LGP, G/242.

62. Lloyd George to Grey, 25 Sept. 1915, FO/800/99; Buxton to Lloyd George, 25 and 30 Sept. 1915, and memorandum, "The Balkan Situation," LGP, D/17/19/3 and 4. O'Beirne favoured an active policy to prevent Bulgaria joining the Central Powers. (O'Beirne to Foreign Office, 15 Sept., LGP, D/19/2/2, and O'Beirne to Grey, 31 Oct. 1915, FO/800/43.)

negotiations with Bulgaria were obviously pointless.[63] She had joined the enemy.

Noel Buxton and Robert Cecil pronounced appropriately on the episode. The former assured Lloyd George that the Foreign Office now realized that he had been correct all along. The Entente could have secured Bulgarian intervention at the crucial point in March. Cecil agreed with Grey that they could not have thrown over Serbia in order to attract Bulgaria. Furthermore, he accepted the ruling that they must protect the Balkans from further activity by the brothers Buxton.[64]

The whole episode was revealing in many ways, not least with regard to the changing relationship between Lloyd George and Grey.[65] A significant degree of disenchantment had developed which would not be irrelevant in December 1916.

63. Asquith to Grey, 1 Oct., and Drummond to Grey, 2 Oct. 1915, FO/800/100; Lloyd George memorandum, 14 Oct. 1915, Cab 37/136/9; Cecil to Grey, 11 Nov. 1915, FO/800/195; Grey to Sir A. Davidson, 16 Nov. 1915, FO/800/103.

64. Cecil note, 7 Dec. 1915, LGP, D/19/2/4.

65. C. Addison, *Four and a Half Years: A Personal Diary from June 1914 to January 1919* (London, 1934), I, 132–36.

# 13

## Prelude

In the winter of 1915 two rather eccentric and indiscreet ladies offered their observations on the political situation. In Margot Asquith's opinion, "no one but God could put Herbert out."[1] To the Duchess of Hamilton, dire times lay ahead. "We have a War Committee comprising of [sic] 3 lawyers, 1 philosopher and 1 merchant. Ye Gods!"[2] Earlier, however, the Duchess had exempted one of the lawyers and, in terms reminiscent of Milner's observations in April 1903, had pointed in his direction. Lloyd George had performed impressively since the outbreak of war, she wrote, in sharp contrast to the years when he had spread his doctrines of hate across the land. The nation was in need of "a strong man—a leader—aristocrat, autocrat, democrat—no matter."[3] By December 1916 the nation had a new leader and the irreverent interlude in twentieth-century British politics had begun. In November 1922 the new political orthodoxy, to be

1. Page to Wilson, 31 Dec. 1915, Page Papers, correspondence with President Wilson, vol. III.
2. Duchess of Hamilton to Garvin, 30 Nov. 1915, Garvin Papers, box 55.
3. Duchess of Hamilton to Garvin, 27 June 1915, Garvin Papers, box 48, and A. M. Gollin, *Proconsul in Politics*, 46. Milner wrote, "the system is hopeless . . . Perhaps a great Charlatan—political scallywag, buffoon, liar—and in other respects popular favourite—may some day arise, who is nevertheless a statesman—and who, having attained power by popular art, may use it for national ends."

enjoyed or deplored, was confirmed; Labour confronted a Conservative government.

The intricate process by which Lloyd George replaced Asquith is beyond the scope of this study. Differences over a mosaic of issues began to divide Lloyd George from his Liberal colleagues and eventually convinced him that he must do as Scott had advised in June 1916, "keep Asquith and sterilise him." At the same time he was pulled closer to the Unionists and the Milner-ites, but not consistently so. Trends did not emerge before the fall of 1915 and even then seemed forfeit to new influences rather than irreversible. The debate over strategy and military questions was one such issue, and Lloyd George's disillusionment with Grey was directly related to Asquith's political demise.

From December 1914, when Lloyd George made his first serious attempt to influence strategy, he failed to secure the support of Asquith, Grey, or any other Liberal of consequence except perhaps Churchill. Kitchener was unimpressed, whatever superficial levels of cordiality were in evidence.[4] Between December 1914 and February 1915, and then in the discussions culminating in September, only Churchill accorded any importance to the Balkan theatre and to the idea of a Salonika expeditionary force. Grey was both sceptical and mildly sarcastic. Between September 1915 and January 1916 Crewe joined Churchill in supporting Lloyd George over the Salonika force, but neither wanted to abandon the Dardanelles, although Crewe wavered. In the final discussions involving the Balkan theatre, from June 1916, Lloyd George operated without the sustained assistance of any Liberal minister. Lloyd George's divorce from his Liberal colleagues over Rumania was the logical outcome, for they blamed the Rumanians themselves and Russia for Rumania's collapse.

On the other hand, from September 1915 Lloyd George found sympathy among certain Unionists over strategic questions, with Bonar Law the most conspicuous and significant supporter. His scepticism over the salvaging of Rumania in October 1916 was the only deviation of note, and it was purely temporary. In contrast Curzon, like Austen Chamberlain, secretary of state for India from May 1915, disparaged Lloyd George's strategic schemes and was particularly opposed to the evacuation from the Dardanelles. So

4. M. Gilbert, *Winston S. Churchill*, III, 384; A. J. P. Taylor, ed., *Lloyd George: A Diary*, 5, 7, 21, 29, 45, 59, 71, 91, 101; Asquith, *Memories and Reflections*, 57–58.

were Balfour and Lansdowne, but the former supported Lloyd George briefly in January 1916 and saw merit in a Salonika offensive in the spring. Balfour deprecated, however, his attitude toward Greece. Conversely, Curzon supported Lloyd George's proposals to deal with Greece in September 1916. Even Walter Long and Robert Cecil shared his concern over military developments at Salonika and the Dardanelles.[5]

Edward Carson, attorney-general from May to October 1915, stood with him over both the Dardanelles and the Balkans while in office, and remained sympathetic.[6] Lord Milner was concerned about the Eastern Front proper and feared lest Russia collapse. His group rapidly became disenchanted with the operations on the Western Front and preferred other theatres. Leopold Amery, for instance, in 1916 advocated an attack through the Balkans to open the path to Hungary and to dispose of the Turk. They did not share all of Lloyd George's views; Milner supported the Greeks and the Serbs against Bulgaria, and Amery denounced both the "whoring after the Bulgars" and the Treaty of London. In general, however, the debate over strategy tended to bring them together. As Waldorf Astor reported to Garvin, "I hear that Leo is beginning to speak well of L.G.—probably one of the most humorous outcomes of this queer war."[7]

In the day to day conduct of the war the Foreign Office, not unnaturally, gave precedence to the War Office viewpoint. Lloyd George deplored what he regarded as an act of abdication, and levelled a charge of craven political subservience to the military.

---

5. Bonar Law to Lloyd George, 28 June, LGP, D/17/8/2, and Bonar Law to Henry Wilson, 15 July 1915, Bonar Law Papers, 53/6/33; Lloyd George to Bonar Law and Carson, 25 Sept. 1915, LGP, D/20/2/30 and D/17/8/8; K. A. Murdock to Lloyd George, 23 and 25 Sept. 1915, LGP, D/20/2/27 and 30; Long to Bonar Law, 14 Oct. 1915, Bonar Law Papers, 117/1/21; Carson to Bonar Law, 5 and 7 Sept., 13 Oct., and 13 Nov. 1915, ibid., 51/3/5 and 7, 51/4/26, and 51 /5/22; Asquith to Bonar Law, 5 Nov., Balfour to Bonar Law, 7 Nov., and Crewe to Bonar Law, 5 Nov. 1915, ibid., 51/5/7 and 15, 53/6/47, and 51/5/8; Cecil memoranda, 20 Sept. and 17 Oct., Cecil Papers, Add. 51105, and Cecil to Asquith, 22 Oct. 1915, FO/800/196.

6. Riddell diary, Oct. 1915, 30 July, and 1 Oct. 1916, Lord Riddell, *War Diary, 1914–1918*, 124–31, 205–06, 213; Scott diary, 18 Feb. 1916, Scott Papers, Add. 50902; H. M. Hyde, *Carson*, 392–95.

7. Astor to Garvin, 16 Nov. 1915, Garvin Papers, box 48; Amery to Cecil, 9 Jan. 1914, Cecil Papers, Add. 51072; Amery to Milner, 27 April and 2 June 1915, and 20 and 27 Oct. 1916, Milner Papers, files 140 and 143; Amery to Cecil, 12 Feb. 1916, FO/800/196; Milner to Carson, 26 Oct., and Milner to Lansdowne, 5 Dec. 1915, Milner Papers, file 141.

Lloyd George's distrust of the military mind and its supposed expertise had been apparent since the Boer War. He permitted exceptions: perhaps Sir John French, commander-in-chief of the BEF, initially Sir William Robertson, and Admiral Fisher. Generals and admirals, however, were all too frequently un-imaginative strategists, inefficient businessmen, and incompetent administrators. The slaughter in France, recruiting problems, and the shell shortage were tragic testimonies to their inadequacy. Lloyd George condemned the War Office under Kitchener, to whom Asquith seemed devotedly bound, on one further count. When it did not indulge in secrecy it misled the government and the nation with false statistics on munitions production and casualties, in an attempt to conceal its own failures. Lloyd George came to disparage Kitchener and made the War Office the symbol of all the frailties of Asquith's administration.[8]

Lloyd George found it incredible, therefore, that Asquith could inform him in July 1916 that the War Office was sound and ready to welcome him as its head.[9] Lloyd George expressed his dis-enchantment in a typical piece of paradox. The Liberals were now Tories because of their defence of the War Office and the Admir-alty; Asquith had become a Conservative because he worshipped generals and admirals. He himself remained the true radical, sceptical of the military.

Whether Lloyd George could function effectively at the War Office would depend largely on his relations with Robertson, the CIGS, whom Asquith described as first-rate. Momentarily, during the Somme offensive, they were in unison.[10] Very rapidly, how-ever, Lloyd George began to wrestle with Robertson in order to define his own powers and assert his authority.[11] By October 1916

8. War Policy Committee, Aug. and Sept., 1915, Cab 27/2; Bonar Law to Lloyd George, 1 Nov. 1915, LGP, D/17/8/9; Lloyd George to his brother, 15 April 1916, W. George, *My Brother and I*, 354; Lloyd George to Asquith, 30 May 1916, LGP, D/18/2/11; House diary, 2 June 1915; Scott diary, 11 March, 1–3 Sept., 1–2 Nov., 11–15 Dec. 1915, Scott Papers, Add. 50901 and 50902.

9. Lloyd George to Asquith, 17 June 1916, LGP, D/18/2/18 and 19, and Asquith Papers, file 30; Asquith to Lloyd George, 6 July 1916, LGP, E/2/23/2.

10. W. George to Lloyd George, 25 June 1916, LGP, I/2/1/45; T. H. Darlow, *William Robertson Nicoll*, 256–57; Sir W. Robertson, *Soldiers and Statesmen, 1914–1918*, I, 175.

11. Robertson–Lloyd George correspondence, 24 and 26 June 1916, LGP, D/18/8/18, 19, and 20, and 11 Oct. 1916, Asquith Papers, file 30; Robertson to Grey, 24 June, and Grey to Robertson, 27 June 1916, FO/800/102; Scott diary, 10, 11, 13, and 14 June 1916, Scott Papers, Add. 50902; R. Blake, ed., *The Private*

they were openly in disagreement over strategy,[12] each charging the other with bad faith and worse practice.[13] To be sure, Lloyd George had agreed with Robertson in August that they must attempt to detach Bulgaria; he had even indulged in faint praise of the CIGS in September in order to dispatch him to Russia. They were also united in their opposition to Lansdowne and temporarily over the question of French assistance to the Arab revolt. The War Committee soon witnessed, however, their differences over the Russian mission,[14] as well as over the Salonika front and the pressing need to defeat Bulgaria and preserve Rumania. Robertson was scarcely *persona grata* with Lloyd George by December, but he was not likely to lose his position during the change of government. However, the malaise at the War Office undoubtedly had served to undermine Asquith's position.

Lloyd George's almost pathological distrust of Joffre likewise had a divisive effect.[15] He condemned Joffre persistently and unreservedly from January 1915. Only when Joffre's views sustained Lloyd George over Balkan strategy did the assault waver. Joffre was not only a symbol of military obtuseness; he personified the process by which the French dominated allied military

---

*Papers of Douglas Haig 1914–1919* (London, 1952), 172. Lloyd George insisted that the CIGS keep him fully informed and not place recommendations before the War Committee without consulting him. Lloyd George demanded, however, that he have an independent voice in the War Committee; he could not be a mere puppet.

12. Lloyd George to D.M.O., 4 Sept. 1916, Carson Papers, D/1507/1, 1916/52, and LGP, E/1/5/6; Robertson, *Soldiers and Statesmen*, I, 179, and II, 127–29.

13. On the Rabegh question Robertson charged Lloyd George with disregarding his advice, consulting junior officers behind his back, and generally failing to support him. Lloyd George accused Robertson of making no criticism of his independent views on Rumania in their private discussions and yet disagreeing with him in the War Committee, of threatening him with a press campaign, and of failing to restrain his subordinates who were leaking to the press. (Lloyd George to Robertson, 12 Oct. 1916, Asquith Papers, file 30.)

14. Lloyd George proposed that Robertson and Reading lead the mission to Russia, but the CIGS and others, quite rightly, were suspicious of his motives. (Lloyd George to Asquith, 26 Sept., LGP, E/2/23/5, Robertson to Lloyd George, 27 Sept., ibid., E/1/5/2, and War Committee, 21, 24, and 27 Nov. 1916, Cab 42/25/2, 8, and 10.) According to Lord Derby, Robertson feared he would be ousted if he went to Russia, and insisted that he would not go unless Joffre accompanied him. (Derby to Lloyd George, 12 Nov. 1916, LGP, E/1/1/9.)

15. Lloyd George commented on a Joffre statement on manpower, "What a traitor to his country and his army thus to imperil their safety." (Lloyd George to Churchill, 17 April 1915, LGP, C/3/16/30.)

planning and dictated to London. A letter from Mark Bonham Carter, Asquith's private secretary, in August 1915, illustrates the point. Joffre had induced a reluctant but pliable Kitchener to launch the new offensive, against Churchill's advice; Asquith had persuaded the cabinet to acquiesce.[16] Lloyd George concluded, from these and other instances, that Asquith, Grey, and Kitchener were not a match for their French or even their Russian counterparts.[17] Lloyd George saw a further refinement here. He frequently praised the magnitude of France's war effort in comparison with that of Britain. The disparity was a source of anger and frustration to him and in turn helped explain why France dominated allied debate.

Lloyd George's disenchantment with Grey also had significant consequences. The foreign secretary and the prime minister were tied indissolubly together, even though the former had become weary of office. They would attempt to close Liberal ranks and to survive together, however feeble Grey's contribution to the act.[18] If Lloyd George lost faith in either one, the credibility of the other would suffer. If he shunted Asquith aside, Grey would leave office for he would serve no other leader.

The prewar rapport between Lloyd George and Grey was based almost exclusively on a consensus over foreign policy, political considerations, and Lloyd George's belief that Grey was an effective foreign secretary. Their regard had weathered the 1914 crisis, but several factors caused it to evaporate.

In the first place Grey had reverted to some extent to the secrecy and deviousness of earlier days. This error, reinforced by a desire to avoid contention and offence, made it appear that the foreign secretary was frank only with Asquith, Haldane, and selected officials. Lloyd George, for instance, told Colonel House that

16. M. Bonham Carter to Lloyd George, 21 Aug. 1915, ibid., D/18/2/5; Riddell diary, 29 Oct. 1915, Riddell, *War Diary*, 130.

17. Paris Conference, 26–28 March 1916, Cab 37/144/77 and Cab 28/1; War Committee, 22 Aug. 1916, Cab 42/18/4. Lloyd George, while deploring the results, actually applauded Asquith's performance at the Paris conference in November 1916. The reason, he told his brother, was that Asquith was removed temporarily from the debilitating environment of London. (Lloyd George draft of P.M.'s statement for, and minutes of the conference, 15–16 Nov., Cab 28/1, War Committee, 21 Nov., Cab 42/25/2, and Lloyd George to his brother, 18, 22, and 27 Nov. 1916, W. George, 255–56.)

18. Grey had offered his resignation in December 1915, along with Runciman, McKenna, and Simon, regretting that he had not joined Haldane in May. (Grey to Asquith, 29 Dec. 1915, Asquith Papers, file 28; Scott diary, 3 Sept. and 26 Oct. 1915, Scott Papers, Add. 50901 and 50902.) Grey's role in December

he had not been informed of the reasons for House's return to England in February 1916. Grey seemed excessively concerned to preserve the authority of the Foreign Office and to retain an exclusive grip on information. He discouraged cabinet interference and avoided coordinating policy with other departments, especially with the Colonial and India Offices. This situation Lloyd George and others found increasingly difficult to tolerate.[19]

While Grey's critics deplored these developments they also lamented the ineffectiveness of the Foreign Office.[20] An overstrained Sir Arthur Nicolson, the permanent under-secretary, had deteriorated to the point of virtual impotence and was replaced in June 1916. Sir Eyre Crowe, the assistant under-secretary, was transferred to the War Department at the outbreak of war and from December 1914 dealt with blockade matters. Eric Drummond replaced Sir William Tyrrell as Grey's private secretary in April 1915 when Tyrrell suffered a nervous breakdown.

Grey himself, visibly aging, periodically ill, sorely troubled by failing eyesight, insomnia, and a guilt complex, seemed to some observers to drift perceptibly into a mood of pessimism.[21] There was an evident loss of skill and confidence, and Lloyd George began to question his nerve and stamina. On matters apparently vital to the Foreign Office Grey seemed unsure and excessively reticent in face of the allies; an unhappy combination of deviousness and ineffectiveness. Conscious that his vigour was suspect, he was forced onto the defensive. Grey felt it necessary to justify himself and to reiterate his devotion to the war effort and to the pursuit of victory.[22] Such protestations served only to arouse

---

1916 remains obscure. He was with Lansdowne on 2 and 3 December and among those Liberals advising Asquith during the next three days.

19. Montagu to Grey, 9 April 1915, FO/800/101; Montagu to Drummond, 26 Feb. 1916, S. D. Waley, *Edwin Montagu* (London, 1964), 92. In October 1915 the cabinet pressed Grey on his failure to consult them over the promise to cede Cyprus to Greece. Grey pleaded the absence of time and the need for unfettered and speedy negotiations. (Crewe report of cabinet meeting, 21 Oct. 1915, Cab 37/136/26.)

20. M. Ekstein-Frankl, "The Development of British War Aims, 1914–15," and K. J. Calder, "National Self-Determination in British Government Policy during the First World War."

21. Riddell diary, 10 Oct. and 22 Nov. 1914, Riddell, *War Diary*, 34, 42. See, however, Runciman to his wife, 11 Aug. 1915, Runciman Papers, box 18.

22. Grey to Lloyd George, 8 Sept. 1915, LGP, D/16/17/5. Lloyd George became less impressed with Grey's expressions of optimism; for example, his

suspicion that he was clinging obstinately to office, and was unwilling to rise to the occasion and surrender power in the national interest.[23]

On the fundamental questions of the degree of compulsion that the state should impose on various aspects of national life in wartime, and the rate at which extraordinary powers could be assumed, Grey stood closer to McKenna and Walter Runciman, president of the board of trade, than to Lloyd George. This difference would have weighed less heavily had Grey fulfilled other expectations, but as Lloyd George wrote, "Grey's Balkan policy is like a man trying to reconcile his wife to his taking a mistress."[24] Moreover, Balkan questions had confirmed for Lloyd George that Grey was unimaginative and rigid, preferring exclusive control to the chance of success.[25]

The conduct of Anglo-American relations, however, did not significantly divide Grey and Lloyd George. Irritants emerged; Grey refused to repatriate Spring-Rice from the Washington embassy, and rejected Lloyd George's proposal to send Gilbert Murray to the United States for propaganda purposes.[26] They carried, however, little sting. There were differences in the impact and power of imagery of their oratory about war aims, evident in, for instance, Lloyd George's effective use of *Pilgrim's Progress* and *Holy War*.[27] There were variations in emphasis, Lloyd George being more insistent in demanding the destruction of the Ottoman Empire, but he and Grey served the same ends.

Indeed, if the question of war aims divided Lloyd George from Grey it did so only over tactics. It also demonstrated Lloyd George's unease lest her allies dictate to Britain. In March 1915

---

wager of one hundred cigars valued at not less than £1 that the war would end within one year from May 1915. (Grey to Lloyd George, 3 May 1915, LGP, C/13; Harcourt to Buxton, 17 March 1915, Harcourt Papers, C.O. 2/34.) Yet as late as October 1916 Lloyd George described Grey as second to himself in public popularity. He also included him in a possible War Committee of three Liberals and three Unionists.

23. Scott diary, 3 Sept., 1, 14–15, and 17 Oct., 1–2 Nov. 1915, and 13–20 April, 10 May, and 14 June 1916, Scott Papers, Add. 50901 and 50902.

24. Lloyd George, cabinet note, n.d. (while munitions minister), LGP, C/13.

25. Dardanelles Commission of Enquiry, 2 April 1917, Cab 19/33.

26. Drummond to F. Stevenson, 2 Nov. 1916, FO/800/102. Grey supported the Washington embassy in its opposition to propaganda excursions by the likes of Gilbert Murray. (Barclay to Foreign Office, 31 Oct. 1916, ibid.)

27. Lloyd George, cabinet notes, LGP, C/13.

he urged the government to spell out Britain's peace desiderata to France and Russia at a foreign ministers' conference.[28] Grey rejected the proposal as one likely to produce interallied irritants, as had the negotiations with France over Alexandretta, and as impracticable because it would take him away from London for two or three weeks.

Neither gave satisfaction to dissenting groups and this was particularly true of Lloyd George.[29] On two issues, the suppression of unpatriotic newspapers such as *Vanguard* and *Forward*, and the restricting of the civil rights of conscientious objectors, he appeared particularly brutal. Any newspaper which undermined the war effort must be crushed. The authorities must not, by acts of unpardonable weakness, permit the likes of Charles Trevelyan and Bertrand Russell to deliver poisonous speeches, paralysing the nation, and injuring recruitment. Furthermore, Lloyd George argued, the tribunals must scrutinize relentlessly the motives of all men who opposed the war, be ruthless with the sham objector, and show what services the sincere could render the nation in its greatest hour of peril. Lloyd George's apparent extremism never faltered, at least publicly, and became part of his support for compulsory war measures. Historically, he argued, all great democracies had resorted to compulsion as an act of self-defence. He was neither the enemy of nor a traitor toward liberalism.[30]

Lloyd George could serve the Foreign Office's interests, as it could his, on occasion.[31] Nevertheless he came to regard Grey as a tired liability to be moved aside with Asquith. Analysing the choice of Grey's successor is the first step in attempting to explain Lloyd George's celebrated lack of respect for the Foreign Office when he was prime minister, supposedly out of sheer caprice and

28. War Council, 10 March 1915, Cab 42/2/5.
29. Bertrand Russell, article, "Clifford Allen and Mr. Lloyd George," 17 Aug. 1916, in *The Tribunal*. The Courtney, Morel, Lansbury, and Russell Papers reveal little on this point.
30. Statements, 22 March, *Parl. Deb.*, LXXXI, 302–308, Oct., LXXXVI, 539–40, and 28 Nov. 1916, LXXXVIII, 295–97; Lloyd George, *War Memoirs*, I, 439–49. Asquith reported in March 1915 that Lloyd George, Kitchener, and Churchill proposed the jailing of men who would not work. (Gilbert, *Winston S. Churchill*, III, 330.)
31. Drummond to Davies, 6 Nov. 1915, FO/800/99. He enclosed an outline of a statement requested by Lloyd George, and which Grey wished to issue under Lloyd George's name. Eustace Percy had drafted the statement in reply to Theodore Roosevelt's criticism of the British war effort in comparison with that of France, in the *Metropolitan Magazine*, 29 Oct. 1915.

because of his unorthodox proclivities. In fact the Foreign Office had done little to maintain his respect during the war. His regard for it had evaporated. After pronouncing Balfour unfit for the Admiralty, Lloyd George installed him in Grey's place, without a formal seat in the War Cabinet.[32] He, like the Foreign Office, would have to prove himself in the new administration. In fact, as will appear, Balfour did so more to the satisfaction of Lloyd George than to that of Curzon.

Lloyd George bore up physically under the strain of war far better than Asquith or Grey. His recuperative powers were remarkable, and emotionally disturbing family bereavements were behind or ahead of him. He rose from the wreckage of both of Asquith's wartime administrations, an object as much as an initiator of disruptive intrigue. Lloyd George did not become prime minister as a result of a sordid conspiracy against a genteel and gallant leader. Asquith went out as he had come into office in 1905, struggling for control to the tune of his wife's exhortations. If it is possible to distinguish between concern for issues, policies, and solutions on the one hand, and driving ambition and the ruthless grasping at office on the other, the evidence favours Lloyd George. At four decisive points, in May 1915, in April, June, and again in December 1916, this was so.[33] His will to preserve Asquith diminished from the spring of 1916, but at most he was guilty of assuming, along with many others, that executive reconstruction, efficient government, and his own accumulation of power were synonymous. A consensus of élite opinion regarded Lloyd George as an almost indispensable part of any War Directory. Even Neville Chamberlain agreed that, despite his defects, Lloyd George was the best man available. He would give the nation fresh hope and he enjoyed a great reputation at home and abroad.[34]

32. War Committee, 1 March, 10 May, and 28 Nov. 1916, Cab 42/10/1, Cab 42/13/6, and Cab 42/26/1; Scott diary, 3 Sept. 1915 and 5–8 June 1916, Scott Papers, Add. 50901 and 50902; B. E. C. Dugdale, *Arthur James Balfour*, II, 39–40; Lloyd George, *War Memoirs*, I, 596–97, 604–607. Lloyd George also clashed with Balfour over Admiral Fisher's value, and aircraft production.

33. A Chamberlain diary, 18 May 1915; C. Hazlehurst, *Politicians at War, July 1914 to May 1915*, 227–60; T. Wilson, *The Downfall of the Liberal Party, 1914–1935* (London, 1966), 69, 76, 80–85, 381; C. Addison, *Four and a Half Years*, 136–37; Lloyd George to Asquith, 30 May and 17 June 1916, LGP, D/18/2/11, 18, and 19, and Asquith Papers, file 30; Lloyd George to Asquith, 2 Dec. 1916, LGP, E/2/23/11.

34. N. Chamberlain to A. Chamberlain, 13 Dec. 1916, A. Chamberlain Papers, AC/15/3/1–44.

Of course, it was recognized that he might fail and become expendable.[35]

By November 1916 the War Committee was disintegrating under the sheer weight of unresolved problems and a damaging lack of success. Dissatisfaction with it was widespread,[36] but political realities militated against a more revolutionary reorganization and redistribution of offices and power, as envisaged, for example, by Arthur Lee and the Milnerites. There was, however, no reprieve for Asquith who had retained power long after he had ceased to deserve it. His record convicted him. As Viscount Devonport noted, the prime minister "exudes weakness at every pore."[37]

December 1916 saw the final, decisive political change of the war. If Asquith's critics had assessed the nation's predicament accurately, to take charge of the government at that point was an act of courage. The Archbishop of Canterbury, not an admirer, conceded that Lloyd George had taken on a "literally tremendous burden," probably without parallel, and noted, "your call, at perhaps the most critical hour in English History, to the place you hold is an event which would be solemn to any man, and to a man of your temperament and 'make' must be, in the most literal sense, almost overwhelming."[38]

Lloyd George's accession to power brought significant deviations in method, style, procedures, tone, levels of dignity, if not of morality, personnel, and even policy. These changes, however, were often less decisive than contemporaries expected or subsequently recorded. Not everything changed substantively, let alone improved, in the conduct of the war. Yet Lloyd George was prime minister; the government's failures were his to defend, its successes his to enjoy. On 6 December 1916, Wales ruled England and that was revolution enough.

35. J. W. Lowther, A *Speaker's Commentaries* (London, 1925), II, 202; *Esher Journals*, IV, 71–72.

36. Asquith to Lloyd George, 30 Oct. 1916, LGP, E/2/23/7. The prime minister wrote, "I have today something like six threatened resignations from colleagues wanting in their sense of proportion." In his memoirs, Lloyd George described Asquith as feeble, strained, unfit, and overwhelmed, but he made no mention of his unconventional social behaviour. He maintained that he could have been much harsher and more truthful about Asquith. (Lloyd George, *War Memoirs*, I, 602–603.)

37. Devonport to Lloyd George, 20 April 1916, LGP, D/6/11/3.

38. Davidson to Lloyd George, 10 Dec. 1916, G. K. A. Bell, *Randall Davidson*, II, 793–94.

# BIBLIOGRAPHY

*Government Records* (Public Record Office, London)

Files of the Board of Trade, 1905–1908
Files of the Treasury, 1908–1915
Files of the Ministry of Munitions, 1915–1916
Files of the War Office, 1916
Files of the Admiralty, 1911
Files of the Committee of Imperial Defence, 1906–1914
Files of the Cabinet Office, including the files of the War Council,
    the Dardanelles Committee, and the War Committee
Files of the Foreign Office, 1905–1916

*The Papers of:*

H. H. Asquith, Bodleian Library, Oxford
Arthur J. Balfour, British Museum, London
Lord Bertie of Thame, Public Record Office, London
W. Beveridge (Ministry of Munitions), London School of
    Economics Library
A. Bonar Law, Beaverbrook Memorial Library, London
Sir Robert Borden, Public Archives of Canada, Ottawa
J. Bryce, Bodleian Library
J. Burns, British Museum
N. Buxton, McGill University Library, Montreal
Sir H. Campbell-Bannerman, British Museum
Sir E. Carson, Ulster Record Office, Belfast
Lord Robert Cecil, British Museum
Sir Austen Chamberlain, University of Birmingham Library
Lord Courtney, London School of Economics Library
Lord Crewe, Cambridge University Library
D. R. Daniel, National Library of Wales, Aberystwyth
W. H. Dawson, University of Birmingham Library

Viscount Elibank, incorporating the papers of A. C. Murray and Murray of Elibank, National Library of Scotland, Edinburgh
T. E. Ellis, National Library of Wales
B. G. Evans, National Library of Wales
Lord Emmott, Nuffield College Library, Oxford
H. A. L. Fisher, Bodleian Library
J. L. Garvin, University of Texas, Austin
Sir Edward Grey, Public Record Office
E. Ellis-Griffith, National Library of Wales
E. T. John, National Library of Wales
Earl Haig, National Library of Scotland
R. B. Haldane, National Library of Scotland
Lord Hankey, Public Record Office and Churchill College, Cambridge
Sir Lewis Harcourt, in the possession of Viscount Harcourt
Lord Hardinge of Penshurst, Cambridge University Library and Public Record Office
F. S. Harrison, London School of Economics Library
E. M. House, Yale University Library
G. Lansbury, London School of Economics Library
Thomas Jones, National Library of Wales
Sir Wilfrid Laurier, Public Archives of Canada
Lord Lee of Fareham, Beaverbrook Memorial Library
J. H. Lewis, National Library of Wales
Sir B. Liddell Hart, while in his possession
D. Lloyd George, Beaverbrook Memorial Library and National Library of Wales
R. McKenna, Cambridge University Library
R. McNeil, Ulster Record Office
Lord Milner, Bodleian Library
E. D. Morel, London School of Economics Library
Viscount Morley, India Office Library, London
Lord Mottistone, Nuffield College, Oxford
Gilbert Murray, Bodleian Library
Sir A. Nicolson, Public Record Office
Walter Hines Page, Harvard University Library
Lord Passfield, London School of Economics Library
Lord Ponsonby of Shulbrede, Bodleian Library
Lord Ripon, British Museum
T. Roosevelt, Harvard University Library
Lord Rosebery, National Library of Scotland

Lord Runciman, University of Newcastle Library
Bertrand Russell, McMaster University Library, Hamilton, Ontario
Lord Samuel, House of Lords Record Office, London
C. P. Scott, British Museum
Lord Simon, in the possession of Viscount Simon
J. A. Spender, British Museum
W. T. Stead, in the possession of Professor J. O. Baylen, Georgia State University, Atlanta, Georgia
J. St. Loe Strachey, Beaverbrook Memorial Library
Sir F. Villiers, Public Record Office


*Government Documents*

*Documents diplomatiques français, 1871–1914.* Paris, 1930–53.
Gooch, G. P., Temperley, H., and Penson, L. M., eds., *British Documents on the Origins of the War, 1898–1914.* London, 1926–38.
Mendelssohn-Barthöldy, A., Lepsius, I., and Thimme, F., eds., *Die Grosse Politik der Europäischen Kabinette.* Berlin, 1922–27.
*Parliamentary Debates,* House of Commons, fourth and fifth series.


*Newspapers and Journals*

*The Times*
*Manchester Guardian*
*Round Table*


*Publications and Collected Speeches of Lloyd George*

*The Budget, the Land and the People.* London: Hodder and Stoughton, 1909.
*The People's Budget.* London: Hodder and Stoughton, 1909.
*The People's Insurance.* London: Hodder and Stoughton, 1911.
*Better Times.* London: Hodder and Stoughton, 1910.
*Honour and Dishonour.* London: Methuen, 1914.
*Through Terror to Triumph.* London: Hodder and Stoughton, 1915.
*The Great Crusade.* London: Hodder and Stoughton, 1918.
*Where Are We Going?* New York: Doran, 1923.
*Is It Peace?* London: Hodder and Stoughton, 1923.
*Liberalism and Liberty.* London, 1924.
*Coal and Power.* London: Hodder and Stoughton, 1924.

*301*

*Land and the Nation*. London, 1925.

*Towns and the Land*. London, 1927.

*Britain's Industrial Future*. London, 1928.

*Slings and Arrows*. Edited by P. Guedalla. Toronto: Ryerson Press, 1929.

*The Truth about Reparations and War Debts*. London: Heinemann, 1932.

*The War Memoirs of David Lloyd George*. 6 vols. London: Nicholson and Watson, 1933–36.

*Organising Prosperity*. London: Nicholson and Watson, 1935.

" Mr. Churchill on his Contemporaries," *The Listener*, xvii, 457 (13 October 1937). Autumn Book Supplement, iii–iv (review of *Great Contemporaries*).

*The Truth About the Peace Treaties*. 2 vols. London: Gollancz, 1938.


*Biographies of Lloyd George*

Anon. *Lloyd George and the War. By an Independent Liberal*. London: Hutchinson, 1917.

Bardoux, J. *Lloyd George et la France*. Paris, 1923.

Burbidge, W. F. *The Wizard of Wales*. London: Crowther, 1943.

Clarke, T. *My Lloyd George Diary*. London: Methuen, 1939.

Davies, Sir A. T. *The Lloyd George I Knew*. London: Walter, 1948.

Davies, W. W. *Lloyd George: 1863–1914*. London: Constable, 1939.

Dilnot, F. *Lloyd George: The Man and His Story*. New York: Harper, 1917.

du Parcq, H. *Life of David Lloyd George*. 4 vols. London: Caxton, 1912–13.

Edwards, J. H. *The Life of David Lloyd George*. 5 vols. London: Waverley, 1913–24.

Edwards, J. H. and Hughes, S. L. *From Village Green to Downing Street: Life of the Rt. Hon. David Lloyd George*. London: Newnes, 1909.

Evans, B. G. *The Life Romance of David Lloyd George*. London: Everyman, 1916.

George, W. *My Brother and I*. London: Eyre and Spottiswoode, 1958.

Gilbert, M. ed. *Lloyd George*. Englewood Cliffs, N.J.: Prentice-Hall, 1968.

Grigg, J. *The Young Lloyd George*. London: Eyre Methuen, 1973.

Humphreys, E. M. *David Lloyd George*. Llandebie: Llyfrau'r Dryw, No. 19, 1943.

Jones, J. *The Man David*. London: Hamish Hamilton, 1944.

Jones, T. *Lloyd George*. London: Oxford University Press, 1951.

Lloyd George, R. *My Father, Lloyd George*. New York: Crown Publishers, 1961.

Mallet, Sir C. E. *Mr. Lloyd George, A Study*. London: Benn, 1930.

McCormick, D. *The Mask of Merlin: A Critical Study of Lloyd George*. London: Macdonald, 1963.

Mills, J. Saxon. *David Lloyd George, War Minister*. London: Cassell, 1924.

Morgan, K. O. *David Lloyd George: Welsh Radical as World Statesman*. Cardiff: University of Wales Press, 1963.

Mowat, C. L. *Lloyd George*. London: Oxford University Press, 1964.

Murray, B. *"L.G."* London: Sampson Low, 1932.

Owen, F. *Tempestuous Journey*. London: Hutchinson, 1954.

Raine, G. E. *The Real Lloyd George*. London: Allen, 1913.

Raymond, E. T. *Mr. Lloyd George: A Biography*. London: Collins, 1922.

Roch, W. F. *Mr. Lloyd George and the War*. London: Chatto and Windus, 1920.

Robertson, J. M. *Mr. Lloyd George and Liberalism*. London: Chapman and Dodd, 1923.

Spender, H. E. *The Prime Minister*. London: Hodder and Stoughton, 1920.

Sylvester, A. J. *The Real Lloyd George*. London: Cassell, 1947.

Taylor, A. J. P. *Lloyd George: Rise and Fall*. Cambridge University Press, 1961.

Thomson, M. *David Lloyd George: The Official Biography*. London: Hutchinson, 1948.

West, G. *Lloyd George's Last Fight*. London: Alston Rivers, 1930.

Walters, E. W. *The "New" Lloyd George and the Old*. London: Joseph Johnson, 1916.

*Articles on and Studies of Lloyd George*

Ayling, S. E. *Portraits of Power*. New York: Barnes and Noble, 1961.

Beaverbrook, Lord. *The Decline and Fall of Lloyd George*. London: Collins, 1963.

Begbie, H. *The Mirrors of Downing Street*. New York: Putnams, 1921.

Brook, S. "Mr. Lloyd George and the War," *Living Age*, 287 (27 November 1915), 515–26.
——. "The Meaning of the Lloyd George Ministry," *North American Review*, 205 (January 1917), 31–35.
——. "The Paradox of the Premier," *Nineteenth Century*, 832 (June 1918), 1319–26.
Cecil, A. "Mr. Lloyd George: A Page of History," *Quarterly Review*, 238, no. 473 (October 1922), 279–305.
"Centurion". *The Man Who Didn't Win the War*. London, 1923.
Chirol, V. "Four Years of Lloyd Georgian Foreign Policy," *The Edinburgh Review*, 237, no. 483 (January 1923), 1–20.
Conacher, W. M. "The Lloyd Georgics," *Queen's Quarterly*, 42 (1935), 43–54.
Cosgrove, R. A. "A Note on Lloyd George's Speech at the Mansion House, 21 July 1911," *The Historical Journal*, 12, no. 4 (1969), 698–701.
Costigan, G. *Makers of Modern England*. New York: MacMillan, 1969.
Davies, Sir J. *The Prime Minister's Secretariat 1916–1920*. Newport: R. H. Johns, 1951.
Derry, J. W. *The Radical Tradition*. London: MacMillan, 1967.
Gardiner, A. G. *Prophets, Priests and Kings*. London, 1914.
——. "The British Cabinet," *Atlantic Monthly*, 115 (1915), 672–82.
Grainger, J. H. *Character and Style in British Politics*. Cambridge: The University Press, 1969.
Grant, W. L. "The Prime Minister of Great Britain," *Queen's Quarterly*, 28 (1920), 138–44.
Harden, M. *I Meet My Contemporaries*. New York: Holt, 1925.
Huddleston, S. *Those Europeans*. New York: Putnams, 1924.
Jones, T. "Lloyd George: Some Personal Memories," *Contemporary Review*, 953 (May 1945), 262–64.
——. "David Lloyd George," in *The Dictionary of National Biography 1941–1950*. Edited by L. G. Wickham Legg and E. T. Williams. London: Oxford University Press, 1959. Pp. 515–29.
Keynes, J. M. *Essays in Biography*. London: MacMillan, 1933.
Kinnear, M. *The Fall of Lloyd George*. London: MacMillan, 1973.
Lucy, Sir H. "The Canonisation of Lloyd George," *The Nation*, 100 (18 March 1915), 312–13.
Lloyd George, Frances. *The Years That Are Past*. London: Hutchinson, 1967.

Mallet, C. "Liberalism and Mr. Lloyd George," *Contemporary Review*, 117 (June 1920), 774–82.

Massingham, H. W. "Lloyd George and His Government," *The Yale Review*, 6 (1916–17), 727–37.

Masterman, C. F. G. "The Coalition, Liberalism and Labour," *Contemporary Review*, 119 (May 1921), 608–17.

Masterman, L. "Recollections of David Lloyd George," *History Today*, 9, nos. 3 and 4 (March and April 1959), 160–66, 274–78.

Maxse, L. J. "The Chameleon of the Rue Nitot," *National Review*, 63 (May 1919).

Morgan, K. O. "Lloyd George's Premiership: A Study in 'Prime Ministerial Government'," *The Historical Journal*, 13, no. 1 (1970), 130–57.

Needham, H. B. "Mr. Lloyd George on the War," *Pearson's Magazine* (March 1915), 258–67.

Nevinson, H. W. "Lloyd George: The Leader of British Liberals," *Foreign Affairs*, 9, no. 3 (April 1931), 457–68.

Nicolson, H. "Lloyd George's Mesmerism," *The Observer*, 19 October 1958.

Raymond, E. T. "The Future of Mr. Lloyd George," *Atlantic Monthly*, 127 (April 1921), 433–39.

Sidebotham, H. "Mr. Lloyd George. An Appreciation," *Atlantic Monthly*, 124 (November 1919), 691–700.

Snow, C. P. "London Diary," *The New Statesman and Nation*, 53, no. 1354 (23 February 1957), 226–27.

Spender, H. "David Lloyd George," in *Encyclopedia Britannica*. 12th ed. Chicago: University of Chicago Press, 1929. Vol. 14.

Taylor, A. J. P., ed., *Lloyd George: A Diary by Frances Stevenson*. London: Hutchinson, 1971.

———. *Lloyd George: Twelve Essays*. London: Hamish Hamilton, 1971.

*The Times*, 27 March 1945.

"Watchman". "Is There an Alternative Government?", *Contemporary Review*, 120 (July 1921), 35–44.

Willson, F. M. G. "The Routes of Entry of New Members of the British Cabinet, 1868–1958," *Political Studies*, 7, no. 3 (1959), 222–32.

*Theses on Lloyd George*

Cornwell, E. E., Jr. "Lloyd George: A Study in Political Leadership." Ph.D. diss., Harvard University, 1953.

Ernst, D. J. "The Social Policies of David Lloyd George." Ph.D. diss., University of Wisconsin, 1942.

Pugh, U. R. "David Lloyd George and Coalition Government: A Study in English History and Politics 1915–1922." Ph.D. diss., University of Colorado, 1941.

# INDEX